The World's Classics

CCLXXXIII

LETTERS OF THOMAS GRAY

LETTERS OF
THOMAS GRAY

SELECTED

WITH AN INTRODUCTION

BY

JOHN BERESFORD

HUMPHREY MILFORD
OXFORD UNIVERSITY PRESS
London   Edinburgh   Glasgow   Copenhagen
New York   Toronto   Melbourne   Cape Town
Bombay   Calcutta   Madras   Shanghai

THOMAS GRAY

Born, Cornhill, London . . . 26 December 1716
Died, Cambridge . . . . . 30 July 1771

This selection of Gray's letters was first published in 'The World's Classics' in 1925.

PRINTED IN ENGLAND
AT THE OXFORD UNIVERSITY PRESS
BY FREDERICK HALL

INTRODUCTION

AFTER Gray's death, a ' Sketch of his own Character '
was found in one of his pocket-books; it had been
written in 1761 :

Too poor for a bribe, and too proud to importune,
He had not the method of making a fortune :
Could love, and could hate, so was thought somewhat
  odd ;
No very great wit, he believed in a God :
A place or a pension he did not desire,
But left Church and State to Charles Townshend and
  Squire.

Gray's description of himself in these lines provides
an interpretation of his character which the reader will
find unfolded with wonderful fidelity and complete-
ness in these letters. The letters, indeed, contain not
only the most charming, but the only really adequate
account of a personality, fascinating in an extraordinary
degree. For purposes of biographical summary, however, and because I have always found this kind of
bird's-eye view of help in my own case, I abstract the
following salient dates from *Alumni Cantabrigienses* by
J. and J. A. Venn, now in course of issue, from the
Cambridge University Press.

' Gray, Thomas. Admitted pensioner (age 18) at
Peterhouse, July 4, 1734 ; Fellow Commoner 1742.
Son of Philip, scrivener, of Cornhill. Baptized at
St. Michael's, Cornhill, December 26, 1716. School,
Eton. Scholar, 1734 ; LL.B. 1744. Migrated to Pem-
broke, March 6, 1756. Appointed Regius Professor of
History and Modern Languages, 1768. Admitted at

the Inner Temple, November 22, 1735. . . . Travelled on the Continent with Horace Walpole, 1739–41. Made Cambridge his head-quarters for the rest of his life. . . . Died July 30, 1771. Buried at Stoke Poges.'

Into this biographical framework it will be found that the Letters fit themselves in the form of a very complete and beautiful picture. For Gray's life, though it was marked by a certain pleasing melancholy, was disfigured by no tragedy which makes such painful reading in the case of poets so different as Cowper, Shelley, and Byron. He combined with his shining literary genius a genius for friendship which gave him the first affection of Richard West, whose early promise was too soon buried in the grave; the lifelong admiration of Horace Walpole[1] brilliant and famous, of Thomas Wharton charming and obscure, of James Brown academic and lovable, of William Mason clever, kind, and worldly; finally, during his later years, the youthful and enduring love of Norton Nicholls and Charles de Bonstetten.

To these friends, and to his mother, to whom he was devoted, though, unfortunately, only the letters written to her while he was travelling on the Continent have (with one exception) survived, Gray wrote the majority of his Letters which cover the long period from 1734 to 1771.

---

[1] Gray's and Walpole's friendship was interrupted for four years (from 1741 to 1745) owing to the quarrel which caused their separation at Reggio in May 1741. Walpole has generously acknowledged that the fault was his: he was, at the time, too conscious that he was the son of the Prime Minister, and Gray, with natural dignity, resented his behaviour.

These letters are notable for many reasons : in the first place and perhaps pre-eminently for their literary quality, in the second place for critical acumen and wit, in the third place for their practical wisdom, and lastly, but by no means least, for a rare and marvellous quality of sympathy.

For literary style and quality the reader has only to turn, for example, to the letters written from abroad in 1739–41, to the letters describing his later travels in England, his description of Netley Abbey (in 1764) for instance, or the Kent Country (in 1766), or to the Journal of his visit to the Lakes in 1769 ; for critical judgement, to the letter to West (in April 1742) containing the famous passage beginning : ' The language of the age is never the language of poetry ', or the letter to Stonehewer (August 18, 1758) on Shaftesbury and Bolingbroke, or the letter to Wharton (August 5, 1763) referring to Rousseau's *Émile*, or the letter to Walpole (February 25, 1768) speaking of his own writing, and containing also an amusing criticism of Boswell ; for practical wisdom, to almost any of the letters, his reiterated advice, for example, that ' to be employed is to be happy ' ; for his sympathy, to those beautiful letters to Walpole (August 1737), to Wharton (April 9, 1758), to Norton Nicholls (September 23, 1766), to Mason (March 28, 1767).

The letters last named show Gray's power of sympathy in any sorrow that befell his friends. But he also possessed an artistic sympathy combined with critical acuteness which enabled him to recognize what was of permanent excellence in the literary work of his contemporaries.

For Gray was a man of letters who was ' essentially

a scholar',[1] and his praise is all the more valuable because it is discriminating. The criticism and praise of Fielding's *Joseph Andrews* (letter to West, April 1742) is an excellent illustration, so is his favourable criticism of Sterne's *Tristram Shandy* (to Wharton, June 1760), so is the letter to Walpole (1748) in which he passes in review the various Poets included in Dodsley's *Collection*. When Norton Nicholls read to him Goldsmith's *Deserted Village*, he exclaimed, 'This man is a poet'. He immediately recognized the merit of Collins, thought that both he and Joseph Warton deserved to last some years, but feared they would not : as to this, in the case of Collins, he was fortunately wrong—the *Ode to Evening* and *How Sleep the Brave* having secured Collins a permanent niche in the temple of fame. For Richardson he had the highest regard. Though the attitude of Voltaire and Rousseau to religion was repugnant to him he greatly admired their literary genius. Again he welcomed enthusiastically Montesquieu's *Esprit des Lois*, and the monumental work of Diderot. As to Johnson's and Gray's attitude to one another, though it is clear they were temperamentally rather incompatible, it is only fair to point out that while Johnson disliked Gray's Odes, except the Hymn to Adversity, he profoundly admired the Elegy,[2] and that Gray warmly praised Johnson's *London*.

But I need not here labour the point further. This selection of the Letters will indeed have been made in

[1] As Professor Saintsbury justly describes him (*A Letter Book*, p. 37).

[2] See the Essay on Gray in Johnson's *Lives of the Poets*.

vain if the reader does not see for himself that an unsympathetic attitude towards his English and French contemporaries in literature is the last thing of which Gray can be accused.[1]

Gray's Journal of his visit to the Lake District which I have included in this Selection, as it rather resembles a very long and charming letter than a regular Journal, is remarkable in showing that he was one of the first in that artificiality-loving eighteenth century to admire Nature in its wild and unelaborate beauty. The difficult Wordsworth has beautifully praised this account of a country, which he regarded almost as his own, in his *Guide to the Lakes*.[2]

Finally, the Letters of Gray are notable as illustrating the extraordinary extent of his knowledge on a great variety of subjects. Writing a year after his death his friend the Reverend William Temple described him as ' perhaps the most learned man in Europe ; he was equally acquainted with the elegant and profound parts of Science, and not superficially, but thoroughly. He knew every branch of history, both natural and civil ; had read all the original historians of England, France, and Italy, and was a great antiquarian. Criticism, metaphysics, morals, politics, made a principal part of his plan of study. Voyages and travels of all sorts were his favourite amusement, and he had a fine taste in painting, prints, architecture, and gardening. . . .

---

[1] I have emphasized this point as I find myself unable to agree in this respect with Sir Edmund Gosse's criticism, pp. 49–50 and p. 216 of his popular life of Gray in the English Men of Letters series.

[2] pp. 69–70. Edited by Ernest de Sélincourt, published 1906 by Henry Frowde.

But he was also a good man, a well-bred man, a man of virtue and humanity.' [1]

Of the singular nobility of Gray's character Matthew Arnold [2] has said all that need be said : indeed it is impossible to read the letters as a whole without experiencing that refreshment of spirit which communion with a beautiful mind alone can bring. That this refreshment is so abundant in the case of Gray's Letters comes, I think, in the main from a swift realization—for one need not read far before feeling it—that he gave full measure of love, pressed down and running over, to his friends. As Dr. Johnson saw, ' he was a man likely to love much where he loved at all '.

In truth, the second verse of the Epitaph at the end of the Elegy written, perhaps, by Gray when he was thinking of his friend Richard West, is also the last word on himself :

Large was his bounty, and his soul sincere,
Heav'n did a recompense as largely send :
He gave to Mis'ry all he had, a tear,
He gain'd from Heav'n ('twas all he wish'd) a friend.

JOHN BERESFORD.

Ashwell End,
  Baldock,
    Herts.

---

[1] Quoted in Sir Edmund Gosse's *Gray*, pp. 211-12.
[2] In *Essays in Criticism*, Second Series.

NOTE ON THE TEXT

THE text of this selection, which ranges over the whole and actually contains about one-half of all Gray's letters, is based partly on the Rev. D. C. Tovey's standard edition in three volumes of the *Letters of Thomas Gray*, published (1900–12) by George Bell & Sons, and partly on Dr. Paget Toynbee's *The Correspondence of Gray, Walpole, West, and Ashton* (1734–71) in two volumes published by the Clarendon Press in 1915. (See list of Letters and foot-note thereto.) For leave to make use of the text of those editions I am indebted to the publishers.

There have been five main editions of Gray's Letters, namely, by the Rev. William Mason (1775); the Rev. John Mitford (1816–53); Mr. (now Sir) Edmund Gosse (1884); the Rev. D. C. Tovey; and Dr. Paget Toynbee. To all these editors for various reasons, and in varying measure, gratitude is due, but especially to Mitford, Tovey, and Paget Toynbee. To Tovey's edition the reader must turn if he desires to understand Gray's time thoroughly, as that edition contains very complete and scholarly notes and appendices. To Dr. Paget Toynbee's edition he must turn if he desires to learn something of Walpole, West, and Ashton from their letters, and also if he desires to supplement his knowledge of Gray's life in various details, which the eighty-nine new (Gray) letters printed therein furnish. That edition also contains fifteen letters then printed in full for the first time. I am indebted to Mr. F. Page, of the Oxford University Press, for the headlines, and to Dr. Arnold Chaplin for identifying the Medical Society on page 132.

J. B.

LIST OF LETTERS SELECTED

LETTER   PAGE

1. To Walpole [April 16, 1734]. *Text*[1]: P.T., vol. i, Letter 1* 1

2. To Walpole [Oct. 31, 1734]. P.T., vol. i, Letter 2* 2

3. To Walpole [Nov. 17, 1734]. P.T., vol. i, Letter 3* 4

4. To Walpole [Dec. 8, 1734]. P.T., vol. i, Letter 4* 7

5. To Walpole [Jan. 12, 1735]. P.T., vol. i, Letter 7* 8

6. To Walpole [Jan. 21, 1735]. P.T., vol. i, Letter 9* 9

7. To Walpole [Feb. 4, 1735]. P.T., vol. i, Letter 12* 10

8. To West [Dec. 1735]. P.T., vol. i, Letter 21 . 11

9. To Walpole, Dec. 24 [1735]. P.T., vol. i, Letter 22* 12

10. To Walpole, Jan. 3 [1736]. P.T., vol. i, Letter 23* 13

11. To Walpole [Aug. 1736]. P.T., vol. i, Letter 39   15

12. To Walpole [Sept. 26, 1736]. P.T., vol. i, Letter 43 17

13. To Walpole [Oct., 1736]. P.T., vol. i, Letter 45*   17

14. To West, Dec., 1736. P.T., vol. i, Letter 48 .   18

15. To West, March, 1737. P.T., vol. i, Letter 55 .   19

16. To West, Aug. 22, 1737. P.T., vol. i, Letter 63   20

17. To Walpole [Aug., 1737]. P.T., vol. i, Letter 64*   21

18. To Walpole [Nov., 1737]. P.T., vol. i, Letter 66*   21

[1] The text of this selection is based on the Rev. D. C. Tovey's standard edition of *The Letters of Thomas Gray*, vol. i, 2nd edition, 1909, vol. ii, 1913, vol. iii, 1912, published by George Bell & Sons, and on Dr. Paget Toynbee's *The Correspondence of Gray, Walpole, West, and Ashton, 1734–1771*, in two volumes, published by the Clarendon Press, 1915. I indicate the source of the text in each case by T. and P.T. respectively.

* An asterisk indicates the new letters discovered by Dr. Paget Toynbee, and first published in 1915.

LETTER   PAGE

19. To Walpole, March 7 [1738]. P.T., vol. i,
      Letter 77*   23
20. To Walpole, March 20 [1738]. P.T., vol. i,
      Letter 78*   24
21. To West, Sept., 1738. P.T., vol. i, Letter 84 .   25
22. To his Mother, April 1, 1739. T., vol. i,
      Letter XIV   25
23. To West, April 12, 1739. P.T., vol. i, Letter 87   27
24. To Ashton, April 21 [1739]. P.T., vol. i,
      Letter 89   30
25. To West, May 22, 1739. P.T., vol. i, Letter 91   32
26. To his Mother, June 21, 1739. T., vol. i,
      Letter XIX   34
27. To West, Sept. 18, 1739. P.T., vol. i, Letter 99   36
28. To his Mother, Oct. 13, 1739. T., vol. i,
      Letter XXIV   38
29. To his Father, Oct. 25, 1739. T., vol. i,
      Letter XXV   40
30. To his Mother, Nov. 7, 1739. T., vol. i,
      Letter XXVI   42
31. To West, Nov. 16, 1739. P.T., vol. i, Letter 105   44
32. To West, Nov. 21, 1739. P.T., vol. i, Letter
      106   46
33. To his Mother, Dec. 9, 1739. T., vol. i,
      Letter XXIX   48
34. To his Mother, Dec. 19, 1739. T., vol. i,
      Letter XXX   49
35. To Wharton, March 12 [1740]. T., vol. i,
      Letter XXXII   51
36. To his Mother, April 2, 1740. T., vol. i,
      Letter XXXIV   56
37. To his Mother, April 15, 1740. T., vol. i,
      Letter XXXV   59
38. To West, May 20, 1740. P.T., vol. i, Letter 118   60
39. To West, May, 1740. T., vol. i, Letter XXXIX   63
40. To his Mother, June 17, 1740. T., vol. i,
      Letter XL   66
41. To his Father, July 16, 1740. T., vol. i,
      Letter XLI   68
42. To West, July 16, 1740. P.T., vol. i, Letter 124   70
43. Postscript to Letter from Walpole to West,
      July 31, 1740. T., vol. i, Letter XLIII .   73

LETTER   PAGE

44. To his Mother, Aug. 21, 1740. T., vol. i,
        Letter XLIV   74
45. To his Father, Oct. 9, 1740. T., vol. i, Letter
        XLVI   75
46. To his Father, Jan. 12, 1741. T., vol. i, Letter
        XLVII   77
47. To West, April 21, 1741. P.T., vol. ii, Letter
        134   78
48. To West [Jan., 1742]. P.T., vol. ii, Letter 139   80
49. To West, April [1742]. P.T., vol. ii, Letter 143   82
50. To West, May 8, 1742. P.T., vol. ii, Letter 149   85
51. To Chute, May [24, 1742]. T., vol. i, Letter LVI   86
52. To Ashton, June 17, 1742. P.T., vol. ii,
        Letter 153   89
53. To Wharton, April [26, 1744]. T., vol. i,
        Letter LX   90
54. To Wharton [Dec. 27, 1744]. T., vol. i, Letter
        LXII   92
55. To Walpole, Feb. 3, 1746. P.T., vol. ii, Letter
        154   93
56. To Walpole, Oct. 20 [1746]. P.T., vol. ii,
        Letter 157*   95
57. To Wharton [1746]. T., vol. i, Letter LXVI   .   97
58. To Wharton, Dec. 11 [1746]. T., vol. i, Letter
        LXXI   102
59. To Walpole, Dec. [1746]. P.T., vol. ii, Letter 158   104
60. To Walpole [1747]. P.T., vol. ii, Letter 164   .   105
61. To Wharton, Nov. 30 [1747]. T., vol. i,
        Letter LXXX   107
62. To Walpole [1748]. P.T., vol. ii, Letter 168   .   110
63. To Wharton, April 25 [1749]. T., vol. i,
        Letter LXXXVII   114
64. To Wharton, Aug. 8 [1749]. T., vol. i, Letter
        LXXXVIII   117
65. To his Mother, Nov. 7, 1749. T., vol. i, Letter
        LXXXIX   119
66. To Walpole, June 12, 1750. P.T., vol. ii,
        Letter 170   120
67. To Walpole [Feb. 11, 1751]. P.T., vol. ii,
        Letter 171   121
68. To Walpole [Feb. 20, 1751]. P.T., vol. ii,
        Letter 172   122

LETTER   PAGE

69. To Walpole, March 3, 1751. P.T., vol. ii,
      Letter 173   123

70. To Walpole, Sept. 8 [1751]. P.T., vol. ii,
      Letter 175   124

71. To Walpole [July 8, 1752]. P.T., vol. ii,
      Letter 179   127

72. To Walpole, Feb. 13, 1753. P.T., vol. ii,
      Letter 182   127

73. To Wharton, March 15 [1753]. T., vol. i,
      Letter CIII   128

74. To Wharton, July 14, 1753. T., vol. i, Letter CV   129

75. To Mason, July 24, 1753. T., vol. i, Letter CVI   129

76. To Mason, Sept. 21, 1753. T., vol. i, Letter CVII   130

77. To Mason, Nov. 5, 1753. T., vol. i, Letter CXII   131

78. To Wharton, Aug. 13 [1754]. T., vol. i, Letter
      CXIII   132

79. To Wharton, Sept. 18, 1754. T., vol. i, Letter
      CXIV   134

80. To Wharton, Dec. 26, 1754. T., vol. i, Letter
      CXVI   137

81. To Wharton, March 9, 1755. T., vol. i, Letter
      CXVIII   138

82. To Wharton, Aug. 6, 1755. T., vol. i, Letter
      CXX   140

83. To Wharton, Aug. 21, 1755. T., vol. i, Letter
      CXXIII   141

84. To Wharton [Oct. 18, 1755]. T., vol. i, Letter
      CXXV   145

85. To Wharton, Jan. 9, 1756. T., vol. i, Letter
      CXXVIII   146

86. To Wharton, March 25, 1756. T., vol. i,
      Letter CXXIX   149

87. To Mason, July 25, 1756. T., vol. i, Letter
      CXXXI   150

88. To Walpole, Sept. 8, 1756. P.T., vol. ii,
      Letter 199*   152

89. To Wharton, Oct. 15, 1756. T., vol. i, Letter
      CXXXIII   153

90. To Mason, April 23, 1757. T., vol. i, Letter
      CXXXIX   154

91. To Walpole, July 11, 1757. P.T., vol. ii,
      Letter 204   156

LETTER   PAGE

92. To the Rev. James Brown, July 25, 1757. T., vol. i, Letter CXLIII 156

93. To Mason, Aug. 1 [1757]. T., vol. i, Letter CXLIV 157

94. To the Rev. James Brown, Aug. 14, 1757. T., vol. i, Letter CXLV * 158

95. To Wharton, Aug. 17, 1757. T., vol. i, Letter CXLVI 159

96. To Richard Hurd, Aug. 25, 1757. T., vol. i, Letter CXLVII 159

97. To Mason [1757]. T., vol. i, Letter CXLVIII . 161

98. To Wharton, Sept. 7 [1757]. T., vol. i, Letter CXLIX 162

99. To Wharton, Oct. 7, 1757. T., vol. i, Letter CLI 164

100. To Wharton, Dec. 8, 1757. T., vol. i, Letter CLIV 165

101. To Mason, Dec. 19, 1757. T., vol. i, Letter CLVI 166

102. To L. Brockett [1757]. T., vol. ii, Letter CLVII 167

103. To Mason, Jan. 3, 1758. T., vol. ii, Letter CLVIII 168

104. To Mason, Jan. 13, 1758. T., vol. ii, Letter CLX 170

105. To Wharton, March 8, 1758. T., vol. ii, Letter CLXIV 172

106. To Mason [March 24] 1758. T., vol. ii, Letter CLXV 173

107. To Wharton, April 9, 1758. T., vol. ii, Letter CLXVI 175

108. To Wharton, June 18, 1758. T., vol. ii, Letter CLXVII 176

109. To Mason, June 20, 1758. T., vol. ii, Letter CLXVIII 177

110. To Mason, Aug. 11, 1758. T., vol. ii, Letter CLXX 179

111. To Stonehewer, Aug. 18, 1758. T., vol. ii, Letter CLXXI 180

112. To William Palgrave, Sept. 6, 1758. T., vol. ii, Letter CLXXIII 182

113. To Mason, Nov. 9, 1758. T., vol. ii, Letter CLXXVIII 183

114. To Mason, Jan. 18, 1759. T., vol. ii, Letter CLXXXII 184

115. To Mason, April 10, 1759. T., vol. ii, Letter CLXXXVI 186

LETTER   PAGE

116. To Wharton, July 21, 1759. T., vol. ii, Letter
      CLXXXVII 187
117. To William Palgrave, July 24, 1759. T., vol. ii,
      Letter CLXXXIX 191
118. To the Rev. James Brown, Aug. 8, 1759. T.,
      vol. ii, Letter CXC 192
119. To the Rev. James Brown, Aug. 9, 1759. T.,
      vol. ii, Letter CXCI 193
120. To Wharton, Sept. 18, 1759. T., vol. ii, Letter
      CXCII 195
121. To Wharton, Jan. 23, 1760. T., vol. ii, Letter
      CXCVII 198
122. To Wharton, April 22, 1760. T., vol. ii,
      Letter CC 203
123. To Mason, June 7, 1760. T., vol. ii, Letter CCI 207
124. To Wharton [June, 1760]. T., vol. ii, Letter CCII 208
125. To Stonehewer, June 29, 1760. T., vol. ii,
      Letter CCIV 213
126. To Mason, Aug. 7, 1760. T., vol. ii, Letter CCVII 215
127. To Wharton, Oct. 21, 1760. T., vol. ii, Letter
      CCIX 218
128. To the Rev. James Brown, Oct. 25, 1760. T.,
      vol. ii, Letter CCXI 220
129. To Mason, Jan. 22, 1761. T., vol. ii, Letter
      CCXVII 220
130. To Wharton, Jan. 31, 1761. T., vol. ii, Letter
      CCXVIII 223
131. To the Rev. James Brown, Feb. 9, 1761. T.,
      vol. ii, Letter CCXIX 230
132. To Wharton, June 23, 1761. T., vol. ii, Letter
      CCXXII 232
133. To Mason, Aug., 1761. T., vol. ii, Letter CCXXV 234
134. To the Rev. James Brown, Sept. 24, 1761. T.,
      vol. ii, Letter CCXXIX 235
135. To Wharton, Jan., 1762. T., vol. ii, Letter
      CCXXXVII 239
136. To Walpole, Feb. 28, 1762. P.T., vol. ii,
      Letter 220 241
137. To Mason, March 17, 1762. T., vol. ii, Letter
      CCXL 243
138. To Wharton, June 4, 1762. T., vol. ii, Letter
      CCXLI 244

LETTER   PAGE

139. To John Chute [1762 ?]. T., vol. ii, Letter
CCXLIV 245

140. To Wharton, Dec. 4, 1762. T., vol. ii, Letter
CCXLV 245

141. To Mason, Dec. 21, 1762. T., vol. ii, Letter
CCXLVI 248

142. To the Rev. James Brown, Feb. 17, 1763. T.,
vol. iii, Letter CCXLIX 250

143. To Mason, 1763. T., vol. iii, Letter CCLII . 250

144. To Wharton, Aug. 5, 1763. T., vol. iii, Letter
CCLIII 252

145. To Count Algarotti, Sept. 9, 1763. T., vol. iii,
Letter CCLIV 255

146. To Wharton, Feb. 21, 1764. T., vol. iii, Letter
CCLVIII 258

147. To Wharton, July 10, 1764. T., vol. iii, Letter
CCLIX 260

148. To the Rev. James Brown [1764]. T., vol. iii,
Letter CCLX 263

149. To the Rev. James Brown, Oct. 13, 1764. T.,
vol. iii, Letter CCLXI 265

150. To Norton Nicholls, Nov. 19, 1764. T., vol. iii,
Letter CCLXIV 267

151. To Walpole, Dec. 30, 1764. P.T., vol. ii,
Letter 231 269

152. To Mason, 1765. T., vol. iii, Letter CCLXVI . 270

153. To Mason, 1765 [? 1763]. T., vol. iii, Letter
CCLXVIII 273

154. To Wharton, April 29, 1765. T., vol. iii,
Letter CCLXIX 274

155. To the Rev. James Brown, 1765. T., vol. iii,
Letter CCLXX 276

156. To Mason, May 23 [1765]. T., vol. iii, Letter
CCLXXI 277

157. To Mason, July 16, 1765. T., vol. iii, Letter
CCLXXIII 278

158. To Wharton [1765]. T., vol. iii, Letter CCLXXVII 279

159. To James Beattie, Oct. 2, 1765. T., vol. iii,
Letter CCLXXVIII 286

160. To Mason, 1765. T., vol. iii, Letter CCLXXIX . 287

161. To Walpole [Nov., 1765]. P.T., vol. ii, Letter
232* 289

LETTER   PAGE

162. To Walpole, Dec. 13, 1765. P.T., vol. ii,
Letter 234   290

163. To Wharton, March 5, 1766. T., vol. iii,
Letter CCLXXXI   292

164. To Norton Nicholls, Aug. 26, 1766. T., vol. iii,
Letter CCLXXXIII   296

165. To Wharton, Aug. 26, 1766. T., vol. iii,
Letter CCLXXXIV   298

166. To Mason [Aug., 1766]. T., vol. iii, Letter
CCLXXXV   301

167. To Norton Nicholls, Sept. 23, 1766. T., vol. iii,
Letter CCLXXXVI   302

168. To Norton Nicholls [1766 ?]. T., vol. iii,
Letter CCLXXXIX   303

169. To the Rev. James Brown, Nov. 18, 1766.
T., vol. iii, Letter CCXCI . . .   304

170. To Mason, Jan. 27, 1767. T., vol. iii, Letter
CCXCIII   305

171. To Mason, Feb. 15, 1767. T., vol. iii, Letter
CCXCV   306

172. To Mason, March 28, 1767. T., vol. iii, Letter
CCXCVI   308

173. To the Rev. James Brown, May, 1767. T.,
vol. iii, Letter CCXCIX . . .   309

174. To the Rev. James Brown, June 2, 1767. T.,
vol. iii, Letter CCC   310

175. To Wharton, June 21, 1767. T., vol. iii,
Letter CCCIII   310

176. To Mason, Sept. 11, 1767. T., vol. iii, Letter
CCCXI   311

177. To Norton Nicholls, Nov. 5, 1767. T., vol. iii,
Letter CCCXIII   312

178. To James Beattie, Dec. 24, 1767. T., vol. iii,
Letter CCCXIV   313

179. To Wharton, Dec. 28, 1767. T., vol. iii, Letter
CCCXV   315

180. To Mason, Jan. 8, 1768. T., vol. iii, Letter
CCCXVII   318

181. To William Taylor Howe, Jan. 12, 1768. T.,
vol. iii, Letter CCCXVIII . . .   319

182. To James Beattie, Feb. 1, 1768. T., vol. iii,
Letter CCCXX   321

LETTER   PAGE

183. To Norton Nicholls, Jan. 28, 1768. T., vol. iii,
Letter CCCXXI 322

184. To Walpole, Feb. 14, 1768. P.T., vol. ii,
Letter 238 323

185. To Walpole, Feb. 25, 1768. P.T., vol. ii,
Letter 240 326

186. To Walpole, March 6, 1768. P.T., vol. ii,
Letter 242 329

187. To the Rev. James Brown, April 27, 1768.
T., vol. iii, Letter CCCXXVII 331

188. To Mary Antrobus, July 29, 1768. T., vol. iii,
Letter CCCXXX 332

189. To Mason, Aug. 1 [1768]. T., vol. iii, Letter
CCCXXXII 333

190. To Norton Nicholls, Aug. 3, 1768. T., vol. iii,
Letter CCCXXXIII 334

191. To James Beattie, Oct. 31, 1768. T., vol. iii,
Letter CCCXXXVII 335

192. To Norton Nicholls, Nov. 8, 1768. T., vol. iii,
Letter CCCXXXVIII 336

193. To Norton Nicholls, Jan. 2, 1769. T., vol. iii,
Letter CCCXLI 338

194. To Norton Nicholls, June 24, 1769. T., vol. iii,
Letter CCCXLVII 338

195. To James Beattie, July 16, 1769. T., vol. iii,
Letter CCCXLVIII 340

196. To Mason, Aug. 26, 1769. T., vol. iii, Letter
CCCL 341

197. To the Rev. James Brown, Oct. 10, 1769. T.,
vol. iii, Letter CCCLI 342

198. Journal 1, 2, 3, and 4, Sept. 30 to Oct. 15, 1769.
T., vol. iii, pp. 232–64 343

199. To Stonehewer, Nov. 2, 1769. T., vol. iii,
Letter CCCLII 366

200. To Norton Nicholls, Jan. 6, 1770. T., vol. iii,
Letter CCCLVI 367

201. To [Norton Nicholls ?], March 20, 1770. T.,
vol. iii, Letter CCCLVII 368

202. To Norton Nicholls, April 4, 1770. T., vol. iii,
Letter CCCLVIII 369

203. To Charles de Bonstetten, April 12, 1770. T.,
vol. iii, Letter CCCLIX 370

rusticity of my simile) in short, I have tryed and condemned you in my mind, all that you can alledge to save yourself won't do; for I find by your excuses you are brought to your derniere Chemise; and as you stand guilty, I adjudge you to be drawn to the place of execution, your chamber; where taking pen in hand, you shall write a letter as long as this, to him, who is nothing, when not

your sincere friend
& most devoted humble Servt

[   ]   T: GRAY

To the Hon^{rble} Mr Horatio [Wal]pole at the house of th[e right] honourable Sr Robert [Walpole] in St James's Square Lond[on]

2. TO WALPOLE

[Cambridge, Oct. 31, 1734]

[   ] For Gods sake send me your Quære's, & I'll do my best to get information upon those Points, you don't understand: I warrant, you imagine that People in one College, know the Customs of others; but you mistake, they are quite little Societies by themselves: ye Dresses, Language, Customs &c are different in different Colledges: what passes for Wit in one, would not be understood if it were carried to another: thus the Men of Peter-house, Pembroke & Clare-hall of course must be Tories; those of Trinity, Rakes; of Kings, Scholars; of Sidney, Wigs; of St Johns, Worthy men & so on: now what to say about this Terra Incognita, I don't know; First then it is a great old Town, shaped like a Spider, with a nasty lump in the middle of it, & half a dozen scambling long legs: it has 14 Parishes, 12 Colledges, & 4 Halls, these Halls only entertain Students, who after a term of years, are elected into the Colledges: there are 5 ranks in the University, subordinate to the Vice-chancellour, who is chose annually: these are [Masters, Fellows, Fellow-Commoners, Pensione]rs, & Sizers; The Masters of Colledges are twelve grey-hair'd Gentlefolks, who are all mad with Pride ; the Fellows are sleepy, drunken, dull, illiterate Things ; the Fellow-Com : are imitatours of the Fellows, or else Beaux, or else nothing : the Pension : grave, formal Sots, who would be thought old ; or else drink Ale, & sing Songs against ye Excise. The Sizers are Graziers Eldest Sons, who come to get good Learning, that they may all be Archbishops of Canterbury : these 2 last Orders are qualified to take Scholarships ; one of which, your humble Servt has had given him : first they led me into the hall, & there I swore Allegiance to ye King ; then I went to a room, where I took 50000 Latin Oaths, such as, to wear a Square Cap, to make 6 verses upon the Epistle or Gospel every Sunday morning, to chant very loud in Chappel, to wear a clean Surplice, &c : &c : Now as to eating : the Fellow-Com : dine at the Fellows Table, their Commons is worth 6^s–4^d a-week, the Pensioners pay but 2^s–4^d ; if any body don't like their Commons, they send down into the Kitchen to know, what's for Sizing ; the Cook sends up a Catalogue of what there is ; & they chuse, what they please : they are obliged to pay for Commons, whither they eat it, or no : there is always Plenty enough : the Sizers feast upon the leavings of the rest ; as to dress, the Fell : Commoners usually wear a Prunella Gown with Sleeves, a hat & no band ; but their proper habit has its Sleeves trimmed with Gold-lace, this they only wear at publick Ceremonies ; neither do the Noblemen use their pr : Habit commonly, but wear only a black Padesoy Gown : the Men of Kings are a sort of University by themselves ; & differ in Customs from all the rest ; every body hates 'em & when Almanzor comes to me, our Peoples stare at him, like a Lord-mayors Show, & wonder to see a human Creature among them : if I tell you, I never stir out, perhaps you won't believe me ; especially when you know, there's a Club of Wits kept at the Mitre, all such as come from Eton ; where Alm : would introduce me, if I so pleased :—yet you will not think it strange, that I don't go abroad, when I tell you, that I am got into a room ; such [a] hugeous

one, that little i is quite lost in it; so [that] when I
get up in the morning, I begin to travel [tow]ards
the middle of it with might & main, & with much ado
about noon bate at a great Table, which stands half-way
it: so then, by that time, (after having pursued my
journey full speed); that I arrive at the door, it is so
dark & late, & I am so tired, that I am obliged to turn
back again: so about Midnight I get to the bedside:
then, thinks you, I suppose, he goes to sleep: hold
you a bit; in this Country it is so far from that, that
we go to bed to wake, & rise to sleep: in short, those
that go along the street, do nothing but walk in their
sleep: they run against every Post they meet: but
I beg pardon, for talking so much of myself, since that's
not, what you care for—(To be continued)

To the Honᵣᵇˡᵉ Horace Walpole Esq at the house of
the right Honᵣᵇˡᵉ Sᵗ Robert Walpole in Sᵗ James's
Square London

3. To Walpole

With care   To mie Nuss att London   Present
Carridge pade   These

[Cambridge] 23ᵈ Sundʸ after Trin:
[Nov. 17, 1734]

HONNER'D NURSE,—this comes to let you know, that
I am in good health; but that I should not have been
so, if it had not been for your kind promise of coming
to tend me yourself, & see the effect of your own
Prescription: and I should desire of you, so please you,
as how that, you would be so good as to be so kind, as
to do me the favour of bringing down with you a
quantity of it, prepared as your Grandmothers Aunt,
poor Mʳˢ Hawthorn (God rest her soul, for she was as
well a natured, a good Gentlewoman, as ever broke
bread, or trod upon Shoe-leather; though I say it,
that should not say it; for you know, she was related
to me, & marry! not a jot the worse, I trow) used to
make it: now I would not put you to this trouble, if
I could provide myself of the Ingredients here; but

truly, when I went to the Poticaries for a drachm of
Spirit of Ridicule ; the saucy Jackanapes of a Prentice-
Boy fleered at me, I warrant ye, as who should say,
you don't know your Errand : so by my troth, away
ambles me I (like a fool as I came) home again, & when
I came to look of your Receipt ; to be sure, there was
Sp^t of RIDICULE in great Letters, as plain as the nose
in one's face : & so, back hurries I in a making-Water-
while, as one may say, & when I came there, says I ;
you stripling, up-start, worsted-stocking, white-liver'd,
lath-backed, impudent Princox, says I ; abuse me !
that am your betters every day in the week, says I ;
you ill-begotten, pocky, rascally, damned Son of a
Bitch, says I—for you know, when he put me in such
a perilous Passion, how could one help telling him his
own—why, 'twould have provoked any Christian in
the world, tho' twere a Dog—to speak ; & so if you'll
be so kind, I'll take care you shall be satisfied for your
trouble : so, this is all at present from

your ever-dutiful & most
obedient & most affectionate,
loving God-daughter
PRU : OROSMADES

A Discourse

Πάντα κόνις, καὶ πάντα πιὸς,
  καὶ πάντα τόβακκο

If I should undertake to prove to you, that everything is Tobacco, it might be looked upon as an
Absurdity after the rev^rd & learn^d D^n Swift has made it
so manifest, that every thing is a Pudding : but I conceive it will not be so difficult to shew, that Tobacco
is every thing (at least here) for there is not a soul in
our Colledge (a body I should say) who does not smoke
or chew : there's nothing but Whiffing from Fellow to
Sizer ; nay, even the very Chimnies, that they may'nt
be thought partic'lar, must needs smoke, like the rest :
whilst unfashionable I labour thro' clouds of it, with as
much pains, as Milton's poor Devil took, when he
travel'd through Chaos :—but, as to the Guzzling

affair, you mistook in thinking it was the Old fellows,
that were with me ; no 'twas a thousand times worse ;
they were all young ones—do but imagine me pent up in
a room hired for the purpose, & none of the largest, from
7 a-clock at night, till 4 in the morning ! 'midst hogs-
heads of Liquor & quantities of Tobacco, surrounded
by 30 of these creatures, infinitely below the meanest
People you could even form an Idea off ; toasting
bawdy healths & deafned with their unmeaning Roar ;
Jesus ! but I must tell you of a fat Mortal, who stuck
close to me, & was as drunk (as Miss Edwards—which
story I'm afraid by the by, was too well-fancied, to
be real) well ! he was so maudlin & so loving & told me
long Stories, interrupted by the sourest Interjections,
with moral Discourses upon God knows what ! that
I was almost drunk too : oh—I must just beg lea[ve
to men]tion one more, who, they tell me, has no fault,
but that, he's a little too *foppish* & talks like a London-
Rake ; this fine Gentleman is quite master of the
Spectator & retails it for ever ; among the rest, he
gave his humble Opinion of the present state of the
Play-house ; that Stevens had a very graceful Motion,
spoke well, &c, but that he must needs give his Voice
for Mᵣ Quin ; Mᵣˢ Thurmond too was in great favour
with him : as for the Opera's he could not understand
them, but had heard Margaretta & Nicolini highly
commended by those, that were judges : by God, says
another, those Opera's are the ruin of the nation ; no
honest people can go to 'em, & those, that do, are
ashamed of themselves ; else why should they go in
Masques & Disguises thither—no body in the company
found out his blunder, so nobody laugh'd but I, which
was taken for applause. you'll think it a strange
compliment, when I tell you how often I thought of
you, all the while : but will forgive me, when you
recollect, that 'twas a great piece of Philosophy in me,
to be able, in yᵉ midst of Noise & Disturbance, to call
to mind the most agreeable thing in nature : when
you could give me so much Pleasure, absent ; what
must you do, when with me ? tho' perhaps its policy in

you to stay away so long, that you may increase my
Desire of seeing you : in your next send me word,
how soon you design, to come to the relief

of your [   ]

4. To Walpole

[Cambridge, Dec. 8, 1734]

[   ] I (tho' I say it) had too much modesty to
venture answering your dear, diverting Letter, in the
Poetical Strain myself : but, when I was last at the
Devil, meeting by chance with the deceased M^r
Dennis there, he offer'd his Service, &, being tip'd with
a Tester, wrought, what follows—

From purling Streams & the Elysian Scene,
From Groves, that smile with never-fading Green
I reascend ; in Atropos' despight
Restored to Celadon, & upper light :
Ye gods, that sway the Regions under ground,
Reveal to mortal View your realms profound ;
At his command admit the eye of Day ;
When Celadon commands, what God can disobey ?
Nor seeks he your Tartarean fires to know,
The house of Torture, & th' Abyss of Woe ;
But happy fields & Mansions free from Pain,
Gay Meads, & springing flowers best please ye gentle
    Swain :
    That little, naked, melancholy thing
My Soul, when first she tryed her flight to wing ;
Began with speed new Regions to explore,
And blunder'd thro' a narrow Postern door ;
First most devoutly having said its Prayers,
It tumbled down a thousand pair of [Stairs],
Thro' Entries long, thro' Cellars vast & deep,
Where ghostly Rats their habitations keep,
Where Spiders spread their Webs, & owlish Goblins
    sleep.
After so many Chances had befell,
It came into a mead of Asphodel :
Betwixt the Confines of ye light & dark
It lies, of 'Lyzium ye St James's park :
Here Spirit-Beaux flutter along the Mall,

And Shadows in disguise scate o'er yᵉ Iced Canal :
Here groves embower'd, & more sequester'd Shades,
Frequented by yᵉ Ghosts of Ancient Maids,
Are seen to rise : the melancholy Scene
With gloomy haunts, & twilight walks between
Conceals the wayward band : here spend their time
Greensickness Girls, that died in youthful prime,
Virgins forlorn, all drest in Willow-green-i
With Queen Elizabeth and Nicolini.
    More to reveal, or many words to use
Would tire alike your patience & my muse.
Believe, that never was so faithful found
Queen Proserpine to Pluto under ground,
Or Cleopatra to her Marc-Antony
As Orozmades to his Celadony.

P : S :

Lucrece for half a crown will shew you fun,
But Mʳˢ Oldfield is become a Nun.
Nobles & Cits, Prince Pluto & his Spouse
Flock to the Ghost of Covent-Garden house :
Plays, which were hiss'd above, below revive ;
When dead applauded, that were damn'd alive :
The People, as in life, still keep their Passions,
But differ something from the world in Fashions.
Queen Artemisia breakfasts on Bohea,
And Alexander wears a Ramilie.

To the Honᵇˡᵉ Horatio Walpole Esq at the house
of the right honᵇˡᵉ Sʳ Robert Walpole in Sᵗ James's
Square London

5. To Walpole

[Cambridge] Jan : 12 [1735]

How severe is forgetful old Age
To confine a poor Devil so ?
That I almost despair
To see even the Air ;
Much more my dear Damon—hey ho !

Thou dear envious Imp, to set me a longing with
accounts of Plays & Opera's, & Masquerades after
hearing of which, I can no more think of Logick &
Stuff, than you could of Divinity at a Ball, or of Caudle

& Carraway-Comfits after having been stuffed at a
Christening : heaven knows ! we have nobody in
our Colledge, that has seen London, but one ; and he,
I believe comes out of Vinegar-yard, & looks like
toasted Cheshire cheese, strewed with brown Sugar. I
beg you, give me the minutest Circumstances of your
Diversions & your Indiversions ; tho' if it is as great a
trouble to you to write, as it is a pleasure to me to get
'em by heart, I fear I shan't hear from you once in a
twelve-month, & dear now, be very punctual & very
long : if I had the least particle of pleasure, you should
know it ; & so you should if I had any thing troublesome ; tho' in Cambridge there is nothing so troublesome, as that one has nothing to trouble one. every
thing is so tediously regular, so samish, that I expire
for want of a little variety. I am just as I was, & so
is every thing about me ; I hope you'll forgive my
formality, in being just the same

Friend of yours, & just
the same Servant

OROZMADES.

To the Honble Horace Walpole Esq at his house in
St James's Square London

6. TO WALPOLE

[Cambridge] Sunday : Jan : 21 [19] [1735]

[   ] You have perform'd your promise as
fully, as I could have wish'd it : there seems to have
been no occasion for ushering it in with an Apology,
since I have long learnt to be more than contented
with whatever comes from a hand so dear. the things,
that are to be deliver'd by word of mouth, give me so
much impatience, that I would desire you to send
down your mouth by the coach, if I were not apprehensive what a loss it would be to the next Masquerade,
& what a dearth of pretty things it might occasion
in town ; however I hope you'll not fail to send your
thoughts by the post, without a Masque. you are
extremely good in making me a feast every other day ;

B 3

I have kept myself alive all this long Christmas by the help of your letters, & a few Mince-pyes, which an old Gentlewoman in this town sends me, & in whose favour I have made no small progress, I can assure you. you must know, I make my Addresses to her by calling her, Grandmother ; in so much, that she sends her Niece every day to know how I do : N : B : the other [day she] was dying, as every one thought, but herself : and when the Physician told her how dangerous her case was ; she fell into a violent passion with him : marry come up ! she dye ! no, indeed wouldn't she ; dye quotha ! she'd as soon be hang'd : in short she was so resolutely bent upon not dying, that she really did live, & is now as well as

your sincerest friend

OROZMADES

P : S : Punch is more smart, than ordinary.

To the Honble Mr Horace Walpole at his house in St James's Square London

7. To Walpole

[Cambridge, Feb. 4, 1735]

[   ] I have so little to write, & so much to say ; that, when you really do come, you may expect for the first fortnight to do nothing, but hearken to my Questions ; & to spend the next month in answering them : nay, I assure you, I limit the time only that you may rest a while, to take breath ; otherwise I could listen to you for the whole two years with an infinite deal of pleasure. I am forming the image to myself of your journey hither ; I suppose you will come down Essex way, & if you do, first you must cross Epping forest, & there you must be rob'd : then you go a long way, & at last you come to Gog-magog hills, and then you must be overturn'd : I hope, you have not hurt yourself ; but you must come at last to Foulmoor fields, & then you must fall Squash into a bog, pray, don't be frighted, for in about an hour and half you may chance to get out ; now perhaps if

it is not dark, you m[ay see the t]op of King's Chappel ;
tho' if it should be night, it is very likely, you won't
be able to see at all : however at last you get into
Cambridge, all bemudded & tired, with three wheels
and a half to the coach, four horses lame, and two
blind : the first thing, that appears, is a row of Alms-
houses, & presently on the right-hand you'll see a thing
like two Presbyterian Meeting-houses with the backside
of a little Church between them, & here you must find
out by Sympathy, that this is Peter-house, & that I am
but a little way off, I shall soon feel how near you are ;
then you should say—no, no, I should say—but I
believe I shall be too much overjoy'd to say anything,
well ; be that, as it will, I still hope, you will be almost
as much so : dear S^r, you are welcome to Cambridge ;
what d'ye think ? Pilk Hale about 3 months ago had
a great inclination to visit Malepert, but thought it
would not be well-bred not to let him know it beforehand ; & being at a loss, who he should send ; I persuaded him to go himself, & let him know Mr Hale
would wait upon him in the afternoon. and so he
did : Mal : promised to return it very soon ; & ever
since the other has staid at home with all his fine things
set out to the best advantage, & is quite sure he'll
come, & expects him every hour :—

[To] the H[on^{ble} Horace Walp]ole Esq a[t his house
in S^t J]ames's Squa[re London]

8. To Richard West

[Dec. 1735]

When you have seen one of my days, you have
seen a whole year of my life ; they go round and
round like the blind horse in the mill, only he has
the satisfaction of fancying he makes a progress, and
gets some ground ; my eyes are open enough to see
the same dull prospect, and to know that having made
four-and-twenty steps more, I shall be just where I
was ; I may, better than most people, say my life is but
a span, were I not afraid lest you should not believe

that a person so short-lived could write even so long a
letter as this ; in short, I believe I must not send you
the history of my own time, till I can send you that
also of the reformation. However, as the most un-
deserving people in the world must sure have the vanity
to wish somebody had a regard for them, so I need
not wonder at my own, in being pleased that you care
about me. You need not doubt, therefore, of having
a first row in the front box of my little heart, and I
believe you are not in danger of being crouded there ;
it is asking you to an old play, indeed, but you will
be candid enough to excuse the whole piece for the
sake of a few tolerable lines.

9. To Walpole

Dec: 24 [1735]—Peter-house

[   ] After having been very piously at S^t
Mary's church yesterday ; as I was coming home ;
somebody told me, that you was come, & that your
Servant had been to enquire for me : whereupon
throwing off all the Pruderie & Reserve of a Cambridge
Student, in a great extasie, I run in a vast hurry to
set the Bells a-ringing, & kindle a thousand Bonfires—
when amidst these Convulsions of Joy, I was stopt by
one of our Colledge, who inform'd me, that a fine
Gentleman in a laced hat & scarlet Stockings wanted
me : so, you may conclude, as soon as I set eyes on
him, I was ready to eat him for having your Livery on ;
but he soon checked me by acquainting me 'twas not
You, that was come ; but—Your Service : now undoubtedly after being so terribly bauked ; one could
not have lived, but by the help of Hartshorn, Hungary-
Water, & your Journal, which gives one a greater
Flow of Spirits, than ei[ther of them.] [but, dear
Celadon], nothing gave me half so much pleasure, as
to find ; that after the toil of the day was over, you
could be so good as to throw away a moment in thinking
of me, & had Spirits enough left, to make all the
hideosities you underwent agreable by describing

them :—by all that's frightful, I was in agonies for
you, when I saw you planted at the upper end of a
Table so elegantly set out ; like the King of Monsters
in the Fairy-tales : never was any one's curiosity half
so much raised by a blot, as mine is by that in your
Diary : 'tis so judicious a Scratch, so genteel a Blurr,
that I shall never be easy, till I know what it conceals ;
no more than I shall be, till I receive the things that
are to come by word of mouth, w^{ch} (if 'twere possible)
would make me wish to see you more than ever : sure
West is as much improved as he says Plato is ; since
you could have the conscience to persuade him to
come to Cambridge . . . . .

10. To Walpole

Jan : 3—[1736] London

[   ] A thousand thanks for the thousand
happy New-years you sent me, & which, I suppose, a
thousand good-natured people have made you a present
of, in the overflowings of their zeal :

—May each revolving year
With blessings crown'd, like this, returning smile
On [? Celadon], the happiest of his Kind—

I need not wish anything further, since (as I wish,
what you do) to be sure you know my wishes already :
Wise folks say the wise mans happiness is in himself ;
pray, are you the wise man ? they tell you too, that
mortal happiness is not of long continuance ; heaven
send, yours may last, till you wish for a little misery ;
nay ! and longer still : I can't tell whither our situations are much changed, since this time twelvemonth ;
certain I am however, that there is a great alteration ;
I don't succeed to your diversions in town, I believe,
& yet am absent from Cambridge without regret, nay
with pleasure, tho' not infinitely happier here :—I have
very little to tell you, as to the place, call'd London :
Adriano expired a few days ago, & his auncient Pre-
decessour Artaxerxes succeeds him for the present, w^{ch}
I think to visit to night : the [Town (in submissio]n

to your judgement) don't much admire Delane; Mrs Porter acts in ye Albion Queens, but I shall stay for another Play, before I see her; neither have I much inclination for old Cibber in Sr Courtly Nice, nor for young Mrs Cibber in Voltaire's Zara, in wch she performs the principal part for ye first time of her appearance in that way: I went to King Arthur last night, which is exceeding fine; they have a new man to [suppl]y Delane's place, one Johnson, with ye finest person & face in the world to all appearance; but as awkward, as a Button-maker; in short, if he knew how to manage his Beauties to advantage, I should not wonder, if all the Women run mad for him: the inchanted part of the play, is not Machinery, but actual magick: the second scene is a British temple enough to make one go back a thousand years, & really be in ancient Britain: the Songs are all Church-musick, & in every one of ye' Chorus's Mrs Chambers sung ye chief part, accompanied with

Roarings, Squawlings & Squeakations dire

Mrs Giffard is by way of Emmeline, & should be blind, but, heaven knows! I would not wish to see better than she does, & seems to do; for when Philidel restores her to sight, her eyes are not at all better than before; she is led in at first, by a Creature, yt was more like a Devil by half, than Grimbald himself; she took herself for Madame la Confidente, but every body else took her to be in the Circumstances of Damnation: when Emmeline comes to her sight, she beholds this Mrs Matilda first, & cries out

Are Women all like thee? such glorious Creatures!

which set the people into such a laugh, as lasted the whole Act: the Frost Scene is excessive fine; the first Scene of it is only a Cascade, that seems frozen; with the Genius of Winter asleep & wrapt in furs, who upon the approach of Cupid, after much quivering, & shaking sings the finest song in the Play: just after, the Scene opens, & shows a view of arched rocks coverd with Ice & Snow to ye end of ye Stage; between the

12. To Walpole

[Burnham, Sept. 26, 1736]

[   ] It rains, 'tis Sunday, this is the country;
three circumstances so dull in conjunction with the
dulness of my nature are like to give birth to an admirable production; I hope you will receive it, as you
would a Michaelmas Goose from a Tenant; since I
send it, not that I believe you have a taste for an
awkward fat creature, but because I have no better
way of showing my good-will: your name, I assure
you, has been propagated in these countries by a
Convert of yours, one Cambridge; he has brought
over his whole family to you; they were before pretty
good Whigs, but now they are absolute Walpolians:
we have hardly any body in the Parish, but knows
exactly the Dimensions of the hall & Saloon at Houghton, & begins to believe, that the Lanthorn is not quite
so great a Consumer of the fat of the land, as disaffected
persons have said: for your reputation we keep to
ourselves that, of your not Hunting, nor drinking
Hogan; e'er a one of which would be sufficient here
to lay your honour in the Dust: I received a little
Billet from my dear Horace, as if he had not heard from
me: whereas I wrote last Sunday; we have not so
good an opportunity here, as I could wish, not lying
conveniently for the Post; but to [morrow sennight]
I hope to be in town, & not long after at Cambridge.

yours most faithfully

T: G:

P: S: my love to Ashton

To the Honble Horatio Walpole, Esq of Kings College
Cambridge

13. To Walpole

[London, October, 1736]

[   ] The best News from Cornhill-shire is,
that I have a little fever, which denies me the pleasure
of seeing either You, or Alexander, or Downing-Street
to day, but when that leaves me at my own Disposal,

I shall be at yours; Covent-Garden has given me a
Sort of Surfeit of Mr Rich & his Cleverness, for I was
at the Way of the World, when the Machine broke
t'other Night; the House was in Amaze for above
a Minute, & I dare say a great many in the Galleries
thought it very dextrously perform'd, & that they
scream'd as naturally, as heart could wish; till they
found it was no jest by their calling for Surgeons; of
whom several luckily happen'd to be in the Pit: I
stayed to see the poor creatures brought out of the
House, & pity poor Mrs Buchanan not a little, whom
I saw put into a Chair in such a fright, that as she is
big with child, I question whether it may not kill her,

I am

Yours ever

T : G :

To the Honble Mr Horace Walpole at Chelsea

14. To West

You must know that I do not take degrees, and,
after this term, shall have nothing more of college
impertinencies to undergo, which I trust will be some
pleasure to you, as it is a great one to me. I have
endured lectures daily and hourly since I came last,
supported by the hopes of being shortly at full liberty
to give myself up to my friends and classical companions, who, poor souls! though I see them fallen
into great contempt with most people here, yet I
cannot help sticking to them, and out of a spirit of
obstinacy (I think) love them the better for it; and
indeed, what can I do else? Must I plunge into
metaphysics? Alas, I cannot see in the dark; nature
has not furnished me with the optics of a cat. Must
I pore upon mathematics? Alas, I cannot see in too
much light; I am no eagle. It is very possible that
two and two make four, but I would not give four
farthings to demonstrate this ever so clearly; and if
these be the profits of life, give me the amusements
of it. The people I behold all around me, it seems,

know all this and more, and yet I do not know one of them who inspires me with any ambition of being like him. Surely it was of this place, now Cambridge, but formerly known by the name of Babylon, that the prophet spoke when he said, ' the wild beasts of the desert shall dwell there, and their houses shall be full of doleful creatures, and owls shall build there, and satyrs shall dance there ; their forts and towers shall be a den for ever, a joy of wild asses ; there shall the great owl make her nest, and lay and hatch and gather under her shadow ; it shall be a court of dragons ; the screech owl also shall rest there, and find for herself a place of rest '. You see here is a pretty collection of desolate animals, which is verified in this town to a tittle, and perhaps it may also allude to your habitation, for you know all types may be taken by abundance of handles ; however, I defy your owls to match mine.

If the default of your spirits and nerves be nothing but the effect of the hyp, I have no more to say. We all must submit to that wayward Queen ; I too in no small degree own her sway,

I feel her influence while I speak her power.

But if it be a real distemper, pray take more care of your health, if not for your own at least for our sakes, and do not be so soon weary of this little world : I do not know what refined friendships you may have contracted in the other, but pray do not be in a hurry to see your acquaintance above ; among your terrestrial familiars, however, though I say it that should not say it, there positively is not one that has a greater esteem for you than

Yours most sincerely, &c.

Peterhouse, December, 1736.

15. To West

Cambridge, March, 1737.

*   *

I learn Italian like any dragon, and in two months am got through the 16th book of Tasso, whom I hold in great admiration : I want you to learn too, that I may know your opinion of him ; nothing can be easier than that language to any one who knows Latin and French already, and there are few so copious and expressive.

*   *   *

16. To West

After a month's expectation of you, and a fortnight's despair, at Cambridge, I am come to town, and to better hopes of seeing you. If what you sent me last be the product of your melancholy, what may I not expect from your more cheerful hours ? For by this time the ill health that you complain of is (I hope) quite departed ; though, if I were self-interested, I ought to wish for the continuance of any thing that could be the occasion of so much pleasure to me. Low spirits are my true and faithful companions ; they get up with me, go to bed with me, make journeys and returns as I do ; nay, and pay visits, and will even affect to be jocose, and force a feeble laugh with me ; but most commonly we sit alone together, and are the prettiest insipid company in the world. However, when you come, I believe they must undergo the fate of all humble companions, and be discarded. Would I could turn them to the same use that you have done, and make an Apollo of them. If they could write such verses with me, not hartshorn, nor spirit of amber, nor all that furnishes the closet of an apothecary's widow, should persuade me to part with them : But, while I write to you, I hear the bad news of Lady Walpole's death on Saturday night last. Forgive me if the thought of what my poor Horace must feel on that account, obliges me to have done in reminding you that I am

Yours, &c.

London, Aug. 22, 1737.

17. To Walpole

[London, August, 1737]

Forgive me, my poor dear Horace, if I intrude upon your Grief, sooner possibly than I ought; yet hardly soon enough for the Anxiety I am in upon your account; far from having any such confidence in myself, as to imagine any thing I can say should lighten your affliction; I fear your own good Sense, and Resignation to Him, who has spared so long the best of Mothers to you, is hardly able to support you under it; I can the easier imagine the Situation you are in from the fears, which are continually before my eyes, of a like misfortune in my own case; if that were really to happen, I know not the least Shadow of comfort, that could come to me, but what I perhaps might find in my dearest Horace's compassion, & that pity, he never denies the unhappy: would to God, I might alleviate in some measure his Sorrows, in the part I willingly would bear in them, & in that commiseration, which I should feel for any one in such circumstances, how much more then for him whose friendship has been my greatest joy, & I hope shall continue so many years: for God's sake, as soon as melancholy reflection shall give you any intermission, let me hear of your welfare; let me have the pleasure of a line, or the sight of you, as soon as it can be proper: believe, I shall not enjoy a moments ease, till I have some information of your condition; I am, my dearest Walpole, with the greatest truth, your faithful friend, & servant,

T : G :

18. To Walpole

[London, November, 1737]

[   ] We were all here in mighty consternation this morning in imagination that the Queen was dead, not out of a joke, as she died you know a while ago, but seriously gone to the Stygian ferry; however now they say she is only very bad, & in a fair way;

as we have been twice bauk'd, she will have much ado
to persuade us, that she's dead in earnest & perhaps
she will survive her funeral no small time in the breasts
of her good subjects : I shall take care to be as sorry,
as one of my diminutiveness ought to be, not for
myself, but in charity to my superiours ; I saw her a
little while ago at the Opera in a green Velvet Sac
embroider'd κατὰ the facings & sleeves with Silver,
a little French Cap, a long black hood, & her hair
in Curls round her face ; but you see, Crown'd heads,
& heads Moutonnées, scald heads, & lousy heads,
Quack heads & Cane heads must all come together to
the Grave, as the famous Abou-saïd has elegantly
hinted, in his Persian Madrigals : for my part I shall
wear her image long imprinted in my mind, tho' I hope
for all this to refresh it frequently, & retouch it from
the living Original : I don't know whether I should
not debase the dignity of my Subject [after this by]
telling you anything of Sig^r Cafarelli, so leaving him,
as all the World has done, to screech by himself ;
we shall descend more gradually, & talk of West,
who is just gone to Oxford again : as soon as Ashton
told me he was in town, I went to Mr Periam's in
Hatton-Garden ; but Mr Periam had left his house
(& consequently Mrs West, as a Lodger) & was removed to Thavies Inn ; at Thavies Inn instead of
Mr Periam, I could find nothing but a Note in the
key-hole, directing me to Mr Greenaways ; but M^r
Greenaways key-hole sent me to Mr Herriot ; & there
I found one of the blood of the Periams, who was so
good as to inform me, he knew nothing of the matter ;
ibi omnis effusus labor : but in a few days more he
came to me himself ; then I went to supper with him,
where he entertain'd me with all the product of his
brain, Verses upon Stow, Translations of Catullus,
& Homer, Epick Epigrams, & Odes upon the New-
Year, Wild Ducks, & Petits Pâtés : we are to write
to each other every post, if not oftener : he corresponds
with Tozhy Cole, & Quid Prinsep : the transactions
of Mr Fleetwood & Rich I defer to my next, or to

word of mouth, for I shall be at Cambridge on Tuesday
night, tho' I fear my not meeting with you there ;
I am, S^r,

yours most sincerely,

T : GRAY

19. To WALPOLE

[   ] I did not allow myself time to rejoyce
with Ashton upon his good fortune, till after I had
ransacked all his informations, as to you ; & with him
admired your judgement & conduct ; for these virtues
(I find, you are resolved to shew us) you are as well
acquainted with, as we knew you were with their
Sisters : what ! will no less than the whole family
serve your turn ; sure one of 'em might have contented
any moderate stomach ! there's Miss Temperance,
Miss Constance & the rest of 'em ; e'er a one, i'gad, a
match for an emperour : these, it is well known, or
the world much belies you, you have Had ; deny it,
if you can ; and must poor Miss Prue go to pot too ?
well, I say no more, but it's too much in all conscience,
methinks, for one man to be fit equally for this world,
& the next. they tell me you are to be here once more
in a little while ; dear now, don't let it be much longer.
in the mean time have you seen Comus, & what figure
does it make after cutting for the simples ? have you
read yourself to sleep with Dr Swift's conversation, as
I did ? that confounded Lady Answerall, tho' she says
less than any body, is the devil to me ! pray did you
ever see an elephant ! I have. if you han't, you never
saw an ugly thing. I would not be Aurengzebe for the
world ; they say, he rid upon one : that's

All.

yours ever,

T : G :

March, 7, [1738] Cantab :
To the Honble Horace Walpole Esq at the Treasury
St James's

20. To Walpole

[   ] Thank God, I had a very good night's
rest, and am sufficiently awake to answer your letter,
tho' likely to be more dull, than you that write in your
sleep : and indeed I do not believe, that you ever are
so much asleep, but you can write to a relation, play a
sober game at Picquet, keep up a tete á tete conversation, sell a bargain, or perform any of the little offices
of life with tolerable spirit ; certain I am, there are
many people in the world, who in their top spirits are
no better eveillés, than you are at four in the morning,
reclined upon your pillow, I believe, I partly guess
[what is] your hopeful branch ; I fancy you may find
the first letters of both somewhere between H & T
inclusive ; if I interpret your hieroglyphs aright. as
to my journey to London, which you are so good as to
press, alas ! what can I do ? if I come, it is for good &
all, & I don't know how it is, I have a sort of reluctance to leave this place, unamiable as it may seem ;
'tis true Cambridge is very ugly, she is very dirty, &
very dull ; but I'm like a cabbage, where I'm stuck,
I love to grow ; you should pull me up sooner, than
any one, but I shall be ne'er the better for transplant-
ing : poor Mr Cornwallis is here, sadly alter'd, so that
one can very hardly know him ; Towers still stands
out, & refuses to admit him ; so that they have called
in their visitours, that is the Vice-chancellour, Dr
Bently, & Dr Ashton ; but nothing is yet determined :
the Assizes are just over, I was there ; but I a'nt to
be transported : Adieu,

yours sincerely

T: GRAY

Cam : March : 20 [1738]
To the Honble Horatio Walpole, Esq at the Treasury
St James's

21. To West

I am coming away all so fast, and leaving behind me, without the least remorse, all the beauties of Sturbridge Fair. Its white bears may roar, its apes may wring their hands, and crocodiles cry their eyes out, all's one for that ; I shall not once visit them, nor so much as take my leave. The university has published a severe edict against schismatical congregations, and created half a dozen new little procterlings to see its orders executed, being under mighty apprehension lest Henley and his gilt tub should come to the Fair and seduce their young ones ; but their pains are to small purpose, for lo, after all, he is not coming.

I am at this instant in the very agonies of leaving college, and would not wish the worst of my enemies a worse situation. If you knew the dust, the old boxes, the bedsteads, and tutors that are about my ears, you would look upon this letter as a great effort of my resolution and unconcernedness in the midst of evils. I fill up my paper with a loose sort of version of that scene in Pastor Fido that begins, Care selve beate.

[Cambridge] Sept. 1738.

22. To His Mother

Amiens, April 1, N. S. 1739.

As we made but a very short journey to-day, and came to our inn early, I sit down to give you some account of our expedition. On the 29th (according to the style here) we left Dover at twelve at noon, and with a pretty brisk gale, which pleased everybody mighty well, except myself, who was extremely sick the whole time : we reached Calais by five : The weather changed, and it began to snow hard the minute we got into the harbour, where we took the boat and soon landed. Calais is an exceeding old, but very pretty town, and we hardly saw any thing there that was not so new and so different from England, that it surprised us agreeably. We went the next morning

to the great Church, and were at high Mass (it being
Easter Monday). We saw also the Convents of the
Capuchins, and the Nuns of St. Dominic ; with these
last we held much conversation, especially with an
English Nun, a Mrs. Davis, of whose work I sent you
by the return of the Pacquet, a letter-case to remember
her by. In the afternoon we took a post-chaise (it
still snowing very hard) for Boulogne, which was only
eighteen miles further. This chaise is a strange sort
of conveyance, of much greater use than beauty,
resembling an ill-shaped chariot, only with the door
opening before instead of the side ; three horses draw
it, one between the shafts, and the other two on each
side, on one of which the postillion rides, and drives
too : This vehicle will upon occasion, go fourscore
miles a-day, but Mr. Walpole, being in no hurry,
chooses to make easy journies of it, and they are easy
ones indeed ; for the motion is much like that of a
sedan, we go about six miles an hour, and commonly
change horses at the end of it : It is true they are no
very graceful steeds, but they go well, and through
roads which they say are bad for France, but to me
they seem gravel walks and bowling-greens ; in short
it would be the finest travelling in the world, were it
not for the inns, which are mostly terrible places indeed.
But to describe our progress somewhat more regularly,
we came into Boulogne when it was almost dark, and
went out pretty early on Tuesday morning ; so that
all I can say about it is, that it is a large, old, fortified
town, with more English in it than French. On
Tuesday we were to go to Abbéville, seventeen leagues,
or fifty-one short English miles ; but by the way we
dined at Montreuil, much to our hearts' content, on
stinking mutton cutlets, addled eggs, and ditch water.
Madame the hostess made her appearance in long
lappets of bone lace and a sack of linsey-woolsey. We
supped and lodged pretty well at Abbéville, and had
time to see a little of it before we came out this morning.
There are seventeen convents in it, out of which we
saw the chapels of Minims and the Carmelite Nuns. We

are now come further thirty miles to Amiens, the chief
city of the province of Picardy. We have seen the
cathedral, which is just what that of Canterbury must
have been before the reformation. It is about the
same size, a huge Gothic building, beset on the outside
with thousands of small statues, and within adorned
with beautiful painted windows, and a vast number of
chapels dressed out in all their finery of altar-pieces,
embroidery, gilding, and marble. Over the high altar
are preserved, in a very large wrought shrine of massy
gold, the relicks of St Firmin, their patron saint. We
went also to the chapels of the Jesuits and Ursuline
Nuns, the latter of which is very richly adorned. To-
morrow we shall lie at Clermont, and next day reach
Paris. The country we have passed through hitherto
has been flat, open, but agreeably diversified with
villages, fields well-cultivated, and little rivers. On
every hillock is a windmill, a crucifix, or a Virgin Mary
dressed in flowers, and a sarcenet robe ; one sees not
many people or carriages on the road ; now and then
indeed you meet a strolling friar, a countryman with
his great muff, or a woman riding astride on a little
ass, with short petticoats, and a great head-dress of
blue wool. * *

    *   *   *   *   *

23. To West

Paris, April 12, 1739.

Enfin donc me voici à Paris. Mr. Walpole is gone
out to supper at Lord Conway's, and here I remain
alone, though invited too. Do not think I make a
merit of writing to you preferably to a good supper ;
for these three days we have been here, have actually
given me an aversion to eating in general. If hunger
be the best sauce to meat, the French are certainly the
worst cooks in the world ; for what tables we have
seen have been so delicately served, and so profusely,
that, after rising from one of them, one imagines it
impossible ever to eat again. And now, if I tell you

all I have in my head, you will believe me mad, mais n'importe, courage, allons! for if I wait till my head grow clear and settle a little, you may stay long enough for a letter. Six days have we been coming hither, which other people do in two; they have not been disagreeable ones; through a fine, open country, admirable roads, and in an easy conveyance; the inns not absolutely intolerable, and images quite unusual presenting themselves on all hands. At Amiens we saw the fine cathedral, and eat paté de perdrix; passed through the park of Chantilly by the Duke of Bourbon's palace, which we only beheld as we passed; broke down at Lusarche; stopt at St. Denis, saw all the beautiful monuments of the Kings of France, and the vast treasures of the abbey, rubies, and emeralds as big as small eggs, crucifixes, and vows, crowns and reliquaries, of inestimable value; but of all their curiosities the thing the most to our tastes, and which they indeed do the justice to esteem the glory of their collection, was a vase of an entire onyx, measuring at least five inches over, three deep, and of great thickness. It is at least two thousand years old, the beauty of the stone and sculpture upon it (representing the mysteries of Bacchus) beyond expression admirable; we have dreamed of it ever since. The jolly old Benedictine, that showed us the treasures, had in his youth been ten years a soldier; he laughed at all the reliques, was very full of stories, and mighty obliging. On Saturday evening we got to Paris, and were driving through the streets a long while before we knew where we were. The minute we came, voila Milors Holdernesse, Conway, and his brother; all stayed supper, and till two o'clock in the morning, for here nobody ever sleeps; it is not the way: Next day go to dine at my Lord Holdernesse's, there was the Abbé Prevôt, author of the Cleveland, and several other pieces much esteemed: The rest were English. At night we went to the Pandore; a spectacle literally, for it is nothing but a beautiful piece of machinery of three scenes. The first represents the chaos, and by degrees the separation of the elements. The second, the temple of Jupiter, and the giving of the box to Pandora. The third, the opening of the box, and all the mischiefs that ensued. An absurd design, but executed in the highest perfection, and that in one of the finest theatres in the world ; it is the grande sale des machines in the Palais des Tuileries. Next day dined at Lord Waldegrave's ; then to the opera. Imagine to yourself for the drama four acts entirely unconnected with each other, each founded on some little history, skilfully taken out of an ancient author, e. g. Ovid's Metamorphoses, &c., and with great address converted into a French piece of gallantry. For instance, that which I saw, called the Ballet de la Paix, had its first act built upon the story of Nireus. Homer having said he was the handsomest man of his time, the poet, imagining such a one could not want a mistress, has given him one. These two come in and sing sentiment in lamentable strains, neither air nor recitative ; only, to one's great joy, they are every now and then interrupted by a dance, or (to one's great sorrow) by a chorus that borders the stage from one end to the other, and screams, past all power of simile to represent. The second act was Baucis and Philemon. Baucis a beautiful young shepherdess, and Philemon her swain. Jupiter falls in love with her, but nothing will prevail upon her ; so it is all mighty well, and the chorus sing and dance the praises of Constancy. The two other acts were about Iphis and Ianthe, and the judgment of Paris. Imagine, I say, all this transacted by cracked voices, trilling divisions upon two notes and a half, accompanied by an orchestra of humstrums, and a whole house more attentive than if Farinelli sung, and you will almost have formed a just notion of the thing. Our astonishment at their absurdity you can never conceive ; we had enough to do to express it by screaming an hour louder than the whole dramatis personæ. We have also seen twice the Comedie Françoise ; first, the Mahomet Second, a tragedy that has had a great run of late ; and the thing itself does not want its beauties, but the actors are beyond measure delightful. Mademoiselle Gaussin (Mr. Voltaire's Zara) has with a charming (though little) person the most pathetic tone of voice, the finest expression in her face, and most proper action imaginable. There is also a Dufrêne, who did the chief character, a handsome man and a prodigious fine actor. The second we saw was the Philosophe marié, and here they performed as well in comedy ; there is a Mademoiselle Quinault, somewhat in Mrs. Clive's way, and a Monsieur Grandval in the nature of Wilks, who is the genteelest thing in the world. There are several more would be much admired in England, and many (whom we have not seen) much celebrated here. Great part of our time is spent in seeing churches and palaces full of fine pictures, &c., the quarter of which is not yet exhausted. For my part, I could entertain myself this month merely with the common streets and the people in them. * * *

24. To Thomas Ashton

Dear Ashton,—You and West have made us happy to night in a heap of letters, & we are resolved to repay you ten-fold. Our English perhaps may not be the best in the World, but we have the Comfort to know that it is at least as good as our French. So to begin. Paris is a huge round City, divided by the Seine, a very near relation (if we may judge from the resemblance) of your old acquaintance, that ancient river, the river Cam. Along it on either side runs a key of perhaps as handsome buildings, as any in the World. the view down which on either hand from the Pont Neuf is the charming'st Sight imaginable. There are infinite Swarms of inhabitants & more Coaches than Men. The Women in general dressd in Sacs, flat Hoops of 5 yards wide nosegays of artificial flowers, on one shoulder, and faces dyed in Scarlet up to the Eyes. The Men in bags, roll-upps, Muffs and Solitaires. our Mornings have been mostly taken up in Seeing Sights : few Hotels or Churches have escapd us, where there is anything remarkable as to building, Pictures or Statues.

Mr Conway is as usual, the Companion of our travels, who, till we came, had not seen anything at all; for it is not the fashion here to have Curiosity. We had at first arrival an inundation of Visits pouring in upon us, for all the English are acquainted, and herd much together & it is no easy Matter to disengage oneself from them, so that one sees but little of the French themselves.

To be introduced to the People of high quality, it is absolutely necessary to be master of the Language, for it is not to be imagined that they will take pains to understand anybody, or to correct a stranger's blunders. Another thing is, there is not a House where they don't play, nor is any one at all acceptable, unless they do so too . . a professed Gamester being the most advantageous Character a Man can have at Paris. The Abbés indeed & Men of learning are a People of easy access enough, but few English that travel have knowledge enough to take any great Pleasure in their Company, at least our present Set of travellers have not. We are, I think to remain here no longer than Ld Conway stays, and then set out for Rheims, there to reside a Month or two, & then to return hither again. this is our present design & very often little hankerings break out, so that I am not sure, we shall not come back tomorrow.

We are exceedingly unsettled & irresolute, don't know our own Minds for two Moments together, profess an utter aversion for all Manner of fatigue, grumble, are ill natured & try to bring ourselves to a State of perfect Apathy in which [we] are so far advanced, as to declare we have no Notion of caring for any mortal breathing but ourselves. In short I think the greatest *evil* could have happen'd to us, is our liberty, for we are not at all capable to determine our own actions.

My dear Ashton I am ever

Yours sincerely   T : G :

Paris—Hotel de Luxembourg. Rue des petits Augustins April 21. N. S. [1739]

25. To West

Paris, May 22, 1739.

After the little particulars aforesaid I should have proceeded to a journal of our transactions for this week past, should have carried you post from hence to Versailles, hurried you through the gardens to Trianon, back again to Paris, so away to Chantilly. But the fatigue is perhaps more than you can bear, and moreover I think I have reason to stomach your last piece of gravity. Supposing you were in your soberest mood, I am sorry you should think me capable of ever being so dissipé, so evaporé, as not to be in a condition of relishing any thing you could say to me. And now, if you have a mind to make your peace with me, arouse ye from your megrims and your melancholies, and (for exercise is good for you) throw away your night-cap, call for your jack-boots, and set out with me, last Saturday evening, for Versailles—and so at eight o'clock, passing through a road speckled with vines, and villas, and hares, and partridges, we arrive at the great avenue, flanked on either hand with a double row of trees about half a mile long, and with the palace itself to terminate the view ; facing which, on each side of you is placed a semi-circle of very handsome buildings, which form the stables. These we will not enter into, because you know we are no jockies. Well ! and is this the great front of Versailles ? What a huge heap of littleness ! it is composed, as it were, of three courts, all open to the eye at once, and gradually diminishing till you come to the royal apartments, which on this side present but half a dozen windows and a balcony. This last is all that can be called a front, for the rest is only great wings. The hue of all this mass is black, dirty red, and yellow ; the first proceeding from stone changed by age ; the second, from a mixture of brick ; and the last, from a profusion of tarnished gilding. You cannot see a more disagreeable tout-ensemble ; and, to finish the matter, it is all stuck over in many places with small busts of a tawny hue between every window. We pass through this to go into the garden, and here the case is indeed altered ; nothing can be vaster and more magnificent than the back front ; before it a very spacious terrace spreads itself, adorned with two large basons ; these are bordered and lined (as most of the others) with white marble, with handsome statues of bronze reclined on their edges. From hence you descend a huge flight of steps into a semi-circle formed by woods, that are cut all round into niches, which are filled with beautiful copies of all the famous antique statues in white marble. Just in the midst is the bason of Latona ; she and her children are standing on the top of a rock in the middle, on the sides of which are the peasants, some half, some totally changed into frogs, all which throw out water at her in great plenty. From this place runs on the great alley, which brings you into a complete round, where is the bason of Apollo, the biggest in the gardens. He is rising in his car out of the water, surrounded by nymphs and tritons, all in bronze, and finely executed, and these, as they play, raise a perfect storm about him ; beyond this is the great canal, a prodigious long piece of water, that terminates the whole : All this you have at one coup d'oeil in entering the garden, which is truly great. I cannot say as much of the general taste of the place ; every thing you behold savours too much of art ; all is forced, all is constrained about you ; statues and vases sowed every where without distinction ; sugar-loaves and minced-pies of yew ; scrawl-work of box, and little squirting jets-d'eau, besides a great sameness in the walks, cannot help striking one at first sight, not to mention the silliest of labyrinths, and all Æsop's fables in water ; since these were designed in usum Delphini only. Here then we walk by moonlight, and hear the ladies and the nightingales sing. Next morning, being Whitsunday, make ready to go to the Installation of nine Knights du Saint Esprit, Cambis is one : high mass celebrated with music, great croud, much incense, King, Queen, Dauphin, Mesdames,

Cardinals, and Court : Knights arrayed by his majesty ;
reverences before the altar, not bows, but curtsies ;
stiff hams ; much tittering among the ladies ; trumpets,
kettle-drums and fifes. My dear West, I am vastly
delighted with Trianon, all of us with Chantilly ; if
you would know why, you must have patience, for
I can hold my pen no longer, except to tell you that
I saw Britannicus last Night ; all the characters,
particularly Agrippina and Nero, done to perfection ;
to-morrow Phædra and Hippolitus. We are making
you a little bundle of petites pieces ; there is nothing
in them, but they are acting at present ; there are too
Crebillon's Letters, and Amusemens sur le langage
des Bêtes, said to be of one Bougeant, a Jesuit ; they
are both esteemed, and lately come out. This day
se'nnight we go to Rheims.

26. To His Mother

Rheims, June 21, N. S. 1739.

We have now been settled almost three weeks in
this city, which is more considerable upon account of
its size and antiquity, than from the number of its
inhabitants, or any advantages of commerce. There
is little in it worth a stranger's curiosity, besides the
cathedral church, which is a vast Gothic building of
a surprising beauty and lightness, all covered over with
a profusion of little statues, and other ornaments.
It is here the Kings of France are crowned by the
Archbishop of Rheims, who is the first Peer, and the
Primate of the kingdom : The holy vessel made use
of on that occasion, which contains the oil, is kept in
the church of St. Nicasius hard by, and is believed to
have been brought by an angel from heaven at the
coronation of Clovis, the first christian king. The
streets in general have but a melancholy aspect, the
houses all old ; the public walks run along the side
of a great moat under the ramparts, where one hears
a continual croaking of frogs ; the country round
about is one great plain covered with vines, which

at this time of the year afford no very pleasing prospect, as being not above a foot high. What pleasures the place denies to the sight, it makes up to the palate; since you have nothing to drink but the best champaigne in the world, and all sort of provisions equally good. As to other pleasures, there is not that freedom of conversation among the people of fashion here, that one sees in other parts of France; for though they are not very numerous in this place, and consequently must live a good deal together, yet they never come to any great familiarity with one another. As my Lord Conway had spent a good part of his time among them, his brother, and we with him, were soon introduced into all their assemblies: As soon as you enter, the lady of the house presents each of you a card, and offers you a party at quadrille; you sit down, and play forty deals without intermission, excepting one quarter of an hour, when every body rises to eat of what they call the gouter, which supplies the place of our tea, and is a service of wine, fruits, cream, sweetmeats, crawfish and cheese. People take what they like, and sit down again to play; after that, they make little parties to go to the walks together, and then all the company retire to their separate habitations. Very seldom any suppers or dinners are given; and this is the manner they live among one another; not so much out of any aversion they have to pleasure, as out of a sort of formality they have contracted by not being much frequented by people who have lived at Paris. It is sure they do not hate gaity any more than the rest of their country-people, and can enter into diversions, that are once proposed, with a good grace enough: for instance, the other evening we happened to be got together in a company of eighteen people, men and women of the best fashion here, at a garden in the town to walk; when one of the ladies bethought herself of asking, Why should not we sup here? Immediately the cloth was laid by the side of a fountain under the trees, and a very elegant supper served up; after which another said, Come, let us

sing; and directly began herself: From singing we
insensibly fell to dancing, and singing in a round;
when somebody mentioned the violins, and immediately
a company of them was ordered: Minuets were begun
in the open air, and then came country-dances, which
held till four o'clock next morning; at which hour the
gayest lady there proposed, that such as were weary
should get into their coaches, and the rest of them
should dance before them with the music in the van;
and in this manner we paraded through all the principal
streets of the city, and waked every body in it.   Mr.
Walpole had a mind to make a custom of the thing,
and would have given a ball in the same manner next
week; but the women did not come into it; so I
believe it will drop, and they will return to their dull
cards, and usual formalities.   We are not to stay
above a month longer here, and shall then go to Dijon,
the chief city of Burgundy, a very splendid and very
gay town; at least such is the present design.

27. To West

Lyons, Sept. 18, N. S. 1739.

Scavez vous bien, mon cher ami, que je vous hais,
que je vous deteste ? voila des termes un peu forts; and
that will save me, upon a just computation, a page
of paper and six drops of ink; which, if I confined
myself to reproaches of a more moderate nature, I
should be obliged to employ in using you according
to your deserts.   What! to let any body reside three
months at Rheims, and write but once to them ?
Please to consult Tully de Amicit. page 5, line 25, and
you will find it said in express terms, ' Ad amicum
inter Remos relegatum mense uno quinquies scriptum
esto; ' nothing more plain, or less liable to false inter-
pretations.   Now because, I suppose, it will give you
pain to know we are in being, I take this opportunity
to tell you that we are at the ancient and celebrated
Lugdunum, a city situated upon the confluence of the
Rhône and Saône (Arar, I should say) two people, who,

though of tempers extremely unlike, think fit to join hands here, and make a little party to travel to the Mediterranean in company; the lady comes gliding along through the fruitful plains of Burgundy, incredibili lenitate, ita ut oculis in utram partem fluit judicari non possit; the gentleman runs all rough and roaring down from the mountains of Switzerland to meet her; and with all her soft airs she likes him never the worse; she goes through the middle of the city in state, and he passes incog. without the walls, but waits for her a little below. The houses here are so high, and the streets so narrow, as would be sufficient to render Lyons the dismallest place in the world, but the number of people, and the face of commerce diffused about it, are, at least, as sufficient to make it the liveliest: Between these two sufficiencies, you will be in doubt what to think of it; so we shall leave the city, and proceed to its environs, which are beautiful beyond expression; it is surrounded with mountains, and those mountains all bedroped and bespeckled with houses, gardens, and plantations of the rich Bourgeois, who have from thence a prospect of the city in the vale below on one hand, on the other the rich plains of the Lyonnois, with the rivers winding among them, and the Alps, with the mountains of Dauphiné, to bound the view. All yesterday morning we were busied in climbing up Mount Fourviere, where the ancient city stood perched at such a height, that nothing but the hopes of gain could certainly ever persuade their neighbours to pay them a visit: Here are the ruins of the Emperors' palaces, that resided here, that is to say, Augustus and Severus; they consist in nothing but great masses of old wall, that have only their quality to make them respected. In a vineyard of the Minims are remains of a theatre; the Fathers, whom they belong to, hold them in no esteem at all, and would have showed us their sacristy and chapel instead of them: The Ursuline Nuns have in their garden some Roman baths, but we having the misfortune to be men, and heretics, they did not think proper to admit us. Hard by are eight arches of

a most magnificent aqueduct, said to be erected by
Antony, when his legions were quartered here: There
are many other parts of it dispersed up and down the
country, for it brought the water from a river many
leagues off in La Forez. Here are remains too of
Agrippa's seven great roads which met at Lyons; in
some places they lie twelve feet deep in the ground:
In short, a thousand matters that you shall not know,
till you give me a description of the Païs de Tombridge,
and the effect its waters have upon you.

28. To His Mother

Lyons, Oct. 13, N. S. 1739

It is now almost five weeks since I left Dijon, one
of the gayest and most agreeable little cities of France,
for Lyons, its reverse in all these particulars. It is
the second in the kingdom in bigness and rank, the
streets excessively narrow and nasty; the houses
immensely high and large; (that, for instance, where
we are lodged, has twenty-five rooms on a floor, and
that for five stories) it swarms with inhabitants like
Paris itself, but chiefly a mercantile people, too much
given up to commerce, to think of their own, much
less of a stranger's diversions. We have no acquaintance in the town, but such English as happen to be
passing through here, in their way to Italy and the
south, which at present happen to be near thirty in
number. It is a fortnight since we set out from hence
upon a little excursion to Geneva. We took the longest
road, which lies through Savoy, on purpose to see a
famous monastery, called the grand Chartreuse, and
had no reason to think our time lost. After having
travelled seven days very slow (for we did not change
horses, it being impossible for a chaise to go post in
these roads) we arrived at a little village, among the
mountains of Savoy, called Echelles; from thence
we proceeded on horses, who are used to the way, to
the mountain of the Chartreuse: It is six miles to
the top; the road runs winding up it, commonly not

six feet broad ; on one hand is the rock, with woods of pine trees hanging over head ; on the other, a monstrous precipice, almost perpendicular, at the bottom of which rolls a torrent, that sometimes tumbling among the fragments of stone that have fallen from on high, and sometimes precipitating itself down vast descents with a noise like thunder, which is still made greater by the echo from the mountains on each side, concurs to form one of the most solemn, the most romantic, and the most astonishing scenes I ever beheld : Add to this the strange views made by the craggs and cliffs on the other hand ; the cascades that in many places throw themselves from the very summit down into the vale, and the river below ; and many other particulars impossible to describe ; you will conclude we had no occasion to repent our pains. This place St. Bruno chose to retire to, and upon its very top founded the aforesaid convent, which is the superior of the whole order. When we came there, the two fathers, who are commissioned to entertain strangers, (for the rest must neither speak one to another, nor to any one else) received us very kindly ; and set before us a repast of dried fish, eggs, butter and fruits, all excellent in their kind, and extremely neat. They pressed us to spend the night there, and to stay some days with them ; but this we could not do, so they led us about their house, which is, you must think, like a little city ; for there are 100 fathers, besides 300 servants, that make their clothes, grind their corn, press their wine, and do every thing among themselves : The whole is quite orderly and simple ; nothing of finery, but the wonderful decency, and the strange situation, more than supply the place of it. In the evening we descended by the same way, passing through many clouds that were then forming themselves on the mountain's side. Next day we continued our journey by Chamberry, which, though the chief city of the duchy, and residence of the king of Sardinia, when he comes into this part of his dominions, makes but a very mean and insignificant appearance ; we

lay at Aix, once famous for its hot baths, and the next
night at Annecy ; the day after, by noon, we got to
Geneva. I have not time to say any thing about it,
nor of our solitary journey back again. * * *

29. To His Father

Lyons, Oct. 25, N. S. 1739.

In my last I gave you the particulars of our little
journey to Geneva : I have only to add, that we
stayed about a week, in order to see Mr. Conway
settled there : I do not wonder so many English choose
it for their residence ; the city is very small, neat,
prettily built, and extremely populous ; the Rhône
runs through the middle of it, and it is surrounded
with new fortifications, that give it a military compact
air ; which, joined to the happy, lively countenances
of the inhabitants, and an exact discipline always as
strictly observed as in time of war, makes the little
republic appear a match for a much greater power ;
though perhaps Geneva, and all that belongs to it,
are not of equal extent with Windsor and its two
parks. To one that has passed through Savoy, as we
did, nothing can be more striking than the contrast,
as soon as he approaches the town. Near the gates of
Geneva runs the torrent Arve, which separates it
from the King of Sardinia's dominions ; on the other
side of it lies a country naturally, indeed, fine and
fertile ; but you meet with nothing in it but meagre,
ragged, bare-footed peasants, with their children, in
extreme misery and nastiness ; and even of these no
great numbers ; You no sooner have crossed the
stream I have mentioned, but poverty is no more ;
not a beggar, hardly a discontented face to be seen ;
numerous and well-dressed people swarming on the
ramparts ; drums beating, soldiers, well clothed and
armed, exercising ; and folks, with business in their
looks, hurrying to and fro ; all contribute to make
any person, who is not blind, sensible what a difference
there is between the two governments, that are the

causes of one view and the other. The beautiful lake, at one end of which the town is situated; its extent; the several states that border upon it; and all its pleasures, are too well known for me to mention them. We sailed upon it as far as the dominions of Geneva extend, that is, about two leagues and a half on each side; and landed at several of the little houses of pleasure, that the inhabitants have built all about it, who received us with much politeness. The same night we eat part of a trout, taken in the lake, that weighed thirty-seven pounds; as great a monster as it appeared to us, it was esteemed there nothing extraordinary, and they assured us, it was not uncommon to catch them of fifty pounds; they are dressed here and sent post to Paris upon some great occasions; nay, even to Madrid, as we were told. The road we returned through was not the same we came by: We crossed the Rhône at Seyssel, and passed for three days among the mountains of Bugey, without meeting with any thing new: At last we came out into the plains of La Bresse, and so to Lyons again. Sir Robert has written to Mr. Walpole, to desire he would go to Italy; which he has resolved to do; so that all the scheme of spending the winter in the south of France is laid aside, and we are to pass it in a much finer country. You may imagine I am not sorry to have this opportunity of seeing the place in the world that best deserves it; Besides as the Pope (who is eighty-eight, and has been lately at the point of death) cannot probably last a great while, perhaps we may have the fortune to be present at the election of a new one, when Rome will be in all its glory. Friday next we certainly begin our journey; in two days we shall come to the foot of the Alps, and six more we shall be in passing them. Even here the winter is begun; what then must it be among those vast snowy mountains where it is hardly ever summer? We are, however, as well armed as possible against the cold, with muffs, hoods, and masks of beaver, fur-boots, and bear skins. When we arrive at Turin, we shall rest after the fatigues of the journey. * * *

30. To His Mother

Turin, Nov. 7, N. S. 1739.

I am this night arrived here, and have just set down to rest me after eight days tiresome journey : For the three first we had the same road we before passed through to go to Geneva ; the fourth we turned out of it, and for that day and the next travelled rather among than upon the Alps ; the way commonly running through a deep valley by the side of the river Arc, which works itself a passage, with great difficulty and a mighty noise, among vast quantities of rocks, that have rolled down from the mountain tops. The winter was so far advanced, as in great measure to spoil the beauty of the prospect ; however, there was still somewhat fine remaining amidst the savageness and horror of the place : The sixth we began to go up several of these mountains ; and as we were passing one, met with an odd accident enough : Mr. Walpole had a little fat black spaniel, that he was very fond of, which he sometimes used to set down, and let it run by the chaise side. We were at that time in a very rough road, not two yards broad at most ; on one side was a great wood of pines, and on the other a vast precipice ; it was noon-day, and the sun shone bright, when all of a sudden, from the wood-side, (which was as steep upwards, as the other part was downwards) out rushed a great wolf, came close to the head of the horses, seized the dog by the throat, and rushed up the hill again with him in his mouth. This was done in less than a quarter of a minute ; we all saw it, and yet the servants had not time to draw their pistols, or do any thing to save the dog. If he had not been there, and the creature had thought fit to lay hold of one of the horses ; chaise, and we, and all must inevitably have tumbled above fifty fathoms perpendicular down the precipice. The seventh we came to Lanebourg, the last town in Savoy ; it lies at the foot of the famous mount Cenis, which is so situated as to allow no room for any way but over the very top of it. Here the chaise was forced to be pulled to pieces, and the baggage and that to be carried by mules : We ourselves were wrapped up in our furs, and seated upon a sort of matted chair without legs, which is carried upon poles in the manner of a bier, and so begun to ascend by the help of eight men. It was six miles to the top, where a plain opens itself about as many more in breadth, covered perpetually with very deep snow, and in the midst of that a great lake of unfathomable depth, from whence a river takes its rise, and tumbles over monstrous rocks quite down the other side of the mountain. The descent is six miles more, but infinitely more steep than the going up ; and here the men perfectly fly down with you, stepping from stone to stone with incredible swiftness in places where none but they could go three paces without falling. The immensity of the precipices, the roaring of the river and torrents that run into it, the huge craggs covered with ice and snow, and the clouds below you and about you, are objects it is impossible to conceive without seeing them ; and though we had heard many strange descriptions of the scene, none of them at all came up to it. We were but five hours in performing the whole, from which you may judge of the rapidity of the men's motion. We are now got into Piedmont, and stopped a little while at La Ferriere, a small village about three quarters of the way down, but still among the clouds, where we began to hear a new language spoken round about us ; at last we got quite down, went through the Pas de Suse, a narrow road among the Alps, defended by two fortresses, and lay at Bossolens : Next evening through a fine avenue of nine miles in length, as straight as a line, we arrived at this city, which, as you know, is the capital of the Principality, and the residence of the King of Sardinia. * * * We shall stay here, I believe, a fortnight, and proceed for Genoa, which is three or four days journey to go post. I am, etc.

31. To WEST

Turin, Nov. 16, N. S. 1739.

After eight days journey through Greenland, we arrived at Turin. You approach it by a handsome avenue of nine miles long, and quite strait. The entrance is guarded by certain vigilant dragons, called Douäniers, who mumbled us for some time. The city is not large, as being a place of strength, and consequently confined within its fortifications; it has many beauties and some faults; among the first are streets all laid out by the line, regular uniform buildings, fine walks that surround the whole, and in general a good lively clean appearance: But the houses are of brick plaistered, which is apt to want repairing; the windows of oiled paper, which is apt to be torn; and every thing very slight, which is apt to tumble down. There is an excellent Opera, but it is only in the Carnival: Balls every night, but only in the Carnival: Masquerades, too, but only in the Carnival. This Carnival lasts only from Christmas to Lent; one half of the remaining part of the year is passed in remembering the last, the other in expecting the future Carnival. We cannot well subsist upon each slender diet, no more than upon an execrable Italian Comedy, and a Puppet-Show, called Rappresentazione d'un' anima dannata, which, I think, are all the present diversions of the place; except the Marquise de Cavaillac's Conversazione, where one goes to see people play at Ombre and Taroc, a game with 72 cards all painted with suns, and moons, and devils and monks. Mr. Walpole has been at court; the family are at present at a country palace, called La Venerie. The palace here in town is the very quintessence of gilding and looking-glass; inlaid floors, carved pannels, and painting, wherever they could stick a brush. I own I have not, as yet, any where met with those grand and simple works of Art, that are to amaze one, and whose sight one is to be the better for: But those of Nature have astonished me beyond expression. In our little journey up to the

Grande Chartreuse, I do not remember to have gone
ten paces without an exclamation, that there was no
restraining : Not a precipice, not a torrent, not a cliff,
but is pregnant with religion and poetry. There are
certain scenes that would awe an atheist into belief,
without the help of other argument. One need not
have a very fantastic imagination to see spirits there
at noon-day : You have Death perpetually before
your eyes, only so far removed, as to compose the mind
without frighting it. I am well persuaded St. Bruno
was a man of no common genius, to choose such a
situation for his retirement ; and perhaps should have
been a disciple of his, had I been born in his time.
You may believe Abelard and Heloïse were not forgot
upon this occasion : If I do not mistake, I saw you
too every now and then at a distance among the trees ;
il me semble, que j'ai vu ce chien de visage là quelque
part. You seemed to call to me from the other side
of the precipice, but the noise of the river below was
so great, that I really could not distinguish what you
said ; it seemed to have a cadence like verse. In your
next you will be so good to let me know what it was.
The week we have since passed among the Alps, has
not equalled the single day upon that mountain,
because the winter was rather too far advanced, and
the weather a little foggy. However, it did not want
its beauties ; the savage rudeness of the view is incon-
ceivable without seeing it : I reckoned in one day,
thirteen cascades, the least of which was, I dare say,
one hundred feet in height. I had Livy in the chaise
with me, and beheld his ' Nives cœlo propè immistæ,
tecta informia imposita rupibus, pecora jumentaque
torrida frigore, homines intonsi & inculti, animalia
inanimaque omnia rigentia gelu ; omnia confragosa,
præruptaque '. The creatures that inhabit them are,
in all respects, below humanity ; and most of them,
especially women, have the tumidum gutter, which
they call goscia. Mont Cenis, I confess, carries the
permission mountains have of being frightful rather
too far ; and its horrors were accompanied with too

much danger to give one time to reflect upon their beauties. There is a family of the Alpine monsters I have mentioned, upon its very top, that in the middle of winter calmly lay in their stock of provisions and firing, and so are buried in their hut for a month or two under the snow. When we were down it, and got a little way into Piedmont, we began to find 'Apricos quosdam colles, rivosque prope sylvas, & jam humano cultu digniora loca'. I read Silius Italicus too, for the first time ; and wished for you according to custom. We set out for Genoa in two days time.

32. To West

Genoa, Nov. 21, 1739.

Horridos tractus, Boreæq; linquens
Regna Taurini fera, molliorem
Advehor brumam, Genuæq; amantes
    Littora soles.

At least if they do not, they have a very ill taste ; for I never beheld any thing more amiable : Only figure to yourself a vast semicircular bason, full of fine blue sea, and vessels of all sorts and sizes, some sailing out, some coming in, and others at anchor ; and all round it palaces and churches peeping over one another's heads, gardens and marble terrases full of orange and cypress trees, fountains, and trellis-works covered with vines, which altogether compose the grandest of theatres. This is the first coup d'oeil, and is almost all I am yet able to give you an account of, for we arrived late last night. To-day was, luckily, a great festival, and in the morning we resorted to the church of the Madonna delle Vigne, to put up our little orisons ; (I believe I forgot to tell you, that we have been sometime converts to the holy Catholic church) we found our Lady richly dressed out, with a crown of diamonds on her own head, another upon the child's, and a constellation of wax lights burning before them : Shortly after came the Doge, in his robes of crimson damask, and a cap of the same, followed by the Senate in black. Upon his approach began a fine concert of music, and among the rest two eunuchs' voices, that were a perfect feast to ears that had heard nothing but French operas for a year. We listened to this, and breathed nothing but incense for two hours. The Doge is a very tall, lean, stately, old figure, called Costantino Balbi; and the Senate seem to have been made upon the same model. They said their prayers, and heard an absurd white friar preach, with equal devotion. After this we went to the Annonciata, a church built by the family Lomellini, and belonging to it; which is, indeed, a most stately structure, the inside wholly marble of various kinds, except where gold and painting take its place. From hence to the Palazzo Doria. I should make you sick of marble, if I told you how it was lavished here upon the porticoes, the balustrades, and terrases, the lowest of which extends quite to the sea. The inside is by no means answerable to the outward magnificence; the furniture seems to be as old as the founder of the family. There great imbossed silver tables tell you, in bas-relief, his victories at sea; how he entertained the Emperor Charles, and how he refused the sovereignty of the Commonwealth when it was offered him; the rest is old-fashioned velvet chairs, and gothic tapestry. The rest of the day has been spent, much to our hearts' content, in cursing French music and architecture, and in singing the praises of Italy. We find this place so very fine, that we are in fear of finding nothing finer. We are fallen in love with the Mediterranean sea, and hold your lakes and your rivers in vast contempt. This is

> The happy country where huge lemons grow,

as Waller says; and I am sorry to think of leaving it in a week for Parma, although it be

> The happy country where huge cheeses grow.

33. To His Mother

Bologna, Dec. 9, N. S. 1739.

Our journey hither has taken up much less time than
I expected. We left Genoa (a charming place, and
one that deserved a longer stay) the week before last ;
crossed the mountains, and lay that night at Tortona,
the next at St. Giovanni, and the morning after came
to Piacenza. That city (though the capital of a Dutchy)
made so frippery an appearance, that instead of spending some days there, as had been intended, we only
dined, and went on to Parma ; stayed there all the
following day, which was passed in visiting the famous
works of Correggio in the Dome, and other churches.
The fine gallery of pictures, that once belonged to the
Dukes of Parma, is no more here ; the King of Naples
has carried it all thither, and the city had not merit
enough to detain us any longer, so we proceeded
through Reggio to Modena ; this, though the residence
of its Duke, is an ill built melancholy place, all of brick,
as are most of the towns in this part of Lombardy :
He himself lives in a private manner, with very little
appearance of a court about him ; he has one of the
noblest collections of paintings in the world, which
entertained us extremely well the rest of that day and
a part of the next ; and in the afternoon we came to
Bologna. So now you may wish us joy of being in
the dominions of his Holiness. This is a populous
city, and of great extent : All the streets have porticoes
on both sides, such as surround a part of Covent-
Garden, a great relief in summer-time in such a climate ;
and from one of the principal gates to a church of the
Virgin, [where is a wonder-working picture, at three
miles distance] runs a corridore of the same sort, lately
finished, and indeed a most extraordinary performance.
The churches here are more remarkable for their
paintings than architecture, being mostly old struc-
tures of brick ; but the palaces are numerous, and fine
enough to supply us with somewhat worth seeing
from morning till night. The country of Lombardy,

hitherto, is one of the most beautiful imaginable; the roads broad, and exactly straight, and on either hand vast plantations of trees, chiefly mulberries and olives, and not a tree without a vine twining about it and spreading among its branches. This scene, indeed, which must be the most lovely in the world during the proper season, is at present all deformed by the winter, which here is rigorous enough for the time it lasts; but one still sees the skeleton of a charming place, and reaps the benefit of its product, for the fruits and provisions are admirable; in short, you find every thing that luxury can desire in perfection. We have now been here a week, and shall stay some little time longer. We are at the foot of the Appennine mountains; it will take up three days to cross them, and then we shall come to Florence, where we shall pass the Christmas. Till then we must remain in a state of ignorance as to what is doing in England, for our letters are to meet us there: If I do not find four or five from you alone, I shall wonder.

34. To His Mother

Florence, Dec. 19, N. S. 1739.

We spent twelve days at Bologna, chiefly (as most travellers do) in seeing sights; for as we knew no mortal there, and as it is no easy matter to get admission into any Italian house, without very particular recommendations, we could see no company but in public places; and there are none in that city but the churches. We saw, therefore, churches, palaces, and pictures from morning to night; and the 15th of this month set out for Florence, and began to cross the Appennine mountains; we travelled among and upon them all that day, and, as it was but indifferent weather, were commonly in the middle of thick clouds, that utterly deprived us of sight of their beauties: For this vast chain of hills has its beauties, and all the valleys are cultivated; even the mountains themselves are many of them so within a little of their very tops.

They are not so horrid as the Alps, though pretty near
as high ; and the whole road is admirably well kept,
and paved throughout, which is a length of fourscore
miles, and more : We left the pope's dominions, and
lay that night in those of the Grand Duke at Fioren-
zuola, a paltry little town, at the foot of Mount Giogo,
which is the highest of them all. Next morning we
went up it ; the post-house is upon its very top, and
usually involved in clouds, or half-buried in the snow.
Indeed there was none of the last at the time we were
there, but it was still a dismal habitation. The descent
is most excessively steep, and the turnings very short
and frequent ; however, we performed it without any
danger, and in coming down could dimly discover
Florence, and the beautiful plain about it, through
the mists, but enough to convince us, it must be one
of the noblest prospects upon earth in summer. That
afternoon we got thither ; and Mr. Mann, the resident,
had sent his servant to meet us at the gates, and conduct us to his house. He is the best and most obliging
person in the world. The next night we were introduced at the Prince of Craon's assembly (he has the
chief power here in the Grand Duke's absence). The
princess, and he, were extremely civil to the name of
Walpole, so we were asked to stay supper, which is as
much as to say, you may come and sup here whenever
you please ; for after the first invitation this is always
understood. We have also been at the Countess
Suarez's, a favourite of the late Duke, and one that
gives the first movement to every thing gay that is
going forward here. The news is every day expected
from Vienna of the Great Duchess's delivery ; if it
be a boy, here will be all sorts of balls, masquerades,
operas, and illuminations ; if not, we must wait for
the Carnival, when all those things come of course.
In the mean time it is impossible to want entertainment ; the famous gallery, alone, is an amusement
for months ; we commonly pass two or three hours
every morning in it, and one has perfect leisure to
consider all its beauties. You know it contains many

hundred antique statues, such as the whole world cannot match, besides the vast collection of paintings, medals, and precious stones, such as no other prince was ever master of ; in short, all that the rich and powerful house of Medicis has in so many years got together. And besides this city abounds with so many palaces and churches, that you can hardly place yourself any where without having some fine one in view, or at least some statue or fountain, magnificently adorned ; these undoubtedly are far more numerous than Genoa can pretend to ; yet, in its general appearance, I cannot think that Florence equals it in beauty. Mr. Walpole is just come from being presented to the Electress Palatine Dowager ; she is a sister of the late Great Duke's ; a stately old lady, that never goes out but to church, and then she has guards, and eight horses to her coach. She received him with much ceremony, standing under a huge black canopy, and, after a few minutes talking, she assured him of her good will, and dismissed him : She never sees any body but thus in form ; and so she passes her life, poor woman ! * * *

35. To Thomas Wharton

Proposals for printing by Subscription, in

THIS LARGE

LETTER,

The Travels of T: G: Gent:

which will consist of the following Particulars.

Chap: 1:

The Author arrives at Dover ; his conversation with the Mayor of that Corporation ; sets out in the Pacquet-Boat, grows very sick ; the Author spews, a very minute account of all the circumstances thereof : his arrival at Calais ; how the inhabitants of that country speak French, & are said to be all Papishes ; the Author's reflexions thereupon.

2

How they feed him with Soupe, and what Soupe is.
how he meets with a Capucin; & what a Capucin is.
how they shut him up in a Post-Chaise, & send him
to Paris; he goes wondring along dureing 6 days;
& how there are Trees, & Houses just as in England.
arrives at Paris without knowing it.

3

Full account of the river Seine, & of the various
animals & plants its borders produce. Description of
the little Creature called an Abbé, its parts, & their
uses; with the reasons why they will not live in England, and the methods, that have been used to propagate them there. a Cut of the inside of a Nunnery;
its Structure, wonderfully adapted to the use of the
animals, that inhabit it: a short account of them, how
they propagate without the help of a Male, and how
they eat up their own young ones, like Cats and
Rabbets. supposed to have both sexes in themselves,
like a Snail. Dissection of a Dutchess with Copper-
Plates, very curious.

4

Goes to the Opera; grand Orchestra of Humstrums,
Bag-pipes, Salt-boxes, Tabours, & Pipes. Anatomy
of a French Ear, shewing the formation of it to be
entirely different from that of an English one, & that
Sounds have a directly contrary effect upon one & the
other. Farinelli at Paris said to have a fine manner,
but no voice. Grand Ballet, in which there is no seeing
the dance for Petticoats. Old Women with flowers,
& jewels stuck in the Curls of their grey Hair; Red-
heel'd Shoes & Roll-ups innumerable, Hoops, & Paniers
immeasurable, Paint unspeakable. Tables, wherein
is calculated with the utmost exactness, the several
Degrees of Red, now in use, from the riseing blush of
an Advocate's Wife to the flameing Crimson of a
Princess of the blood; done by a Limner in great
vogue.

5

The Author takes unto him a Taylour; his Character. how he covers him with Silk, & Fringe, & widens his figure with buckram a yard on each side; Wastcoat, & Breeches so strait, he can neither breath, nor walk. how the Barber curls him en Bequille, & à la negligee, & ties a vast Solitaire about his Neck; how the Milliner lengthens his ruffles to his finger's ends, & sticks his two arms into a Muff. how he cannot stir, & how they cut him in proportion to his Clothes.

6

He is carried to Versailles; despises it infinitely. a dissertation upon Taste. goes to an Installation in the Chappel-royal. enter the King & 50 Fiddlers Solus. Kettle-Drums & Trumpets, Queens, & Dauphins, Princesses, & Cardinals, Incense, & the Mass. Old Knights makeing Curtsies; Holy-Ghosts & Fiery-tongues.

7

Goes into the country to Rheims in Champagne. stays there 3 Months, what he did there (he must beg the reader's pardon, but) he has really forgot.

8

Proceeds to Lyons. Vastness of that City. Can't see the Streets for houses. how rich it is, & how much it stinks. Poem upon the Confluence of the Rhône & the Sâone, by a friend of the Author's; very pretty!

9

Makes a journey into Savoy, & in his way visits the Grand Chartreuse; he is set astride upon a Mule's back, & begins to climb up the Mountain. Rocks & Torrents beneath; Pine-trees, & Snows above; horrours, & terrours on all sides. the Author dies of the Fright.

10

He goes to Geneva. his mortal antipathy to a Presbyterian, and the cure for it. returns to Lyons.

gets a surfeit with eating Ortolans, & Lampreys ; is
advised to go into Italy for the benefit of the air. . . .

11

Sets out the latter end of November to cross the
Alps. he is devoured by a Wolf, & how it is to be
devoured by a Wolf. The 7th day he comes to the foot
of Mount Cenis. how he is wrap'd up in Bear Skins,
& Beaver-Skins, Boots on his legs, Caps on his head,
Muffs on his hands, & Taffety over his eyes ; he is
placed on a Bier, & is carried to heaven by the savages
blindfold. how he lights among a certain fat nation,
call'd Clouds : how they are always in a Sweat, and
never speak, but they f—t. how they flock about him,
& think him very odd for not doing so too. he falls
plump into Italy.

12

Arrives at Turin ; goes to Genoa, & from thence to
Placentia ; crosses the River Trebia : the Ghost of
Hannibal appears to him ; & what it, & he, say upon
the occasion. locked out of Parma in a cold winter's
night : the author by an ingenious stratagem, gains
admittance. despises that City, & proceeds through
Reggio to Modena. how the Duke, & Duchess lie over
their own Stables, and go every night to a vile Italian
Comedy ; despises them, & it ; & proceeds to Bologna.

13

Enters into the Dominions of the Pope o' Rome.
meets the Devil, & what he says on the occasion. very
publick, & scandalous doings between the Vines & the
Elm-trees, and how the Olive-trees are shock'd thereupon. Author longs for Bologna-Sausages, & Hams ;
& how he grows as fat as a Hog.

14

Observations on Antiquities. the Author proves,
that Bologna was the ancient Tarentum ; that the
battle of Salamis, contrary to the vulgar opinion, was
fought by Land, and that not far from Ravenna.

that the Romans were a colony of the Jews, & that
Eneas was the same with Ehud.

15

Arrival at Florence. is of opinion, that the Venus
of Medicis is a modern performance, & that a very
indifferent one, and much inferiour to the K: Charles
at Charing-Cross. Account of the City, & manners
of the inhabitants. A learned Dissertation on the
true situation of Gomorrah. . . .

And here will end the first part of these instructive
& entertaining voyages. the Subscribers are to pay
20 Guineas ; 19 down, & the remainder upon delivery
of the book. *N: B:* A few are printed on the softest
Royal Brown paper for the use of the Curious.

MY DEAR, dear WHARTON,—(Which is a dear more
than I give anybody else. it is very odd to begin with
a Parenthesis, but) You may think me a Beast, for
not haveing sooner wrote to you, & to be sure a Beast
I am. now, when one owns it, I don't see what you
have left to say. I take this opportunity to inform
you (an opportunity I have had every week this
twelvemonth) that I am arrived safe at Calais, and
am at present at Florence, a city in Italy in I don't
know how many degrees N: latitude. under the line
I am sure it is not, for I am at this instant expireing
with Cold. You must know, that not being certain
what circumstances of my History would particularly
suit your curiosity, & knowing that all I had to say to
you would overflow the narrow limits of many a good
quire of Paper, I have taken this method of laying
before you the contents, that you may pitch upon what
you please, & give me your orders accordingly to
expatiate thereupon : for I conclude you will write
to me ; won't you ? oh ! yes, when you know, that in
a week I set out for Rome, & that the Pope is dead,
& that I shall be (I should say, God willing ; & if
nothing extraordinary intervene ; & if I'm alive, &
well ; & in all human probability) at the Coronation

of a new one. now as you have no other correspondent
there, & as if you do not, I certainly shall not write
again (observe my impudence) I take it to be your
interest to send me a vast letter, full of all sorts of
News, & Bawdy, & Politics, & such other ingredients,
as to you shall seem convenient with all decent expedition. only do not be too severe upon the Pretender ;
& if you like my Style, pray say so. this is à la Françoise ; and if you think it a little too foolish, & impertinent, you shall be treated alla Toscana with a
thousand Signoria Illustrissima's. in the meantime
I have the honour to remain

Your lofing Frind tell Deth, T: GRAY

Florence, March. 12. N: S: [1740].

P:S: This is à l'Angloise. I do'nt know where you
are ; if at Cambridge, pray let me know all, how, &
about it ; and if my old friends, Thompson, or Clark
fall in your way, say I am extremely theirs. but if
you are in town, I entreat you to make my best compliments to Mrs. Wharton. Adieu, Yours Sincerely
a second time.

36. To His Mother

Rome, April 2, N. S. 1740.

This is the third day since we came to Rome, but
the first hour I have had to write to you in. The
journey from Florence cost us four days, one of which
was spent at Sienna, an agreeable, clean, old city, of
no great magnificence or extent ; but in a fine situation,
and good air. What it has most considerable is its
cathedral, a huge pile of marble, black and white laid
alternately, and laboured with a gothic niceness and
delicacy in the old-fashioned way. Within too are
some paintings and sculpture of considerable hands.
The sight of this, and some collections that were
shewed us in private houses, were a sufficient employment for the little time we were to pass there : and
the next morning we set forward on our journey
through a country very oddly composed ; for some
miles you have a continual scene of little mountains

cultivated from top to bottom with rows of olive-trees,
or else elms, each of which has its vine twining about
it, and mixing with the branches ; and corn sown
between all the ranks. This diversified with numerous
small houses and convents, makes the most agreeable
prospect in the world : But, all of a sudden, it alters
to black barren hills, as far as the eye can reach, that
seem never to have been capable of culture, and are
as ugly as useless. Such is the country for some time
before one comes to Mount Radicofani, a terrible
black hill, on the top of which we were to lodge that
night. It is very high, and difficult of ascent ; and
at the foot of it we were much embarrassed by the
fall of one of the poor horses that drew us. This
accident obliged another chaise, which was coming
down, to stop also ; and out of it peeped a figure in
a red cloak, with a handkerchief tied round its head,
which, by its voice and mien, seemed a fat old woman :
but upon its getting out, appeared to be Senesino,
who was returning from Naples to Sienna, the place
of his birth and residence. On the highest part of
the mountain is an old fortress, and near it a house
built by one of the Grand Dukes for a hunting-seat,
but now converted into an inn ; It is the shell of a
large fabric, but such an inside, such chambers, and
accommodations, that your cellar is a palace in comparison ; and your cat sups and lies much better than
we did ; for, it being a saint's eve, there was nothing
but eggs. We devoured our meagre fare ; and, after
stopping up the windows with the quilts, were obliged
to lie upon the straw beds in our clothes. Such are the
conveniences in a road, that is, as it were, the great
thoroughfare of all the world. Just on the other side
of this mountain, at Ponte-Centino, one enters the
patrimony of the church ; a most delicious country,
but thinly inhabited. That night brought us to
Viterbo, a city of a more lively appearance than any we
had lately met with ; the houses have glass windows,
which is not very usual here ; and most of the streets
are terminated by a handsome fountain. Here we

had the pleasure of breaking our fast on the leg of an old hare and some broiled crows. Next morning, in descending Mount Viterbo, we first discovered (though at near thirty miles distance) the cupola of St. Peter's, and a little after began to enter on an old Roman pavement, with now and then a ruined tower, or a sepulchre on each hand. We now had a clear view of the city, though not to the best advantage, as coming along a plain quite upon a level with it; however it appeared very vast, and surrounded with magnificent villas and gardens. We soon after crossed the Tiber, a river that ancient Rome made more considerable than any merit of its own could have done: However, it is not contemptibly small, but a good handsome stream; very deep, yet somewhat of a muddy complexion. The first entrance of Rome is prodigiously striking. It is by a noble gate, designed by Michael Angelo, and adorned with statues; this brings you into a large square, in the midst of which is a vast obelisk of granite, and in front you have at one view two churches of a handsome architecture, and so much alike that they are called the twins; with three streets, the middlemost of which is one of the longest in Rome. As high as my expectation was raised, I confess, the magnificence of this city infinitely surpasses it. You cannot pass along a street but you have views of some palace, or church, or square, or fountain, the most picturesque and noble one can imagine. We have not yet set about considering its beauties, ancient and modern, with attention; but have already taken a slight transient view of some of the most remarkable. St. Peter's I saw the day after we arrived, and was struck dumb with wonder. I there saw the Cardinal d'Auvergne, one of the French ones, who upon coming off his journey, immediately repaired hither to offer up his vows at the high altar, and went directly into the Conclave; the doors of which we saw opened to him, and all the other immured Cardinals came thither to receive him. Upon his entrance they were closed again directly. It is supposed they will not come to an agreement about a Pope till after Easter, though the confinement is very disagreeable. I have hardly philosophy enough to see the infinity of fine things, that are here daily in the power of any body that has money, without regretting the want of it; but custom has the power of making things easy to one. I have not yet seen his majesty of Great-Britain, etc. though I have the two boys in the gardens of the Villa Borgese, where they go a-shooting almost every day; it was at a distance, indeed, for we did not choose to meet them, as you may imagine. This letter (like all those the English send or receive) will pass through the hands of that family, before it comes to those it was intended for. They do it more honour than it deserves; and all they will learn from thence will be, that I desire you to give my duty to my father, and wherever else it is due, and that I am, etc.

37. To His Mother

Rome, April 15, 1740.   Good Friday.

To-day I am just come from paying my adoration at St. Peter's to three extraordinary relics, which are exposed to public view only on these two days in the whole year, at which time all the confraternities in the city come in procession to see them. It was something extremely novel to see that vast church, and the most magnificent in the world, undoubtedly, illuminated (for it was night) by thousands of little crystal lamps, disposed in the figure of a huge cross at the high altar, and seeming to hang alone in the air. All the light proceeded from this, and had the most singular effect imaginable as one entered the great door. Soon after came one after another, I believe, thirty processions, all dressed in linen frocks, and girt with a cord, their heads covered with a cowl all over, only two holes to see through left. Some of them were all black, others red, others white, others party-coloured; these were continually coming and going with their tapers and crucifixes before them; and to

each company, as they arrived and knelt before the
great altar, were shown from a balcony at a great
height, the three wonders, which are, you must know,
the head of the spear that wounded Christ ; St.
Veronica's handkerchief, with the miraculous impression of his face upon it ; and a piece of the true
cross, on the sight of which the people thump their
breasts, and kiss the pavement with vast devotion.
The tragical part of the ceremony is half a dozen
wretched creatures, who with their faces covered, but
naked to the waist, are in a side chapel disciplining
themselves with scourges full of iron prickles ; but
really in earnest, as our eyes can testify, which saw
their backs and arms so raw we should have taken it
for a red satin doublet torn, and shewing the skin
through, had we not been convinced of the contrary
by the blood which was plentifully sprinkled about
them. It is late ; I give you joy of Port-Bello, and
many other things, which I hope are all true. * * * *

38. To West

Tivoli, May 20, 1740.

This day being in the palace of his Highness the
Duke of Modena, he laid his most serene commands
upon me to write to Mr. West, and said he thought it
for his glory, that I should draw up an inventory of all
his most serene possessions for the said West's perusal.
—Imprimis, a house, being in circumference a quarter
of a mile, two feet and an inch ; the said house containing the following particulars, to wit, a great room.
Item, another great room ; item, a bigger room ; item,
another room ; item, a vast room ; item, a sixth of
the same ; a seventh ditto ; an eighth as before ;
a ninth as abovesaid ; a tenth (see No. 1.) ; item, ten
more such, besides twenty besides, which, not to be
too particular, we shall pass over. The said rooms
contain nine chairs, two tables, five stools, and a
cricket. From whence we shall proceed to the garden,
containing two millions of superfine laurel hedges, a

clump of cypress trees, and half the river Teverone, that pisses into two thousand several chamberpots. Finis.—Dame Nature desired me to put in a list of her little goods and chattels, and, as they were small, to be very minute about them. She has built here three or four little mountains, and laid them out in an irregular semi-circle ; from certain others behind, at a greater distance, she has drawn a canal, into which she has put a little river of hers, called Anio ; she has cut a huge cleft between the two innermost of her four hills, and there she has left it to its own disposal ; which she has no sooner done, but, like a heedless chit, it tumbles headlong down a declivity fifty feet perpendicular, breaks itself all to shatters, and is converted into a shower of rain, where the sun forms many a bow, red, green, blue and yellow. To get out of our metaphors without any further trouble, it is the most noble sight in the world. The weight of that quantity of waters, and the force they fall with, have worn the rocks they throw themselves among into a thousand irregular craggs, and to a vast depth. In this channel it goes boiling along with a mighty noise till it comes to another steep, where you see it a second time come roaring down (but first you must walk two miles farther) a greater height than before, but not with that quantity of waters ; for by this time it has divided itself, being crossed and opposed by the rocks, into four several streams, each of which, in emulation of the great one, will tumble down too ; and it does tumble down, but not from an equally elevated place ; so that you have at one view all these cascades intermixed with groves of olive and little woods, the mountains rising behind them, and on the top of one (that which forms the extremity of one of the half-circle's horns) is seated the town itself. At the very extremity of that extremity, on the brink of the precipice, stands the Sybils' temple, the remains of a little rotunda, surrounded with its portico, above half of whose beautiful Corinthian pillars are still standing and entire ; all this on one hand. On the other, the open Campagna

of Rome, here and there a little castle on a hillock,
and the city itself on the very brink of the horizon,
indistinctly seen (being 18 miles off) except the dome
of St. Peter's ; which, if you look out of your window,
wherever you are, I suppose, you can see. I did not
tell you that a little below the first fall, on the side of
the rock, and hanging over that torrent, are little
ruins which they shew you for Horace's house, a
curious situation to observe the

> Præceps Anio, & Tiburni lucus, & uda
> Mobilibus pomaria rivis.

Mæcenas did not care for such a noise, it seems, and
built him a house (which they also carry one to see) so
situated that it sees nothing at all of the matter, and for
any thing he knew there might be no such river in the
world. Horace had another house on the other side of
the Teverone, opposite to Mæcenas's ; and they told
us there was a bridge of communication, by which
' andava il detto Signor per trastullarsi coll' istesso
Orazio.' In coming hither we crossed the Aquæ
Albulæ, a vile little brook that stinks like a fury, and
they say it has stunk so these thousand years. I forgot
the Piscina of Quintilius Varus, where he used to keep
certain little fishes. This is very entire, and there is a
piece of the aqueduct that supplied it too ; in the
garden below is old Rome, built in little, just as it was,
they say. There are seven temples in it, and no houses
at all : They say there were none.

May 21.

We have had the pleasure of going twelve miles out of
our way to Palestrina. It has rained all day as if heaven
and us were coming together. See my honesty, I do
not mention a syllable of the temple of Fortune, because
I really did not see it ; which, I think, is pretty well
for an old traveller. So we returned along the Via
Prænestina, saw the Lacus Gabinus and Regillus,
where, you know, Castor and Pollux appeared upon a
certain occasion. And many a good old tomb we left
on each hand, and many an Aqueduct,

> Dumb are whose fountains, and their channels dry.

There are, indeed, two whole modern ones, works of
Popes, that run about thirty miles a-piece in length ;
one of them conveys still the famous Aqua Virgo to
Rome, and adds vast beauty to the prospect. So we
came to Rome again, where waited for us a splendi-
dissimo regalo of letters ; in one of which came You,
with your huge characters and wide intervals, staring.
I would have you to know, I expect you should take
a handsome crow-quill when you write to me, and not
leave room for a pin's point in four sides of a sheet
royal. Do you but find matter, I will find spectacles.

I have more time than I thought, and I will employ
it in telling you about a Ball that we were at the other
evening. Figure to yourself a Roman villa ; all its
little apartments thrown open, and lighted up to the
best advantage. At the upper end of the gallery, a fine
concert, in which La Diamantina, a famous virtuosa,
played on the violin divinely, and sung angelically ;
Giovannino and Pasqualini (great names in musical
story) also performed miraculously. On each side were
ranged all the secular grand monde of Rome, the
Ambassadors, Princesses, and all that. Among the rest
Il Serenissimo Pretendente (as the Mantova gazette
calls him) displayed his rueful length of person, with
his two young ones, and all his ministry around him.
' Poi nacque un grazioso ballo,' where the world
danced, and I sat in a corner regaling myself with iced
fruits, and other pleasant rinfrescatives.

39. To West

Rome, May, 1740.

I am to-day just returned from Alba, a good deal
fatigued ; for you know the Appian is somewhat tiresome. We dined at Pompey's ; he indeed was gone
for a few days to his Tusculan, but, by the care of his
Villicus, we made an admirable meal. We had the
dugs of a pregnant sow, a peacock, a dish of thrushes,
a noble scarus just fresh from the Tyrrhene, and some
conchylia of the Lake with garum sauce : For my part

I never eat better at Lucullus's table. We drank half-a-dozen cyathi a-piece of ancient Alban to Pholoë's health ; and, after bathing, and playing an hour at ball, we mounted our essedum again, and proceeded up the mount to the temple. The priests there entertained us with an account of a wonderful shower of birds' eggs, that had fallen two days before, which had no sooner touched the ground, but they were converted into gudgeons ; as also that the night past, a dreadful voice had been heard out of the Adytum, which spoke Greek during a full half-hour, but no body understood it. But quitting my Romanities, to your great joy and mine, let me tell you in plain English, that we come from Albano. The present town lies within the inclosure of Pompey's Villa in ruins. The Appian way runs through it, by the side of which, a little farther, is a large old tomb, with five pyramids upon it, which the learned suppose to be the burying-place of the family, because they do not know whose it can be else. But the vulgar assure you it is the sepulchre of the Curiatii, and by that name (such is their power) it goes. One drives to Castel Gondolfo, a house of the Pope's, situated on the top of one of the Collinette, that forms a brim to the basin, commonly called the Alban lake. It is seven miles round ; and directly opposite to you, on the other side, rises the Mons Albanus, much taller than the rest, along whose side are still discoverable (not to common eyes) certain little ruins of the old Alba longa. They had need be very little, as having been nothing but ruins ever since the days of Tullus Hostilius. On its top is a house of the Constable Colonna's, where stood the temple of Jupiter Latialis. At the foot of the hill Gondolfo, are the famous outlets of the lake, built with hewn stone, a mile and a half under ground. Livy, you know, amply informs us of the foolish occasion of this expence, and gives me this opportunity of displaying all my erudition, that I may appear considerable in your eyes. This is the prospect from one window of the palace. From another you have the whole

Campagna, the City, Antium, and the Tyrrhene sea
(twelve miles distant) so distinguishable, that you may
see the vessels sailing upon it. All this is charming.
Mr. Walpole says, our memory sees more than our
eyes in this country. Which is extremely true ; since,
for realities, Windsor, or Richmond Hill, is infinitely
preferable to Albano or Frescati. I am now at home,
and going to the window to tell you it is the most
beautiful of Italian nights, which, in truth, are but
just begun (so backward has the spring been here, and
every where else, they say.) There is a moon ! there
are stars for you ! Do not you hear the fountain ?
Do not you smell the orange flowers ? That building
yonder is the convent of S. Isidore ; and that eminence,
with the cypress trees and pines upon it, the top of
M. Quirinal. This is all true, and yet my prospect is
not two hundred yards in length. We send you some
Roman inscriptions to entertain you. The first two
are modern, transcribed from the Vatican library by
Mr. Walpole.

> Pontifices olim quem fundavere priores,
>   Præcipuâ Sixtus perficit arte tholum ;
> Et Sixti tantum se gloria tollit in altum,
>   Quantum se Sixti nobile tollit opus :
> Magnus honos magni fundamina ponere templi,
>   Sed finem cæptis ponere major honos.
>
> Saxa agit Amphion, Thebana ut mænia condat :
>   Sixtus & immensæ pondera molis egit.
> Saxa trahunt ambo longè diversa : sed arte
>   Hæc trahit Amphion ; Sixtus & arte trahit.
> At tantum exsuperat Dircæum Amphiona Sixtus,
>   Quantum hic exsuperat cætera saxa lapis.

Mine is ancient, and I think not less curious. It is
exactly transcribed from a sepulchral marble at the villa
Giustiniani. I put stops to it, when I understand it.

> Dis Manibus
> Claudiæ, Pistes
> Primus Conjugi
> Optumae, Sanctae,
> Et Piae, Benemeritate.

Non æquos, Parcae, statuistis stamina vitæ.
Tam bene compositos potuistis sede tenere.
Amissa est conjux · cur ego & ipse moror ?
Si · bella · esse mî · iste · mea · vivere · debuit ·
Tristia contigerunt qui amissâ conjuge vivo.
Nil est tam miserum, quam totam perdere vitam.
Nec vita enasci dura peregistis crudelia pensa, sorores,
Ruptaque deficiunt in primo munere fusi.
O nimis injustæ ter denos dare munus in annos,
Deceptus · grautus · fatum · sic · pressit · egestas ·
Dum vitam tulero, Primus Pistes lugea conjugium.

40. To His Mother

Naples, June 17, 1740.

Our journey hither was through the most beautiful
part of the finest country in the world ; and every
spot of it on some account or other, famous for these
three thousand years past. The season has hitherto
been just as warm as one would wish it ; no unwhole-
some airs, or violent heats, yet heard of : The people
call it a backward year, and are in pain about their
corn, wine, and oil ; but we, who are neither corn,
wine, nor oil, find it very agreeable. Our road was
through Velletri, Cisterna, Terracina, Capua, and
Aversa, and so to Naples. The minute one leaves his
Holiness's dominions, the face of things begins to
change from wide uncultivated plains to olive groves
and well-tilled fields of corn, intermixed with ranks of
elms, every one of which has its vine twining about it,
and hanging in festoons between the rows from one
tree to another. The great old fig-trees, the oranges
in full bloom, and myrtles in every hedge, make
one of the delightfullest scenes you can conceive ;
besides that, the roads are wide, well-kept, and full
of passengers, a sight I have not beheld this long time.
My wonder still increased upon entering the city,
which I think for number of people, outdoes both
Paris and London. The streets are one continued
market, and thronged with populace so much that
a coach can hardly pass. The common sort are a

jolly lively kind of animals, more industrious than Italians usually are; they work till evening; then take their lute or guitar (for they all play) and walk about the city, or upon the sea-shore with it, to enjoy the fresco. One sees their little brown children jumping about stark-naked, and the bigger ones dancing with castanets, while others play on the cymbal to them. Your maps will show you the situation of Naples; it is on the most lovely bay in the world, and one of the calmest seas: it has many other beauties besides those of nature. We have spent two days in visiting the remarkable places in the country round it, such as the bay of Baiæ, and its remains of antiquity; the lake Avernus, and the Solfatara, Charon's grotto, etc. We have been in the Sybil's cave and many other strange holes under ground (I only name them because you may consult Sandy's travels); but the strangest hole I ever was in, has been to-day at a place called Portici, where his Sicilian Majesty has a country-seat. About a year ago, as they were digging, they discovered some parts of ancient buildings above thirty feet deep in the ground: Curiosity led them on, and they have been digging ever since; the passage they have made, with all its turnings and windings, is now more than a mile long. As you walk you see parts of an amphi-theatre, many houses adorned with marble columns, and incrusted with the same; the front of a temple, several arched vaults of rooms painted in fresco. Some pieces of painting have been taken out from hence finer than any thing of the kind before discovered, and with these the king has adorned his palace; also a number of statues, medals, and gems; and more are dug out every day. This is known to be a Roman town, that in the emperor Titus's time was over-whelmed by a furious eruption of Mount Vesuvius, which is hard by. The wood and beams remain so perfect that you may see the grain! but burnt to a coal, and dropping into dust upon the least touch. We were to-day at the foot of that mountain, which at present smokes only a little, where we saw the materials

that fed the stream of fire, which about four years
since ran down its side. We have but a few days longer
to stay here ; too little in conscience for such
a place. * * *

41. To His Father

Florence, July 16, 1740.

At my return to this city, the day before yesterday,
I had the pleasure of finding yours dated June the 9th.
The period of our voyages, at least towards the South,
is come as you wish. We have been at Naples, spent
nine or ten days there, and returned to Rome, where
finding no likelihood of a Pope yet these three months,
and quite wearied with the formal assemblies and
little society of that great city, Mr. Walpole determined
to return hither to spend the summer, where he imagines
he shall pass his time more agreeably than in the
tedious expectation of what, when it happens, will
only be a great show. For my own part, I give up the
thoughts of all that with but little regret ; but the
city itself I do not part with so easily, which alone
has amusements for whole years. However, I have
passed through all that most people do, both ancient
and modern ; what that is you may see better than
I can tell you, in a thousand books. The Conclave
we left in greater uncertainty than ever ; the more
than ordinary liberty they enjoy there, and the unusual coolness of the season, makes the confinement
less disagreeable to them than common, and, consequently maintains them in their irresolution. There
have been very high words, one or two (it is said) have
come even to blows ; two more are dead within this
last month, Cenci and Portia ; the latter died distracted : and we left another (Altieri) at the extremity : Yet nobody dreams of an election till the
latter end of September. All this gives great scandal
to all good catholics, and every body talks very freely
on the subject. The Pretender (whom you desire an
account of) I have had frequent opportunities of seeing
at church, at the corso, and other places ; but more

particularly, and that for a whole night, at a great ball given by Count Patrizii to the Prince and Princess Craon, (who were come to Rome at that time, that he might receive from the hands of the Emperor's minister there, the order of the golden fleece) at which he and his two sons were present. They are good fine boys, especially the younger, who has the more spirit of the two, and both danced incessantly all night long. For him, he is a thin, ill-made man, extremely tall and awkward, of a most unpromising countenance, a good deal resembling King James the Second, and has extremely the air and look of an idiot, particularly when he laughs or prays. The first he does not often, the latter continually. He lives private enough with his little court about him, consisting of Lord Dunbar, who manages every thing, and two or three of the Preston Scotch Lords, who would be very glad to make their peace at home.

We happened to be at Naples on Corpus Christi Day, the greatest feast in the year, so had an opportunity of seeing their Sicilian Majesties to advantage. The King walked in the grand procession, and the Queen (being big with child) sat in a balcony. He followed the Host to the church of St. Clara, where high mass was celebrated to a glorious concert of music. They are as ugly a little pair as one can see : she a pale girl, marked with the smallpox ; and he a brown boy with a thin face, a huge nose, and as ungain as possible.

We are settled here with Mr. Mann in a charming apartment ; the river Arno runs under our windows, which we can fish out of. The sky is so serene, and the air so temperate, that one continues in the open air all night long in a slight nightgown without any danger ; and the marble bridge is the resort of every body, where they hear music, eat iced fruits, and sup by moonlight ; though as yet (the season being extremely backward every where) these amusements are not begun. You see we are now coming northward again, though in no great haste ; the Venetian and Milanese territories, and either Germany or the South

of France, (according to the turn the war may take)
are all that remain for us, that we have not yet seen ; as
to Loretto, and that part of Italy, we have given over
all thoughts of it.

42. To West

Florence, July 16, 1740.

You do yourself and me justice, in imagining that
you merit, and that I am capable of sincerity. I have
not a thought, or even a weakness, I desire to conceal
from you ; and consequently on my side deserve to be
treated with the same openness of heart. My vanity
perhaps might make me more reserved towards you, if
you were one of the heroic race, superior to all human
failings ; but as mutual wants are the ties of general
society, so are mutual weaknesses of private friendships,
supposing them mixt with some proportion of good
qualities ; for where one may not sometimes blame, one
does not much care ever to praise. All this has the
air of an introduction designed to soften a very harsh
reproof that is to follow ; but it is no such matter : I
only meant to ask, Why did you change your lodging ?
Was the air bad, or the situation melancholy ? If so,
you are quite in the right. Only, is it not putting
yourself a little out of the way of a people, with whom
it seems necessary to keep up some sort of intercourse
and conversation, though but little for your pleasure or
entertainment, (yet there are, I believe, such among
them as might give you both) at least for your information in that study, which, when I left you, you
thought of applying to ? for that there is a certain study
necessary to be followed, if we mean to be of any use
in the world, I take for granted ; disagreeable enough
(as most necessities are) but, I am afraid, unavoidable.
Into how many branches these studies are divided in
England, every body knows ; and between that which
you and I had pitched upon, and the other two, it was
impossible to balance long. Examples shew one that it
is not absolutely necessary to be a blockhead to succeed

in this profession. The labour is long, and the elements dry and unentertaining; nor was ever any body (especially those that afterwards made a figure in it) amused, or even not disgusted in the beginning; yet, upon a further acquaintance, there is surely matter for curiosity and reflection. It is strange if, among all that huge mass of words, there be not somewhat intermixed for thought. Laws have been the result of long deliberation, and that not of dull men, but the contrary; and have so close a connexion with history, nay, with philosophy itself, that they must partake a little of what they are related to so nearly. Besides, tell me, Have you ever made the attempt? Was not you frighted merely with the distant prospect? Had the Gothic character and bulkiness of those volumes (a tenth part of which perhaps it will be no further necessary to consult, than as one does a dictionary) no ill effect upon your eye? Are you sure, if Coke had been printed by Elzevir, and bound in twenty neat pocket volumes, instead of one folio, you should never have taken him up for an hour, as you would a Tully, or drank your tea over him? I know how great an obstacle ill spirits are to resolution. Do you really think, if you rid ten miles every morning, in a week's time you should not entertain much stronger hopes of the Chancellorship, and think it a much more probable thing than you do at present? The advantages you mention are not nothing; our inclinations are more than we imagine in our own power; reason and resolution determine them, and support under many difficulties. To me there hardly appears to be any medium between a public life and a private one; he who prefers the first, must put himself in a way of being serviceable to the rest of mankind, if he has a mind to be of any consequence among them: Nay, he must not refuse being in a certain degree even dependent upon some men who already are so. If he has the good fortune to light on such as will make no ill use of his humility, there is no shame in this: If not, his ambition ought to give place to a reasonable pride, and he should apply to the cultivation of his own mind those abilities which he has not been permitted to use for others' service. Such a private happiness (supposing a small competence of fortune) is almost always in every one's power, and the proper enjoyment of age, as the other is the employment of youth. You are yet young, have some advantages and opportunities, and an undoubted capacity, which you have never yet put to the trial. Set apart a few hours, see how the first year will agree with you, at the end of it you are still the master; if you change your mind, you will only have got the knowledge of a little somewhat that can do no hurt, or give you cause of repentance. If your inclination be not fixed upon any thing else, it is a symptom that you are not absolutely determined against this, and warns you not to mistake mere indolence for inability. I am sensible there is nothing stronger against what I would persuade you to, than my own practice; which may make you imagine I think not as I speak. Alas! it is not so; but I do not act what I think, and I had rather be the object of your pity, than you should be that of mine; and, be assured, the advantage I may receive from it, does not diminish my concern in hearing you want somebody to converse with freely, whose advice might be of more weight, and always at hand. We have some time since come to the southern period of our voyages; we spent about nine days at Naples. It is the largest and most populous city, as its environs are the most deliciously fertile country, of all Italy. We sailed in the bay of Baiæ, sweated in the Solfatara, and died in the grotta del Cane, as all strangers do; saw the Corpus Christi procession, and the King and the Queen, and the city underground, (which is a wonder I reserve to tell you of another time) and so returned to Rome for another fortnight; left it (left Rome!) and came hither for the summer. You have seen an Epistle to Mr. Ashton, that seems to me full of spirit and thought, and a good deal of poetic fire. I would know your opinion. Now I talk of verses, Mr. Walpole and I have frequently wondered

you should never mention a certain imitation of
Spencer, published last year by a namesake of yours,
with which we are all enraptured and enmarvailed.

43.   POSTSCRIPT TO LETTER FROM WALPOLE TO WEST

Florence, July 31, 1740 N. S.

Though far unworthy to enter into so learned and
political a correspondence, I am employed pour
barbouiller une page de sept pouces et demie en
hauteur, et cinq en largeur ; and to inform you that
we are at Florence, a city of Italy, and the capital of
Tuscany ; the latitude I cannot justly tell, but it is
governed by a Prince called Great Duke ; an excellent
place to employ all one's animal sensations in, but
utterly contrary to one's rational powers.   I have
struck a medal upon myself : the device is thus, O,
and the motto *Nihilissimo*, which I take in the most
concise manner to contain a full account of my person,
sentiments, occupations, and late glorious successes.
If you choose to be annihilated too, you cannot do
better than undertake this journey.   Here you shall
get up at twelve o'clock, breakfast till three, dine till
five, sleep till six, drink cooling liquors till eight, go
to the bridge till ten, sup till two, and so sleep till
twelve again.

> Labore fessi venimus ad larem nostrum
> Desideratoque acquiescimus lecto :
> Hoc est, quod unum est, pro laboribus tantis.
> O quid solutis est beatius curis ?

We shall never come home again ; a universal war is
just upon the point of breaking out ; all out-lets will
be shut up.   I shall be secure in my nothingness, while
you that will be so absurd as to exist, will envy me.
You don't tell me what proficiency you make in the
noble science of defence.   Don't you start still at the
sound of a gun ?   Have you learned to say Ha ! ha ! and
is your neck clothed with thunder ?   Are your whiskers
of a tolerable length ?   And have you got drunk yet
with brandy and gunpowder ?   Adieu, noble Captain !

T. GRAY.

44. To His Mother

Florence, Aug. 21, N. S. 1740.

It is some time since I have had the pleasure of writing to you, having been upon a little excursion cross the mountains to Bologna. We set out from hence at sun-set, passed the Appennines by moon-light travelling incessantly till we came to Bologna at four in the afternoon next day. There we spent a week agreeably enough, and returned as we came. The day before yesterday arrived the news of a Pope; and I have the mortification of being within four days journey of Rome, and not seeing his coronation, the heats being violent, and the infectious air now at its height. We had an instance, the other day, that it is not only fancy. Two country fellows, strong men, and used to the country about Rome, having occasion to come from thence hither, and travelling on foot, as common with them, one died suddenly on the road; the other got hither, but extremely weak, and in a manner stupid; he was carried to the hospital, but died in two days. So, between fear and laziness, we remain here, and must be satisfied with the accounts other people give us of the matter. The new Pope is called Benedict XIV. being created Cardinal by Benedict XIII. the last Pope but one. His name is Lambertini, a noble Bolognese, and Archbishop of that city. When I was first there I remember to have seen him two or three times; he is a short, fat man, about sixty-five years of age, of a hearty, merry countenance, and likely to live some years. He bears a good character for generosity, affability, and other virtues; and, they say, wants neither knowledge nor capacity. The worst side of him is, that he has a nephew or two; besides a certain young favourite, called Melara, who is said to have had, for some time, the arbitrary disposal of his purse and family. He is reported to have made a little speech to the Cardinals in the Conclave, while they were undetermined about an election, as follows : ' Most eminent Lords, here are three Bolognese

of different characters, but all equally proper for the
Popedom. If it be your pleasures to pitch upon a
Saint, there is Cardinal Gotti; if upon a Politician,
there is Aldrovandi; if upon a Booby, here am I.'
The Italian is much more expressive, and, indeed not
to be translated; wherefore, if you meet with any
body that understands it, you may show them what
he said in the language he spoke it. ' Emin^ssimi. Sigr^l.
Ci siamo tré, diversi sì, mà tutti idonei al Papato. Si
vi piace un Santo, c' è l'Gotti; se volete una testa
scaltra, e Politica, c' è l'Aldrovandé; se un Coglione,
ecco mi!' Cardinal Coscia is restored to his liberty,
and, it is said, will be to all his benefices. Corsini
(the late Pope's nephew) as he has had no hand in this
election, it is hoped, will be called to account for all
his villanous practices. The Pretender, they say, has
resigned all his pretensions to his eldest boy, and will
accept of the Grand Chancellorship, which is thirty
thousand crowns a-year; the pension he has at present
is only twenty thousand. I do not affirm the truth of
this article; because, if he does, it is necessary he
should take the ecclesiastical habit, and it will sound
mighty odd to be called his Majesty the Chancellor.——
So ends my Gazette.

45. To His Father

Florence, Oct. 9, 1740.

The beginning of next spring is the time determined
for our return at furthest; possibly it may be before
that time. How the interim will be employed, or what
route we shall take is not so certain. If we remain
friends with France, upon leaving this country we shall
cross over to Venice, and so return through the cities
north of the Po to Genoa; from thence take a felucca
to Marseilles, and come back through Paris. If the
contrary fall out, which seems not unlikely, we must
take the Milanese, and those parts of Italy, in our way
to Venice; from thence pass through the Tirol into
Germany, and come home by the Low-Countries.

As for Florence, it has been gayer than ordinary for this last month, being one round of balls and entertainments, occasioned by the arrival of a great Milanese Lady; for the only thing the Italians shine in, is their reception of strangers. At such times every thing is magnificence: The more remarkable, as in their ordinary course of life they are parsimonious, even to a degree of nastiness. I saw in one of the vastest palaces in Rome (that of Prince Pamfilio) the apartment which he himself inhabited, a bed that most servants in England would disdain to lie in, and furniture much like that of a soph at Cambridge, for convenience and neatness. This man is worth £30,000 sterling a year. As for eating, there are not two Cardinals in Rome that allow more than six paoli, which is three shillings a day, for the expence of their table: and you may imagine they are still less extravagant here than there. But when they receive a visit from any friend, their houses and persons are set out to the greatest advantage, and appear in all their splendour; it is, indeed, from a motive of vanity, and with the hopes of having it repaid them with interest, whenever they have occasion to return the visit. I call visits going from one city of Italy to another; for it is not so among acquaintance of the same place on common occasions. The new Pope has retrenched the charges of his own table to a sequin (ten shillings) a meal. The applause which all he says and does meets with, is enough to encourage him really to deserve fame. They say he is an able and honest man; he is reckoned a wit too. The other day, when the Senator of Rome came to wait upon him, at the first compliments he made him, the Pope pulled off his cap: His Master of the Ceremonies, who stood by his side, touched him softly, as to warn him that such a condescension was too great in him, and out of all manner of rule: Upon which he turned to him and said, ' Oh! I cry you mercy, good Master, it is true, I am but a Novice of a Pope; I have not yet so much as learned ill manners.' * * *

46. To His Father

Florence, Jan. 12, 1741.

We still continue constant at Florence, at present
one of the dullest cities in Italy. Though it is the
middle of the Carnival there are no public diversions ;
nor is masquerading permitted as yet. The Emperor's
obsequies are to be celebrated publicly the 16th of this
month ; and after that, it is imagined every thing will
go on in its usual course. In the mean time, to employ
the minds of the populace, the Government has thought
fit to bring into the city in a solemn manner, and at
a great expence, a famous statue of the Virgin called
the Madonna dell'Impruneta, from the place of her
residence, which is upon a mountain seven miles off.
It never has been practised but at times of public
calamity ; and was done at present to avert the ill
effects of a late great inundation, which it was feared
might cause some epidemical distemper. It was
introduced a fortnight ago in procession, attended by
the Council of Regency, the Senate, the Nobility, and
all the Religious Orders, on foot and bare-headed, and
so carried to the great church, where it was frequented
by an infinite concourse of people from all the country
round. Among the rest I paid my devotions almost
every day, and saw numbers of people possessed with
the devil who were brought to be exorcised. It was
indeed in the evening, and the church-doors were always
shut before the ceremonies were finished, so that I
could not be eye-witness of the event ; but that they
were all cured is certain, for one never heard any more
of them the next morning. I am to-night just returned
from seeing our Lady make her exit with the same
solemnities she entered. The show had a finer effect
than before ; for it was dark ; and every body (even
those of the mob that could afford it) bore a white
wax flambeau. I believe there were at least five
thousand of them, and the march was near three hours
in passing before the window. The subject of all this
devotion is supposed to be a large Tile with a rude

figure in bas-relief upon it. I say supposed, because since the time it was found (for it was found in the earth in ploughing) only two people have seen it; the one was, by good luck, a saint; the other was struck blind for his presumption. Ever since she has been covered with seven veils; nevertheless, those who approach her tabernacle cast their eyes down, for fear they should spy her through all her veils. Such is the history, as I had it from the Lady of the house where I stood to see her pass; with many other circumstances; all which she firmly believes, and ten thousand besides.

We shall go to Venice in about six weeks, or sooner. A number of German troops are upon their march into this State, in case the King of Naples thinks proper to attack it. It is certain he has asked the Pope's leave for his troops to pass through his country. The Tuscans in general are much discontented, and foolish enough to wish for a Spanish government, or any rather than this. * * * *

47. To West

Florence, April 21, 1741.

I know not what degree of satisfaction it will give you to be told that we shall set out from hence the 24th of this month, and not stop above a fortnight at any place in our way. This I feel, that you are the principal pleasure I have to hope for in my own country. Try at least to make me imagine myself not indifferent to you; for I must own I have the vanity of desiring to be esteemed by somebody, and would choose that somebody should be one whom I esteem as much as I do you. As I am recommending myself to your love, methinks I ought to send you my picture (for I am no more what I was, some circumstances excepted, which I hope I need not particularize to you); you must add then, to your former idea, two years of age, reasonable quantity of dullness, a great deal of silence, and something that rather resembles, than is, thinking; a confused notion of many strange and fine things that have swum before my eyes for some time, a want of love for general society, indeed an inability to it. On the good side you may add a sensibility for what others feel, and indulgence for their faults or weaknesses, a love of truth, and detestation of every thing else. Then you are to deduct a little impertinence, a little laughter, a great deal of pride, and some spirits. These are all the alterations I know of, you perhaps may find more. Think not that I have been obliged for this reformation of manners to reason or reflection, but to a severer school-mistress, Experience. One has little merit in learning her lessons, for one cannot well help it ; but they are more useful than others, and imprint themselves in the very heart. I find I have been haranguing in the style of the Son of Sirach, so shall finish here, and tell you that our route is settled as follows : First to Bologna for a few days, to hear the Viscontina sing ; next to Reggio, where is a Fair. Now, you must know, a Fair here is not a place where one eats gingerbread or rides upon hobby-horses ; here are no musical clocks, nor tall Leicestershire women ; one has nothing but masquing, gaming, and singing. If you love operas, there will be the most splendid in Italy, four tip-top voices, a new theatre, the Duke and Dutchess in all their pomps and vanities. Does not this sound magnificent ? Yet is the city of Reggio but one step above Old Brentford. Well ; next to Venice by the 11th of May, there to see the old Doge wed the Adriatic Whore. Then to Verona, so to Milan, so to Marseilles, so to Lyons, so to Paris, so to West, &c. in sæcula sæculorum. Amen.

Eleven months, at different times, have I passed at Florence ; and yet (God help me) know not either people or language. Yet the place and the charming prospects demand a poetical farewell, and here it is.

* * Oh Fæsulæ amœna
Frigoribus juga, nec nimiùm spirantibus auris!
Alma quibus Tusci Pallas decus Apennini
Esse dedit, glaucâque suâ canescere sylvâ !

Non ego vos posthàc Arni de valle videbo
Porticibus circum, & candenti cincta coronâ
Villarum longè nitido consurgere dorso,
Antiquamve Ædem, et veteres præferre Cupressus
Mirabor, tectisque super pendentia tecta.

I will send you, too, a pretty little Sonnet of a Sig^r.
Abbate Buondelmonte, with my imitation of it.

> Spesso Amor sotto la forma
> D'amistà ride, e s'asconde :
> Poi si mischia, e si confonde
> Con lo sdegno, e col rancor.
> In Pietade ei si trasforma ;
> Par trastullo, e par dispetto :
> Mà nel suo diverso aspetto
> Sempr' egli, è l'istesso Amor.

Lusit amicitiæ interdum velatus amictu,
  Et benè compositâ veste fefellit Amor.
Mox iræ assumsit cultus, faciemque minantem,
  Inque odium versus, versus & in lacrymas :
Ludentum fuge, nec lacrymanti, aut crede furenti ;
  Idem est dissimili semper in ore Deus.

Here comes a letter from you.—I must defer giving
my opinion of Pausanias till I can see the whole, and
only have said what I did in obedience to your commands. I have spoken with such freedom on this
head, that it seems but just you should have your
revenge ; and therefore I send you the beginning not
of an Epic Poem, but of a Metaphysic one. Poems
and Metaphysics (say you, with your spectacles on) are
inconsistent things. A metaphysical poem is a contra-
diction in terms. It is true, but I will go on. It is
Latin too to increase the absurdity. It will, I suppose,
put you in mind of the man who wrote a treatise of
Canon Law in Hexameters. Pray help me to the
description of a mixt mode, and a little Episode about
Space.

48. To West

[Jan. 1742].

As I know you are a lover of Curiosities, I send you
the following, which is a true & faithful Narrative
of what passed in my Study on Saturday the 16th,

instant. I was sitting there very tranquil in my chair, when I was suddenly alarmd with a great hubbub of Tongues. In the street, you suppose ? No ! in my Study, Sir. In your Study say you ? Yes & between my books, which is more. For why should not books talk as well as Crabs & Mice & files & Serpents do in Esop. But as I listened with great attention so as to remember what I heard pretty exactly, I shall set down the whole conversation as methodically as I can, with the names prefixd.

Mad: Sevigné. . Mon cher Aristote ! do get a little farther or you'll quite suffocate me.

Aristotle. . Οὐδέποτε γυνὴ . . . I have as much right to be here as you, and I shan't remove a jot.

M. Sevigné. . Oh ! the brute ! here's my poor Sixth tome is squeezed to death : for God's sake, Bussy, come & rescue me.

Bussy Rabutin. . Ma belle Cousine ! I would fly to your assistance. Mais voici un Diable de Strabon qui me tue : I have nobody in my neighbourhood worth conversing with here but Catullus.

Bruyere. . Patience ! You must consider we are but books & so can't help ourselves. for my part, I wonder who we all belong to. We are a strange mixture here. I have a Malebranche on one Side of me, and a Gronovius on t'other.

Locke. . Certainly our owner must have very confusd ideas, to jumble us so strangely together. he has associated me with Ovid & Ray the Naturalist.

Virgil. . ' Me vero primum dulces ante omnia Musæ Accipiant ! '

Hen: More. . Of all the Speculations that the Soul of Man can entertain herself withall ; there is none of greater Moment than this of her immortality.

Cheyne. . Every Man after fourty is a fool or a Physician.

Euclid. . Punctum est, cujus nulla est—

Boileau. . Peste soit de cet homme avec son Punctum ! I wonder any Man of Sense will have a Mathematician in his Study.

Swift. . In short let us get the Mathematicians
banishd first; the Metaphysicians and Natural
Philosophers may follow them. &c.

Vade Mecum. . Pshaw ! I and the Bible are enough
for any one's library.

This last ridiculous Egotism made me laugh so
heartily that I disturbed my poor books & they talk'd
no more.

49. To West

London, April, Thursday [1742].

You are the first who ever made a Muse of a Cough ;
to me it seems a much more easy task to versify in one's
sleep, (that indeed you were of old famous for) than
for want of it. Not the wakeful nightingale (when she
had a cough) ever sung so sweetly. I give you thanks
for your warble, and wish you could sing yourself to
rest. These wicked remains of your illness will sure
give way to warm weather and gentle exercise ; which
I hope you will not omit as the season advances.
Whatever low spirits and indolence, the effect of them,
may advise to the contrary, I pray you add five steps
to your walk daily for my sake ; by the help of which,
in a month's time, I propose to set you on horseback.

I talked of the Dunciad as concluding you had seen
it ; if you have not, do you choose I should get and
send it you ? I have myself, upon your recommendation, been reading Joseph Andrews. The incidents
are ill laid and without invention ; but the characters
have a great deal of nature, which always pleases even
in her lowest shapes. Parson Adams is perfectly well ;
so is Mrs. Slipslop, and the story of Wilson ; and
throughout he shews himself well read in Stage-Coaches,
Country Squires, Inns, and Inns of Court. His reflections upon high people and low people, and misses
and masters, are very good. However the exaltedness
of some minds (or rather as I shrewdly suspect their
insipidity and want of feeling or observation) may
make them insensible to these light things, (I mean

such as characterize and paint nature) yet surely they are as weighty and much more useful than your grave discourses upon the mind, the passions, and what not. Now as the paradisaical pleasures of the Mahometans consist in playing upon the flute and lying with Houris, be mine to read eternal new romances of Marivaux and Crebillon.

You are very good in giving yourself the trouble to read and find fault with my long harangues. Your freedom (as you call it) has so little need of apologies, that I should scarce excuse your treating me any otherwise ; which, whatever compliment it might be to my vanity, would be making a very ill one to my understanding. As to matter of stile, I have this to say : The language of the age is never the language of poetry ; except among the French, whose verse, where the thought or image does not support it, differs in nothing from prose. Our poetry, on the contrary, has a language peculiar to itself ; to which almost every one, that has written, has added something by enriching it with foreign idioms and derivatives : Nay sometimes words of their own composition or invention. Shakespear and Milton have been great creators this way ; and no one more licentious than Pope or Dryden, who perpetually borrow expressions from the former. Let me give you some instances from Dryden, whom every body reckons a great master of our poetical tongue.——Full of *museful mopeings*—unlike the *trim* of love—a pleasant *beverage*—a *roundelay* of love— stood silent in his *mood*—with knots and *knares* deformed—his *ireful mood*—in proud *array*—his *boon* was granted—and *disarray* and shameful rout—*way-ward* but wise—*furbished* for the field—the *foiled doddard* oaks—*disherited*—*smouldring* flames—*retchless* of laws—*crones* old and ugly—the *beldam* at his side— the *grandam-hag*—*villanize* his Father's fame.——But they are infinite : And our language not being a settled thing (like the French) has an undoubted right to words of an hundred years old, provided antiquity have not rendered them unintelligible. In truth, Shakespear's language is one of his principal beauties; and he has no less advantage over your Addisons and Rowes in this, than in those other great excellencies you mention. Every word in him is a picture. Pray put me the following lines into the tongue of our modern Dramatics:

> But I, that am not shaped for sportive tricks,
> Nor made to court an amorous looking-glass:
> I, that am rudely stampt, and want love's majesty
> To strut before a wanton ambling nymph:
> I, that am curtail'd of this fair proportion,
> Cheated of feature by dissembling nature,
> Deform'd, unfinish'd, sent before my time
> Into this breathing world, scarce half made up—

And what follows. To me they appear untranslatable; and if this be the case, our language is greatly degenerated. However, the affectation of imitating Shakespear may doubtless be carried too far; and is no sort of excuse for sentiments ill-suited, or speeches ill-timed, which I believe is a little the case with me. I guess the most faulty expressions may be these—*silken* son of *dalliance*—*drowsier* pretensions—wrinkled *beldams*—*arched* the hearer's brow and *riveted* his eyes in *fearful extasie*. These are easily altered or omitted: and indeed if the thoughts be wrong or superfluous, there is nothing easier than to leave out the whole. The first ten or twelve lines are, I believe, the best; and as for the rest, I was betrayed into a good deal of it by Tacitus; only what he has said in five words, I imagine I have said in fifty lines: Such is the misfortune of imitating the inimitable. Now, if you are of my opinion, una litura may do the business better than a dozen; and you need not fear unravelling my web. I am a sort of spider; and have little else to do but spin it over again, or creep to some other place and spin there. Alas! for one who has nothing to do but amuse himself, I believe my amusements are as little amusing as most folks. But no matter; it makes the hours pass, and is better than ἐν ἀμαθίᾳ καὶ ἀμουσεᾳ κατα-βιῶναι. Adieu.

50. To West

London, May 8, 1742.

I rejoice to see you putting up your prayers to the May : She cannot choose but come at such a call. It is as light and genteel as herself. You bid me find fault ; I am afraid I cannot ; however I will try. The first stanza (if what you say to me in it did not make me think it the best) I should call the worst of the five (except the fourth line). The two next are very picturesque, Miltonic, and musical ; her bed is so soft and so snug that I long to lie with her. But those two lines ' Great Nature ' are my favourites. The exclamation of the flowers is a little step too far. The last stanza is full as good as the second and third ; the last line bold, but I think not too bold. Now, as to myself and my translation, pray do not call names. I never saw Broukhusius in my life. It is Scaliger who attempted to range Propertius in order ; who was, and still is, in sad condition.* * * You see, by what I sent you, that I converse, as usual, with none but the dead : They are my old friends, and almost make me long to be with them. You will not wonder therefore, that I, who live only in times past, am able to tell you no news of the present. I have finished the Peloponnesian war much to my honour, and a tight conflict it was, I promise you. I have drank and sung with Anacreon for the last fortnight, and am now feeding sheep with Theocritus. Besides, to quit my figure, (because it is foolish) I have run over Pliny's Epistles and Martial ἐκ παρέργου ; not to mention Petrarch, who, by the way, is sometimes very tender and natural. I must needs tell you three lines in Anacreon, where the expression seems to me inimitable. He is describing hair as he would have it painted.

> Ἕλικας δ᾽ ἐλευθέρους μοι
> Πλοκάμων ἄτακτα συνθεὶς
> Ἀφὲς ὡς θέλουσι κεῖσθαι.

Guess, too, where this is about a dimple.

> Sigilla in mento impressa Amoris digitulo
> Vestigio demonstrant mollitudinem.

51. To John Chute

My dear Sir,—Three days ago I was in the Coffee-House very deep in advertisements, a servant came in and waked me (as I thought) with the name of Mr. Chute; for half a minute I was not sure, but that it was you transported into England, by some strange chance, the Lord knows how, till he brought me to a coach that seem'd to have lost its way, by looking for a needle in a bottle of hay. In it was a lady who said she was not you, but only a near relation, and was so good to give me a letter, with which I return'd to my den, in order to prey upon it. I had wrote to you but a few days ago, and am glad of so good an excuse to do it again, which I may the better do, as my last was all out, and nothing to the purpose, being design'd for a certain Mr. Chute at Rome, and not him at Florence.

I learn from it that I have been somewhat smarter than I ought, but (to shew you with how little malice) I protest I have not the least idea what it was. My memory would be better, did I read my own letters so often as I do yours : you must attribute it to a sort of kittenish disposition that scratches, where it means to caress. However, I repent neither, if 'tis that has made you write. I know, I need not ask pardon, for you have forgiven me : nay, I have a good mind, to complain myself—How could you say, that I designed to hurt you, because I knew you could feel. I hate the thoughts of it, and would not for the world wound anything that was sensible. 'Tis true, I should be glad to scratch the careless, or the foolish ; but no armour is so impenetrable as indifference, and stupidity, and so I may keep my claws to myself. For another instance of the shortness of my memory, would you believe, I have so little knowledge of the Florentine History, as not to guess who the Lady Errant is, you mention ? sure it can't be the R$^{dl.}$ and her faithful swain, or may be M. G$^{dl.}$ and the little abbé; what you do there so long I have no conception ; if you stay at other places in proportion, I despair of ever seeing you

again. 'Tis true indeed Mr. Mann is not everywhere ;
I am shock'd to think of his sufferings, but he of all
men was born to suffer with a good grace. He is
a Stoick without knowing it, and seems to think pain
a pleasure. I am very sorry to compliment him upon
such an occasion, and wished with all my heart, he
were not so pleased. I much fear his books are gone
already ; but if not, to be sure he shall have *Middleton*
and the *Sofa* ; it seems most people here are not such
admirers of it as I was : but I wont give up an inch of it,
for all that. Did I tell you about Mr. Garrick, that the
town are horn-mad after : there are a dozen Dukes of a
night at Goodmansfields sometimes, and yet I am stiff in
the opposition. Our fifth Opera was the *Olympiade*,
in which they retained most of Pergolesi's songs, and
yet 'tis gone already, as if it had been a poor thing
of Galuppi's. Two nights did I enjoy it all alone, snug
in a nook of the gallery, but found no one in those
regions had ever heard of Pergolesi, nay, I heard several
affirm it was a composition of Pescetti's. Now there
is a 6th sprung up, by the name of *Cephalo and Procri*.
My Lady of Queensbury is come out against my Lady
of Marlborough, and she has her spirit too, and her
originality, but more of the woman, I think, than
t'other. As to the facts, it don't signify two pence
who's in the right ; the manner of fighting, and
character of the combatants is all : 'tis hoped old
Sarah will at her again. A play of Mr. Glover's I am
told, is preparing for the stage, call'd *Boadicea ;* it is
a fine subject, but I have not an extreme opinion of
him. The invalides at Chelsea intend to present
Ranelagh Gardens, as a nuisance, for breaking their
first sleep with the sound of fiddles ; it opens, I think,
to-night. Messieurs the Commons are to ballot for 7
persons to-morrow, commission'd to state the public
accounts, and they are to be such, who have no places,
nor are any ways dependent on the King. The Com-
mittee have petitioned for all papers relating to the
Convention. A bill has pass'd the lower house, for
indemnifying all who might subject themselves to

penalties, by revealing any transaction with regard
to the conduct of my Lord Orford, and to-morrow the
Lords are summon'd about it. The wit of the time
consists in Satyrical Prints; I believe there have been
some hundreds within this month. If you have any
hopeful young designer of caricaturas, that has a
political turn, he may pick up a pretty subsistence
here: let him pass thro' Holland to improve his taste
by the way. We are all very sorry for poor Queen
Hungary: but we know of a second battle (which
perhaps you may never hear of, but from me), as how
Prince Lobbycock came up in the nick of time, and
cut 120,000 of them all to pieces; and how the King
of Prussia narrowly escap'd aboard a ship, and so
got down the Dannub to Wolf-in-Bottle, where Mr.
Mallyboyce lay encamped; and how the Hannoverians,
with Prince Hissy-Castle, at their head, fell upon the
French Mounseers, and took him away with all his
treasure, among which is Pitt's diamond, and the
great cistern—all this is firmly believed here, and
a vast deal more: upon the strength of which we
intend to declare war with France.

You are so obliging as to put me in mind of our last
year's little expeditions; alas! Sir, they are past, and
how many years will it be, at the rate you go on, before
we can possibly renew them in this country: in all
probability I shall be gone first on a long expedition
to that undiscover'd country, from whose bourn no
traveller returns: however (if I can), I will think of
you, as I sail down the *River of Eternity*. I can't help
thinking, that I should find no difference almost
between this world, and t'other (for I converse with
none but the dead here), only indeed I should receive
nor write no more letters (for the Post is not very well
regulated). If you see the King of Naples, pray talk
with him on this subject, for I see he is upon settling
one between his country and Constantinople, and I take
this to be but a little more difficult.

My dab of Musick, and Prints, you are very good to
think of sending with your own, to which I will add

a farther trouble, by desireing you to send me some of the roots of a certain Flower, which I have seen at Florence. It is a huge white Hyacynth tinged with pink (Mr. M. knows what I mean, by the same token that they grow sometimes in the fat Gerina's *Boosom*), I mean if they bear a reasonable price, which you will judge of for me : but don't give yourself any pains about it, for if they are not easily had, and at an easy rate, I am not at all eager for them. Do you talk of *Strumming ?* Oh me, who have not seen the face of a *harpical*, since I came home ; no ! I have hang'd up my Harp on the Willows : however, I look at my musick now and then, that I may not forget it ; for when you return, I intend to sing a song of thanksgiving, and praise the Lord with a cheerful noise of many-stringed instruments. Adieu ! dear Sir, I am sincerely yours,

T. G.

M[ay 24, 1742.] O. S. London. Not forgetting my kiss-hands to Mr. Whithed.

52. To Ashton

MY DEAR ASHTON,—This melancholy day is the first that I have had any notice of my Loss in poor West, and that only by so unexpected a Means as some Verses publishd in a Newspaper (they are fine & true & I believe may be your own.) I had indeed some reason to suspect it some days since from recieving a letter of my own to him sent back unopen'd. The stupid People had put it no Cover, nor thought it worth while to write one Line to inform me of the reason, tho' by knowing how to direct, they must imagine I was his friend. I am a fool indeed to be surprizd at meeting with Brutishness or want of Thought among Mankind ; what I would desire is, that you would have the goodness to tell me, what you know of his death, more particularly as soon as you have any Leisure ; my own Sorrow does not make me insensible to your new Happiness, which I heartily congratulate you upon, as the means of Quiet, and Independence,

& the Power of expressing your benevolence to those
you love. neither my Misfortune, nor my joy shall
detain you longer at a time, when doubtless you are
a good deal employd ; only beleive me sincerely yours
                                        T. GRAY.

P.S. Pray do not forget my impatience,—especially
if you do not happen to be in London. I have no one
to enquire of but yourself. 'tis now three weeks,
that I have been in the Country, but shall return to
Town in 2 days.

June 17—— Stoke. 1742.

53. To Wharton

You write so feelingly to little Mr Brown, and
represent your abandoned condition in Terms so
touching, that, what Gratitude could not effect in
several Months, Compassion has brought about in a
few Days, and broke that strong Attachment, or rather
Allegiance, wch I and all here owe to our sovereign
Lady and Mistress, the President of Presidents, and
Head of Heads (if I may be permitted to pronounce
her Name, that ineffable Octogrammaton) the power
of LAZINESS. you must know she had been pleased to
appoint me (in Preference to so many old Servants of
hers, who had spent their whole lives in qualifying
themselves for the Office) Grand Picker of Straws, and
Push-Pin-Player in ordinary to her Supinity (for that
is her Title) the first is much in the Nature of L^d
President of the Council, & the other, like the Groom-
Porter, only without the Profit. but, as they are both
Things of very great Honour in this Country, I consider'd with myself the Load of Envy attending such
great Charges, & besides (between you & I) I found
myself unable to support the Fatigue of keeping up the
appearance, that Persons of such Dignity must do,
so I thought proper to decline it, & excused myself as
well as I could : however, as you see such an Affair
must take up a good deal of Time, & it has always been
the Policy of this Court to proceed slowly, like the
Imperial, & that of Spain, in the Dispatch of Business ;

in the Career of Glory. far be it from me to hamper the wheels of your gilded Chariot. go on, Sr Thomas ; & when you die (for even Physicians must die) may the Faculty in Warwick Lane erect your statue in Sr John Cutler's own Niche.

As to Cambridge it is, as it was, for all the World ; & the People are, as they were ; & Mr Trollope is as he was, that is, half ill, half well. I wish with all my Heart they were all better, but what can one do ? there is no News, only I think I heard a Whisper, as if the Vice-Chancellour should be with Child (but I beg you not to mention this, for I may come into trouble about it) ; there is some Suspicion, that the Professor of Mathematicks had a Hand in the thing. Dr Dickens says the University will be obliged to keep it, as it was got, in Magistratu.

I was going to tell you how sorry I am for your Illness. but, I hope, it is too late to be sorry now : I can only say, that I really *was* very sorry. may you live a hundred Christmases, & eat as many Collars of brawn stuck with Rosemary. Adieu, I am sincerely Yours   T G:

Dec: 27 [1744] Cambridge . . Wo'nt You come to the Jubilee ? Dr Long is to dance a Saraband & Hornpipe of his own Invention without lifting either Foot once from the Ground.

55. To Walpole

DEAR S^r,—You are so good to enquire after my usual Time of comeing to Town ; it is at a Season, when even You, the perpetual friend of London, will I fear hardly be in it, the Middle of June : and I commonly return hither in September, a Month, when I may more probably find you at home. I do not imagine that any Thing farther can be done with Mr Turner, but You only, who saw the Manner of his promiseing, can judge of that. what he calls the College, is the Master & his Party of Fellows, among wch he himself has been reckon'd latterly : but, I know, it must be from some other Influence, than that

of the Master merely, if he vote with them ; wch if M^r
Brudenel could stand, might very likely be made Use
of (as he is nearly related to several People of Condition)
but he is disqualified at present in every Sense. 'tis
likely indeed he is intended for next Year, & M^r
Turner has had some Application made already, by
his knowing anything about him ; but he mistakes
the Time.

Our Defeat to be sure is a rueful Affair for the
Honour of the Troops, but the Duke is gone, it seems,
with the Rapidity of a Cannon-Bullet to undefeat us
again. the Common-People in Town at least know
how to be afraid : but We are such *uncommon* People
here as to have no more Sense of Danger, then if the
Battle had been fought when & where the Battle of
Cannæ was. the Perception of these Calamities and
of their Consequences, that we are supposed to get
from Books, is so faintly impress'd, that we talk of
War, Famine, & Pestilence with no more Apprehension,
than of a broken Head, or of a Coach overturn'd
between York and Edinburgh. I heard three People,
sensible, middle-aged Men (when the Scotch were said
to be at Stamford, & actually were at Derby) talking
of hireing a Chaise to go to Caxton, (a Place in the high
Road) to see the Pretender & the Highlanders, as they
passed.

I can say no more for Mr Pope, (for what You
keep in Reserve may be worse than all the Rest) it
is natural to wish the finest Writer, one of them, we
ever had should be an honest Man. it is for the
Interest even of that Virtue, whose Friend he profess'd
himself, & whose Beauties he sung, that he should
not be found a dirty Animal. but however this is M^r
Warburton's Business, not mine, who may scribble
his Pen to the Stumps & all in vain, if these Facts are
so. it is not from what he told me about himself
that I thought well of him, but from a Humanity &
Goodness of Heart, ay, & Greatness of Mind, that
runs thro his private Correspondence, not less apparent
than are a thousand little Vanities & Weaknesses

mixed with those good Qualities, for no body ever
took him for a Philosopher.

If you know anything of Mr Mann's State of Health
& Happiness, or the Motions of Mr Chute homewards,
it will be a particular Favour to inform me of them,
as I have not heard this half year from them.

I am sincerely Yours

T GRAY.

Cambr:^{dge} Febr: 3—1746

56. To Walpole

MY DEAR S^r,—I found (as soon as I got hither) a very
kind Letter from Mr Chute, from whence I have Reason
to hope we may all meet in Town about a Week
hence. You have probably been there, since I left
you, & consequently have seen the Mr Barry you
desired some Account of: yet as I am not certain of
this, & should be glad to know whether we agree
about him; I will nevertheless tell you what he is,
& the Impression he made upon me. he is upwards of
six Foot in Height, well & proportionably made, treads
well, & knows what to do with his Limbs; in short
a noble graceful Figure: I can say nothing of his
Face, but that it was all Black, with a wide Mouth
& good Eyes. his Voice is of a clear & pleasing Tone,
something like Delane's, but not so deep-mouth'd,
not so like a Passing Bell. when high strained, it is
apt to crack a little, & be hoarse: but in its common
Pitch, & when it sinks into any softer Passion, particularly expressive & touching. in the first Scenes,
especially where he recounts to the Senate the Progress
of his Love, & the Means he used to win Desdemona,
he was quite mistaken, & I took a Pique against him:
instead of a Cool Narration he flew into a Rant of Voice
& Action, as tho' he were relating the Circumstances
of a Battle that was fought yesterday. I expected
nothing more from him, but was deceived: in the
Scenes of Rage & Jealousy he was seldom inferior to
Quin: in the Parts of Tenderness & Sorrow far above
him. these latter seem to be his peculiarly: his

Action is not very various, but rarely improper, or without Dignity : & some of his Attitudes are really fine. he is not perfect to be sure ; but I think may make a better Player than any now on the Stage in a little while. however to see a Man in one Character, & but once, is not sufficient : so I rather ask your Opinion by this, than give you mine.

I annex (as you desired) another Ode. all it pretends to with you is, that it is mine, & that you never saw it before, & that it is not so long as t'other.

Lo, where the rosie-bosom'd Hours,
Fair Venus' Train, appear,
Disclose the long-expecting Flowers,
And wake the purple Year !
The Attic Warbler pours her Throat
Responsive to the Cuckow's Note,
The untaught Harmony of Spring :
While whisp'ring Pleasure as they fly
Cool Zephyrs thro' the clear blue Sky
Their gather'd Fragrance fling

Where'er the Oak's thick Branches stretch
A broader browner Shade ;
Where'er the rude & moss-grown Beech
O'ercanopies the Glade ;
Beside some Water's rushy Brink
With me the Muse shall sit, & think
(At Ease reclined in rustic State)
How vain the Ardour of the Crowd,
How low, how indigent the Proud,
How little are the Great !

Still is the toiling Hand of Care :
The panting Herds repose.
Yet hark, how thro' the peopled Air
The busy Murmur glow !
The insect-Youth are on the Wing
Eager to tast the honied Spring,
And float amid the liquid Noon :
Some lightly o'er the Current skim,
Some shew their gayly-gilded Trim
Quick-glanceing to the Sun.

To Contemplation's sober Eye
Such is the Race of Man:
And they that creep, & they that fly,
Shall end where they began.
Alike the Busy & the Gay
But flutter thro' Life's little Day,
In Fortune's varying Colours drest:
Brush'd by the Hand of rough Mischance,
Or chill'd by Age, their airy Dance
They leave, in Dust to rest.

Methinks I hear in Accents low
The sportive Kind reply,
Poor Moralist! & what art Thou?
A solitary Fly!
Thy Joys no glittering Female meets,
No Hive hast thou of hoarded Sweets,
No painted Plumage to display:
On hasty Wings thy Youth is flown;
Thy Sun is set; thy Spring is gone:
We frolick, while 'tis May.

My Compliments to Ashton. Adieu, I am sincerely
Yours

T G:

Camb: Oct: 20. [1746]

57. To Wharton

MY DEAR WHARTON,—I am just returned hither from
Town, where I have past better than a Fortnight,
(including an Excursion that I made to Hampton Court,
Richmond, Greenwich, & other Places) & am happily
met by a letter from You, [one from Tuthill,] & another
from Trollope. as I only run over Dr Andrew's
Answers hastily in a Coffee House, all I could judge
was that they seem'd very unfavourable on the whole
to our Cause, & threw everything into the Hands of
a Visitour, for wch Reason I thought they might have
been conceal'd, till the Attorney-General's Opinion
arrived, wch will perhaps raise the Spirits of such, as
the other may have damp'd a little; or leave Room
at least to doubt, whether the Matter be so clear on

283   E

the Master's Side as Andrew would have it. You cant
suppose, that I was in the least uneasy about M^r
Brown's Fortitude, who wants nothing but a Foot in
height & his own Hair, to make him a little old Roman :
with two dozen such I should not hesitate to face an
Army of Heads, tho' they were all as tall as Dr Adams.
I only wish every body may continue in as good
a Disposition as they were ; & imagine, if possible,
Roger will be Fool enough to keep them so. I saw
Trollope for about an Hour in London ; & imagineing
he could not be left in the dark as to your Consulta-
tions, I mention'd, that I had cast an Eye over Andrew's
paper, & that it was not so favourable as we hoped.
he spoke however with Horrour of going to Law ; with
great Passion of the Master ; and with Pleasure of
himself for quitting a Place, where he had not found
a Minute's Ease in I know not how long : yet I perceive
his Thoughts run on nothing else, & he trembled while
he spoke. he writes to me here on the same Subject ;
and after abusing Roger, he adds, Whartoni rubro hæc
subscribe libello.

My Evenings have been chiefly spent at Ranelagh &
Vaux Hall, several of my Mornings, or rather Noons, in
Arlington-Street, & the rest at the Tryal of the Lords.
The first Day I was not there, & only saw the Ld High-
Steward's Parade in going ; the second & third [. . .
Peers were all in their Robes . . . by their wearing Bag-
Wigs and Hats instead of Coronets. My Lord H:
Steward] was the least part of the Shew, as he wore
only his Baron's Robe, & was always asking the
Heralds what he should do next, & bowing or smileing
about to his Acquaintance, as to his Speech, you see it ;
People hold it very cheap, tho' several Incorrectnesses
have been alter'd in the printed Copy. Kilmarnock
spoke in Mitigation of his Crime near half an Hour,
with a decent Courage, and in a strong, but pathetic,
Voice. his Figure would prejudice people in his Favour,
being tall & genteel ; he is upwards of 40, but to the
Eye not above 35 Years of Age. what he said appears
to less Advantage, when read. Cromartie (who is

about the same Age a Man of lower Stature, but much like a Gentleman) was sinking into the Earth with Grief & Dejection. with Eyes cast down & a Voice so low, that no one heard a Syllable, that did not sit close to the Bar, he made a short Speech to raise Compassion. it is now, I see, printed ; & is reckon'd extremely fine. I believe, you will think it touching & well-expressed : if there be any Meanness in it, it is lost in that Sorrow he gives us for so numerous & helpless a Family. Lady Cromartie (who is said to have drawn her husband into these Circumstances) was at Leicester-House on Wednesday with four of her Children ; the Princess saw her, & made no other answer than by bringing in her own Children & placing them by her ; w^{ch} (if true) is one of the prettiest Things I ever heard. she was also at the Duke's, who refused to admit her : but she waited till he came to his Coach & threw herself at his Knees, while her Children hung upon him, till he promised her all his Interest could do ; & before on several Occasions he has been heard to speak very mildly of Cromartie, & very severely of Kilmarnock. so if any be spared, it will probably be the former, tho' he had a pension of 600£ a-Year from the Government, & the order for giveing Quarter to no Englishman was found in his Pocket. As to Balmerino he never had any Hopes from the Beginning: he is an old soldierlike Man of a vulgar Manner & Aspect, speaks the broadest Scotch, & shews an Intrepidity, that some ascribe to real Courage, & some to Brandy. You have heard perhaps, that the first Day (while the Peers were adjourned to consider of his Plea, and he left alone for an Hour & half in the Bar) he diverted himself with the Ax, that stood by him, played with its Tassels & tryed the Edge with his Finger : & some Lord, as he passed by him, saying he was surprised to hear him alledge anything so frivolous, & that could not possibly do him the least Service ; he answer'd, that as there were so many Ladies present, he thought it would be uncivil to give them no Amusement. the D: of Argyle, telling him,

how sorry & how astonish'd he was to see him engaged
in such a Cause. My Lord (says he) for the two Kings
& their Rights I cared not a Farthing, wᶜʰ prevailed :
but I was starveing ; & by God if Mahomet had set up
his Standard in the Highlands, I had been a good
Musselman for Bread, & stuck close to the Party, for
I must eat. the Sollicitor-General came up to speak
to him too ; & he turns about to old Williamson. Who
is that Lawyer, that talks to me ? My Lᵈ, it is Mʳ
Murray. Ha ! Mʳ Murray, my good Friend (says he,
& shook him by the Hand) and how does your good
Mother ? oh, she was of admirable Service to us ;
we should have done nothing without her in Perth-
shire. he recommends (he says) his Peggy ('tis uncertain . . . the favour of the Government, for she
has. . . .

[I have been diverted with an account of old Lovat
in his confinement at] Edinburgh. there was a Captain
Maggett, that is obliged to lie in the Room every Night
with him. when first he was introduced to him, he
made him come to his Bedside where he lay in a hundred
flannel Wastcoats and a furr'd Nightgown, took him in
his Arms, & gave him a long Embrace, that absolutely
suffocated him. he will speak nothing but French ;
insists upon it, that Maggett is a Frenchman & calls
him, Mon cher Capitaine Magot (you know *Magot* is
a Monkey) at his Head lie two Highland Women at his
feet two Highland Men. By his Bedside is a Close-
Stool to which he rises two or three times in a Night,
& always says, Ah, mon cher Capitaine Magot ! vous
m'excuserez, mais la Nature demande que je chie !
he is to be impeached by the House of Commons,
because not being actually in Arms, it would otherwise
be necessary, that the jury of Inverness should find
a Bill of Indictment against him, wᶜʰ it is very sure
they would not do. when the Duke return'd to
Edinburgh they refused to admit Kingston's light
Horse & talked of their Privileges. but they came in
Sword in Hand, & replied, that when the Pretender was
at their gates, they had said nothing of their privileges.

Spirits very notably) will give you an Account of your College Proceedings, if they may be so call'd, where nothing proceeds at all. only the last Week Roger was so wise to declare ex motu proprio, that he took Mr Delaval (who is now a Fell: Commoner) into his own Tuition. this raised the dirty Spirit of his Friend, Mr May (now Tutor in Francis's Room) against him, & even gentle Mr Peele (who never acts but in Conjunction), together with Mr Brown (who pretended to be mighty angry, tho' in reality heartily glad), and they all came to an Eclaircissement in the Parlour. they abused him pretty reasonably, & it ended in threatening them as usual with a Visitor. in short, they are all as rude as may be, leave him at Table by himself, never go into the Parlour, till he comes out ; or if he enters, when they are there, continue sitting even in his own Magisterial Chair. May bickers with him publickly about twenty paltry Matters, & Roger t'other Day told him he was impertinent. what would you have more ? you see they do as one would wish. if you were here, all would be right. I am surprised not to hear you mention, when that will be ; pray give an Account of yourself.—I am very sincerely Yours,

TG:

P: S: When I went to Town Part of my Errand was to sell a little stock I had, to pay off Birkett's old Debt now at Xmas, but it was so low, I should have lost near 12 per Cent, and so it continues. if you think of being here near that Time, and find it not inconvenient to you to lend me 40£, you will save me the Money I mention (as I remember you once offered) but if any Inconvenience attend it you must imagine I don't by any Means desire it ; & you need not be at the Trouble of any Excuse, as I well know, nothing but the not being able would hinder your doing it immediately. let me know, because otherwise I have another Journey to make to Town.

Dec: 11 [1746] . . Cambridge.

59. To Walpole

Cambridge, Dec. Monday [1746].

This comes du fond de ma cellule to salute Mr.
H. W. not so much him that visits and votes, and
goes to White's and to court; as the H. W. in his
rural capacity, snug in his tub on Windsor-hill, and
brooding over folios of his own creation : him that
can slip away, like a pregnant beauty (but a little
oftener), into the country, be brought to bed perhaps
of twins, and whisk to town again the week after with
a face as if nothing had happened. Among the little
folks, my godsons and daughters, I can not choose but
enquire more particularly after the health of one ;
I mean (without a figure) the Memoires : Do they
grow ? Do they unite, and hold up their heads, and
dress themselves ? Do they begin to think of making
their appearance in the world, that is to say, fifty years
hence, to make posterity stare, and all good people
cross themselves ? Has Asheton (who will then be
lord bishop of Killaloe, and is to publish them) thought
of an *aviso al lettore* to prefix to them yet, importing,
that if the words church, king, religion, ministry, &c.
be found often repeated in this book, they are not to
be taken literally, but poetically, and as may be most
strictly reconcileable to the faith then established ;—
that he knew the author well when he was a young
man ; and can testify upon the honour of his function,
that he said his prayers regularly and devoutly,
had a profound reverence for the clergy, and firmly
believed everything that was the fashion in those
days ?

When you have done impeaching my lord Lovat,
I hope to hear *de vos nouvelles*, and moreover, whether
you have got colonel Conway yet ? Whether sir C.
Williams is to go to Berlin ? What sort of a prince
Mitridate may be ?—and whatever other tidings you
choose to refresh an anchoret with. *Frattanto* I send
you a scene in a tragedy : if it don't make you cry, it

will make you laugh ; and so it moves some passion,
that I take to be enough. Adieu, dear sir ! I am
Sincerely yours,
T. GRAY.

60. To WALPOLE
[Cambridge, 1747].

When I received the testimonial of so many considerable personages to adorn the second page of my
next edition, and (adding them to the Testimonium
Autoris de seipso) do relish and enjoy all the conscious
pleasure resulting from six pennyworths of glory,
I cannot but close my satisfaction with a sigh for the
fate of my fellow-labourer in poetry, the unfortunate
Mr. Golding, cut off in the flower or rather the bud
of his honours, who had he survived but a fortnight
more, might have been by your kind offices as much
delighted with himself, as I.   Windsor and Eton
might have gone down to posterity together, perhaps
appeared in the same volume, like Philips and Smith,
and we might have set at once to Mr. Pond for the
frontispiece, but these, alas ! are vain reflections.   To
return to myself.   Nay ! but you are such a wit ! sure
the gentlemen an't so good, are they ? and don't you
play upon the word.   I promise you, few take to it
here at all, which is a good sign (for I never knew
anything liked here, that ever proved to be so any
where else,) it is said to be mine, but I strenuously deny
it, and so do all that are in the secret, so that nobody
knows what to think ; a few only of King's College
gavè me the lie, but I hope to demolish them ; for if
I don't know, who should ? Tell Mr. Chute, I would
not have served him so, for any brother in Christen-
dom, and am very angry. To make my peace with the
noble youth you mention, I send you a Poem that I am
sure they will read (as well as they can) a masterpiece—
it is said, being an admirable improvement on that
beautiful piece called Pugna Porcorum, which begins

Plangite porcelli Porcorum pigra propago ;

but that is in Latin, and not for their reading, but

indeed, this is worth a thousand of it, and unfortunately
it is not perfect, and it is not mine.

THE CHARACTERS OF THE CHRIST-CROSS ROW,
By A CRITIC, To MRS ——.

*　　　*　　　*

Great D draws near—the Dutchess sure is come,
Open the doors of the withdrawing-room ;
Her daughters deck'd most daintily I see,
The Dowager grows a perfect Double D.
E enters next, and with her Eve appears.
Not like yon Dowager deprest with years ;
What Ease and Elegance her person grace,
Bright beaming, as the Evening-star, her face ;
Queen Esther next—how fair e'en after death,
Then one faint glimpse of Queen Elizabeth ;
No more, our Esthers now are nought but Hetties,
Elizabeths all dwindled into Betties ;
In vain you think to find them under E,
They're all diverted into H and B.
F follows fast the fair—and in his rear,
See Folly, Fashion, Foppery, straight appear,
All with fantastic clews, fantastic clothes,
With Fans and Flounces, Fringe and Furbelows.
Here Grub-street Geese presume to joke and jeer,
All, all, but Grannam Osborne's Gazetteer.
High heaves his hugeness H, methinks we see,
Henry the Eighth's most monstrous majesty,
But why on such *mock* grandeur should we dwell,
H mounts to Heaven, and H descends to Hell.

*　　　*　　　*

As H the Hebrew found, so I the Jew,
See Isaac, Joseph, Jacob, pass in view ;
The walls of old Jerusalem appear,
See Israel, and all Judah thronging there.

*　　　*　　　*

P pokes his head out, yet has not a pain ;
Like Punch, he peeps, but soon pops in again ;
Pleased with his Pranks, the Pisgys call him Puck,
Mortals he loves to prick, and pinch, and pluck ;
Now a pert Prig, he perks upon your face,
Now peers, pores, ponders, with profound grimace,

Now a proud Prince, in pompous Purple drest,
And now a Player, a Peer, a Pimp, or Priest ;
A Pea, a Pin, in a perpetual round,
Now seems a Penny, and now shews a Pound ;
Like Perch or Pike, in Pond you see him come,
He in plantations hangs like Pear or Plum,
Pippin or Peach ; then perches on the spray,
In form of Parrot, Pye, or Popinjay.
P, Proteus-like all tricks, all shapes can shew,
The pleasantest Person in the Christ-Cross row.

*   *   *

As K a King, Q represents a Queen,
And seems small difference the sounds between ;
K, as a man, with hoarser accent speaks,
In shriller notes Q like a female squeaks ;
Behold K struts, as might a King become,
Q draws her train along the Drawing-room,
Slow follow all the quality of State,
Queer Queensbury only does refuse to wait.

*   *   *

Thus great R reigns in town, while different far,
Rests in retirement, *little* Rural R ;
Remote from cities lives in lone Retreat,
With Rooks and Rabbit burrows round his seat—
S, sails the Swan slow down the Silver stream.

*   *   *

So big with Weddings, waddles W,
And brings all Womankind before your view ;
A Wench, a Wife, a Widow, and a W—e,
With Woe behind, and Wantonness before.

When you and Mr Chute can get the remainder of
Mariane, I shall be much obliged to you for it—I am
terribly impatient.

61. To WHARTON

MY DEAR WHARTON,—I rejoice to hear you are safe
arrived, tho' drawn by *four wild Horses*, like people
one reads of in the Book of Martyrs. yet I cannot
chuse but lament your Condition, so cooped up in the
Elvet-House with Spirits & Hobgoblins about you,
& pleasure at one Entrance quite shut out ; you must

so much the more set open all the other Avenues to admit it, open your Folio's, open your De L'Isle, & take a Prospect of that World, wᶜʰ the cruel Architect has hid from your corporeal Eyes, & confined 'em to the narrow Contemplation of your own Backside, & Kitchen Garden. Mʳ Keene has been here, but is now gone to Town for a little While, & returns to pass the Winter with us. we are tolerably gracious, & he speaks mighty well of you : but when I look upon his Countenance & his Ways, I can never think of bestowing [? my poor Tuthill] upon him (tho' it were never so advantagious, & they both had a Mind to it) and so I have said nothing to either of them. I found, he had no Hopes of your Petition ; and believe you are right in thinking no farther of it. your mention of Mʳ Vane, reminds me of poor Smart (not that I, or any other Mortal, pity him) about three Weeks ago he was arrested here at the Suit of a Taylor in London for a Debt of about 50£ of three Years standing. the College had about 28£ due to him in their Hands, the rest (to hinder him from going to the Castle, for he could not raise a shilling) Brown, May, & Peele, lent him upon his Note. upon this he remained confined to his Room, lest his Creditors here should snap him ; & the Fellows went round to make out a List of his Debts, wᶜʰ amount in Cambridge to above 350£. that they might come the readier to some Composition, he was advised to go off in the night, and lie hid somewhere or other. he has done so, & this has made the Creditors agree to an Assignment of 50£ per ann: out of his Income, wᶜʰ is above 140£, if he lives at Cambridge (not else). but I am apprehensive, if this comes to the Ears of Mʳ Vane he may take away the 40£ hitherto allowed him by the Duke of Cleveland ; for before all this (last Summer) I know they talked of doing so, as Mʳ Smart (they said) was settled in the World. If you found an Opportunity, possibly you might hinder this (wᶜʰ would totally ruin him now) by representing his absurdity in the best Light it will bear : but at the same Time they should make this a Condition of its Continuance ; that he live in the

College, soberly, & within Bounds, for that upon any Information to the contrary it shall be absolutely stop'd. This would be doing him a real Service, tho' against the Grain : yet I must own, if you heard all his Lies, Impertinence, & Ingratitude in this Affair, it would perhaps quite set you against him, as it has his only friend (Mr Addison) totally. & yet one would try to save him, for Drunkenness is one great Source of all this, & he may change it. I would not tell this matter in the North, were I you, till I found it was known by other Means. we have had an Opinion from the Attor^ny : General in a manner directly contrary to the former. he does not seem to have been clear then ; so that he may possibly not be so now. The King's-Bench (he says) can take no Cognisance of it ; the Visitor must do all, & he is the Vice-Chancellor by K: James's Charter, wch is good. this is sad indeed, & the Fellows, before they acquiesce in it, seem desirous of consulting Dr Lee, who is well acquainted with College-Matters.

Have you seen Lyttelton's Monody on his Wife's Death ? there are Parts of it too stiff & poetical ; but others truly tender & elegiac, as one would wish. Dodsley is publishing three Miscellaneous Volumes ; some new, many that have been already printed. Lyttelton, Nugent, and G: West have given him several Things of theirs. M^r W: has given him three Odes of Mine (wch you have seen before) & one of Mr West's (my friend who is dead) wch in spite of the Subject is excellent : it is on the late Queen's Death. there is a Mr Archibald Bower, a Scotchman bred in Italy, Professour in three Universities there, & of the Inquisition. he was employed by the Court of Rome to write a History of the Popes. as he searched into the Materials, his Eyes were open'd : he came to England, has changed his religion, & continues his Work in our language under the Patronage of Mr Pitt, the Yorks, &c. the Preface is come out with the Proposals, /& promises exceeding well. doubtless there is no part of History more curious, if it be well perform'd.

My best wishes wait upon Mrs. Wharton, and My Compliments to Miss Wharton, & to King Harry the 8th—Brown will write ; . . . Adieu, I am ever yours.

T. G.

Nov: 30 . . Cambridge [1747].

P : S : I said something to Stonhewer, who (I believe) will do what he can. he is now in London.

62. To Walpole

[1748]

I am obliged to you for Mr. Dodsley's book, and, having pretty well looked it over, will (as you desire) tell you my opinion of it. He might, methinks, have spared the Graces in his frontispiece, if he chose to be œconomical, and dressed his authors in a little more decent raiment—not in whited-brown paper and distorted characters, like an old ballad. I am ashamed to see myself ; but the company keeps me in countenance : so to begin with Mr. Tickell. This is not only a state-poem (my ancient aversion), but a state-poem on the peace of Utrecht. If Mr. Pope had wrote a panegyric on it, one could hardly have read him with patience : but this is only a poor short-winded imitator of Addison, who had himself not above three or four notes in poetry, sweet enough indeed, like those of a German flute, but such as soon tire and satiate the ear with their frequent return. Tickell had added to this a great poverty of sense, and a string of transitions that hardly become a schoolboy. However, I forgive him for the sake of his ballad, which I always thought the prettiest in the world. All there is of M. Green here has been printed before : there is a profusion of wit every where ; reading would have formed his judgment, and harmonized his verse, for even his wood-notes often break out into strains of real poetry and music. The Schoolmistress is excellent in its kind, and masterly ; and (I am sorry to differ from you, but) London is to me one of those few imitations, that have all the ease and all the spirit

of an original. The same man's verses at the opening
of Garrick's theatre are far from bad. Mr. Dyer (here
you will despise me highly) has more of poetry in his
imagination, than almost any of our number; but
rough and injudicious. I should range Mr. Bramston
only a step or two above Dr. King, who is as low in my
estimation as in yours. Dr. Evans is a furious mad-
man; and Pre-existence is nonsense in all her altitudes.
Mr. Lyttelton is a gentle elegiac person: Mr. Nugent
sure did not write his own ode. I like Mr. Whitehead's
little poems, I mean the Ode on a tent, the Verses to
Garrick, and particularly those to Charles Townshend,
better than any thing I had seen before of him. I gladly
pass over H. Brown, and the rest, to come at you. You
know I was of the publishing side, and thought your
reasons against it none; for though, as Mr. Chute said
extremely well, the *still small voice* of Poetry was not
made to be heard in a crowd; yet Satire will be heard,
for all the audience are by nature her friends; especially
when she appears in the spirit of Dryden, with his
strength, and often with his versification; such as you
have caught in those lines on the royal unction, on the
papal dominion, and convents of both sexes, on Henry
VIII. and Charles II. for these are to me the shining
parts of your Epistle. There are many lines I could
wish corrected, and some blotted out, but beauties
enough to atone for a thousand worse faults than these.
The opinion of such as can at all judge, who saw it
before in Dr. Middleton's hands, concurs nearly with
mine. As to what any one says, since it came out; our
people (you must know) are slow of judgement; they
wait till some body saves them the trouble, and
then follow his opinion; or stay till they hear what is
said in town, that is at some bishop's table, or some
coffee-house about the Temple. When they are
determined, I will tell you faithfully their verdict. As
for the Beauties, I am their most humble servant.
What shall I say to Mr. Lowth, Mr. Ridley, Mr. Rolle,
the reverend Mr. Brown, Seward, &c.? If I say,
Messieurs! this is not the thing; write prose, write

sermons, write nothing at all; they will disdain me,
and my advice. What then would the sickly peer have
done, that spends so much time in admiring everything
that has four legs, and fretting at his own misfortune
in having but two; and cursing his own politic head
and feeble constitution, that won't let him be such
a beast as he would wish? Mr. S. Jenyns now and
then can write a good line or two—such as these—

> Snatch us from all our little sorrows here,
> Calm every grief, and dry each childish tear, &c.

I like Mr. Ashton Hervey's fable; and an ode (the
last of all) by Mr. Mason, a new acquaintance of mine,
whose Musæus too seems to carry with it the promise
at least of something good to come. I was glad to see
you distinguished who poor West was, before his
charming ode, and called it anything rather than
a Pindaric. The town is an owl, if it don't like Lady
Mary, and I am surprised at it: we here are owls
enough to think her eclogues very bad; but that I did
not wonder at. Our present taste is sir T. Fitz-
Osborne's Letters. I send you a bit of a thing for two
reasons: first, because it is one of your favourites,
Mr. M. Green; and next, because I would do justice.
The thought on which my second ode turns is mani-
festly stole from hence:—not that I knew it at the
time, but, having seen this many Years before, to be
sure it imprinted itself on my Memory, & forgetting
the Author, I took it for my own. the Subject was the
Queen's Hermitage.

*   *   *

> Tho' yet no Palace grace the Shore
> To lodge the Pair you should adore;
> Nor Abbies great in Ruins rise,
> Royal Equivalents for Vice:
> Behold a Grott in Delphic Grove
> The Graces & the Muses love,
> A Temple from Vain-Glory free;
> Whose Goddess is Philosophy;
> Whose Sides such licensed Idols crown,
> As Superstition would pull down:

The only Pilgrimage I know,
That Men of Sense would chuse to go.
W^{ch} sweet Abode, her wisest Choice,
Urania cheers with heavenly Voice:
While all the Virtues gather round
To see her consecrate the Ground.
   If Thou, the God with winged Feet,
In Council talk of this Retreat;
And jealous Gods Resentment shew
At Altars raised to Men below:
Tell those proud Lords of Heaven, 'tis fit
Their House our Heroes should admit.
While each exists (as Poets sing)
A lazy, lewd, immortal, Thing:
They must, or grow in Disrepute,
With Earth's first Commoners recruit.
   Needless it is in Terms unskill'd
To praise, whatever Boyle shall build.
Needless it is the Busts to name
Of Men, Monopolists of Fame;
Four Chiefs adorn the modest Stone
For Virtue, as for Learning, known.
The thinking Sculpture helps to raise
Deep Thoughts, the Genii of the Place:
To the Mind's Ear, & inward Sight,
There Silence speaks, & Shade gives Light:
While Insects from the Threshold preach,
And Minds disposed to Musing teach;
Proud of strong Limbs & painted Hues
They perish by the slightest Bruise
Or Maladies begun within
Destroy more slow Life's frail Machine:
From Maggot-Youth thro' Change of State
They feel like us the Turns of Fate;
Some born to creep have lived to fly,
And changed Earth's Cells for Dwellings high:
And some, that did their six Wings keep,
Before they died, been forced to creep.
They Politicks, like ours, profess:
The greater prey upon the less.
Some strain on Foot huge Loads to bring,
Some toil incessant on the Wing:
Nor from their vigorous Schemes desist
Till Death; & then are never mist.

Some frolick, toil, marry, increase,
Are sick & well, have War & Peace,
And broke with Age in half a Day
Yield to Successors, & away.

*   *   *

Please to tell Mr Chute, that I never borrow'd any
Life of Mahomet (if that be his Meaning) having read
Boulainvillers long ago : but that I have Du Clos'
Louis Onze, & will send it him, if you will be so good
as to send me Directions both to Mr Whithed ; & M^r
Chute (per se) at his Lodgeings, wch I would be glad to
know for more Reasons than this. I hear Lamb-Pye
is dead, & could have wished to be told the Consequences : but both You & He, I doubt, will grow to
regard me in the Light of a *Miscellaneous Writer*.
Adieu, I am

Yours ever

T G:

P:S: If You chance to see a Letter of mine in any
body's hand, this is the History of it. Dr Whalley,
who has hated me ever since that Affair of Mr Turner,
thought fit to intimate to a large Table full of People,
that I was a Kind of Atheist. I wrote to him partly to
laugh at, & partly to reprove him for his Malice ; &
(as what he said was publick) I shew'd my Letter to
several of those, who had heard him ; & threaten'd
(not in earnest, you may imagine) to have it hawk'd
about Streets. they took me literally, & by Way of
Anticipation my Letter has been consign'd to one
Etoffe (a Fiend of a Parson, that you know) to shew
about here, & to carry to Town, if any one will read it.
he makes Criticisms on it, & has found out a false
Spelling, I'm told. Adieu !

63. TO WHARTON

April 25. Cambridge. [1749.]

MY DEAR WHARTON,—I perceive, that Second Parts
are as bad to write, as they can be to read ; for this, w^{ch}
you ought to have had a Week after the first, has been

a full Month in coming forth. The spirit of Lazyness (the Spirit of the Place), begins to possess even me, that have so long declaimed against it : yet has it not so prevail'd, but that I feel that discontent with myself, that *Ennuy*, that ever accompanies it in its Beginnings. Time will settle my Conscience, time will reconcile me to this languid Companion : we shall smoke, we shall tipple, we shall doze together. we shall have our little Jokes, like other People, and our long Stories ; Brandy will finish what Port begun ; & a Month after the time you will see in some Corner of a London Even^ng: Post, Yesterday, died the Rev^nd Mr John Grey, Senior-Fellow of Clare-Hall, a facetious Companion, & well-respected by all that knew him. his death is supposed to have been occasion'd by a Fit of an Apoplexy, being found fall'n out of Bed with his Head in the Chamber-Pot.

I am half ashamed to write University News to you, but as perhaps you retain some little Leven of Pembroke Hall, your nursing Mother, I am in hopes you will not be more than half-ashamed—to read it. Pembroke then is all harmonious & delightful since the Pacification : but I wish you would send them up some Boys, for they are grown extremely thin from their late long Indisposition. Keene's *Implications* have ended queerly, for, contrary to all Common Sense Peter Nourse and two others have joined Rogers, & brought in a shameful low Creature by a Majority. the master appeals to the Visitor against their Choice, as of a Person not qualified. he has received the Appeal, & (I suppose) will put in Brocket (Dr Keene's man) by main Force. Chapman is at present in Town in waiting ; he has just married a Miss Barnwell, niece to one Dr Barnwell, who was Minister of Trompington, with 2000£, a plain Woman, & about his own Age. I hear, that when he sent to Leicester-House to know, when the Prince would be waited upon with the Book of Verses on the Peace the Prince appointed no Day at all ; but order'd the Verses to be sent, & left there. the Design of receiving the University at Newcastle

House is said to be alter'd ; the Duke intending to
come hither (I imagine) after the Parliament is risen.
Rosse's ' Epistles of Tully ad Familiares ' will come
out in about a Week. it is in two handsome 8ᵛᵒ
Volumes, with an Intro:ᵗⁱᵒⁿ & Notes in English, but no
Translation, dedicated to Lᵈ Gower. now I am come
to Books, there is a new edition of Montesquieu's
Work (wᶜʰ I mentioned to you before) publishing in
2 v: 8ᵛᵒ. have you seen old Crebillon's ' Catilina,'
a Tragedy, wᶜʰ has had a prodigious Run at Paris ?
historical Truth is too much perverted by it, wᶜʰ is
ridiculous in a Story so generally known : but if you
can get over this, the Sentiments & Versification are
fine, & most of the Characters (particularly the principal
one) painted with great Spirit. observe, if you chuse
to send for it, not to have Brindley's Edition, which
is all false Prints, but Vaillant's. there is a Work
publishing in Denmark by Subscription (4 guineas)
' Travels in Egypt ' by Capt: Norden. he was once
in England (as Tutor to a young Count Daniskiold,
hereditary Admiral of Denmark) and known to many
Persons for a Man of Sense & that understood Drawing
extremely well : accordingly it is the Plates, that
raise it to such a Price, & are said to be excellent. the
Author himself is dead, & his papers are publish'd by
the Academy at Copenhagen. Mʳ Birch, the inde-
fatigable, has just put out a thick 8ᵛᵒ of original Papers
of Q: Elizabeth's Time. there are many curious Things
in it, particularly Letters from Sʳ Rob: Cecil (Salisbury)
about his Negotiations with Henry the 4ᵗʰ of France ;
the Earl of Monmouth's odd Account of Q: Elizabeth's
Death, several Peculiarities of James 1ˢᵗ, & Pr:ce
Henry, &c. ; and above all an excellent Account of
the State of France with Characters of the King, his
Court & Ministry, by Sʳ G: Carew, Ambassador there.
this, I think, is all new worth mentioning, that I have
seen or heard of, except a natural History of Peru in
Spanish, printed at London by Don —— something, a
Man of Learning, sent thither by that Court on Purpose.
I shall venture to accept of a Part of that kind Offer

you once made me (for my Finances are much disorder'd this Year) by desiring you to lend me twenty Guineas. the sooner you can do this, the more convenient it will be to me, & if you can find a Method to pay it here ; still more so. but if anything should happen, that may defer it, or make this Method troublesome : then I will desire you to make it payable in Town after the first Week in June, when I shall be obliged to go thither.

I want to hear from you, to know of your Health and that of your Family, my best Compliments to Mrs Wharton, Mr Brown comes and throws in his *little comps* too, & we are both very truly

Yours
TG: i: b:

64. To Wharton

MY DEAR WHARTON,—I promised Dr Keene long since to give you an Account of our Magnificences here, but the News-Papers & he himself in Person have got the Start of my Indolence, so that by this Time you are well acquainted with all the Events, that adorned that Week of Wonders. thus much I may venture to tell you, because it is probable no body else has done it, that our Friend Chappy's Zeal & Eloquence surpassed all Power of Description. Vesuvio in an Eruption was not more violent than his Utterance, nor (since I am at my Mountains) Pelion with all its Pine-trees in a Storm of Wind more impetuous than his Action. and yet the Senate-house still stands, & (I thank God) we are all safe & well at your Service. I was ready to sink for him, & scarce dared to look about me, when I was sure it was all over : but soon found I might have spared my Confusion, for all People join'd to applaud him : everything was quite right ; & I dare swear, not three People here but think him a Model of Oratory. for all the Duke's little Court came with a Resolution to be pleased ; & when the Tone was once given, the University, who ever wait for the Judgement of their Betters, struck into it with an admirable Harmony. for the rest of the Performances they were (as usual) very ordinary. every one, while it lasted, was very gay, & very busy in the Morning, & very owlish & very tipsy at Night. I make no exceptions from the Chancellour to Blew-Coat. Mason's Ode was the only Entertainment, that had any tolerable Elegance; & for my own Part, I think it (with some little abatements) uncommonly well on such an Occasion. pray let me know your Sentiments, for doubtless you have seen it. the Author of it grows apace into my good Graces, as I know him more: he is very ingenious with great Good-Nature & Simplicity. a little vain, but in so harmless & so comical a Way, that it does not offend one at all; a little ambitious, but withall so ignorant in the World & its Ways, that this does not hurt him in one's Opinion. so sincere & so undisguised, that no Mind with a Spark of Generosity would ever think of hurting him, he lies so open to Injury. but so indolent, that if he can not overcome this Habit, all his good Qualities will signify nothing at all. after all I like him so well, I could wish you knew him.

[? Tuthill] who was here at the Installation & in high Spirits, will come to settle in Cambridge at Michaelmas. and I have hopes, that these two, with Brown's assistance may bring Pembroke into some Esteem: but then there is no making Bricks without Straw. They have no Boys at all, & unless you can send us a Hamper or two out of the North to begin with, they will be like a few Rats straggling about an old deserted Mansion-House.

I should be glad (as you will see Keene often) if you could throw in a Word, as of your own head merely, about a Fellowship for Stonhewer. he has several times mention'd it himself, as a Thing he would try to bring about either at Queen's or Christ's, where he has interest: but I know not how, it has gone off again, & we have heard no more lately about it. I know it is not practicable here at Peterhouse, because of his County; and though at Pembroke we might possibly get a Majority, yet Roger is an animal, that might play over again all his old Game, & with a better appearance

than before. you would therefore oblige me, if you
would sound him upon this Subject, for it is Stonhewer's Wish, & (I think) would be an Advantage to
him, if he had a Reason for continuing here some time
longer. if you can get Keene to be explicit about it
(but it must seem to be a Thought entirely of your
own) I will desire you to let me know the Result. my
best Wishes, Dear Sr, ever attend on you, & Mrs
Wharton. I am most sincerely & unalterably

Yours

TG:

Aug: 8 Cambridge [1749].

65. To His Mother

Cambridge, November 7, 1749.

The unhappy news I have just received from you
equally surprises and afflicts me. I have lost a person
I loved very much, and have been used to from my
infancy ; but am much more concerned for your loss,
the circumstances of which I forbear to dwell upon, as
you must be too sensible of them yourself ; and will,
I fear, more and more need a consolation that no one
can give, except He who has preserved her to you so
many years, and at last, when it was His pleasure,
has taken her from us to Himself : and perhaps, if we
reflect upon what she felt in this life, we may look
upon this as an instance of His goodness both to her,
and to those that loved her. She might have lan-
guished many years before our eyes in a continual
increase of pain, and totally helpless ; she might have
long wished to end her misery without being able to
attain it ; or perhaps even lost all sense, and yet
continued to breathe ; a sad spectacle to such as
must have felt more for her than she could have done
for herself. However you may deplore your own loss,
yet think that she is at last easy and happy ; and has
now more occasion to pity us than we her. I hope,
and beg, you will support yourself with that resignation
we owe to Him, who gave us our being for our good,

and who deprives us of it for the same reason. I would have come to you directly, but you do not say whether you desire I should or not; if you do, I beg I may know it, for there is nothing to hinder me, and I am in very good health.

66. To Walpole

Stoke, June 12, 1750.

Dear Sir,—As I live in a place, where even the ordinary tattle of the town arrives not till it is stale, and which produces no events of its own, you will not desire any excuse from me for writing so seldom, especially as of all people living I know you are the least a friend to letters spun out of one's brains, with all the toil and constraint that accompanies sentimental productions. I have been here at Stoke a few days (where I shall continue good part of the summer); and having put an end to a thing, whose beginning you have seen long ago, I immediately send it you. You will, I hope, look upon it in the light of a *thing with an end to it*; a merit that most of my writings have wanted, and are like to want, but which this epistle I am determined shall not want, when it tells you that I am ever

Yours,

T. Gray.

Not that I have done yet; but who could avoid the temptation of finishing so roundly and so cleverly in the manner of good queen Anne's days? Now I have talked of writings; I have seen a book, which is by this time in the press, against Middleton (though without naming him), by Asheton. As far as I can judge from a very hasty reading, there are things in it new and ingenious, but rather too prolix, and the style here and there savouring too strongly of sermon. I imagine it will do him credit. So much for other people, now to *self* again. You are desired to tell me your opinion, if you can take the pains, of these lines. I am once more

Ever yours.

67. To Walpole

[Cambridge, Feb. 11. 1751]

My dear Sr,—As you have brought me into a little
Sort of Distress, you must assist me, I believe, to get
out of it, as well as I can. yesterday I had the Misfortune of receiving a Letter from certain Gentlemen (as
their Bookseller expresses it) who have taken the
Magazine of Magazines into their Hands. they tell me,
that an *ingenious* Poem, call'd, *Reflections* in a Country-
Churchyard, has been communicated to them, wch they
are printing forthwith : that they are inform'd, that
the *excellent* Author of it is I by name, & that they beg
not only his *Indulgence*, but the *Honor of his Correspondence*, &c: as I am not at all disposed to be either so
indulgent, or so correspondent, as they desire ; I have
but one bad Way left to escape the Honour they would
inflict upon me. & therefore am obliged to desire you
would make Dodsley print it immediately (wch may be
done in less than a Week's time) from your Copy, but
without my Name, in what Form is most convenient
for him, but in his best Paper & Character. he must
correct the Press himself, & print it without any
Interval between the Stanza's, because the Sense is
in some Places continued beyond them ; & the Title
must be, Elegy, wrote in a Country Church-yard. if he
would add a Line or two to say it came into his Hands
by Accident, I should like it better. if you think fit,
the 102d Line may be read

Awake, & faithful to her wonted Fires.

but if this be worse than before ; it must go, as it was.
in the 126th, for *ancient* Thorn, read *aged*.

If you behold the Mag: of Mag:s in the Light that
I do, you will not refuse to give yourself this Trouble
on my Account, wch you have taken of your own Accord
before now. Adieu, Sr, I am   Yours ever

TG:

If Dodsley don't do this immediately,
he may as well let it alone.

To The Honble Horace Walpole, Esq in Arlington
Street London

68. To Walpole

Ash-Wednesday [Feb. 20], Cambridge, 1751.

MY DEAR SIR,—You have indeed conducted with great decency my little *misfortune* : you have taken a paternal care of it, and expressed much more kindness than could have been expressed from so near a relation. But we are all frail ; and I hope to do as much for you another time. Nurse Dodsley has given it a pinch or two in the cradle, that (I doubt) it will bear the marks of as long as it lives. But no matter : we have ourselves suffered under her hands before now ; and besides, it will only look the more careless, and by *accident* as it were. I thank you for your advertisement, which saves my honour, and in a manner *bien flatteuse pour moi*, who should be put to it even to make myself a compliment in good English.

You will take me for a mere poet, and a fetcher and carrier of singsong, if I tell you that I intend to send you the beginning of a drama, not mine, thank God, as you'll believe, when you hear it is finished, but wrote by a person whom I have a very good opinion of. It is (unfortunately) in the manner of the ancient drama, with choruses, which I am, to my shame, the occasion of ; for, as great part of it was at first written in that form, I would not suffer him to change it to a play fit for the stage, as he intended, because the lyric parts are the best of it, and they must have been lost. The story is Saxon, and the language has a tang of Shakespear, that suits an old-fashioned fable very well. In short, I don't do it merely to amuse you, but for the sake of the author, who wants a judge, and so I would lend him *mine* : yet not without your leave, lest you should have us up to dirty our stockings at the bar of your house for wasting the time and politics of the *nation*. Adieu, sir !

I am ever yours,

T. GRAY.

69. To Walpole

Cambridge, March 3, 1751.

Elfrida (for that is the fair one's name) and her author are now in town together. He has promised me, that he will send a part of it to you some morning while he is there ; and (if you shall think it worth while to descend to particulars) I should be glad you would tell me very freely your opinion about it ; for he shall know nothing of the matter, that is not fit for the ears of a *tender* parent—though, by the way, he has ingenuity and merit enough (whatever his drama may have) to bear hearing his faults very patiently. I must only beg you not to show it, much less let it be copied ; for it will be published, though not as yet.

I do not expect any more editions, as I have appeared in more magazines than one. The chief errata were *sacred* bower for *secret* ; *hidden* for *kindred* (in spite of dukes and classicks) ; and *frowning* as in scorn for *smiling*. I humbly propose, for the benefit of Mr. Dodsley and his matrons, that take *awake* for a verb, that they should read *asleep*, and all will be right. Gil Blas is the Lying Valet in five acts. The Fine Lady has half-a-dozen good lines dispersed in it. Pompey is the hasty production of a Mr. Coventry (cousin to him you knew), a young clergyman : I found it out by three characters, which once made part of a comedy that he showed me of his own writing. Has that miracle of *tenderness and sensibility* (as she calls it) lady Vane given you any amusement ? Peregrine, whom she uses as a vehicle, is very poor indeed with a few exceptions. In the last volume is a character of Mr. Lyttelton, under the name of Gosling Scrag, and a parody of part of his Monody, under the notion of a pastoral on the death of his grandmother.

I am ever yours,

T. GRAY.

70. To Walpole

Hymn to Adversity

Daughter of Jove, relestless Power,
Thou Tamer of the human Breast!
Whose iron Scourge, & torturing Hour,
The bad affright, afflict the best,
Bound in thy adamantine Chain
The Proud are taught to tast of Pain
And purple Tyrants vainly groan
With Pangs unfelt before, unpitied & alone.

When first thy Sire to send on Earth
Virtue, his darling Child, design'd,
To Thee he gave the heav'nly Birth
And bad to form her infant Mind.
Stern rugged Nurse ! thy rigid Lore
With patience many a Year she bore :
What sorrow was thou bad'st her know,
And from her own she learn'd to melt at other's Woe.

Scared at thy Frown terrific, fly
Self-pleasing Folly's idle Brood,
Wild Laughter, Noise, & thoughtless Joy,
And leave us Leisure to be good :
Light they disperse, & with them go
The Summer-Friend, the flatt'ring Foe ;
By vain Prosperity received,
To her they vow their Truth, & are again believed.

Wisdom in sable Garb array'd,
Immers'd in rapturous Thought profound,
And Melancholy, silent Maid,
With leaden Eye, that loves the Ground
Still on thy solemn Steps attend :
Warm Charity, the general Friend,
With Justice, to herself severe,
And Pity, dropping soft the sadly-pleasing Tear.

Oh ! gently on thy Suppliant's Head
Dread Goddess lay thy chast'ning Hand,
Not in thy Gorgon-Terrors clad,
Nor circled with the vengeful Band,
As by the Impious thou art seen,
With thund'ring Voice, & threat'ning Mien,

With screaming Horrour's funeral Cry,
Despair, & fell Disease, & ghastly Poverty.

Thy Form benign, oh Goddess, wear,
Thy milder Influence impart ;
Thy philosophic Train be there
To soften, not to wound, my Heart.
The generous Spark extinct revive,
Teach me to love, & to forgive,
Exact my own Defects to scan,
What others are, to feel, & know myself a Man.

I send you this (as you desire) merely to make up half
a dozen ; tho' it will hardly answer your End in
furnishing out either a Head or Tail-piece. but your
own Fable may much better supply the Place. you
have alter'd it to its Advantage ; but there is still
something a little embarrass'd here & there in the
Expression. I rejoice to find you apply (pardon the
Use of so odious a Word) to the History of your own
Times. speak, & spare not. be as impartial as you
can ; & after all, the World will not believe, you are
so, tho' you should make as many Protestations as
Bishop Burnet. they will feel in their own Breast,
& find it very possible to hate fourscore Persons, yea,
ninety and nine : so you must rest satisfied with the
Testimony of your own Conscience. somebody has
laughed at Mr Dodsley or at me, when they talk'd
of the *Bat* : I have nothing more, either nocturnal or
diurnal, to deck his Miscellany with. we have a Man
here that writes a good Hand ; but he has two little
Failings, that hinder my recommending him to you.
he is lousy, & he is mad : he sets out this Week for
Bedlam ; but if you insist upon it, I don't doubt he
will pay his Respects to you. I have seen two of
Dr M:ldns unpublish'd Works. one is about 44 Pages
in 4to against Dr Waterland, who wrote a very orthodox
Book on the Importance of the Doctrine of ye Trinity,
& insisted, that Christians ought to have no Communion with such as differ from them in Fundamentals.
M:ldn enters no farther into the Doctrine itself than to
shew that a mere speculative Point can never be

call'd a Fundamental; & that the earlier Fathers, on whose concurrent Tradition Wat:^d would build, are so far, when they speak of the three Persons, from agreeing with the present Notion of our Church, that they declare for the Inferiority of the Son, & seem to have no clear & distinct Idea of the H: Ghost at all. the rest is employed in exposing the Folly & Cruelty of Stiffness & Zealotism in Religion, & in shewing that the primitive Ages of the Church, in wch Tradition had its Rise, were (even by Confession of the best Scholars & most orthodox Writers) the *Æra of Nonsense & Absurdity.* it is finish'd, & very well wrote; but has been mostly incorporated into his other Works, particularly the Enquiry: & for this Reason I suppose he has writ upon it, *This wholly laid aside.* the second is in Latin, on Miracles; to shew, that of the two Methods of defending Christianity, one from its intrinsic Evidence, the Holiness and Purity of its Doctrines; the other from its external, the Miracles said to be wrought to confirm it. the first has been little attended to by reason of its Difficulty; the second much insisted upon, because it appear'd an easier Task, but that it can in reality prove nothing at all. ' Nobilis illa quidem Defensio (the first) quam si obtinere potuissent, rem simul omnem expediisse, causamq3 penitùs vicisse viderentur. at causæ hujus defendendæ labor cum tantâ argumentandi cavillandiq3 molestiâ conjunctus ad alteram, quam dixi, defensionis viam, ut commodiorem longé & faciliorem, plerosque adegit——ego veró istiusmodi defensione Religionem nostram non modo non confirmari, sed dubiam potiús suspectamq3 reddi existimo.' he then proceeds to consider Miracles in general, & afterwards those of the Pagans, compared with those of X^t. I only tell you the Plan, for I have not read it out (tho' it is short) but you will not doubt to what Conclusion it tends. there is another Thing, I know not what, I am to see. as to the Treatise on Prayer; they say, it is burnt indeed. Adieu, I am ever

Yours

Sept: 8. [1751] Camb:

71. To Walpole

Wednesday—[July 8, 1752] Stoke.

I am at present at Stoke, to wch I came at half an
Hour's Warning upon the News I received of my
Mother's Illness, & did not expect to have found her
alive : but as I found her much better, & she continues
so, I shall be very glad to make you a Visit at Strawberry, whenever you give me Notice of a convenient
time. I am surprized at the Print, wch far surpasses
my Idea of London Graving. the Drawing itself was
so finished, that I suppose, it did not require all the
Art I had imagined to copy it tolerably. my Aunts just
now, seeing me open your Letter, take it to be a Bury-
ing-Ticket enclosed, & ask, whether any body has left
me a Ring ? and so they still conceive it to be, even
with all their Spectacles on. heaven forbid they should
suspect it to belong to any Verses of mine ; they would
burn me for a Poet. Mr Bentley (I believe) will catch
a better Idea of Stoke-House from any old Barn he
sees, than from my Sketch : but I will try my Skill.
I forbid no Banes ; but am satisfied, if your Design
succeed so well as you intend it. and yet I know, it
will be accompanied with something not at all agreeable
to me. Adieu ! I am

Yours ever

TG:

To The Honble Horace Walpole Esq in Arlington
Street London

72. To Walpole

Camb:^ge Feb: 13. 1753.

Sure You are not out of your Wits ! this I know,
if you suffer my Head to be printed, you infallibly
will put me out of mine. I conjure you immediately
to put a stop to any such design. who is at the Expence
of engraving it, I know not ; but if it be Dodsley,
I will make up the Loss to him. the thing, as it was,
I know will make me ridiculous enough ; but to appear
in proper Person at the head of my works, consisting

of half a dozen Ballads in 30 Pages, would be worse than the Pillory. I do assure you, if I had received such a Book with such a frontispice without any warning, I believe, it would have given me a Palsy. therefore I rejoice to have received this Notice ; & shall not be easy, till you tell me all thoughts of it are laid aside. I am extremely in earnest, & can't bear even the Idea !

I had wrote to Dodsley to tell him, how little I liked the Title he had prefix'd, but your letter has put all that out of my Head. if you think it necessary to print these explanations for the use of People that have no eyes, I could be glad, they were a little alter'd. I am to my shame in your debt for a long letter, but I can not think of anything else, till you have set me at ease. Adieu, I am

Yours ever,
T: G:

73. To Wharton

March 15—Stoke.

MY DEAR WHARTON,—I judge by this time you are in town. the reason that I thought would have deprived me of the pleasure of seeing you is now at an end : my poor Mother, after a long and painful Struggle for life, expired on Sunday morning. when I have seen her buried, I shall come to London, & it will be a particular satisfaction to me to find you there. if you can procure me a tolerable lodging near you, be so good (if you can conveniently) to let me know the night you receive this ; if not, I shall go to my old Landlord in Jermyn Street. I believe, I shall come on Tuesday, & stay a few days, for I must return hither to pay my aunt her Arrears, wch she will demand with great Exactness. Adieu, dear S^r, I am,

Ever yours,
T GRAY.

To me at Mrs Rogers's of Stoke, near Windsor Bucks.

74. To Wharton

Cambridge
Saturday, July 14, 1753.

My dear Doct^r,—This is only to tell you, that we set out on Monday Morning, & shall travel leisurely, not by the direct road, for we intend to see several houses & places as we go ; on Thursday we shall see York, & next morning as early as we can (certainly before ten o'clock) shall hope to meet you at Studley. you will understand all this with Arch-Bishop Potter's Proviso, God willing, & provided nothing hinder, for if we are overturn'd & *tous fracassés,* or if the Mob at Leeds cut us off, as friends to Turnpikes ; or if the Waters be out, & drown us ; or (as Herodotus says) if we can go no farther *for feathers,* in all these cases, & many more, we may chance to fail you. my respects to Mrs Wharton, I am ever

Yours,
T Gray.

By Caxton Bag.

75. To the Rev. William Mason

Durham, July 24, Tuesday, 1753.

Dear Sir,—We performed our journey, a very agreeable one, within the time appointed, and left out scarcely anything worth seeing in or near our way. The Doctor and Mrs. Wharton had expected us about two hours, when we arrived at Studley on Friday. We passed that night at Ripon, and the next at Richmond ; and on Sunday evening got to Durham. I cannot now enter into the particulars of my travels, because I have not yet gathered up my quotations from the Classics to intersperse, like Mr. Addison ; but I hope to be able soon to entertain you with a dish of very choice erudition. I have another reason, too, which is, that the post is just setting out. Suffice it to tell you, that I have one of the most beautiful vales here in England to walk in, with prospects that change every ten steps, and open something new wherever I turn me, all rude and romantic ; in short, the sweetest spot to break your neck or drown yourself in that ever was beheld. I have done neither yet, but I have been twice at the races, once at the assembly, have had a visit from Dr. Chapman, and dined with the Bishop.

I am very shabby, for Stonhewer's box, with my coat in it, which went by sea, is not yet arrived. You are desired therefore to send Lee, the bedmaker at Peterhouse, to the master of the Lynn boats, to enquire what vessel it was sent by, and why it does not come. It was directed to Dr. Stonhewer, of Houghton, to be left with the rector of Sunderland. Another trouble I have to give you, which is to order Barnes to bring any letter Stonhewer or I may have to you, and direct them hither. The Doctor and Mrs. Wharton desire their particular compliments to you, and are sorry you could not be with us. Adieu. I am ever sincerely yours,

T. G.

P.S.—I have left my watch hanging (I believe) in my bed-room : will you be so good as to ask after it.

76. To Mason

Durham, September 21, 1753.

DEAR MASON,—It is but a few days since I was informed by Avison, that the alarm you had on your sister's account served but to prepare you for a greater loss, which was soon to follow. I know what it is to lose a person that one's eyes and heart have long been used to, and I never desire to part with the remembrance of that loss, nor would wish you should. It is something that you had a little time to acquaint yourself with the idea beforehand, if I am informed right, and that he probably suffered but little pain, the only thing that makes death terrible.

It will now no longer be proper for me to see you at Hull, as I should otherwise have tried to do. I shall go therefore to York, with intention to make use of the stage-coach, either on Friday or Monday. I shall be a week at Cambridge, and then pass through London into Buckinghamshire. If I can be of any use to you in anything it will give me great pleasure. Let me have a line from you soon, for I am very affectionately yours,

T. GRAY.

77. TO MASON

Stoke, November 5, 1753.

MY DEAR MASON,—I am not in a way of leaving this place yet this fortnight, and consequently shall hardly see you in town. I rejoice in the meantime to think that you are there, and have left, I hope, a part of your disagreeable reflections in the place where they grew.

Stoke has revived in me the memory of many a melancholy hour that I have passed in it, and, though I have no longer the same cause of anxiety, I do not find myself at all the happier for thinking that I have lost it, as my thoughts now signify nothing to any one but myself. I shall wish to change the scene as soon as ever I can.

I am heartily glad to hear Mr. Hutton is so reasonable, but am rather sorry to find that design is known to so many. Dr. Wharton, who, I suppose, heard it from Avison, mentions it in a letter to me. Were I you, I should have taken some pleasure in observing people's faces, and perhaps in putting their kindness a little to the trial; it is a very useful experiment, and very possibly you will never have it in your power to put it in practice again. Pray make your bargain with all the circumspection and selfishness of an old hunks; when you are grown as rich as Crœsus, do not grow too good-for-nothing,—a little good-for-nothing to be sure you will grow; everybody does so in proportion to their circumstances, else, indeed, what should we do with one's money? My third sentence is, do not anticipate your revenues, and live upon air till you know what you are worth. You bid me write no more than a scrawl to you, therefore I will trouble you, as you are so busy, with nothing more. Adieu.

I am very sincerely and affectionately yours,

T. G.

I should be obliged to you, if you had time, to ask at Robert's, or some place in Jermyn Street, whether I could be there about a fortnight hence. I will not give more than half-a-guinea a week, nor put up with a second floor unless it has a tolerable room to the street. Will you acquaint me of this ?

78. To Wharton
Stoke. Aug: 13 [1754].

My dear Sʳ,—Having been some little time absent from hence I missed of your letter, or I had answer'd it as soon as you desire me. the opportunity of a good House I hope you will not suffer to escape you. whether the rent be too high, you alone can properly judge. there is great comfort to be sure in a good house. some appearance of œconomy I should think would give you a credit in that part of the town you are to be well with : they pride themselves in living much within their income. upon the whole I seem to have a partiality for Mʳ Crumpe, but be sure never to repent. if you think you shall ; by all means settle yourself in the great house. besides I do not know, but some great old Doctor may come & squat himself down there at your elbow (for I suppose there may be some convenience in succeeding to a house of the same Profession) & then you would be horridly out of humour. in short you see with your own eyes, you know the Quarter, & must necessarily be best qualified to decide. Dʳ Fothergill's invitation is very civil. as to the depth of Science, which you seem to dread, it always grows shallower, as one comes nearer, tho' it makes a great noise at a distance. the design of the Society at least is a good one. but if they are warm & profess'd Enemies of the College, I should think the same reason, that makes Hebᵉⁿ withdraw himself, should prevent your admission into it : it will be easy to delay it however on various pretences without disobliging any one.

I am glad you agree with me in admiring Mr Southcote's Paradise, wch whenever you see it again, will improve upon you. do you know, you may have it for 20,000£, but I am afraid, the Lands are not very improveable. you do not say enough of Esher. it is my other favourite place. It was a Villa of Cardinal Wolsey's, of wch nothing but a part of the Gateway remained. Mr Kent supplied the rest, but I think with you, that he had not read the Gothic Classicks with taste or attention. he introduced a mix'd Style, wch now goes by the name of the *Battey-Langley-Manner*. he is an Architect, that has publish'd a book of bad Designs. if you have seen M^r W:^s pray let me hear your opinion, wch I will not anticipate by saying anything about it. to be sure its extreme littleness will be the first thing, that strikes you. by all means see Ld Radnor's again. he is a simple old Phobus, but nothing can spoil so glorious a situation, wch surpasses everything round it. I take it ill, you should say any thing against ye Mole. it is a reflection, I see, cast at the Thames. do you think, that Rivers, wch have lived in London & its neighbourhood all their days, will run roaring & tumbling about, like your Tramontane Torrents in the North. no, they only glide and whisper. in your next expedition you will see Claremont, & Ld Portmore's, wch joins my Ld Lincoln's, & above all Mr Hamilton's, at Cobham in Surrey, wch all the world talks of & I have seen seven years ago. The Year indeed does not behave itself well, but think, what it must be in the North. I suppose the roads are impassable with the deep snow still.

I could write abundance more, but am afraid of losing this Post. pray let me hear from you as soon as you can, & make my Compliments to Mrs Wharton. Mason is by this time in Town again. . . . Brown, I believe, at Cambridge. Adieu, I am ever

Yours,
T. G.

I am obliged to you for sending the Tea. wch is excellent.

79. To Wharton

Stoke, September 18, 1754.

DEAR S^R,—I rejoice to find you at last settled to
your heart's content, & delight to hear you talk of
giving your house *some Gothic ornaments* already. if
you project anything, I hope it will be entirely within
doors ; & don't let me (when I come gaping into
Coleman-street) be directed to the Gentleman's at the
ten Pinnacles, or with the Church-Porch at his door.
I am glad you enter into the Spirit of Strawberry-
Castle. it has a purity & propriety of Gothicism in it
(with very few exceptions) that I have not seen else-
where. the eating-room and library were not compleated, when I was there, & I want to know what
effect they have. My Ld Radnor's Vagaries (I see)
did not keep you from doing justice to his situation,
wch far surpasses everything near it, and I do not
know a more *laughing* Scene, than that about Twickenham & Richmond. Dr Akenside (I perceive) is no
Conjurer in Architecture, especially when he talks of
the Ruins of Persepolis, wch are no more Gothic, than
they are Chinese. the Egyptian Style (see Dr Pococke,
not his discourses, but his prints) was apparently the
Mother of ye Greek ; & there is such a similitude
between the Egyptian, & those Persian Ruins, as gave
room to Diodorus to affirm, that the old buildings of
Persia were certainly perform'd by Egyptian Artists.
as to the other part of his opinion, that the Gothic
manner is the Saracen or Moorish, he has a great
Authority to support him, that of Sr Christ:^{r} Wren,
& yet (I cannot help thinking) is undoubtedly wrong.
the Palaces in Spain, I never saw but in description,
wch gives us little or no idea of things ; but the Doge's
Palace at Venice I have seen (wch is in the Arabesque
manner) & the houses of Barbary you may see in D^r
Shaw's book, not to mention abundance of other
eastern Buildings in Turky, Persia, &c: that we have
views of, & they seem plainly to be corruptions of the
Greek Architecture, broke into little parts indeed,

& cover'd with little ornaments, but in a taste very distinguishable from that we call Gothic. there is one thing that runs thro' the Moorish Buildings, that an Imitator would certainly have been first struck with, & would have tried to copy, & that is the Cupola's, wch cover everything, Baths, Apartments, & even Kitchens. yet who ever saw a Gothic Cupola ? it is a thing plainly of Greek original. I do not see anything but the slender Spires, that serve for steeples, wch may perhaps be borrowed from the Saracen Minarets on their Mosques.

I was in Northamptonshire, when I received your Letter, but am now returned hither. I have been at Warwick, wch is a place worth seeing. the Town is on an eminence surrounded every way with a fine cultivated Valley, through wch the Avon winds, & at the distance of 5 or 6 miles, a circle of hills well wooded, & with various objects crowning them, that close the Prospect. out of the town on one side of it, rises a rock, that might remind one of your rocks at Durham, but that it is not so savage, or so lofty, & that the river, wch washes its foot, is perfectly clear, & so gentle, that its current is hardly visible. upon it stands the Castle, the noble old residence of the Beauchamps & Neville's, & now of Earl Brooke. he has sash'd the great Appartment that's to be sure (I can't help these things) & being since told, that square sash-windows were not Gothic, he has put certain whim-wams within side the glass, wch appearing through are to look like fret-work. then he has scooped out a little Burrough in the massy walls of the place for his little self & his children, wch is hung with Paper & printed Linen, & carved chimney-pieces, in the exact manner of Berkley-square, or Argyle-buildings. what in short can a Lord do now a days, that is lost in a great old solitary Castle, but skulk about & get into the first hole he finds, as a Rat would do in like case. a pretty long old stone-bridge leads you into the town with a Mill at the end of it, over wch the rock rises with the Castle upon it with all its battle-

ments & queer ruined towers, & on your left hand the
Avon strays thro' the Park, whose ancient Elms seem
to remember Sr Philip Sidney, (who often walk'd under
them) and talk of him to this day. the Beauchamp
Earls of Warwick lie under stately Monuments in the
Choir of the great Church, & in our Lady's Chappel
adjoining to it. There also lie Ambrose Dudley, E:
of Warwick; & his Brother, the famous Ld Leicester,
with Lettice, his Countess. this Chappel is preserved
entire, though the Body of the Church was burnt down
60 years ago, & rebuilt by Sir C: Wren. I had heard
often of Guy-Cliff two miles from the town, so I walked
to see it; & of all improvers commend me to M^r
Greathead, its present owner. He shew'd it me
himself, & is literally a fat young Man with a head
& face much bigger than they are usually worn. it
was naturally a very agreeable rock, whose Cliffs
cover'd with large trees hung beetleing over the Avon,
wch twists twenty ways in sight of it. there was the
Cell of Guy, Earl of Warwick, cut in the living stone,
where he died a Hermit (as you may see in a penny
History, that hangs upon the rails in Moorfields) there
were his fountains bubbling out of the Cliff; there
was a chantry founded to his memory in Henry the
6^{th's} time. but behold the Trees are cut down to make
room for flowering shrubs, the rock is cut up, till it is
as smooth & as sleek as sattin; the river has a gravel-
walk by its side; the Cell is a Grotta with cockle-shells
and looking-glass; the fountains have an iron-gate
before them, and the Chantry is a Barn, or a little
House. even the poorest bits of nature, that remain,
are daily threatned, for he says (& I am sure, when the
Greatheads are once set upon a thing, they will do it)
he is determined, it shall be *all new.* These were his
words, & they are Fate. I have also been at Stow, at
Woburn (the Du[ke] of Bedford's), and at Wroxton
(Ld Guilford's) but I defer these chapt[ers] till we meet.
I shall only tell you for your comfort, that the part of
Northampt:^{re}, where I have been, is in fruits, in
flowers [and in] corn very near a fortnight behind this

part of Buckinghamshire, that they have no nightingales, & that the other birds are almost as silent, as at
Durham.   it is rich land, but upon a Clay, and in a
very bleak, high, exposed situation. I hope, you have
had some warm weather, since you last complained
of the South. I have thoughts of seeing you about
Michaelmas, tho' I shall not stay long in town. I
should have been at Cambridge before now, if the
D: of Newc^le: and his foundation-stone would have let
me, but I want them to have done before I go. I am
sorry Mr Brown should be the only one, that has stood
upon Punctilio's with me, & would not write first.
pray tell him so. Mason is (I believe) in town, or at
Chiswick. [? No news of Tuthill.] I wrote a long
letter to him in answer to one he wrote me, but
no reply. Adieu, I am ever yrs.   TG:
Brown call'd here this morning, before I was up,
& breakfasted with me.

80. To Wharton

ODE IN THE GREEK MANNER

. . . . . .

If this be as tedious to You, as it is grown to me,
I shall be sorry that I sent it you. I do not pretend to
debellate any one's Pride : I love my own too well to
attempt it. as to mortifying their Vanity it is too easy
and too mean a task for me to delight in. you are very
good in shewing so much sensibility on my account.
but be assured, my Taste for Praise is not like that of
Children for fruit. If there were nothing but Medlars
and Blackberries in the world, I could be very well
content to go without any at all. I dare say that
M——n (tho' some years younger than I) was as little
elevated with the approbation of L^d D: and L^d M: as
I am mortified by their silence. I desire you would by
no means suffer this to be copied ; nor even shew it,
unless to very few, & especially not to mere Scholars,
that can scan all the measures in Pindar, & say the
Scholia by heart. the oftener (and in spite of poor

Trollope) the *more* you write to me, the happier I shall
be. I envy your Opera. Your Politicks I don't understand, but I think, matters can never continue long in
the situation they now are. Barbarossa I have read,
but I did not cry: at a modern Tragedy it is sufficient
not to laugh. I had rather the King's Arms look'd
askew upon me, than the Mitre; it is enough to be
well-bred to both of them. You do not mention L^d
Strathmore, so that I doubt, if you received my little
Letter about him. Mas^n is still here: we are all
mighty glad he is in Orders: & no better than any of
us. pray inform me, if Dr. Clerke is come to Town,
& where he is fix'd, that I may write to him, angry as
he is. my compliments to my friend Mrs. Wharton, to
your Mother, and all the little Gentry. I am ever,
dear D^r, most sincerely

Yours.

Camb: Dec: 26. 1754.

81. To Wharton

March, 9. 1755. Camb^ge:

My dear Doctor,—According to my reckoning M^rs
Wharton should have been brought to bed before this
time; yet you say not a syllable of it. if you are so
loth to publish *your productions*, you cannot wonder
at the repugnance I feel to spreading abroad mine.
but in truth I am not so much against publishing, as
against publishing *this alone*. I have two or three
ideas more in my head. what is to come of them?
must they too come out in the shape of little six-penny
flams, dropping one after another, till Mr Dodsley
thinks fit to collect them with M^r this's song, and M^r
t'other's epigram, into a pretty Volume? I am sure
Mason must be sensible of this, & therefore can never
mean what he says. to be sure, Doctor, it must be
owned, that Physick, and indeed all Professions, have
a bad effect upon the Mind. this it is my Duty, &
Interest to maintain; but I shall still be very ready
to write a Satyr upon the Clergy, and an Epode against

Historiographers, whenever you are hard press'd;
& (if you flatter me) may throw in a few lines with
somewhat handsome upon Magnesia alba, & Alicant-
soap. as to Humanity you know my aversion to it;
wch is barbarous and inhuman, but I cannot help it.
God forgive me.

I am not quite of your opinion with regard to Strophe
and Antistrophe. setting aside the difficulties, methinks it has little or no effect upon the ear, wch scarce
perceives the regular return of Metres at so great
a distance from one another. to make it succeed, I am
persuaded the stanza's must not consist of above
9 lines each at the most. Pindar has several such odes.

Lord S: is come, & makes a tall genteel figure in our
eyes. his tutors & He appear to like one another mighty
well. when we know more of him than his outside,
You & the Historian shall hear of it. I am going to
ask a favour of you, wch I have no better pretence
for doing, than that I have long been used to give you
trouble. it is, that you would go to the London
Insurance office in Birchin-Lane for me, and pay two
Insurances, one of my House at Wanstead (Policy,
N° 9675.) the other of that in Cornhill (N° 23470.) from
Lady-Day next to Lady-Day 1756. the first is 20
shillings; the 2^d, 12 Shill^gs: & be pleased to enclose
the two Receipts (stamp'd) in a Cover, and send them
to me; the sooner the better for I am always in
a little apprehension during this season of Conflagra-
tions. I know you will excuse me, & therefore will
make no excuses. I cannot think of coming to town,
till some time in April myself.

I know, you have wrote a very obliging Letter [? to
Tuthill,] but as I have not seen it, & he is not in my
way at present, I leave him to answer for himself.
Adieu, dear S^r, & make my Compliments to your
Family.

I am ever
Yours
T GRAY.

82. To Wharton

Stoke, August 6, 1755.

DEAR DOCTOR,—I was just returned from my Hampshire expedition, & going to enquire after your little family, and how they had got over the measles, when I found a letter from Stonhewer, in wch he says nothing on that head ; whence I conclude they are out of danger, & you free from anxiety about them. but he tells me, you expect me in town, for wch I am at a loss to account, having said nothing to that purpose, at least I am sure nothing with that meaning. I said I was to go to Twickenham, & am now expecting a letter from Mr. W: to inform me, when he shall be there. my stay will be at farthest a week with him, and at my return I shall let you know, and if the season be better than it now is, enquire, if you continue inclined to visit Windsor and its Environs. I wished for you often on the Southern Coast, where I have been, & made much the same tour, that Stonhewer did before me. take notice, that the Oaks grow quite down to the Beach, & that the Sea forms a number of Bays little & great, that appear glittering in the midst of thick Groves of them. add to this the fleet (for I was at Portsmouth two days before it sail'd) and the number of Vessels always passing along, or sailing up Southampton River (wch is the largest of these Bays I mention), and enters about ten miles into the Land, and you will have a faint idea of the *South*. from Fareham to South-ampton, where you are upon a level with the coast, you have a thousand such Peeps and delightful Openings, but would you see the whole at once, you must get upon Ports-Down, 5 Mile upon this side Ports-mouth. it is the top of a ridge, that forms a natural Terrass 3 Mile long, literally not three times broader than Windsor-Terrass, with a gradual fall on both sides and covered with a turf like New-Market. to the North opens Hampshire & Berkshire covered with woods, and interspersed with numerous Gentlemen's Houses and Villages. to the South, Portsmouth,

Gosport, &c:, just at your foot in appearance, the
Fleet, the Sea winding, and breaking in bays into the
land, the deep shade of tall Oaks in the enclosures, w^ch
become blue, as they go off to distance, Portchester-
Castle, Carshot-Castle, & all the Isle of Wight, in which
you plainly distinguish the fields, hedge-rows, & woods
next the shore, & a background of hills behind them.
I have not seen a more magnificent or more varied
Prospect.   I have been also at Titchfield, at Netly-
Abbey (a most beautiful ruin in as beautiful a situation)
at Southampton, at Bevis-Mount, at Winchester, &c:
my Gout is gone, but I am not absolutely well yet.
I hear Mason was expected on Monday last, but was
not to speak of it, therefore you will say nothing till
you see him.   I do not understand this, nor what he
means by coming.   It seems wrong to me.   What do
you think of the *Morceau* I sent you, pray, speak your
mind.

My best compliments to Mrs. Wharton. Adieu, I am
Ever Yours,
T. G.

83.   To Wharton

Stoke, August 21, 1755.

DEAR DOCTOR,—Instead of going to Twickenham
I was obliged to send my excuses, & the same day Mr.
W: sent a messenger to say he was confined in Town
with a Fever and a Rash. He has since wrote me word,
that he is well again ; but for me I continue much as
I was, & have been but once out of the house to walk,
since I returned from Hampshire. being much inclined
to bleeding myself, I yet was fearful to venture, least
it should bring on a regular fit of the Gout, so I sent
for advice at last, & expected Dr. Hayes should tell me
presently, whether it were Gout or Rheumatism. in his
talk he treated it rather as the former, but his prescription appears to me to be meant for the latter. you
will judge. He took away 10 or 11 *oz* of blood, &
order'd these draughts night & morning :—*Sal: Absinth.
Succ: Limon. finitâ effervescentiâ add: Aqu: Alexit.*

*Simpl:, Menth. Piperit, Magnes. alb., Tinct: G. Guiac.
Spirituos.* the quantities I can't read ; only I think
there is a Dram of the Tincture, & $\frac{1}{2}$ a Dram of Magnesia
in each draught. The Blood had no sign of Inflammation, but of a bright red : the Serum of a dark yellow
with little transparency, not viscid to the touch.
The draughts (wch I took over night only) made me
sweat almost immediately, & open'd a little in the
morning. the consequence is, that I have still many
slight complaints, broken and unrefreshing sleeps, as
before. less feverish than I was, in a morning :
instead of it a sensation of weariness. a soreness in
both feet, which goes off in the day, a frequent dizziness
and lightness of head. easily fatigued with motion.
sometimes a little pain in my breast, as I had in the
winter. These symptoms are all too slight to make an
illness ; but they do not make perfect health. that is
sure.

Tho' I allow abundance for your kindness & partiality
to me, I am yet much pleased with the good opinion
you seem to have of the *Bard.* You may alter that,
Robed in the sable, &c, almost in your own words, thus,

> With fury pale, and pale with woe,
> Secure of fate, the Poet stood, &c.

Though *haggard*, wch conveys to you the idea of a
Witch, is indeed only a metaphor taken from an
unreclaimed Hawk, which is called a *Haggard*, and
looks wild and *farouche*, & jealous of its liberty. I have
sent now to Stonhewer a bit more of the *prophecy*, and
desire him to shew it you immediately : it is very
rough and unpolish'd at present. Adieu, dear Sir,
I am ever

Truly Yours
T.G.

She-Wolf of France with unrelenting fangs
That tear'st the bowels of thy mangled Mate
From thee be born, who o'er thy country hangs
The Scourge of Heaven. What Terrors round him wait !
Amazement in his Van with Flight combined,
And Sorrow's faded form and Solitude behind.

Ant. 2

   Victor
Mighty Conqu'ror, mighty Lord,
    his
Low on the funeral couch he lies ;
 No   no
What pitying heart, what eye afford
A tear to grace his obsequies ?
Is the sable Warrior fled ?
Thy son is gone. he rests among the dead.
     in thy noontide beam were born
The swarm that *hover'd in thy noontide ray ?* [1]
     morn
Gone to salute the rising *day*
[2] Mirrors of Saxon truth and loyalty,
Your helpless old expiring master view,
They hear not. Scarce Religion dares supply
Her mutter'd Requiems and her holy Dew.
Yet thou, proud Boy, from Pomfret's walls shalt send
A sigh, and envy oft thy happy Grandsire's end.

Epode 2

Fill high the sparkling bowl,
The rich repast prepare,
Reft of a crown he yet may share the feast.
Close by the regal chair
Fell Thirst and Famine scowl
A smile of horror on their baffled guest.
Heard ye the din of battle bray,
Lance to lance and horse to horse !
Long years of havock urge their destined course,
And thro' the kindred squadrons mow their way.

---

 [1] Whatever Gray strikes through is printed in italics.
 [2] On the fourth page of the MS. are given instead of these six lines :

  Fair laughs the Morn, and soft the Zephyr blows
  While proudly riding o'er the azure realm
  In gallant trim the gilded vessel goes,
  Youth in the prow, and Pleasure at the helm,
  Regardless of the sweeping Whirlwind's sway
  That hush'd in grim repose expects his evening-prey.

Ye
Grim towers of Julius, London's lasting shame,
With many a foul and midnight murther fed,
Revere his consort's faith, his Father's fame,
And spare the meek Usurper's hallow'd head
Above, below, the Rose of snow,
Twined with her blushing foe we spread :
The bristled boar in infant gore,
Wallows beneath the thorny shade.
Now, Brothers, bending o'er the accursed loom,
Stamp we our vengeance deep, and ratify his doom.

STROPHE 3

Edward, lo ! to sudden fate,
  (Weave we the woof.   The thread is spun),
Half of thy heart we consecrate
  (The web is wove.   The work is done).
            thus
Stay, oh stay, nor here forlorn
       me unbless'd.   Unpitied here
Leave your despairing Caradoc to mourn !
     track
In yon bright *clouds* that fires the western skies
     melt
They sink, they vanish from my eyes.
    solemn
But ah !   what ∧ scenes *of Heaven* on Snowdon's height
          glitt'ring
Descending slow their golden skirts unroll !
Visions of glory, spare my aching sight,
Ye unborn ages, crowd not on my soul.
From Cambria's thousand hills a thousand strains
Triumphant tell aloud, another Arthur reigns.

ANTIST. 3

Girt with many a
Youthful Knights and Barons bold
Sublime their starry fronts they rear
With dazzling helm and horrent spear
And gorgeous Dames, and Statesmen old,
In bearded majesty appear.
In the midst a Form divine,
Her eye proclaims her of the Briton-Line :

Her   her
A Lyon-port, *an* awe-commanding face,
Attemper'd sweet to virgin-grace.
What strings symphonious tremble in the air !
What strains of vocal transport round her play !
Hear from thy grave, great Taliessin, hear,
They breath a soul to animate thy clay.
Bright Rapture calls, and soaring, as she sings,
Waves in the eye of Heaven her many-coloured wings.

EPODE 3

  The verse adorn again,
    Fierce War, and Faithful Love,
And Truth severe by fairy-Fiction drest.
    In buskin'd measures move
  Pale Grief and pleasing Pain
With Horrour, tyrant of the throbbing breast.
  A voice as of the Cherub-Quire,
    Gales from blooming Eden bear ;
    And distant Warblings lessen on my ear,
  That lost in long futurity expire.
  Fond impious man, think'st thou yon sanguine cloud
    Rais'd by thy breath has quench'd the Orb of day ?
  To-morrow he repairs the golden flood,
    And warms the Nations with redoubled ray
      Enough for me. With joy I see
      The different doom our fates assign,
      Be thine Despair, & scepter'd Care.
      To triumph & to die are mine.
He spoke, & headlong from the mountain's height
Deep in the roaring tide he sunk to endless night.

84. To WHARTON

MY DEAR DOCTOR,—I ought before now to have
thanked you for your kind offer, wch I mean soon to
accept for a reason, wch to be sure can be no reason to
you or Mrs Wharton, and therefore I think it my duty
to give you notice of it. it is a very possible thing
I may be ill again in town, which I would not chuse to
be in a dirty inconvenient lodgeing, where perhaps my
Nurse might stifle me with a pillow, and therefore it is

no wonder, if I prefer your house. but I tell you of this in time, that if either of you are frighted at the thought of a sick body, you may make a handsome excuse, & save yourselves this trouble. You are not to imagine my illness is in *Esse ;* no, it is only in *Posse,* otherwise I should myself be scrupulous of bringing it home to you. I shall be in town in about a fortnight. you will be sorry (as I am) at the destruction of poor . . .'s views, wch promised so fair ; but both he & I have known it this long time, so, I believe, he was prepared, and his old Patron is no bad ressource. I am told, it is the fashion to be totally silent with regard to the ministry. nothing is to be talked of, or even suspected, till the Parliament meets. in the meantime the new *Manager* has taken what appears to me a very odd step. if you do not hear of a thing, which is in it's nature no secret, I cannot well inform you by the Post. to me it is utterly unaccountable.

Pray what is the reason I do not read your name among the Censors of the College ? did they not offer it you, or have you refused it ? I have not done a word more of *Bard*, having been in a very listless, unpleasant, and inutile state of Mind for this long while, for which I shall beg you to prescribe me somewhat strengthning & agglutinant, lest it turn to a confirmed Pthisis. to shew you how epidemical Self-Murther is this year, Lady M. Capel (Ld Essex's Sister) a young person, has just cut the veins of both arms across, but (they say) will not die of it, she was well & in her senses, though of a family that are apt to be otherwise. Adieu, dear Doct^r, I should be glad of a line from you, before I come. believe me ever

Most sincerely Yours,

TG:

85. To Wharton

Jan: 9. Cambridge. 1756.

Dear Doctor,—I am quite of Mr Alderman's opinion ; provided you have a very fair prospect of success (for I do not love repulses, tho' I believe in such cases they are not attended with any disgrace)

such an employment must necessarily give countenance and name to one in your profession, not to mention the use it must be of in refreshing and keeping alive the Ideas of Practise you have already got, & improving them by new observation. it cannot but lead to other business too in a more natural way, than perhaps any other ; for whatever lucky chance may have introduced into the world here and there a Physician of great vogue, the same chance may hardly befall another in an age ; & the indirect & by-ways, that doubtless have succeeded with many, are rather too dirty for you to tread. as to the time it would take up, so much the better. whenever it interferes with more advantageous practise, it is in your power to quit it. in the meantime it will prepare you for that trouble & constant attendance, wch much business requires a much greater degree of. for you are not to dream of being your own master, till Old-age & a satiety of gain shall set you free. I tell you my notions of the matter, as I see it at a distance, which you, who stand nearer, may rectify at your pleasure.

I have continued the Soap every other day from the time I left you, except an interval or two of a week or ten days at a time, wch I allow'd in order to satisfy myself, whether the good effects of it were lasting, or only temporary. I think, I may say it has absolutely cured that complaint I used to mention to you, & (what is more) the ill-habit, wch perhaps was the cause of that, and of the flying pains I have every now and then felt in my joints. whenever I use it, it much increases my appetite, and the Heartburn is quite vanish'd. so I may venture to say, it does good to my Stomach. when I shall speak of its bad effects, you are no longer to treat me as a whimsical body, for I am certain now, that it disorders the head, & much disturbs one's sleep. this I now avoid by taking it immediately before dinner ; & besides these things are trifles compared with the good it has done me. in short, I am so well, it would be folly to take any other medicine : therefore I reserve Lime-water for some more pressing occasion. I should be glad to know the particulars of Ld Northumb:^d and the Archbish:^ps illnesses, & how far it has eased them in the Gout.

I am glad you admire Machiaval, & are entertained with Buffon, & edified with the divine Ashton. the first (they say) was a good Man, as much as he has been abused; and we will hope the best of the two latter. Mr. Bedingfield, who (as Lord Orford sent me word) desired to be acquainted with me, call'd here (before I came down), & would pay a visit to my rooms. he made Dr Long conduct him thither, left me a present of a Book (not of his own writing) & a Note with a very civil Compliment. I wrote to him to thank him, & have received an answer, that fifteen years ago might have turned my head. I know [Mason] will abuse him to you, but I insist he is a Slanderer, & shall write a Satire upon him, if he does not do Justice to my new Admirer. I have not added a line more to old Caradoc; when I do, you will be sure to see it. you who give yourself the trouble to think of my health, will not think me very troublesome if I beg you to bespeak me a Rope-Ladder (for my Neighbours every day make a great progress in drunkenness, wch gives me reason to look about me) it must be full 36 Foot long, or a little more, but as light and manageable as may be, easy to unroll, and not likely to entangle. I never saw one, but I suppose it must have strong hooks, or something equivalent, a-top, to throw over an iron bar to be fix'd within side of my window. however, you will chuse the properest form, & instruct me in the use of it. I see an Ephraim Hadden near Hermitage Stairs Wapping, that advertises them, but perhaps you may find a better Artisan near you. This with a Canister of Tea & another of Snuff, wch I left at your house, and a Pound of Soap from Mr. Field (for mine is not so good here) will fill a Box, wch I beg the favour of you to send, when you can conveniently. my best Compliments to Mrs. Wharton.—I am ever

Yours

TG:

86. To Wharton

March 25. Pemb: Hall. 1756.

DEAR DOCTOR,—Tho' I had no reasonable excuse for myself before I received your last letter, yet since that time I have had a pretty good one, having been taken up in quarrelling with Peter-house, and in removing myself from thence to Pembroke. This may be look'd upon as a sort of Æra in a life so barren of events as mine, yet I shall treat it in Voltaire's manner, & only tell you, that I left my lodgings, because the rooms were noisy, and the People of the house dirty. this is all I would chuse to have said about it ; but if you in private should be curious enough to enter into a particular detail of facts and minute circumstances, Stonhewer who was witness to them will probably satisfy you. all, I shall say more, is, that I am for the present extremely well lodged here, and as quiet as in the Grande Chartreuse ; & that everybody (even the Dr Longs and Dr Mays) are as civil, as they could be to Mary de Valence in person. with regard to any advice I can give as to the Hospital, I freely own it ought to give way to Dr. H^s counsels, who is a much better judge, & (I should think) disinterested. I love refusals no more than you do ; but as to your Effluvia, I maintain, that one sick *rich* has more of pestilence and putre-faction about him, than a whole ward of sick Poor.

You should have received Mason's present as last Saturday. I desire you to tell me your critical opinion of the new Ode : & also whether you have found out two lines, wch he has inserted in another of them, that are superlative. we do not expect, that the world, wch is just going to be *invaded*, will bestow much attention on them. if you hear any thing, you will tell us.

The similitude between the Italian republicks & those of ancient Greece has often struck me, as it does you. I do not wonder, that Sully's Memoirs have highly entertain'd you, but can not agree with you in thinking him or his Master two of the *best Men* in the world. The King was indeed one of the best-natur'd

Men, that ever lived. but it is owing only to chance, that his intended Marriage with Mad. d'Estrées, or with the Marq:ᵉ de Verneuil, did not involve him and the kingdom in the most inextricable confusion; & his design upon the Princess of Condé (in his old age) was worse still. as to the Minister, his base application to Concini after the murther of Henry has quite ruin'd him in my esteem, and destroy'd all the merit of that honest surly Pride, for which I honour'd him before. Yet I own, that as Kings and Ministers go, they were both extraordinary Men. Pray look at the end of Birch's State Papers of Sir T: Edmonde's, for the character of the French Court at that time, written by Sʳ George Carew.

Pray don't suspect me of any such *suspicions*, as you mention. I would hardly believe you were tired of me though you told me so yourself, sensible as I am nevertheless, that you might have reason enough to be so. to prove what I say, I have thoughts of coming to you for three days in April. There is to be a Concerto Spirituale, in wᶜʰ the Mingotti (who has just lain in) & Ricciarelli will sing the *Stabat Mater* of Pergolesi. You and Mason and I are to be at it together, so pray make no excuses, nor put-offs. saving to you however the liberty of saying whether you have a bed to spare (I mean for me, not for him) in your house. Adieu, dear Sir, I am ever faithfully

Yours
T G:

My best compliments to Mrs. Wharton. I give you joy of the Divine Ashton. it is indeed a Conquest you have made.

87. To Mason

Stoke, July 25, 1756.

DEAR MASON,—I feel a contrition for my long silence, and yet perhaps it is the last thing you trouble your head about; nevertheless, I will be as sorry as if you took it ill. I am sorry too to see you so punctilious as to stand upon answers, and never to come near me till

I have regularly left my name at your door, like a
mercer's wife that imitates people who go a visiting.
I would forgive you this, if you could possibly suspect
I were doing anything that I liked better, for then your
formality might look like being piqued at my negligence,
which has somewhat in it like kindness; but you know
I am at Stoke, hearing, seeing, doing, absolutely
nothing, not such a nothing as you do at Tunbridge,
chequered and diversified with a succession of fleeting
colours, but heavy, lifeless, without form and void;
sometimes almost as black as the moral of Voltaire's
'Lisbon,' which angers you so. I have had no more
pores and muscular inflations, and am only troubled
with this depression of mind; you will not expect
therefore I should give you any account of my verve,
which is at best, you know, of so delicate a constitution,
and has such weak nerves, as not to stir out of its
chamber above three days in a year, but I shall enquire
after yours, and why it is off again; it has certainly
worse nerves than mine, if your reviewers have frighted
it. Sure I (not to mention a score of your uncles and
aunts) am something a better judge than all the man
midwives and presbyterian parsons that ever were
born. Pray give me leave to ask you, do you find
yourself tickled with the commendations of such
people? for you have your share of these too. I dare
say not; your vanity has certainly a better taste;
and can, then, the censure of such critics move you?
I own it is an impertinence in these gentry to talk of
one at all either in good or in bad, but this we must all
swallow; I mean not only we that write, but all the
we's that ever did anything to be talked of. I cannot
pretend to be learned without books, nor to know the
Druids from the Pelasgi at this distance from Cambridge.
I can only tell you not to go and take the Mona for the
Isle of Man; it is Anglesey, a tract of plain country,
very fertile, but picturesque only from the view it has
of Caernarvonshire, from which it is separated by the
Menai, a narrow arm of the sea. Forgive me for
supposing in you such a want of erudition.

I congratulate you on our glorious successes in the Mediterranean. Shall we go in time, and hire a house together in Switzerland ? it is a fine poetical country to look at, and nobody there will understand a word we say or write. Pray let me know what you are about ; what new acquaintances you have made at Tunbridge ; how you do in body and in mind ; believe me ever sincerely yours,   T. G.

Have you read Madame Maintenon's *Letters ?* When I saw Lord John in town, he said, if his brother went to Ireland you were to go second chaplain, but it seemed to me not at all certain that the Duke would return thither ; you probably know by this time.

88.   To WALPOLE

                                 Sept: 8. 1756. the Vine

Poor Mr Chute has now had the Gout for these five days with such a degree of pain & uneasiness, as he never felt before. whether to attribute it to Dr La Cour's forcing medicines, or to a little cold he got as soon as he came hither, I know not, but for above forty hours it seem'd past all human suffering, & he lay screaming like a Man upon the rack. the torture was so great, that (against my judgement & even his own) he was forced to have recourse to [an] infusion of Poppy-heads, wch Cocchi used to give him, & in [half] an hours time was easy, fell into a gentle perspiration, [&] slept many hours. this was the night before last, & all yesterday he continued chearful & in spirits. at night (as he expected) the pain returned, not so violent, but in more places, for now it is in one foot, both knees, & one hand, and I hourly dread it will increase again to its former rage. if any thing sudden happen, who can I send to ? here is no assistance nearer than a Dr Langrish at Winchester, of whom he has no great opinion. as to Lacour he is enraged against him, & looks upon him as the cause of all he suffers. I can not think there is any danger, for tho' with all this he is at times in a high Fever, yet it seems to depend upon the Gout entirely, increasing & abating with the pain. but if anything unexpected happen, here are no body but myself & Muntz in the house, would you advise to send to Mrs Pawlet, or to whom ? you will oblige me, if you will answer me in a loose paper, for he must see your Letter. it will be a charity too to insert any thing of news, or whatever you please to tell us, for when he gets any respite from pain, he is capable & desirous of entertainment, & talks with an eagerness of spirits, that seems to make part of his distemper. pray tell us how Mr Man does. I am ever

Yours

TG:

To the Honble Horace Walpole in Arlington Street London

89. To Wharton

Stoke, Oct: 15. 1756.

DEAR DOCTOR,—I have not been dead, but only gone to . . . seized with a cruel fit of the Gout, wch held him five weeks, & as he had no other company in the house it was impossible to leave him in that condition. since my return I have made a visit of four days at Twickenham. I shall probably stay here till the middle of next month & then transplant myself to London, if Mrs Wharton and You *de bon cœur* have no objection to me. If any thing has happened, since I saw you, to make it inconvenient I insist upon being told so. I have heard the story of the *Lyon*, & its consequences, tho' you say not a word about it. pray, inform me how Miss Peggy got over her operation. Leicester House is (as I suppose you know) settling upon its own terms. 40,000£ a year for the P: ; 5000 for P. E^d., no removing to St. J$^{s'}$s ; Earl of Bute Groom of the Stole (there is for you) Mr Stone Controller of the . . . a concession by way of thanks Lords of the Bedchamber I have forgot. Miss Shepherd's, Mr Ingram, and Mr Onslow, the Speaker's Son, Grooms of the Bedchamber. are you upon the list ?

Shew me such another king, as the K: of Prussia.

Everybody used to call him Coxcomb, and to be sure he is one ; but a Coxcomb (it is plain) may make a figure far superior to the ordinary run of Kings. I delight in his treatment of the K: of Poland. when he first informed him of the necessity he was under to make use of Saxony in his way to Bohemia, he added that if his Majesty chose to retire into his Polish Dominions he had order'd Relais on the road, and that all the respect in the world should be shewn him. & his last memorial to the Empress-Queen ended with *point de réponse en stile d'Oracle.*

I recommend two little French Books to you, one called Memoires de M^r: de la Porte. it has all the air of simplicity & truth, and contains some few very extraordinary facts relating to Anne of Austria & Card^l: Mazarin. the other is two small Volumes, *Mem:^es de Madame Staal.* the facts are no great matter, but the manner & vivacity of it make it interesting. she was a sort of Confidente to the late Dutchess of Maine, & imprison'd a long time in the Bastille on her account during the Regency. The first you may buy, & the latter borrow. I desire my Compliments to Mrs Wharton, and am.

Ever yours,

TG:

90. TO MASON

April 23, 1757.

DEAR MASON,—I too am set down here with something greater hopes of quiet than I could entertain when I saw you last ; at least nothing new has happened to give me any disturbance, and the assurances you gave me in your letter from hence are pretty well confirmed by experience. I shall be very ready to take as much of Mr. Delap's dulness as he chooses to part with at any price he pleases, even with his want of sleep and weak bowels into the bargain ; and I will be your curate, and he shall live here with all my wit and power of learning. Dr. Brown's book (I hear) is much admired in town, which I do not understand.

I expected it would be admired here ; but they affect not to like it, though I know they ought. What would you have me do ? There is one thing in it I applaud, which is the dissertation against trade, for I have always said it was the ruin of the nation. I have read the little wicked book about Evil, that settled Mr. Dodsley's conscience in that point, and find nothing in it but absurdity : we call it Soame Jenyns's, but I have a notion you mentioned some other name to me, though I have forgotten it. Stonhewer has done me the honour to send me your friend Lord Nuneham hither, with a fine recommendatory letter written by his own desire, in Newmarket-week. Do not think he was going to Newmarket ; no, he came in a solitaire, great sleeves, jessamine-powder, and a large bouquet of jonquils, within twelve miles of that place, on purpose not to go thither. We had three days' intercourse, talked about the beaux arts, and Rome, and Hanover, and Mason,—whose praises we celebrate *à qui mieux mieux*,—vowed eternal friendship, embraced, and parted. I promised to write you a thousand compliments in his name. I saw also Lord Villiers and Mr. Spencer, who carried him back with them ; *en passant*, they did not like me at all. Here has been too the best of all Johns (I hardly except the Evangelist and the Divine), who is not, to be sure, a bit like my Lord Nuneham, but full as well, in my mind. The Duke of Bedford has brought his son, aye, and Mr. Rigby too ; they were at church on Sunday morning, and Mr. Sturgeon preached to them and the heads, for nobody else was present. Mr. F——n is not his tutor. These are the most remarkable events at Cambridge.

Mr. Bonfoy has been here ; he had not done what you recommended to him before he came out of town, and he is returned thither only the beginning of this week, when he assured me he certainly would do it. Alas ! what may this delay occasion ; it is best not to think. Oh happy Mr. Delap ! Adieu, my best Mason ; I am pleased to think how much I am obliged to you, and that, while I live, I must be ever yours

91. To Walpole

Stoke, July 11, 1757.

I will not give you the trouble of sending your chaise for me. I intend to be with you on Wednesday in the evening. If the press stands still all this time for me, to be sure it is dead in child-bed.

I do not love notes, though you see I had resolved to put two or three. They are signs of weakness and obscurity. If a thing cannot be understood without them, it had better be not understood at all. If you will be vulgar, and pronounce it *Lunnun*, instead of London, I can't help it. Caradoc I have private reasons against ; and besides it is in reality Carādoc, and will not stand in the verse.

I rejoice you can fill all your *vuides* : the Maintenon could not, and that was her great misfortune. Seriously though, I congratulate you on your happiness, and seem to understand it. The receipt is obvious : it is only, Have something to do ; but how few can apply it !— Adieu !

I am ever yours,

T. Gray.

92. To the Rev. James Brown

Stoke, July 25, 1757.

Dear Sir,—I thank you for the second little letter, for your Cambridge Anecdotes, and, suffer me to say too, for the trouble you have had on my account. I am going to add to it, by sending you my poetical cargo to distribute ; though, whatever the advertisement says, it will not be this fortnight yet, for you must know (what you will like no more than I do, yet it was not in my power anyhow to avoid it), Mr. Walpole, who has set up a printing-press in his own house at Twickenham, earnestly desired that he might print it for Dodsley, and, as there is but one hand employed, you must think it will take up some time to despatch 2000 copies. As soon as may be you will have a parcel sent you, which you will dispose of as follows: Mrs. Bonfoy, Mr. Bonfoy, Dr. Long, Gaskarth, and all the Fellows resident; Mr. Montagu and Southwell, if they happen to be there; Master of St. John's (I know he is at Rochester, but it suffices to send it to his lodge); Master of Bennet, Mr. Hurd, Mr. Balguy, Mr. Talbot, Mr. Nourse, Mr. Neville of Jesus, Mr. Bickham, Mr. Hadley, Mr. Newcome. If you think I forget anybody, pray send it them in my name; what remain upon your hands you will hide in a corner. I am sorry to say I know no more of Mason than you do. It is my own fault, I am afraid, for I have not yet answered that letter.

His Prussian Majesty wrote a letter to the King owning himself in a bad situation, from which, he said, nothing but a *coup-de-maître* would extricate him. We have a secret expedition going forward; all I know is, that Lord Ancram, Sir John Mordaunt, and General Conway are to bear a part in it. The Duke has been very ill, with his leg; Ranby was sent for, but countermanded, the Marshall d'Etrées having sent him his own surgeons. I would wish to be like Mr. Bonfoy, and think that everything turns out the best in the world, but it won't do, I am stupid and low-spirited, but ever yours,   T. G.

93. To Mason

Stoke, Monday, August 1.

Dear Mason,—If I did not send you a political Letter forthwith, it was because Lord Holdernesse came in again so soon that it was the same thing as if he had never gone out, excepting one little circumstance, indeed, the anger of old Priam; which, I am told, is the reason, that he has not the blue riband, though promised him before. I have been here this month or more, low-spirited and full of disagreeablenesses, and, to add to them, am at this present very ill, not with the gout, nor stone (thank God), nor with blotches, nor blains, nor with frogs nor with lice, but with a painful infirmity, that has to me the charms of novelty, but would not amuse you much in the description.

I hope you divert yourself much better than I do. You may be sure Dodsley had orders to send you some Odes the instant they were off the spit; indeed I forgot Mr. Fraser, so I fear they will come to Sheffield in the shape of a small parcel by some coach or waggon; but if there is time I will prevent it. They had been out three weeks ago, but Mr. Walpole having taken it into his head to set up a press of his own at Twickenham, was so earnest to handsel it with this new pamphlet that it was impossible to find a pretence for refusing such a trifle. You will dislike this as much as I do, but there is no help; you understand, it is he that prints them, not for me, but for Dodsley. I charge you send me some *Caractacus* before I die; it is impossible this weather should not bring him to maturity.

If you knew how bad I was you would not wonder I could write no more. Adieu, dear Mason; I am ever most truly yours,   T. G.

94. To the Rev. James Brown

August 14, 1757.

DEAR SIR,—Excuse me if I begin to wonder a little that I have heard no news of you in so long a time. I conclude you received Dodsley's packet at least a week ago, and made my presents. You will not wonder therefore at my curiosity, if I enquire of you what you hear said; for, though in anybody in the rest of the world I do not expect to hear that anybody says much, or thinks about the matter, yet among *mes confrères*, the learned, I know there is always leisure, at least to find fault, if not to commend.

I have been lately much out of order, and confined at home, but now I go abroad again. Mr. Garrick and his wife, have passed some days at my Lady Cobham's, and are shortly to return again; they,

and a few other people that I see there, have been my
only entertainment till this week, but now I have
purchased some volumes of the great *French Encyclopedie,* and am trying to amuse myself within doors.
Pray tell me a great deal, and believe me ever most
faithfully yours,   T. G.

95. To Wharton
                                        Aug: 17. 1757.

DEAR DOCTOR,—It feels to me as if it were a long
while, since I heard from you. not a word to flatter
or to abash the vanity of an Author ! suffer me then
to tell you, that I hear, we are not at all popular. the
great objection is obscurity, no body knows what we
would be at. one Man (a Peer) I have been told of,
that thinks the last stanza of the 2ᵈ Ode relates to
Charles the first, and Oliver Cromwell. in short the
Συνετοὶ appear to be still fewer, than even I expected.
    You will imagine all this does not go very deep ;
but I have been almost ever since I was here exceedingly
dispirited, besides being really ill in body. no gout,
but something feverish, that seems to come almost
every morning, & disperses soon after I am up. the
Cobhams are here, and as civil as usual. Garrick and
his Wife have been down with them some days, and
are soon to come again. except the little amusement
they give me, & two volumes of the Encyclopedie now
almost exhausted, I have nothing but my own thoughts
to feed upon, & you know they are of the gloomy
cast. write to me then for *sweet Sᵗ Charity,* and remember, that while I am my own, I am most faithfully
                                   Yours

My best services to Mʳˢ Wharton.   TG.

96. To Richard Hurd
                                   Stoke, August 25, 1757.

DEAR SIR,—I do not know why you should thank
me for what you had a right and title to ; but attribute
it to the excess of your politeness, and the more so

because almost no one else has made me the same compliment. As your acquaintance in the University (you say) do me the honour to admire, it would be ungenerous in me not to give them notice that they are doing a very unfashionable thing, for all people of condition are agreed not to admire, nor even to understand : one very great man, writing to an acquaintance of his and mine, says that he had read them seven or eight times, and that now, when he next sees him, he shall not have above thirty questions to ask. Another, a peer, believes that the last stanza of the Second Ode relates to King Charles the First and Oliver Cromwell. Even my friends tell me they do not succeed, and write me moving topics of consolation on that head ; in short, I have heard of nobody but a player and a doctor of divinity that profess their esteem for them. Oh yes ! a lady of quality, a friend of Mason's, who is a great reader. She knew there was a compliment to Dryden, but never suspected there was anything said about Shakspeare or Milton, till it was explained to her ; and wishes that there had been titles prefixed to tell what they were about.

From this mention of Mason's name you may think, perhaps, we are great correspondents ; no such thing ; I have not heard from him these two months. I will be sure to scold in my own name as well as in yours. I rejoice to hear you are so ripe for the press, and so voluminous,—not for my own sake only, whom you flatter with the hopes of seeing your labours both public and private,—but for yours too, for to be employed is to be happy. This principle of mine, and I am convinced of its truth, has, as usual, no influence on my practice. I am alone and *ennuyé* to the last degree, yet do nothing ; indeed I have one excuse ; my health, which you so kindly enquire after, is not extraordinary, ever since I came hither. It is no great malady, but several little ones, that seem brewing no good to me.

It will be a particular pleasure to me to hear whether Content dwells in Leicestershire, and how she enter-

tains herself there; only do not be too happy, nor
forget entirely the quiet ugliness of Cambridge. I
am, dear sir,
> Your friend and obliged humble servant.
> > T. GRAY.

If Mr. Brown falls in your way, be so good to shew
him the beginning of this letter, and it will save me the
labour of writing the same thing twice. His first
letter, I believe, was in the mail that was robbed, for
it was delayed many days; his second I have just
received.

97. To Mason

DEAR MASON,—You are welcome to the land of
the living, to the sunshine of a court, to the dirt of a
chaplain's table, to the society of Dr. Squire and Dr.
Chapman. Have you set out, as Dr. Cobden ended,
with a sermon against adultery? or do you, with deep
mortification and a Christian sense of your own nothingness, read prayers to Princess Emily while she is putting
on her dress? Pray acquaint me with the whole
ceremonial, and how your first preachment succeeded;
whether you have heard of anybody that renounced
their election, or made restitution to the Exchequer;
whether you saw any woman trample her pompons
under foot, or spit upon her hankerchief to wipe off
the rouge.

I would not have put another note to save the souls
of all the owls in London. It is extremely well as it
is—nobody understands me, and I am perfectly
satisfied. Even the *Critical Review* (Mr. Franklin,
I am told), that is rapt and surprised and shudders
at me, yet mistakes the Æolian lyre for the harp of
Æolus, which, indeed, as he observes, is a very bad
instrument to dance to. If you hear anything (though
it is not very likely, for I know my day is over), you
will tell me. Lord Lyttleton and Mr. Shenstone admire
me, but wish I had been a little clearer. Mr. (Palmyra)
Wood owns himself disappointed in his expectations.
Your enemy, Dr. Brown, says I am the best thing in

the language. Mr. Fox, supposing the Bard sung his song but once over, does not wonder if Edward the First did not understand him. This last criticism is rather unhappy, for though it had been sung a hundred times under his window, it was absolutely impossible King Edward should understand him; but that is no reason for Mr. Fox, who lives almost 500 years after him. It is very well; the next thing I print shall be in Welch,—that's all.

I delight in your Epigram, but dare not show it anybody, for your sake; but I more delight to hear from Mr. Hurd that *Caractacus* advances. Am I not to see Mador's song? Could not we meet some day,— at Hounslow, for example, after your waiting is over? Do tell me time and place. I am most truly yours,

T. G.

P.S.—If you write to Lord Jersey, commend me to him. I was so civil to send a book to Lord Nuneham, but hear nothing of him. Where is Stonhewer? I am grown a stranger to him. You will oblige me by sending to Dodsley's, to say I wonder the third and fourth volumes of the *Encyclopedie* are not come. If you chance to call yourself, you might enquire if many of my 2000 remain upon his hands. He told me a fortnight ago about 12 or 1300 were gone.

You talk of writing a comment. I do not desire you should be employed in any such office; but what if Delap (inspired by a little of your intelligence) should do such a matter; it will get him a shilling; but it must bear no name, nor must he know I mentioned it.

98. To Wharton

Stoke, Sept: 7, 1757.

DEAR DOCT^R,—I am greatly obliged to your care & kindness for considering with more attention, than it deserves, the article of my health. at present I am far better, & take long walks again, have better spirits, & am more capable of amusement. the offer you make me of your lodgings for a time I should gladly embrace,

both for the sake of seeing you, & for variety, & because
it will answer another end by furnishing me with a
reason for not going into the country to *a place, where
I am invited.* (I think, you understand me) but the
truth is, I can not afford to hurry about from place
to place ; so I shall continue, where I am, and trust
to *illness,* or some other cause for an excuse, since to
that place I am positive, I will not go. it hurts me
beyond measure, that I am forced to make these excuses,
but go I cannot, and something must be said. These
are cruel things !

The family you mention near me are full as civil as
ever ; Miss Sp: seems to understand ; and to all such,
as do not, she says—Φωναντα συνετοισι—in so many
words. And this is both my Motto and Comment.
I am afraid, you mistake Mr. Roper's complaisance
for approbation. Dr. Brown (I hear) says, they are
the best Odes in our language. Mr. Garrick, the best
in ours, *or any other.* I should not write this immodest
panegyric, did not you guess at the motive of their
applause. L⁴ Lyttleton & Mʳ Shenstone admire, but
wish they they were a little clearer. L⁴ Barrington's
explanation, I think, I told you before, so will not
repeat it. Mr. Fox thinks, if the Bard sung his song
but once over, King Edward could not possibly understand him. indeed I am of his opinion, and am certain,
if he had sung it fifty times, it was impossible the king
should know a jot the more about Edwᵈ the 3ᵈ, &
Qu: Elizabeth, and Spencer, and Milton, &c . . . Mʳ
Wood (Mʳ Pitt's Wood) is disappointed in his expectations. Dr. Akenside criticises opening a *source* with
a *key.* The Critical Review you have seen, or may
see. He is in raptures (they say, it is Professor Franklin) but mistakes the Æolian Lyre for the *Harp of
Æolus,* & on this mistake founds a compliment & a
criticism. this is, I think, all I have heard, that
signifies.

The *Encyclopedie,* I own, may cloy one, if one sits
down to it. but you will own, that out of one great
good dinner, a number of little good dinners may be

made, that would not cloy one at all.   There is a long
article sur *le Beau* that for my life I cannot understand.
several of the geographical articles are carelessly done,
& some of the antiquities, or ancient history.

My best compliments to Mrs Wharton. I hope the
operation going forward on your children will succeed
to your wishes. Adieu, dear S^{r}, & believe me ever,

Yours

TG :

This letter is to *yourself* only.   Our best Mason, I
suppose you know is in Town, and *in waiting*. Do you
know any thing of St^{r} ? Pray desire Mas^{n} to repeat
an epigram to you.

99. To Wharton

Oct: 7. 1757.

DEAR DOCT^{R},—I heartily rejoice with you, that your
little family are out of danger, and all apprehensions
of that kind over with them for life. yet I have heard,
you were ill yourself, and kept your bed : as this was
(I imagine) only by way of regimen, & not from
necessity ; I hope soon to be told, you have no further
occasion for it. yet take care of yourself, for there
is a bad fever now very frequent. it is among the boys
at Eton, & (I am told), is much spread about London
too. my notion is, that your violent quick pulse, &
soapy diet, would not suit well with feverish disorders.
Though our party at Slough turn'd out so ill, I could
not help being sorry, that you were not with us.

Have you read Mr. Hurd's (printed) letter to Mason,
on the Marks of Imitation ? you do not tell me your
opinion of it. You bid me send you criticisms on myself, and even *compliments*. did I tell you, what the
Speaker says ? the 2^{d} Ode, he says, is a good pretty
tale, but nothing to the *Churchyard*. Mr. Bedingfield
in a golden shower of panegyrick writes me word, that
at York-races he overheard three People, whom by
their dress and manner he takes for Lords, say, that
I was impenetrable & inexplicable, and they wish'd,

I had told them in prose, what I meant in verse, &
then they bought me (wch was what most displeased
him) and put me in their pocket. Dr Warburton is
come to town, and likes them extremely. he says the
World never pass'd so just an opinion upon any thing
as upon them : for that in other things they have
affected to like or dislike, whereas here they own,
they do not understand, which he looks upon to be
very true ; but yet thinks, they understand them as
well as they do Milton or Shakespear, whom they are
obliged by fashion to admire. M^r G:^k's compliment
you have seen ; I am told it was printed in the Chronicle
of last Saturday. The Review I have read, & admire
it, particularly that observation, that the ' Bard ' is
taken from *Pastor*, *cum traheret*, & the advice to be
more an *original*, & in order to be so, the way is (he
says) to cultivate the native flowers of the soil, & not
introduce the exoticks of another climate.

I am greatly pleased with M^ns *Caractacus* in its
present state. The contrivance & arrangement of
events, the manners of the country, the characters
& passions, strike me wonderfully. the difficult part
is now got over, nothing remains but to polish, &
retouch a little : yet only the beginning of the first
Chorus is done of the lyric part. have you seen it ?

Adieu ! dear S^r, and believe me ever

Yours

TG

I shall be in Town probably sooner than you come
to stay there.

100. To Wharton

Dec: 8. 1757.

DEAR DOCTOR,—I have received the draught you
were so good to send me, & the money is paid. you
apprehend too much from my resolutions about
writing : they are only made to be broken, & after
all it will be just as the maggot bites. you have a very
mean opinion of the Epick if you think it consists only
in laying out a Plan. in four and twenty years at a

moderate computation I may have finish'd twelve books, & nine years after I hope to publish. I shall then be 74 years old, and I shall get 500£ for the copy to make me easy for the remainder of my days. somebody has directed a letter to the Rev^d Mr. G: at Strawberry-Hill, wch was sent me yesterday hither. It is anonymous, consists of above nine pages, all about the Bard, and if I would hear as much more about his Companion, I am to direct to the Posthouse at Andover. I do not know but I may have that curiosity, for his observations (whoever it is) are not nonsense. He takes the liberty of a Person unknown, and treats me with abundance of freedom. I guess it to be some *reading* clergyman. Mr Brown & I join in our best compliments to Mrs Wharton. I am, Dear S^r, most sincerely

Yours

TG:

101. To Mason

December 19, 1757.

DEAR MASON,—Though I very well know the bland emollient saponaceous qualities both of sack and silver, yet if any great man would say to me, ' I make you rat-catcher to his Majesty, with a salary of £300 a year and two butts of the best Malaga ; and though it has been usual to catch a mouse or two, for form's sake, in public once a year, yet to you, sir, we shall not stand upon these things,' I cannot say I should jump at it ; nay, if they would drop the very name of the office, and call me Sinecure to the King's Majesty, I should still feel a little awkward, and think everybody I saw smelt a rat about me ; but I do not pretend to blame any one else that has not the same sensations ; for my part I would rather be serjeant trumpeter or pinmaker to the palace. Nevertheless I interest myself a little in the history of it, and rather wish somebody may accept it that will retrieve the credit of the thing, if it be retrievable, or ever had any credit. Rowe was, I think, the last man of character that had it. As to

Settle, whom you mention, he belonged to my lord
mayor not to the king. Eusden was a person of great
hopes in his youth, though at last he turned out a
drunken parson. Dryden was as disgraceful to the
office, from his character, as the poorest scribbler could
have been from his verses. The office itself has always
humbled the professor hitherto (even in an age when
kings were somebody), if he were a poor writer by
making him more conspicuous, and if he were a good
one by setting him at war with the little fry of his own
profession, for there are poets little enough to envy
even a poet-laureat.

I am obliged to you for your news ; pray send me
some more, and better of the sort. I can tell you
nothing in return ; so your generosity will be the
greater ;—only Dick is going to give up his rooms, and
live at Ashwell. Mr. Treasurer sets Sir M. Lamb at
nought, and says he has sent him reasons half a sheet
at a time ; and Mr. Brown attests his veracity as an
eye-witness. I have had nine pages of criticism on
the 'Bard' sent me in an anonymous letter, directed
to the Reverend Mr. G. at Strawberry Hill ; and if
I have a mind to hear as much more on the other
Ode, I am told where I may direct. He seems a good
sensible man, and I dare say a clergyman. He is very
frank, and indeed much ruder than he means to be.
Adieu, dear Mason, and believe me that I am too.

102. To Laurence Brockett

Mr Gray sends his compliments to Mr Brocket.
Shall be extremely obliged to him, if he would make
inquiry (when he has occasion to go into Trin: Library)
after the following old English Books

Paradise of dainty devices 1578 4to & 1585
England's Helicon   4to
W. Webbe's Discourse of Eng: Poetrie 1585 4to
Fr: Mere's Wit's Commonweath : 1598 Lond. &
     1634
Sam: Daniel's Musa, or Defence of Rhyme 1611 8vo
Stephen Hawes' Pastime of Pleasure 1555 4to

Gawen Douglas' Palace of Honour 1533 London 1579
  Edinb:
Earl of Surrey's Ecclesiastes 1567 4to
——————— 2^d & 4th Books of the Æneid 1557
  12mo
Gascoign's Works, 2 v: 4to 1577 & 1587.

If they should not be in the Library, Mr Gray
believes that Professor Torriano could favour him
with a sight of some of them for a few days. he will
take all imaginable care of them.

103. To Mason

Jan. 3, 1758.

DEAR MASON,—A life spent out of the world has
its hours of despondence, its inconveniences, its sufferings, as numerous and as real (though not quite of the
same sort) as a life spent in the midst of it. The power
we have, when we will exert it, over our own minds,
joined to a little strength and consolation, nay, a
little pride we catch from those that seem to love us,
is our only support in either of these conditions. I am
sensible I cannot return to you so much of this assistance as I have received from you. I can only tell you
that one who has far more reason than you (I hope)
will ever have to look on life with something worse
than indifference, is yet no enemy to it, and can look
backward on many bitter moments partly with satisfaction, and partly with patience, and forward too,
on a scene not very promising, with some hope and
some expectations of a better day. The conversation
you mention seems to me to have been in some measure
the cause of your reflection. As you do not describe
the manner (which is very essential, and yet cannot
easily be described,) to be sure I can judge but very
imperfectly of it. But if (as you say) it ended very
amicably, why not take it as amicably? In most
cases I am a great friend to *éclaircissements* ; it is no
pleasant task to enter upon them, therefore it is always
some merit in the person who does so. I am in the

dark too as to what you have said of——. To whom,
where, before whom, how did it come round ? for you
certainly would not do it indiscriminately, nor without
a little reserve. I do not mean on your own account
(for he is an object of contempt, that would naturally
tempt any one to laugh, or——*himself*), but for the
person's sake with whom you so often are, who (merely
from his situation) must neither laugh nor——*himself*,
as you and I might do. Who knows ? any little imprudence (which it is so pleasant to indulge) might
really be disagreeable in its consequences to him ; for
it would be said infallibly, though very unjustly, that
you would not dare to take these liberties without
private encouragement, at least, that he had no aversion to hear in secret what you ventured to say in
public. You do not imagine that the world (which
always concludes wrong about the motives of such
minds as it has not been used to) will think you have
any sentiments of your own : and though you (if you
thought it worth while) might wish to convince them
of their mistake, yet you would not do it at the expense
of another, especially of this other ; in short, I think
(as far as I know) you have no reason from this to
take any such resolution as you meditate. Make use
of it in its season, as a relief from what is tiresome to
you, but not as if it was in consequence of something
you take ill ; on the contrary, if such a conference
had happened about the time of your transmigration,
I would defer it, to avoid that appearance merely : for
the frankness of this proceeding has to me an appearance of friendliness that one would by no means wish
to suppress.

I am ashamed not to have returned Mr. Hurd my
thanks for his book ; pray do it for me in the civilest
manner, and tell him I shall be here till April, when
I must go for a short time to town, but shall return
again thither. I rejoice to hear he is again coming
out, and had no notion of his being so ready for the
press.

I wrote to the man (as you bid me), and had a

second criticism; his name (for I desired to know it) is Butler. He is (he says) of the number of those who live less contented than they ought, in an independent indolence, can just afford himself a horse for airings about Harewood Forest (the scene of Elfrida,) half a score new books in a season, and good part of half an acre of garden-ground for honeysuckles and roses. Did you know that Harewood was near Andover? I think that you had some friend in that neighbourhood, —is it not Mr. Bourne? however, do not inquire, for our correspondence is to be a profound secret. Adieu! I am ever truly yours.

TO MASON

                              T.G.

104. TO MASON

Jan. 13, 1758.

DEAR MASON,—Why you make no more of writing an Ode, and throwing it into the fire, than of buckling and unbuckling your shoe. I have never read Keysler's book, nor you neither, I believe; if you had taken that pains, I am persuaded you would have seen that his Celtic and his septentrional antiquities are two things entirely distinct. There are, indeed, some learned persons who have taken pains to confound what Cæsar and Tacitus have taken pains to separate, the old Druidical or Celtic belief, and that of the old Germans, but nobody has been so learned as to mix the Celtic religion with that of the Goths. Why, Woden himself is supposed not to have been older than Julius Cæsar; but let him have lived when he pleases, it is certain that neither he nor his Valhalla were heard of till many ages after. This is the doctrine of the Scalds, not of the Bards; these are the songs of Hengist and Horsa, a modern new-fangled belief in comparison of that which you ought to possess. After all, I shall be sorry to have so many good verses and good chimæras thrown away. Might we not be permitted (in that scarcity of Celtic ideas we labour under) to adopt some of these foreign whimsies, dropping however all mention of Woden and his Valkhyrian virgins,

&c. ? To settle this scruple of conscience, I must
refer you to Dr. Warburton : if this should be his
opinion (which I doubt), then I go on to tell you (first
premising that a dirge is always a funeral service sung
over persons already dead,) that I would have something striking and uncommon in the measures, the
rhythm, and the expression of this Chorus ; the two
former are not remarkable here, and the third is so
little antiquated, that ' murky ' and ' dank ' look
like two old maids of honour got into a circle of fleering
girls and boys. Now for particulars. I like the first
stanza ; the image of Death in arms is very fine and
gallant, but I banish ' freeborn train,' and ' glory and
luxury ' here (not the ideas, but the words), and
' liberty and freedom's cause,' and several small
epithets throughout. I do not see how one person
can *lift* the voice of another person. The imagery of
the second stanza too is excellent. A dragon *pecks !*
why a cock-sparrow might do as much : in short,
I am pleased with the Gothic Elysium. Do not think
I am ignorant about either that, or the *hell* before, or
the *twilight.* I have been there, and have seen it all
in Mallet's Introduction to the History of Denmark
(it is in French), and many other places. ' Now they
charge,' &c. looks as if the coursers rode upon the men.
A ghost does not fall. These are all my little objections.
but I have a greater. Extreme conciseness of expression, yet pure, perspicuous, and musical, is one of
the grand beauties of lyric poetry ; this I have always
aimed at, and never could attain ; the necessity of
rhyming is one great obstacle to it : another and
perhaps a stronger is, that way you have chosen of
casting down your first ideas carelessly and at large,
and then clipping them here and there, and forming
them at leisure ; this method, after all possible pains,
will leave behind it in some places a laxity, a diffuse-
ness ; the frame of a thought (otherwise well invented,
well turned, and well placed) is often weakened by it.
Do I talk nonsense, or do you understand me ? I am
persuaded what I say is true in my head, whatever

it may be in prose,—for I do not pretend to write prose.

I am extremely pleased with your fashionable Ode, and have nothing to find fault there, only you must say ' portray'st ' in the first stanza ; and ' it looks at best but skin,' in the fourth, is not right. I have observed your orders, but I want to shew it everybody. Pray tell me when I may have the credit of doing so. I have never seen a prettier modernism : let it be seen while it is warm. You are in the road to fame ; but do not tell your name at first, whatever you may venture to do afterwards.

Fobus is a treat ; desire Lord Holdernesse to kiss him on both ears for me. I forgive Lord B. for taking the Tudors for the Restoration. Adieu, dear Mason, and remember me ; and remember too that I have neither company, nor pleasure, nor spirits here, and that a letter from you stands in all the place of all these. Adieu !

So you have christened Mr. Dayrolles' child, and my Lady Y. they say. Oh ! brave Dupp. how comes he to be the Chancellor of the Exchequer ? What is going to be now ?

105. To WHARTON
Cambridge, March 8, 1758.

It is indeed for want of spirits, as you suspect, that my studies lie among the Cathedrals, and the Tombs, and the Ruins. To think, though to little purpose, has been the chief amusement of my days ; and when I would not, or cannot think, I dream. At present I find myself able to write a Catalogue, or to read the Peerage book, or Miller's Gardening Dictionary, and am thankful that there are such employments and such authors in the world. Some people, who hold me cheap for this, are doing perhaps what is not half so well worth while. As to posterity, I may ask, (with some body * whom I have forgot) what has it ever done to oblige me ?

To make a transition from myself to as poor a subject, the Tragedy of Agis; I cry to think that it should be by the Author of Douglas: Why, it is all modern Greek; the story is an antique statue, painted white and red, frized, and dressed in a negligée made by a Yorkshire mantuamaker. Then here is the Miscellany (Mr Dodsley has sent me the whole set gilt and lettered, I thank him). Why, the two last volumes are worse than the four first; particularly Dr Akenside is in a deplorable way. What signifies Learning and the Antients, (Mason will say triumphantly) why should people read Greek to lose their imagination, their ear, and their mother tongue? But then there is Mr Shenstone, who trusts to nature and simple sentiment, why does he do no better? he goes hopping along his own gravel-walks, and never deviates from the beaten paths for fear of being lost.

I have read Dr Swift, and am disappointed. There is nothing of the negotiations that I have not seen better in M. de Torcy before. The manner is careless, and has little to distinguish it from common writers. I met with nothing to please me but the spiteful characters of the opposite party and its leaders. I expected much more secret history.

106. To Mason

Good Friday [Mar. 24th], 1758.

DEAR MASON,—I have full as much *ennui* as yourself though much less dissipation, but I cannot make this my excuse for being silent, for I write to you *pour me désennuyer*, though I have little enough to say. I know not whether I am to condole with you on this Canterbury business, for it is not clear to me that you or the Church are any great losers by it; if you are be so good as to inform me, and I will be sorry; however, there is one good thing in it, it proves the family are mortal.

You do not seem to discover that Mons. Mallet is but a very small scholar, except in the erudition of the Goths. There are, *à propos*, two Dissertations on the Religion and Opinions of the Gauls, published in the Mémoires de l'Acad. des Belles Lettres et des Inscriptions, vol. XXIV. 4to. one by the Abbé Fénel, in which he would shew that, above Tiberius' and Claudius' times the Druids, persecuted and dispersed by the Romans, probably retired into Germany, and propagated their doctrines there. This is to account for some similitude to the Gaulish notions which the religion of Germany seems to bear, as Tacitus has described it, whereas Julius Cæsar makes them extremely different, who lived before this supposed dispersion of the Druids ; the other by Monsieur Freret, is as to shew the reverse of all this,—that there was no such dispersion, no such similitude, and that, if Cæsar and Tacitus disagree, it is because the first knew nothing but of those nations that bordered on the Rhine, and the other was acquainted with all Germany. I do not know whether these will furnish you with any new matter, but they are well enough written and easily read. I told you before, that, in a time of dearth, I would venture to borrow from the Edda without entering too minutely on particulars ; but, if I did so, I would make each image so clear, that it might be fully understood by itself, for in this obscure mythology we must not hint at things, as we do with the Greek fables, that every body is supposed to know at school. However, on second thoughts, I think it would be still better to graft any wild picturesque fable, absolutely of one's own invention, upon the Druid stock ; I mean upon those half-dozen of old fancies that are known to have made their system : this will give you more freedom and latitude, and will leave no hold for the critics to fasten on.

Pray, when did I pretend to finish, or even insert passages into other people's works ? as if it were equally easy to pick holes and to mend them. All I can say is, that your Elegy must not end with the worst line in it ; it is flat, it is prose ; whereas that above all ought to sparkle, or at least to shine. If the sentiment must stand, twirl it a little into an apophthegm, stick a flower in it, gild it with a costly expression; let it strike the fancy, the ear, or the heart, and I am satisfied.

Hodges* is a sad fellow; so is Dr. Akenside, and Mr. Shenstone, our friends and companions. Your story of Garrick is a good one; pray is it true, and what came of it? did the tragic poet call a guard? It was I that hindered Mr. Brown from sending the pamphlet. It is nonsense, and that nonsense all stolen from Dr. Stukeley's book about Abury and Stonehenge; yet if you will have it, you may. Adieu, and let me hear soon from you.

I am ever yours, T.G.

107. To Wharton

Sunday April 9, 1758.

MY DEAR SIR,—I am equally sensible of your affliction, & of your kindness, that made you think of me at such a moment. would to God, I could lessen the one, or requite the other with that consolation, wch I have often received from you, when I most wanted it! but your grief is too just, & the cause of it too fresh, to admit of any such endeavour. what indeed is all human consolation, can it efface every little amiable word or action of an object we loved, from our memory? Can it convince us that all the hopes we had entertain'd, the plans of future satisfaction we had form'd, were ill-grounded & vain, only because we have lost them? The only comfort (I am afraid) that belongs to our condition is to reflect (when time has given us leisure for reflection) that others have suffer'd worse, or that we ourselves might have suffer'd the same misfortune at times & in circumstances, that would probably have aggravated our sorrow. you might have seen this poor child arrive at an age to fulfil all your hopes, to attach you more strongly to him by long habit, by esteem, as well as natural affection, & that towards the decline of your life, when we most stand in need of support, & when he might chance to have been your *only* support ; & then by some unforeseen and deplorable accident, or some painful ling'ring distemper you might have lost him. such has been the fate of many an unhappy Father ! I know, there is a sort of tenderness, wch Infancy & Innocence alone produce, but I think, you must own the other to be a stronger & more overwhelming Sorrow.

I am glad Mrs Wharton has fortitude enough not to suffer this misfortune to prevail over her, and add to the natural weakness of her present condition. Mr Brown sincerely sympathises with you, and begs to be kindly remembered to you both. I have been . . . Town by this time, had I not heard Mason was coming hither soon, and I was unwilling to miss him. Adieu, my dear Wharton, and believe me ever most sincerely yours,

T G:

108. To Wharton

Dear Doctor,—I am much concern'd to hear the account you give of yourself, & particularly for that dejection of spirits, wch inclines you to see everything in the worst light possible, and throw a sort of voluntary gloom not only over your present, but future days, as if even your situation now were not preferable to that of thousands round you, and as if your prospect hereafter might not open as much of happiness to you, as to any Person you know. the condition of our life perpetually instructs us to be rather slow to hope, as well as to despair, & (I know, you will forgive me, if I tell you) you are often a little too hasty in both, perhaps from constitution. it is sure, we have great power over our own minds, when we chuse to exert it ; and tho' it be difficult to resist the mechanic impulse and biass of our own temper, it is yet possible ; and still more so, to delay those resolutions it inclines us to take, wch we almost always have cause to repent.

You tell me nothing of Mrs Wharton's, or your own state of health. I will not talk to you more on this subject, till I hear you are both well, for that is the grand point, & without it we may as well not think at all. You flatter me in thinking, that any thing, I can do, could at all alleviate the just concern your late loss has given you : but I can not flatter myself so far, & know how little qualified I am at present to give any satisfaction to myself on this head, & in this way, much less to you. I by no means pretend to inspiration, but yet I affirm, that the faculty in question is by no means voluntary. it is the result (I suppose) of a certain disposition of mind, wch does not depend on one self, and wch I have not felt this long time. you that are a witness, how seldom this spirit has moved me in my life, may easily give credit to what I say.

I am in hopes of seeing you very soon again in my way to Stoke. Mrs Rogers has been very ill this spring, & my other aunt writes me word, that she herself has had something (wch she takes for a paralytic stroke) which came as she walked in the garden, & is afraid, she shall lose the use of one leg : so that it looks to me, as if I should have perhaps some years to pass in a house with two poor bed-ridden Women, a melancholy object, & one that in common humanity I cannot avoid. I shall be glad to know, whether I can be in Gloucester-street for a week ten or twelve days hence.

I had wrote to you sooner, but that I have been on a little expedition lately to see Ely, Peterborough, Crowland-Abbey, Thorney, Fotheringhey, and many other old places, wch has amused me a little.

Poor Mason is all alone at Aston (for his Curate is gone to be Tutor to somebody) with an inflammation in his eyes, & could scarce see to write me a few lines. Adieu, Dear S^r, I am

Ever yours

June 18, 1758.   TG:

109. TO MASON

June 20, 1758.

DEAR MASON,—I sympathize with your eyes, having been confined at Florence with the same complaint for three weeks, but (I hope) in a much worse degree, for, besides not seeing, I could not sleep in the night for pain ; have a care of old women (who are all great oculists), and do not let them trifle with so tender a part.

I have been exercising my eyes at Peterborough, Crowland, Thorney, Ely, &c. ; am grown a great Fen antiquary ; this was the reason I did not answer you directly, as your letter came in my absence. I own I have been all this while expecting Caractacus, or at least three choruses, and now you do not so much as tell me it is finished : sure your spiritual functions, and even your attentions to the Duchess of Norfolk and Sir Conyers, might have allowed you some little intervals for poetry ; if not (now Queen Hecuba is gone), I utterly despair, for (say what you will) it was not retirement, it was not leisure, or the summer, or the country, that used to make you so voluminous ; it was emulation, it was rivalry, it was the collision of tragedy against tragedy, that kindled your fires, and set old Mona in a blaze. You do not say who succeeds her Trojan Majesty ; it ought to be well considered. Let me have none of your prosaic curates. I shall have you write sermons and private forms, and ' heaven's open to all men.'

That old *fizzling* Duke is coming here again (but I hope to be gone first,) to hear speeches in his new library, with the Bishop of Bristol, to air his close-stool ; they have fitted it up—not the close-stool, nor the Bishop, but the library, with classes, that will hold anything but books, yet books they must hold, and all the bulky old Commentators, the Synopses and Tractatus Tractatuums, are washed with white-of-eggs, gilt and lettered, and drawn up in review before his Grace. Your uncle Balguy takes his doctor's degree, and preaches the commencement sermon at Dr. Green's request.

Mr. Brown sends his love, and bids me tell you that Dr. Warburton has sent you his New Legation, with its dedication to Lord Mansfield ; would you have it sent you ? Lord Strathmore goes to-morrow into

the North to come of age. I keep an owl in the garden
as like me as it can stare ; only I do not eat raw meat,
nor bite people by the fingers. This is all the news
of the place. Adieu, dear Mason ! and write to me
directly if it will not hurt you, or I shall think you
worse than you are. I am ever yours.   T. G.

110. To Mason

Stoke, August 11, 1758.

DEAR MASON,—I was just leaving Cambridge at the
time when I received your last letter, and have been
unfixed and flitting about almost ever since, or you
had heard of me sooner. You do not think I could
stay to receive Fobus ; no more did Mr. Hurd, he was
gone into Leicestershire long before. As to uncle
Balguy, pray do him justice ; he stayed, indeed, to
preach the commencement sermon, but he assured me
(in secret) it was an old one, and had not one word
in it to the purpose. The very next morning he set
out for Winchester, and I do really think him much
improved since he had his residence there ; freer and
more open, and his heart less set upon the mammon
of unrighteousness. *A propos*,—would you think it ?
—Fobus has wit. He told Young, who was invited
to supper at Doctor L.'s. and made all the company
wait for him,—' Why, Young, you make but an awkward figure now you are a bishop ; this time last year
you would have been the first man here.'   I cannot
brag of my spirits, my situation, my employments,
or my fertility ; the days and the nights pass, and I
am never the nearer to anything but that one to which
we are all tending. Yet I love people that leave some
traces of their journey behind them, and have strength
enough to advise you to do so while you can. I expect
to see ' Caractacus ' completed, not so much from
the opinion I entertain of your industry as from the
consideration that another winter approaches, which
is the season of harvest to an author ; but I will conceal the secret of your motives, and join in the common

applause. The books you inquire after are not worth your knowledge. Parnell is the dunghill of Irish Grub-street. I did hear who Lancelot Temple was, but have really forgot. I know I thought it was Mr. Grenville. Avon is nothing but a type. The Duchess of Queensberry's advertisement has moved my impatience ; yet, after all, perhaps she may curl her gray hair with her grandfather's golden periods. Another object of my wishes is, the King of Prussia's account of the Campaign, which Niphausen talked of six weeks ago as just coming over, but it is not come : perhaps he waits for a better catastrophe. The Twickenham Press is in labour of two or three works (not of the printer's own). One of them is an Account of Russia by a Lord Whitworth, who, I think, was minister there from King William.

I seem to have told you all I know, which you will think very little, but *a nihilo nil fit*. If I were to coin my whole mind into phrases they would profit you nothing, nor fill a moderate page. Compassionate my poverty, show yourself noble in giving me better than I bring, and ever believe me

Most sincerely yours,

T. G.

I find you missed of Stonhewer by going to Sir Conyers Darcy's. Can you tell me if he is still at Harrowgate, for I do not know how to direct to him there ?

111. To Richard Stonehewer

Cambridge, August 18, 1758.

I am as sorry as you seem to be, that our acquaintance harped so much on the subject of materialism, when I saw him with you in town, because it was plain to which side of the long-debated question he inclined. That we are indeed mechanical and dependent beings, I need no other proof than my own feelings ; and from the same feelings I learn, with equal conviction, that we are not *merely* such : that there is a power within that struggles against the force and bias of that mechanism, commands its motion, and, by frequent practice, reduces it to that ready obedience which we call *Habit*; and all this in conformity to a preconceived opinion (no matter whether right or wrong), to that least material of all agents, a Thought. I have known many in his case who, while they thought they were conquering an old prejudice, did not perceive they were under the influence of one far more dangerous; one that furnishes us with a ready apology for all our worst actions, and opens to us a full license for doing whatever we please; and yet these very people were not at all the more indulgent to other men (as they naturally should have been); their indignation to such as offended them, their desire of revenge on anybody that hurt them was nothing mitigated: in short, the truth is, they wished to be persuaded of that opinion for the sake of its convenience, but were not so in their heart; and they would have been glad (as they ought in common prudence) that nobody else should think the same, for fear of the mischief that might ensue to themselves. His French author I never saw, but have read fifty in the same strain, and shall read no more. I can be wretched enough without them. They put me in mind of the Greek Sophist that got immortal honour by discoursing so feelingly on the miseries of our condition, that fifty of his audience went home and hanged themselves; yet he lived himself (I suppose) many years after in very good plight.

You say you cannot conceive how Lord Shaftesbury came to be a Philosopher in vogue; I will tell you: First, he was a Lord; 2dly, he was as vain as any of his readers; 3dly, men are very prone to believe what they do not understand; 4thly, they will believe anything at all, provided they are under no obligation to believe it; 5thly, they love to take a new road, even when that road leads nowhere; 6thly, he was reckoned a fine writer, and seemed always to mean more than he said. Would you have any more reasons? An interval of above forty years has pretty well destroyed the charm. A dead Lord ranks but with Commoners: Vanity is no longer interested in the matter, for the new road has become an old one. The mode of free-thinking is like that of Ruffs and Farthingales, and has given place to the mode of not thinking at all; once it was reckoned graceful, half to discover and half conceal the mind, but now we have been long accustomed to see it quite naked: primness and affectation of style, like the good breeding of Queen Anne's Court, has turned to hoydening and rude familiarity.

112. To WILLIAM PALGRAVE

Stoke, September 6, 1758.

I do not know how to make you amends, having neither rock, ruin, or precipice near me to send you; they do not grow in the South: but only say the word, if you would have a compact neat box of red brick with sash windows, or a grotto made of flints and shell-work, or a walnut-tree with three mole-hills under it, stuck with honeysuckles round a basin of gold-fishes, and you shall be satisfied; they shall come by the Edinburgh coach.

In the meantime I congratulate you on your new acquaintance with the *savage*, the *rude*, and the *tremendous*. Pray, tell me, is it anything like what you had read in your book, or seen in two-shilling prints? Do not you think a man may be the wiser (I had almost said the better) for going a hundred or two of miles; and that the mind has more room in it than most people seem to think, if you will but furnish the apartments? I almost envy your last month, being in a very insipid situation myself; and desire you would not fail to send me some furniture for my Gothic apartment, which is very cold at present. It will be the easier task, as you have nothing to do but transcribe your little red books, if they are not rubbed out; for I conclude you have not trusted everything to memory, which is ten times worse than a lead pencil: half a word fixed upon or near the spot, is worth a cartload of recollection. When we trust to the picture that objects draw of themselves on our minds, we deceive ourselves; without accurate and particular observation, it is but ill-drawn at first, the outlines are soon blurred, the colours every day grow fainter; and at last, when we would produce it to anybody, we are forced to supply its defects with a few strokes of our own imagination. God forgive me, I suppose I have done so myself before now, and misled many a good body that put their trust in me. Pray, tell me (but with permission, and without any breach of hospitality), is it so much warmer on the other side of the Swale (as some people of honour say) than it is here? Has the singing of birds, the bleating of sheep, the lowing of herds, deafened you at Rainton! Did the vast old oaks and thick groves of Northumberland keep off the sun too much from you? I am too civil to extend my enquiries beyond Berwick. Everything, doubtless, must improve upon you as you advanced northward. You must tell me, though, about Melross, Rosslin Chapel, and Arbroath. In short, your Port-feuille must be so full, that I only desire a loose chapter or two, and will wait for the rest till it comes out.

113. To Mason

Stoke, November 9, 1758.

DEAR MASON,—I should have told you that *Caradoc* came safe to hand, but my critical faculties have been so taken up in dividing nothing with ' The Dragon of Wantley's Dam,' that they are not yet composed enough for a better and more tranquil employment; shortly, however, I will make them obey me. But am I to send this copy to Mr. Hurd, or return it to you? Methinks I do not love this travelling to and again of manuscripts by the post. While I am writing, your second packet is just arrived. I can only tell you in gross that there seem to me certain passages altered, which might as well have been let alone ; and that I shall not be easily reconciled to Mador's own song. I must not have my fancy raised to that agreeable pitch of heathenism and wild magical enthusiasm, and then have you let me drop into moral philosophy and cold good sense. I remember you insulted me when I saw you last, and affected to call that which delighted my imagination nonsense. Now I insist that sense is nothing in poetry but according to the dress she wears, and the scene she appears in. If you should lead me into a superb Gothic building with a thousand clustered pillars, each of them half a mile high, the walls all covered with fretwork, and the windows full of red and blue saints, that had neither head nor tail, and I should find the Venus of Medici in person perked up in a long niche over the high altar, as naked as ever she was born, do you think it would raise or damp my devotions ? I say that Mador must be entirely a Briton, and that his pre-eminence among his companions must be shewn by superior wildness, more barbaric fancy, and a more striking and deeper harmony, both of words and numbers. If British antiquity be too narrow, this is the place for invention ; and if it be pure invention, so much the clearer must the expression be, and so much the stronger and richer the imagery—there's for you now.

I am sorry to hear you complain of your eyes. Have a care of candle-light, and rather play at hot-cockles with the children than either read or write. Adieu ! I am truly and ever yours,   T. G.

114. To Mason

London, January 18, 1759.

DEAR MASON,—You will think me either dead, or in that happy state which is that of most people alive, of forgetting everything they ought to remember ; yet I am neither one nor the other. I am now in town, having taken leave of Stoke, and hoping to take leave of my other incumbrances in a few months hence.

I send you in short my opinion of Caractacus, so far,
I mean, as I have seen of it; I shall only tell you
further, that I am charmed with the idea you give
me of your fourth Ode; it is excellently introduced,
and the specimen you send me even sublime. I am
wrapped in it; but the last line of the stanza falls off,
and must be changed, 'Courage was in his van,'
etc., for it is ordinary when compared with the rest;
to be sure, the immortality of the soul and the happiness
of dying in battle are Druid doctrines; you may dress
them at pleasure, so they do but look wild and
British.

I have little to say from hence but that Cleone has
succeeded very well at Covent Garden, and that people
who despised it in manuscript went to see it, and
confess—they cried so. For fear of crying too I did
not go. Poor Smart is not dead, as was said, and
Merope is acted for his benefit this week, with a new
farce, *The Guardian*. Here is a very agreeable opera
of Cocchi's, the *Cyrus*, which gave me some pleasure;
do you know I like both Whitehead's Odes in great
measure, but nobody else does.

I hear matters will be made up with the Dutch, and
there will be no war. The King of Portugal has slily
introduced troops into Lisbon, under pretence of
clearing away the rubbish, and seized the unsuspecting
conspirators in their own houses; they are men of
principal note, in particular the family of Tavora,
who have some pretensions to the crown; and it is
thought the Jesuits have made use of their ambition
to execute their own revenge. The story of the king's
gallantries, and the jealousy of some man of quality,
who contrived the assassination, is said to be all false.

Adieu! I rejoice to hear you use your eyes again.
Write to me at Dr. Wharton's, for perhaps I may go
to Cambridge for some weeks, and he will take care
I shall have your letter.

115. To Mason

April 10, 1759.

DEAR MASON,—This is the third return of the gout in the space of three months, and worse than either of the former. It is now in a manner over, and I am so much the nearer being a cripple, but not at all the richer. This is my excuse for long silence ; and, if you had felt the pain, you would think it an excuse for a greater fault. I have been all the time of the fit here in town, and doubtless ought to have paid my court to you and to Caractacus. But a critic with the gout is a devil incarnate, and you have had a happy escape. I cannot repent (if I have really been any hindrance) that you did not publish this spring. I would have it mellow a little longer, and do not think it will lose anything of its flavour ; to comfort you for your loss, know that I have lost above £200 by selling stock.

I half envy your situation and your improvements (though I do not know Mr. Wood), yet am of your opinion as to prudence ; the more so because Mr. Bonfoy tells me he saw a letter from you to Lady H., and that she expressed a sort of kindness ; to which my Lord added, that he should write a rattling epistle to you that was to fetch you out of the country. Whether he has or not don't much signify : I would come and see them.

I shall be here this month at least against my will, unless you come. Stonhewer is here with all his sisters, the youngest of which has got a husband. Two matches more (but in a superior class) are going to be soon :— Lord Weymouth to the Duchess of Portland's homely daughter, Lady Betty, with £35,000 ; and Lord Waldegrave to Miss Maria Walpole with £10,000. It is impossible for two handsomer people ever to meet.

All the cruelties of Portugal are certainly owing to an amour of the King's (of long standing) with the younger Marquess of Tavora's wife. The Jesuits made their advantage of the resentments of that family. The disturbances at Lisbon are all false.

This is my whole little stock of news.

Here is a very pretty opera, the *Cyrus;* and here is the Museum which is indeed a treasure. The trustees lay out £1400 a-year, and have but £900 to spend. If you would see it you must send a fortnight beforehand, it is so crowded. Then here are Murdin's *Papers*, and Hume's *History of the Tudors*, and Robertson's *History of Mary Stuart and her Son* and what not. Adieu, dear Mason, I am most faithfully yours,   T. G.

116. To Wharton

Saturday, July 21. 1759

DEAR DOCTOR,—I have at last found rest for the sole of my gouty foot in your own old Dining-room, and hope in spite of the damnation denounced by the bishop's two Chaplains, that you may find at least an equal satisfaction & repose at Old-Park. if your Bog prove as comfortable as my Oven, I shall see no occasion to pity you; and only wish that you may *brew* no worse, than I *bake*. You totally mistake my talents, when you impute to me any magical skill in planting roses. I know, I am no Conjuror in these things; when they are done, I can find fault, & that is all. Now this is the very reverse of Genius, and I feel my own littleness. reasonable People know themselves better, than is commonly imagined; and therefore (tho' I never saw any instance of it) I believe Mason, when he tells me he understands planting better, than anything whatever. The *prophetic eye of Taste* (as Mr. Pitt call'd it) sees all the beauties, that a Place is susceptible of, long before they are born; and when it plants a seedling, already sits under the shadow of it, & enjoys the effect it will have from every point of view, that lies in prospect. You must, therefore invoke Caractacus, and he will send his spirits from the top of Snowdon to Cross-Fell or Warden-Low.

The Thermometer is in the Passage-Window (where

the sun never comes) near the head of the Back-Stairs. since you went, I have never observed it lower than 68, most part of the day at 74, & yesterday at 5 in ye afternoon it was at 79, the highest I have ever seen it. it now is prepared to correspond regularly with you at the hours you mention. the weather for this fortnight has been broiling without interruption, one thunder-shower excepted, wch did not cool the air at all. Rye (I am told) is begun to be cut near London. in Cambridgeshire a fortnight ago the promise of harvest was the finest I ever saw, but the Farmers complain (I hear) that the ears do not fill for want of wet : the Wheat was then turning yellow. Duke-Cherries are over in London ; three days ago they sold for half-a-crown a Pound. Caroons and Black-Hearts very large and fine drive about the streets in wheel-barrows a penny a pound. Raspberries a few are yet remaining, but in a manner over. Melons are ripe, and apricots and Orleans-Plums are to be seen in the fruit shops. Roses are (I think) over a week ago. The jessamine (at Mrs Dod's, on a S:W: Wall) was in full bloom (if you remember) long before you went from hence, & so it continues. That below in the Garden on a N:E: Wall has been all this week cover'd with flowers. my nosegays from Covent-Garden consist of nothing but Scarlet-Martagons, Everlasting-Peas, Double-Stocks, Pinks, and flowering Marjoram. As I have kept no exact account hitherto this year, I can say no more of July, that now is. therefore, I shall annex one for the year 1754, which I observed day by day at Stoke. observe, it had been then a cold rainy summer.

The heat was very moderate this month, & a great deal of rain fell. The sown Hay was all got in by the first day, but the meadow-hay was not before ye 23^d. It was very good & in plenty, but sold at 40 shillings a load in the field on account of the scarcity the year preceding. Barley was in ear on the first day ; grey and white Peas in bloom. The Bean flowers were going off. Duke-Cherries in plenty on the 5th ; Hearts were also ripe. green Melons on the 6th, but watry,

& not sweet. Currants begun to ripen on the 8th, & red Goose-berries had changed colour; Tares were then in flower, and meadow-Hay cutting. Lime-trees in full bloom on the 9th, Mushrooms in perfection on the 17th. Wheat & Oats had changed colour, and Buck-Wheat was in bloom on the 19th. the Vine had then open'd its blossoms, & the end of the month Grapes were near ye size of small Pease. Turneps appear'd above ground on the 22d; and Potatoes were in flower. Barley had changed its hue, & Rye was almost ripe on the 23d. The Pine-apple-Strawberry was then in perfection. Black Caroons were ripe, & some Duke-Cherries still remained on walls the 26th, but the Hearts were then all spoil'd by the rain. Goose-berries red and white were then ripe, and Currants in abundance.

Haws turned red		
Broom-flower went off	On ye	
Honey-suckles in full bloom	first	
Phlomis, or yellow Tree-Sage	2d	
Virginia flowering Raspberry blew		
Shrub-Cinquefoil	3d	
Spiræa-frutex		
Sweet-Briar		
Syringa went off		
Balm of Gilead blowing	7th	
Common Jasmine blew		
Moss-Provence Rose	8th	
Yellow and Austrian, Rose goe off		
Yellow Jasmine blows		
White, and Gum-Cistus		
Tamarisk in flower		
Coccygria		
Virginia-Sumach	9th	
Tutsan, or Park-leaves.		
Spanish-Broom		
Scarlet, & Painted Geraniums		
Pyracantha, in berry		
Mountain-Ash		
White-Beam	11th	
Orange flowering		
Winter-Cherry		
Single-Velvet-Rose goes off	15th	

Lavender and Marjoram blow	22d
Damask, Red, Moss, and Double Velvet, Roses go off	26th
Rosa-Mundi, and Rose without thorns, go off	28th
White Rose goes off	31st

These were all the flowering Shrubs observed by me.

GARDEN-FLOWERS

Convolvulus minor blows	
Garden-Poppy	
Single Rose-Campion	
Double Larkspur	2d
Candy-Tuft	
Common Marigold	
Pansies continue blowing	
Lupines blew, and white blow	
Purple Toads-flax	5th
White, and blew Campanula	
Double-scarlet Lychnis blows	
Tree-Primrose	
White Lilly	9th
Willow-Bay	
Scarlet-Bean	
French Marigold	

Yellow Lupine blows .	⎫	
Tree-Mallow . . .	⎬ 11th	
Amaranthus Cat's-tail	⎭	
Striped Lilly blows .	⎫	
Fairchild's Mule . .	⎬ 19th	
Double rose-Campion .		
African Ragwort . .	⎭	
Whole Carnations blow	23d	
Double white Stock in bloom	24th	

In the fields Scabious, St. John's Wort, Trefoil, Yarrow, Bugloss, Purple Vetch, Wild-thyme, Pale Wood-Orchis, Betony, & white Clover, flowering on yᵉ first. Large blew Cranesbill the 9th; Ragwort, Mothmullein, and Brambles, the 20th. Knapweed all the month. there was rain (more or less) 13 days out of yᵉ 31, this month ; and 17 days out of 30 in June preceding.

I was too late for the Post on Saturday, so I continue on Monday. It is now 6 in the afternoon, & the therm: is mounted to 80, tho' the wind is at N. E. by N: . . the gay Lady Essex is dead of a Fever during her lieing-in ; and Mrs. Charles York last week, with one of her children, of the Sore throat. Heberden, and (I think) Taylor attended her ; the latter had pronounced her out of danger ; but Heb:ⁿ doubted about her. the little boy was at Acton, & escaped the infection.

Everybody continues as quiet about the invasion, as if a Frenchman, as soon as he set his foot on our coast, would die, like a Toad in Ireland. Yet the King's Tents & Equipage are order'd to be ready at an hour's warning. no body knows positively, what is the damage, that Rodney has done, whether much or little : he can only guess himself ; and the French have kept their own secret, as yet. of the 12 Millions, raised for the year, eight are gone already, and the old Party assure us, there is no more to be had for next year. you may easily guess at the source of my intelligence, and therefore will not talk of it. News is hourly expected of a battle in Westphalia, for Pr: Ferdinand is certainly preparing to fight the French, who have taken Minden by storm.

I hear the D: of N: is much broke ever since his sister Castle-comer died, not that he cared for her, or saw her above once a year ; but she was the last of the brood, that was left ; & he now goes regularly to Church, which he never did before.

I hope Mrs Wharton's native Air will be more civil

to her, when they are better acquainted: my best
Compliments to her. I am glad the Children are well.
Adieu, I am ever
Yours

117. To William Palgrave

London, July 24, 1759.

I am now settled in my new territories commanding
Bedford Gardens, and all the fields as far as Highgate
and Hampstead, with such a concourse of moving
pictures as would astonish you; so *rus-in-urbe-ish*, that
I believe I shall stay here, except little excursions and
vagaries, for a year to come. What though I am
separated from the fashionable world by broad St.
Giles's, and many a dirty court and alley, yet here is
air, and sunshine, and quiet, however, to comfort you:
I shall confess that I am basking with heat all the
summer, and I suppose shall be blown down all the
winter, besides being robbed every night; I trust,
however, that the Musæum, with all its manuscripts
and rarities by the cart-load, will make ample amends
for all the aforesaid inconveniences.

I this day past through the jaws of the great leviathan
into the den of Dr. Templeman, superintendant of the
reading-room, who congratulated himself on the sight
of so much good company. We were, first, a man
that writes for Lord Royston; 2dly, a man that writes
for Dr. Burton, of York: 3dly, a man that writes for
the Emperor of Germany, or Dr. Pocock, for he speaks
the worst English I ever heard; 4thly, Dr. Stukeley,
who writes for himself, the very worst person he could
write for; and, lastly, I, who only read to know if
there be anything worth writing, and that not without
some difficulty. I find that they printed 1000 copies
of the *Harleian Catalogue*, and have only sold fourscore;
that they have £900 a year income, and spend £1300,
and are building apartments for the under-keepers;
so I expect in winter to see the collection advertised
and set to auction.

Have you read Lord Clarendon's Continuation of

his History ? Do you remember Mr. ——'s account
of it before it came out ? How well he recollected all
the faults, and how utterly he forgot all the beauties.
Surely the grossest taste is better than such a sort of
delicacy.

118. To the Rev. James Brown

August 8, 1759.

DEAR SIR,—The season for triumph is at last come ;
I mean for our allies, for it will be long enough before
we shall have reason to exult in any great actions of
our own, and therefore, as usual, we are proud for our
neighbours. Contades' great army is entirely defeated :
this (I am told) is undoubted, but no particulars are
known as yet ; and almost as few of the other victory
over the Russians, which is lost in the splendour of this
greater action. So much for war ; and now come and
see me in my peaceful new settlement, from whence
I have the command of Highgate, Hampstead, Bedford
Gardens, and the Museum ; this last (as you will
imagine) is my favourite domain, where I often pass
four hours in the day in the stillness and solitude of
the reading-room, which is uninterrupted by anything
but Dr. Stukeley the antiquary, who comes there to
talk nonsense and coffee-house news ; the rest of the
learned are (I suppose) in the country, at least none
of them come there, except two Prussians, and a man
who writes for Lord Royston. When I call it peaceful,
you are to understand it only of us visitors, for the
society itself, trustees and all, are up in arms, like the
fellows of a college. The keepers have broke off all
intercourse with one another, and only lower a silent
defiance as they pass by. Dr. Knight has walled up
the passage to the little house, because some of the
rest were obliged to pass by one of his windows in the
way to it. Moreover the trustees lay out £500 a-year
more than their income ; so you may expect all the
books and the crocodiles will soon be put up to auction ;
the University (we hope) will buy.

I have not (as you silently charge me) forgot Mosheim. I enquired long ago, and was told there were none in England, but Nourse expects a cargo every day, and as soon as it comes, you shall have it. Mason never writes, but I hear he is well, from Dr. Gisburne. Do not pout, but pray let me hear from you, and above all, do come and see me, for I assure you I am not uncomfortably situated for a lodger; and what are we but lodgers? Adieu, dear Sir, I am ever yours,   T. G.

At Mr. Jauncey's, Southampton Row, Bloomsbury.

119. TO THE REV. JAMES BROWN

Saturday, August 9, 1759.

I retract a part of my yesterday's intelligence, having to-day had an opportunity of hearing more, and from the best hand.

The merit of Prince Ferdinand's policy and conduct is not a little abated by this account. He made a detachment of 4 or 5000 men, under the hereditary Prince of Brunswick, which had got between the main French army and the town of Herwart, where their principal magazine lay. The fear they were under on that account obliged Contades to begin the attack, and he accordingly began his march at midnight, in eight columns. Very early in the morning, before the Prince had time to make the proper dispositions, they were upon him. He had only his first line formed when the battle began, and of that line the English infantry made a considerable part; Contades' troops (joined by the Duke of Broglio's corps) amounting to near fourscore thousand: the Prince had only forty battalions with him, half of which only engaged (as I said) for want of time. The French artillery at first did terrible execution, and it was then our four regiments suffered so much, 68 of their officers (all, I think, below a captain in degree) being killed or wounded; 267 private men killed, and above 900 wounded. The rest of the line were Hanoverians (who behaved very bravely), and, as their number was much greater, it is

H

likely they suffered still more ; but of their loss I have no particular account. In the village of Tonhausen, near at hand, were all the Hessian artillery, which being now turned upon the French, soon silenced their cannon, and gave an opportunity to come to close engagement. The conflict after this lasted but an hour and a quarter. The French made a poor and shameful resistance, and were dispersed and routed on all sides. The Marshal himself (having detached a body of men to try if they could save or turn Herwart) retreated along the Weser toward Rintelen and Corvey, but wrote a letter to the Prince to say that, as Minden must now soon fall into the hands of his victorious troops, he doubted not but he would treat the wounded and sick (who were all lodged there) with his usual humanity. Accordingly he entered Minden the next day. Eight thousand only of the French were slain in the field, twenty pieces of cannon (sixteen-pounders) taken, and twelve standards. The number of prisoners and the slaughter of the pursuit not so great as it might have been, for the English horse (though they received orders to move) stirred not a foot, nor had any share in the action. This is unaccountable, but true ; and we shall soon hear a greater noise about it. (Lord G. Sackville.)

The Prince of Brunswick fell in with the party sent towards Herwart, entirely routed it, took five pieces of cannon, the town, and all the magazines.

The loss of the Russians is not what has been reported. Their march towards Silesia, however, was stopped ; and the King of Prussia is gone in person to attack them.

The story of Durell is all a lie.

Lord H. is blamed for publishing General Yorke's and Mitchell's letters so hastily.

Don't quote me for all this Gazette. The Prussians have had a very considerable advantage over General Harsch.

120. To WHARTON

DEAR DOCT^R,—I cannot say anything to you about Mason, whose motions I am entirely a stranger to, and have not once heard from him since he left London ; till (the 3^d of this month) a letter came, in wch he tells me, that Gaskarth is at Aston with him, & that the latter end of the month, or the beginning of the next, he shall be in town as he goes into waiting the last fortnight in October. Ld H. has sent him no less than four Expresses (literally so) with public News good & bad, wch has made him of infinite importance in the eyes of that neighbourhood. I can not pretend therefore to guess, whether he will be able to come to you. I am sorry to tell you that I try in vain to execute your commission about tapestry. what is so bad, as wry-mouthed histories ? and yet for this they ask me at least double the price you talk of. I have seen nothing neither, that would please me at any price : yet I allow tapestry (if at all tolerable) to be a very proper furniture for your sort of house ; but doubt, if any bargain of that kind is to be met with, except at some old mansion-sale—in the country, where People will disdain tapestry, because they hear, that Paper is all the fashion. Stonhewer has been in Northamptonshire till now : as you told me the subject of your letter, I did not send it thither to him, besides that he was every day expected in Town. at last he is come, and has it ; but I have not yet seen him : he is gone to-day (I believe) to Portsmouth to receive a Morocco Embassador, but returns very shortly. there is one advantage in getting into your Abbey at Christmastime : that it will be at its worst, and if you can bear it then, you need not fear for the rest of the year. M^r W: has lately made a new Bed-chamber, wch as it is in the best tast of anything he has yet done, & in your own Gothic way, I must describe a little. you enter by a peaked door at one corner of the room (out of a narrow winding passage, you may be sure) into an Alcove, in which the bed is to stand, formed by a

screen of pierced work opening by one large arch in
the middle to the rest of the chamber, wch is lighted
at the other end by a bow-window of three bays, whose
tops are of rich painted glass in mosaic. the cieling
is coved & fretted in star and quatrefoil compartments,
with roses at the intersections, all in papier-maché.
the chimney on your left is the high-altar in the
cathedral of Rouen (from whence the Screen also is
taken) consisting of a low surbased Arch between two
octagon Towers, whose pinnacles almost reach the
Cieling, all of nich-work. the chairs and dressing-table
are real carved ebony, pick'd up at auctions. the
hangings uniform purple paper, hung all over with
the court of Henry, ye 8th, copied after the Holbein's
in the Queen's Closet at Kensington, in black & gold
frames. the bed is to be either from Burleigh (for
Ld Exeter is new furnishing it, and means to sell some
of his original household-stuff) of the rich old tarnish'd
embroidery; or if that is not to be had, & it must be
new, it is to be a cut velvet with a dark purple pattern
on a stone-colour sattin ground, & deep mixt fringes
& tassels. there's for you, but I want you to see it.
in the meantime I live in the Musæum, & write volumes
of antiquity. I have got (out of the original Ledger-
book of the Signet) K: Richard 3^d's oath to Elizabeth,
late *calling herself Queen of* England; to prevail upon her
to come out of Sanctuary with her 5 daughters. his
Grant to Lady Hastings & her Son, dated 6 weeks
after he had cut off her Husband's head. a letter to
his Mother; another to his Chancellor, to persuade
his Sollicitor General not to marry Jane Shore then in
Ludgate by his command. Sr Tho: Wyat's Defence
at his Tryal, when accused by B^p Bonner of high-
treason; Lady Purbeck and her Son's remarkable
Case, and several more odd things unknown to our
Historians. when I come home, I have a great heap
of the Conway Papers (wch is a secret) to read, & make
out. in short, I am up to the ears.

The Fish you mention is so accurately described
that I know it at sight. It is the *Ink-fish*, or Loligo

of the Romans. in Greek Τευθὸς, in Italian, Calamaio. in French, Calmar. you will find it ranged by Linnæus in the class of *Vermes*, the order of *Mollusca*, the genus of *Sepia*, Nº 4, pag: 659. The smaller ones are eaten as a delicacy fried, with their own ink for sauce, by the Italians and others. you may see it in Aldrovandus.

I do not see much myself of the face of nature here, but I enquire. Wheat was cutting in Kent the 23d of July. the 25th at Enfield. the 27th Wheat, Barley, & oats cutting all at once about Windsor: the forward Pease all got in, ground plough'd. and turnips sow'd. 9th of August, Harvest still continued in Buck:re. The 27th about Kennington it was just over, being delay'd for want of hands. in some places 50 mile from London it is but just over now for the same reason. the 3d of Aug: Catherine-pears, Muscle-Plums, and small black Cherries were sold in wheel barrows. Filberds in plenty the 8th. Mulberries, & fine green-gage plums the 19th. fine Nectarines & Peaches, the 27th. the 4th of Sept: Melons and Perdrigon-plums. the 8th, Walnuts 20 a penny. this is all I know about fruit. My Weather is not very compleat.

July
20, 1759. London. Therm: 5 in the afternoon, at 79
21 .
22 . same hour 76
23 Wind N.N.E. . d:° 80 ⎧ Grass
24 . d:° — ⎨ burnt
25 . d:° 78 ⎩ up
26 wd N:N:W. brisk at noon . 71
27 Wind laid at night .
28 wd N: fair, white flying clouds, 9 in morng —
29 ,, S.S.W. still & cloudy sunshine d:° 68
30. gloomy & hot. wd W:S:W: shower at night d:° 69
31. 8 hours rain. wd S:W: moonshiny night d:° 70
Aug: d:° 70
1. cloudy. W:S:W: brisk and chill, bright eveng
d:° 66
2. Cloudy sun, W:S:W: chill. a little rain. night clear . d:° 65

Aug:

3. Fine, w^d N:W: cool	.	.	d:°	64

3. Fine, w^d N:W: cool . . . . d:° . 64
4. gloomy. S:W: high. seven hours
        heavy rain . . . d:° . 64
5. cloudy. N:W: hard rain at night . d:° . 66
6. Clouds & sunshine. w^d N:W: brisk . Therm: at 9 . 64
7. w^d S:W: fair . . . . d:° . 66
8. W: clear and hot . . . . ,, . 74
9. S:S:W: very hot . . . . ,, . 76
10. d°. hot and foggy . . . ,, . 74
11.   clear and extreme hot . . ,, . 76
12. N:N:W: small rain. evening fine . ,, . 66
13. N:N:E: brisk. fine day . . . ,, . 66
14.   cloudy . . . . ,, . 64
15. N:N:W: clouds & sun . . . ,, . 68
16.   very fine . . . . ,, . 64
17. S:W: overcast. some rain . . ,, . 68
18.   very fine . . . . ,, . 64
19. W:N:W: cloudy, but fair. at night hard rain . 64
20. W:S:W: overcast. at night much rain ,, . 66

I go no farther than you do: but it is down in my book.

what do you say to all our victories? The night we rejoiced for Boscawen, in the midst of squibs and bonfires arrived Lord G. Sackville. He sees company: & to-day has put out a short address to the Publick, saying, he expects a Court-Martial (for no one abroad had authority to try him) and desires people to suspend their judgement. I fear, it is a rueful case.

I believe, I shall go on Monday to Stoke for a time, where Lady Cobh^m has been dying. My best respects to Mrs Wharton. Believe me ever faithfully

                              Yours

Southampton-Row, Sept: 18. 1759.   TG:

121. To Wharton

London, Thursday, Jan. 23, 1760.

DEAR DOCTOR,—I am much obliged to you for your antique news: Froissard is a favourite book of mine (tho' I have not attentively read him, but only dip'd

here and there) & it is strange to me that people who
would give thousands for a dozen Portraits (Originals
of that time) to furnish a gallery, should never cast
an eye on so many moving pictures of the life, actions,
manners, & thoughts of their ancestors done on the
spot, & in strong tho' simple colours. In the succeeding
century Froissard (I find) was read with great satisfaction by everybody, that could read ; & on the same
footing with King Arthur, Sr Tristram, & Archbishop
Turpin : not because they thought him a fabulous
Writer, but because they took them all for true and
authentic Historians. to so little purpose was it in
that age for a Man to be at the pains of writing truth !
pray, are you come to the four Irish Kings, that went
to school to K. Richard the 2d.'s Master of the Ceremonies ; and the Man who informed Froissard of all
he had seen in St Patrick's Purgatory ?

You ask after Quebec. Gen: Townsend says, it is
much like Richmond-Hill, and the river as fine (but
bigger) & the Vale as *riant*, as rich, & as well cultivated.
no great matters are attributed to his conduct. the
Officer, who brought over the news, when the Pr: of
W: ask'd, how long Gen: T: commanded in the action
after Wolfe's death ? answer'd, a Minute, S^r. it is
certain, he was not at all well with Wolfe, who for
some time had not cared to consult with him, or communicate any of his designs to him. he has brought
home an Indian Boy with him (designed for L^d G:
Sackville, but he did not chuse to take him) who goes
about in his own dress, & is brought into the room to
divert his company. the Gen: after dinner one day
had been shewing them a box of scalps & some Indian
arms & utensils. when they were gone, the Boy got
to the box, and found a scalp, wch he knew by the hair
belong'd to one of his own nation. he grew into a
sudden fury (tho' but eleven years old) & catching up
one of the scalping-knives made at his Master with
intention to murther him, who in his surprise hardly
knew how to avoid him, & by laying open his breast,
making signs, & with a few words of French Jargon,

that the Boy understood, at last with much difficulty pacified him. the first rejoicing night he was terribly frighted, and thought the bonefire was made for him, & that they were going to torture and devour him. he is mighty fond of venison blood-raw; & once they caught him flourishing his knife over a dog that lay asleep by the fire, because (he said) it was *bon manger*.

You have heard of the Irish disturbances (I reckon); never were two Houses of Parliament so bep——d & s——upon. this is not a figure, but literally so. they placed an old Woman on the Throne, & called for pipes & tobacco; made my Lord Chief-Justice administer an oath (wch they dictated) to my Ld Chancellor; beat the B^p of Killaloe black and blew; play'd at football with Chenevix, the old refugié B^p of Waterford; roll'd my Ld Farnham in the Kennel; pulled Sr Tho: Prendergast by the nose (naturally large) till it was the size of a Cauliflower; and would have hanged Rigby, if he had not got out of a window. all this time *the Castle* remain'd in perfect tranquillity. at last the Guard was obliged to move (with orders not to fire), but the Mob threw dirt at them. then the horse broke in upon them, cutting & slashing, and took 17 prisoners: next morning they were all set at liberty, and said to be poor silly people, that knew nothing of the matter. the same night there was a Ball at the Castle, and Play till four in the morning. this tumult happened two days before the news of Hawke's victory got to Dublin; & there was another some time before, when first it was known that the Brest Fleet had sail'd. warning was given (from the *best hands* in England) six weeks before that time, that there would be a *rising of the Papists* in Ireland; & the first person whom the Mob insulted was a Mr Rowley, a Member always in opposition to the Court, but a *Presbyterian.* it is strange (but, I am assured, true) that the Government have not yet received any account of the matter from thence, & all the Irish here are ready to fight a Man, that says there has been any riot at all at Dublin. the notion, that had possess'd the crowd, was, that a Union was to be voted between the two nations, & they should have no more Parliaments there.

Prince. F: has done a strange thing in Germany. we have always studiously avoided doing anything to incur the Ban of the Empire. he has now (without waiting for commands from hence) detach'd 14000 men, the Flower of his flock, to assist the K: of Prussia in Saxony against the Empress-Queen & the Empire. The old Gentleman does not know how to digest it after giving him 2000£ a year on the Irish Establishment, & 20000£ for the Battle of Minden (not out of his own pocket; don't mistake: but out of yours under the head of Extraordinaries). a great Fleet is preparing, & an expedition going forward; but nobody knows whereto: some say Martinico, others Minorca. all thought of a Congress is vanished, since the Empress has shew'd herself so cool to our proposal.

Mr. Pitt (not the Great, but the little one, my acquaintance) is setting out on his travels. he goes with my Ld Kinnoul to Lisbon; then (by Sea still) to Cales, then up the Guadalquiver to Seville & Cordova, and so perhaps to Toledo, but certainly to Granada; and after breathing the perfumed air of Andalusia, and contemplating the remains of Moorish Magnificence, re-embarks at Gibraltar or Malaga, and sails to Genoa. sure an extraordinary good way of passing a few winter-months, & better than dragging through Holland, Germany, & Switzerland, to the same place. now we have been contriving to get my Ld Str: (for whose advantage it will be in several respects) to bear a part in this expedition, & to-day we have brought it about, and they will go in a fortnight: but this is a secret, and you must not tell, for fear my Lady should be frighted at so much Sea.

The Attorney and Sollic:^r General (to whom it was refer'd) have declared that L^d G: S: may be tried by a Court-Martial. L^d H^sse: has wrote him a letter to inform him of this, & *desires* to know (these are the words) how his L^dp *would have* them proceed, as there is no *specific charge* against him. I am told, he has answer'd, that he cannot pretend to prescribe how a Court, that sits in judgement upon him, is to proceed against him. that he well knows, nothing can justly be alledged against him ; but doubts not from Pr: Ferdinand's treatment of him, that there was some charge against him, especially as he finds himself *dismiss'd from all his employments.* I hear too, that (whatever the lawyers have said) the General Officers insist, they will not have anything to do with his cause, as he is no longer of the Army. so (I suppose) after a little bustle the matter will drop.

Here is a new farce of Macklin the Player's, that delights the Town much, Love-a-la-Mode, a Beau-Jew, an English Gentleman-Jockey, a Scotch Baronet, & an Irish Officer in the Prussian-Service, that make love to a Merchant's Niece. the Irishman is the Heroe, and the happy Man, as he deserves ; for Sr Reilichan O'Callaghan is a modest, brave, & generous Soldier ; yet with the manners, the Brogue, & the understanding, of an Irishman, wch makes a new Character. the K: is so pleased with the Scotch character (which is no compliment to that nation) that he has sent for a copy of the piece, for it is not printed, to read.

I am sorry to hear, you have reason to complain of Mr Bell, because he seem'd to have some taste in Gothick, and it may not be easy to find such another. It is for my sake, not from your own judgement, that you see the *affair I* mentioned to you in so good a light ; I wish, I could foresee any such consequences, as you do : but fear, it will be the very reverse, & so do others than I. The Musæum goes on as usual : I have got the Earl of Huntingdon & Sr George Bowes's letters to Cecil about the Rebellion in the North. Heberden has married Miss Wollaston of Charterhouse square, this week, whom he formerly courted, but could not then afford to have ; for she has (they say) but 2000£ fortune. I have not yet seen her.

My best respects to Mrs. Wharton. I am, ever
Yours,
TG:

122. To Wharton

April 22, 1760. London.

DEAR DOCTOR,—I am not sorry to hear, you are exceeding busy, except as it has deprived me of the pleasure I should have in hearing often from you, & as it has been occasion'd by a little vexation & disappointment. to find oneself business (I am persuaded) is the great art of life ; & I am never so angry, as when I hear my acquaintance wishing they had been bred to some poking profession, or employ'd in some office of drudgery, as if it were pleasanter to be at the command of other People, than at one's own ; & as if they could not go, unless they were wound up. yet I know and feel, what they mean by this complaint : it proves, that some spirit, something of Genius (more than common) is required to teach a Man how to employ himself. I say *a Man*, for Women commonly speaking never feel this distemper : they have always something to do ; time hangs not on their hands (unless they be fine ladies) a variety of small inventions & occupations fill up the void & their eyes are never open in vain.

I thank you heartily for the Sow. if you have no occasion for her, I have ; & if his L^{dp} will be so kind as to drive her up to Town, will gladly give him 40 shillings and the Chitterlings into the bargain. I could repay you with the Story of my Lady F^r:, but (I doubt) you know my Sow already, especially as you dwell near Raby. however I'll venture : it may happen, you have not heard it. About two months ago Mr. Creswick (the D: of Cleveland's managing Man) received an anonymous letter as from a Lady, offering him (if he would bring about a match between her & his Lord) 3000£ to be paid after marriage out of the Estate. if he came into the proposal, a place was named, where he might speak with the Party. He carried the letter directly to the old Lady Darlington & they agreed, he should go to the Lady. he did so, and found there a Man, Agent for the Lady : but refusing to treat with any but Principals, after a little difficulty was con-

ducted to her in person, and found it was my Lady F:
(S^r Ev: F:^{s} fine young Widow). what passed between
them, I know not : but that very night she was at
Lady Darl:$^{n's}$ Assembly (as she had used to be) and
no notice taken. the next morning she received a card
to say, Lady D: had not expected to see her, *after what
had passed :* otherwise she would have ordered her
Porter not to let her in. the whole affair was immediately told to every body. yet she has continued
going about to all public places *tête levée*, and solemnly
denying the whole to her acquaintance. since that
I hear she owns it, & says, her Children were unpro-
vided for, & desires to know, wch of her Friends would
not have done the same ? but as neither of these
expedients succeed very well, she has hired a small
house, & is going into the Country for the summer.

Here has just been a Duel between the Duke of
Bolton and Mr. Stuart (a Candidate for the County
of Hampshire at the late Election) what the quarrel
was, I do not know : but they met near Marybone,
& the D: in making a pass over-reached himself, fell
down, & hurt his knee. The other bid him get up,
but he could not. then he bid him ask his life, but he
would not. so he let him alone, and that's all. Mr.
Steuart was slightly wounded.

The old Pundles, that sat on L^d G: Sackville (for
they were all such, but two, Gen: Cholmondeley, &
Ld Albermarle) have at last hammer'd out their
sentence. he is declared disobedient, and unfit for
all military command. it is said, that 9 (out of the
15) were for death, but as two-thirds must be unani-
mous, some of them came over to the merciful side.
I do not affirm the truth of this. what he will do with
himself, nobody guesses. the poor old Duke went into
the country some time ago, & (they say) can hardly
bear the sight of anybody. the unembarrass'd countenance, the looks of sovraign contempt & superiority,
that his L^d bestow'd on his Accusers during the tryal,
were the admiration of all : but his usual Talents and
Art did not appear, in short his cause would not support

him. be that as it will, everybody blames *somebody*,
who has been out of all temper, & intractable during
the whole time. Smith (the Aid-de-Camp, and principal
Witness for L^d G:) had no sooner finish'd his evidence,
but he was forbid to mount guard, & order'd to sell
out. The Court & the Criminal went halves in the
expence of the short-hand Writer, so L^d G: has already
publish'd the Tryal, before the authentic Copy appears;
and in it are all the foolish questions, that were asked,
and the absurdities of his Judges. you may think
perhaps that he intends to go abroad, & hide his head.
au contraire, all the World visits him on his condemna-
tion. he says himself, his situation is better, than ever
it was. the Scotch have all along affected to take him
under their protection; his Wife has been daily walking
with Lady Augusta (during the tryal) in Leicester-
Gardens, and L^d B^s chariot stands at his door by the
hour.

Ld Ferrers has entertained the Town for three days.
I was not there, but Mason and Stonhewer were in
the D: of Ancaster's gallery and in the greatest danger
(wch I believe they do not yet know themselves) for
the Cell underneath them (to wch the prisoner retires)
was on fire during the tryal, & the D: of Anc^r: with
the Workmen by sawing away some timbers & other
assistance contrived to put it out without any alarm
given to the Court: several now recollect they smelt
burning & heard a noise of sawing, but no one guest
at the cause. Miss Johnson, Daughter to the murthered
Man, appeared so cool, & gave so gentle an evidence,
that at first sight every one concluded, she was bought
off: but this could do him little good. the Surgeon
and his own Servants laid open such a scene of barbarity
& long-meditated malice, as left no room for his plea
of Lunacy, nor any thought of pity in the hearers.
the oddest thing was this plea of temporary Lunacy,
and his producing two Brothers of his to prove it,
one a Clergyman (suspended for Methodism by the
B^p of London) the other a sort of Squire, that goes in
the country by the name of *Ragged & Dangerous*. he

managed the cause himself with more cleverness than
any of his Counsell, & (when found guilty) asked pardon
for his plea, & laid it upon the persuasions of his family.
Mrs Shirley (his mother) Lady Huntingdon, & others
of the relations were at Court yesterday with a petition
for mercy ; but on the 5th of May he is to be hang'd
at Tyburn.

The town are reading the K: of Prussia's poetry, (Le
Philosophe sans Souci) and I have done, like the town,
they do not seem so sick of it, as I am. It is all the
scum of Voltaire and Ld Bolingbroke, the *Crambe
recocta* of our worst Free-thinkers, toss'd up in German-
French rhyme. Tristram Shandy is still a greater
object of admiration, the Man as well as the Book.
One is invited to dinner, where he dines, a fortnight
beforehand. his portrait is done by Reynolds, and
now engraving. Dodsley gives 700£ for a second
edition, & two new volumes not yet written ; & to-
morrow will come out two Volumes of Sermons by
him. Your friend, Mr. Hall has printed two Lyric
Epistles, one to my Cousin Shandy on his coming to
Town, the other to the grown gentlewomen, the Misses
of York : they seem to me to be absolute madness.
these are the best lines in them :—

> I'll tell you a story of Elijah—
> Close by a Mob of Children stood,
> Commenting on his sober mood. &c. :
> And backed them (their opinions) like such sort of folks
> With a few stones & a few jokes :
> Till, weary of their pelting & their prattle,
> He order'd out his Bears to battle.
> It was delightful fun
> To see them run
> And eat up the young Cattle.

The 7th Vol of Buffon is come over : do you chuse
to have it ?

Poor Lady Cobham is at last deliver'd from a painful
life. she has given Miss Speed above 30,000£.

Mr Brown is well : I heard from him yesterday,
and think of visiting him soon. Mason & Stonhewer

are both in Town, & (if they were here) would send their best comp:^ts to you & Mrs. Wh:^n with mine. you see, I have left no room for weather : yet I have observed the birth of the spring, w^ch (tho' backward) is very beautiful at present. mind, from this day the Therm^r : goes to its old place below in the yard, & so pray let its Sister do. Mr Stillingfleet (with whom I am grown acquainted) has convinced me, it ought to do so. Adieu !

123. To Mason

London, June 7, 1760.

DEAR MASON,—First and foremost pray take notice of the paper on which I am writing to you ; it is the first that ever was made of silk rags upon the encouragement given by your Society of Arts ; and (if this were all the fruits) I think you need not regret your two guineas a-year. The colour and texture you see ; and besides I am told it will not burn (at least will not flame) like ordinary paper, so that it may be of great use for hanging rooms ; it is uncommonly tough, and, though very thin, you observe, is not transparent. Here is another sort of it, intended for the uses of drawing.

You have lately had a visit where you are that I am sure bodes no good, especially just at the time that the Dean of Canterbury and Mr. Blacowe died ; we attribute it to a miff about the garter, and some other humps and grumps that he has received. Alas ! I fear it will never do. The Condé de Fuentes was much at a loss, and had like to have made a quarrel of it, that he had nobody but the D. of N. to introduce him ; but Miss Chudleigh has appeased him with a ball.

I have sent Musæus to Mr. Fraser, scratched here and there ; and with it I desired him to inclose a bloody satire, written against no less persons than you and me by name. I concluded at first it was Mr. Pottinger, because he is your friend and my humble servant ; but then I thought he knew the world too well to call us the favourite minions of taste and of fashion, especially as to Odes, for to them his abuse is confined. So it is not Secretary Pottinger, but Mr. Colman, nephew to my Lady Bath, author of ' The Connoisseur ', a member of some [? one] of the inns of court, and a particular acquaintance of Mr. Garrick's. What have you done to him ? for I never heard his name before. He makes very tolerable fun with me, where I understand him, which is not every-where, but seems more angry with you. Lest people should not understand the humour of the thing (which indeed to do they must have our lyricisms at their fingers' ends), he writes letters in Lloyd's Evening Post to tell them who and what it was that he meant, and says that it is like to produce a great *combustion* in the literary world ; so if you have any mind to *combustle* about it well and good ; for me, I am neither so literary nor so *combustible*.

I am going into Oxfordshire for a fortnight to a place near Henley, and then to Cambridge, if that owl Fobus does not hinder me, who talks of going to fizzle there at the commencement.

What do you say to Lord Lyttelton, your old patron, and Mrs. Montagu, with their secondhand Dialogues of the Dead ? And then there is your friend the little black man ; he has written one supplemental dialogue, but I did not read it.

Do tell me of your health, your doings, your designs, and your golden dreams, and try to love me a little better in Yorkshire than you did in Middlesex.—For I am ever yours
                                                          T G :

124. To Wharton

[June 1760]

DEAR DOCTOR,—I heard yesterday from your old friend Mr. Field, that Mrs Wharton had brought you a Son, and as I sincerely hope this may be some addition to your happiness, I heartily congratulate you both on the occasion. another thing I rejoice in is, to know, that you not only grow reconciled to your scene, but discover beauties round you, that once were deformities. I am persuaded the whole matter is to have always something going forward. Happy they, that can create a rose-tree, or erect a honey-suckle, that can watch the brood of a Hen, or see a fleet of their own ducklings launch into the water ! It is with a sentiment of envy I speak it, who never shall have even a thatch'd roof of my own, nor gather a strawberry but in Covent-Garden. I will not believe in the *vocality* of Old-Park till next summer, when perhaps I may trust my own ears.

I remain (bating some few little excursions, that I have made) still in Town, though for these three weeks I have been going into Oxfordshire with Madam Speed ; but her affairs, as she says, or her vagaries, as I say, have obliged her to alter her mind ten times within that space : no wonder, for she has got at least 30,000£ with a house in Town, plate, jewels, china, and old-japan infinite, so that indeed it would be ridiculous for her to know her own mind. I, who know mine, do intend to go to Cambridge, but that Owl Fobus is going thither to the commencement, so that I am forced to stay till his Nonsense is at an end. Chapman you see is dead at last, wch signifies not much, I take it, to any body, for his family (they say) are left in good circumstances. I am neither sorry, nor glad, for M: (I doubt) will scarce succeed to his Prebend. The old Creature is down at Aston, where my Lord has paid him a visit lately, as the Town says, in *a miff*, about the garter, and other *Trumps*, he has met with of late. I believe, this at least is certain, that he has deserted his old attachments, & worships another idol, who receives his incense with a good deal of coldness and negligence.

I can tell you but little of St Germain. He saw Monsieur D'Affry at the Hague, who, in a day or two (on receiving a Courier from his own Court) ask'd the State's leave to apprehend him, but he was gone, & arrived safe in St Mary Ax, where he had lodgings

(I fancy) at his old Friend La-Cour's, the Jew-Physician.
after some days a Messenger took charge of him, & he
was examined (I believe), before Mr Pitt. They however dismissed him, but with orders to leave England
directly, yet I know care was taken, that he should
be furnish'd with proper passports to go safe through
Holland to Hamb'rough: wch gives some room to
believe, what many at first imagined, that he was
charged with some proposal from the French Court.
he is a lively person enough to make them believe at
Paris, that he could somehow serve them on such an
occasion.

We are in great alarms about Quebec. the force in
the town was not 3000 Men, sufficient to defend the
place (naturally strong) against any attack of the
French forces, unfurnish'd as they must be for a formal
siege: but by no means to meet them in the field.
This however is what Murray has chose to do, whether
from rashness, or deceived by false intelligence, I can
not tell. the returns of our loss are undoubtedly false,
for we have above 100 officers killed or taken. all
depends upon the arrival of our garrison from Louïs-
bourg, wch was daily expected, but even that (unless
they bring provisions with them) may increase the
distress, for at the time, when we were told of the
plenty and cheapness of all things at Quebec, I am
assured, a piece of fresh meat could not be had for
20 Guineas.

If you have seen Stonhewer he has probably told
you of my old Scotch (or rather Irish) poetry. I am
gone mad about them. they are said to be translations
(literal & in prose) from the *Erse*-tongue, done by one
Macpherson, a young Clergyman in the High-lands.
he means to publish a Collection he has of these
specimens of antiquity, if it be antiquity: but what
plagues me is, I cannot come at any certainty on that
head. I was so struck, so *extasié* with their infinite
beauty, that I writ into Scotland to make a thousand
enquiries. The letters I have in return are ill-wrote,
ill-reasoned, unsatisfactory, calculated (one would

imagine) to deceive one, & yet not cunning enough
to do it cleverly. in short, the whole external evidence
would make one believe these fragments (for so he calls
them, tho' nothing can be more entire) counterfeit :
but the internal is so strong on the other side, that
I am resolved to believe them genuine, spite of the
Devil & the Kirk. It is impossible to convince me,
that they were invented by the same Man, that writes
me these letters. on the other hand it is almost as
hard to suppose, if they are original, that he should
be able to translate them so admirably. what can
one do ? since St:ʳ went, I have received another of
a very different & inferior kind (being merely descriptive) much more modern than the former (he says)
yet very old too ; this too in its way is extremely
fine. In short this Man is the very Demon of Poetry,
or he has lighted on a treasure hid for ages. the
Welch Poets are also coming to light : I have seen
a Discourse in MS. about them (by one Mr Evans,
a Clergyman) with specimens of their writings. this
is in Latin, and tho' it don't approach the other, there
are fine scraps among it.

You will think I am grown mighty poetical of a
sudden ; you would think so still more, if you knew,
there was a Satyr printed against me & Mason jointly.
it is call'd *Two Odes* : the one is inscribed to Obscurity
(that is me) the other to Oblivion. it tells me what
I never heard before, for (speaking of himself) the
Author says, tho' he has,

> Nor the Pride, nor Self-Opinion,
> That possess the happy pair,
> Each of Taste the fav'rite Minion,
> Prancing thro' the desert air :
> Yet shall he mount, with classick housings graced,
> By help mechanick of equestrian block ;
> And all unheedful of the Critick's mock
> Spur his light Courser o'er the bounds of Taste.

The writer is a Mr Coleman, who publish'd the
Connoisseur, nephew to the late Lady Bath, & a Friend
of Garrick's. I believe his Odes sell no more than

mine did, for I saw a heap of them lie in a Bookseller's window, who recommended them to me as a very pretty thing.

If I did not mention Tristram to you, it was because I thought I had done so before. There is much good fun in it, & humour sometimes hit & sometimes mist. I agree with your opinion of it, & shall see the two future volumes with pleasure. have you read his Sermons (with his own comic figure at the head of them)? they are in the style I think most proper for the pulpit, and shew a very strong imagination and a sensible heart: but you see him often tottering on the verge of laughter, & ready to throw his periwig in the face of his audience. now for my season.

April 10. I observed the Elm putting out.
    12. That, & the Pear looked green. Therm: at 62.
    13. very fine; White-Poplar & Willow put out.
    15. Standard-Pear (shelter'd) in full bloom.
    18. Lime & Horn-beam green.
    19. Swallows flying.
    20. Th: at 60. w^d S:W: Sky-Lark, Chaffinch, Thrush, Wren, & Robin singing. Horse-Chesnut, Wild-Bryar, Bramble, and Sallow had spread their leaves. Haw-thorn & Lilac had formed their blossoms. Black-thorn, double-flowered Peach, & Pears in full bloom; Double Jonquils, Hyacinths, Anemones, single Wall-flowers, & Auriculas in flower. In the fields, Dog-Violets, Daisies, Dandelion, Butter-cups, Red-Archangel, & Shepherd's Purse.
    21. Almond out of bloom, & spreading its leaves.
    26. Lilacs flow'ring.
May 1. Gentianella in flower.
    2. Pear goes off; Apple blooms. Th: at 63. W^d N:E: still fair and dry.
    3. Evening & all night hard rain.
    4. Th: at 40. W^d N:E:, rain.
    11. Very fine. W^d N:E: Horse-Chesnut in full bloom. Wallnut & Vine spread. Lilacs, Persian Jasmine, Tulips, Wall-flowers, Phea-sant-eye, Lilly in the Valley in flower. In the

<pre>
                fields, Furze, Cowslips, Harebells, and Cow-
                  Parsnip.
May 13. Jasmine and Acacia spread. fine weather.
    18. Show'ry. w^d high.
    19. Same. Therm: at 56.
    20. Thunder, Rain. . . 54.
    21. Rain. w^d N:E: 52.
    31. Green Peas 15d a Quart.
June 1. . . . . . .   at 78.
      2. Scarlet Strawberries, Duke-Cherries ; hay-
                making here.
      3. w^d S:S:E: Therm: at 84 (the highest I ever saw
                it) it was at Noon. since wch till last week we
                had hot dry weather. now it rains like mad.
                Cherries and Strawberries in bushels.
</pre>

I believe, there is no fear of War with Spain.

125. To Stonehewer

London, June 29, 1760.

Though you have had but a melancholy employ-ment, it is worthy of envy, and (I hope) will have all the success it deserves. It was the best and most natural method of cure, and such as could not have been administered by any but your gentle hand. I thank you for communicating to me what must give you so much satisfaction.

I too was reading M. D'Alembert, and (like you) am totally disappointed in his Elements. I could only taste a little of the first course : it was dry as a stick, hard as a stone, and cold as a cucumber. But then the letter to Rousseau is like himself ; and the ' Dis-courses on Elocution ', and on the ' Liberty of Music ', are divine. He has added to his translations from Tacitus ; and (what is remarkable) though that author's manner more nearly resembles the best French writers of the present age, than anything, he totally fails in the attempt. Is it his fault, or that of the language ?

I have received another Scotch packet with a third specimen, inferior in kind (because it is merely description), but yet full of nature and noble wild imagination. Five Bards pass the night at the Castle of a Chief (himself a principal Bard) ; each goes out in his turn to observe the face of things, and returns with an extempore picture of the changes he has seen ; it is an October night (the harvest-mouth of the Highlands). This is the whole plan ; yet there is a contrivance, and a preparation of ideas, that you would not expect. The oddest thing is, that every one of them sees Ghosts (more or less). The idea, that struck and surprised me most, is the following. One of them (describing a storm of wind and rain) says

> Ghosts ride on the tempest to-night :
> Sweet is their voice between the gusts of wind ;
> *Their songs are of other worlds !*

Did you never observe (*while rocking winds are piping loud*) that pause, as the gust is recollecting itself, and rising upon the ear in a shrill and plaintive note, like the swell of an Æolian harp ? I do assure you there is nothing in the world so like the voice of a spirit. Thomson had an ear sometimes : he was not deaf to this ; and has described it gloriously, but given it another different turn, and of more horror. I cannot repeat the lines : it is in his 'Winter'. There is another very fine picture in one of them. It describes the breaking of the clouds after the storm, before it is settled into a calm, and when the moon is seen by short intervals.

> The waves are tumbling on the lake,
> And lash the rocky sides.
> The boat is brim-full in the cove
> The oars on the rocking tide.
> Sad sits a maid beneath a cliff,
> And eyes the rolling stream :
> Her lover promised to come,
> She saw his boat (when it was evening) on the lake ;
> *Are these his groans in the gale ?*
> *Is this his broken boat on the shore ?*

126. To Mason

August 7, 1760, Pembroke Hall.

Dear Mason,—Your packet, being directed to me here, lay some days in expectation of my arrival (for I did not come till about ten days since); so, if the letter inclosed to Dr. Zachary Howlet were not delivered so soon as it ought to have been, you must not lay the fault to my charge.

It is a great misfortune that I dare not present your new seal to the senate in congregation assembled, as I long to do. Not only the likeness, but the character of the fowl is so strongly marked, that I should wish it were executed in marble, by way of bas-relief, on the pedestal of George the Second, which his Grace proposes soon to erect in the Theatre. Mr. Brown and I think we discover beauties which perhaps the designer never intended. There is a brave little mitred Madge already on the wing, who is flying, as it were, in the face of his parent; this, we say, is Bishop K.: then there is a second, with ingratitude in its face, though not in its attitude, that will do the same as soon as it is fledged and has the courage; this is Bishop Y.: a third, that looks mighty modest, and has two little ears sprouting, but no mitre yet, we take for Dean G.: the rest are embryos that have nothing distinguishing, and only sit and pull for a bit of mouse; they won't be prebends these five days, grace of God, and if the nest is not taken first.

Your friend Dr. Ch: died of a looseness: about a week before, he eat five large mackerel, full of roe, to his own share; but what gave the finishing stroke was a turbot, on Trinity Sunday, of which he left but very little for the company. Of the mackerel I have eyewitnesses, so the turbot may well find credit. He has left, I am told, £15,000 behind him.

The Erse Fragments have been published five weeks ago in Scotland, though I had them not (by a mistake) till last week. As you tell me new things do not soon reach you at Aston, I inclose what I can; the rest shall follow when you tell me whether you have not got it already. I send the two which I had before, for Mr. Wood, because he has not the affectation of not admiring. I continue to think them genuine, though my reasons for believing the contrary are rather stronger than ever: but I will have them antique, for I never knew a Scotchman of my own time that could read, much less write, poetry; and such poetry too! I have one (from Mr. Macpherson) which he has not printed: it is mere description, but excellent, too, in its kind. If you are good, and will learn to admire, I will transcribe it. Pray send to Sheffield for the last *Monthly Review*: there is a deal of stuff about us and Mr. Colman. It says one of us, at least, has always borne his faculties meekly. I leave you to guess which that is: I think I know. You oaf, you must be meek, must you? and see what you get by it!

I thank you for your care of the old papers: they were entirely insignificant, as you suspected.

Billy Robinson has been married near a fortnight to a Miss Richardson (of his own age, he says, and not handsome), with £10,000 in her pocket; she lived with an (unmarried) infirm brother, who (the first convoy that sails) sets out with the bride and bridegroom in his company for Naples; you see it is better to be curate of Kensington than rector of Aston.

Lord J: C: called upon me here the other day; young Ponsonby, his nephew, is to come this year to the University, and, as his Lordship (very justly) thinks that almost everything depends on the choice of a private tutor, he desires me to look out for such a thing, but without engaging him to anything. Now I am extremely unacquainted with the younger part of Cambridge, and consequently can only enquire of other people, and (what is worse) have nobody now here whose judgment I could much rely on. In my own conscience I know no one I should sooner recommend than Onley, and besides (I own) should wish to bring him to this college; yet I have scruples, first because I am afraid Onley should not answer my lord's expectations (for what he is by way of a scholar I cannot tell), and next because the young man (who is high-spirited and unruly) may chance to be more than a match for Mr. B:, with whom the authority must be lodged. I have said I would enquire, and mean (if I could) to do so without partiality to any college : but believe, after all, I shall find no better. Now I perceive you have said something to Lord J: already to the same purpose, therefore tell me what I shall do in this case. If you chance to see his lordship you need not mention it, unless he tell you himself what has passed between us.

Adieu, dear Mason, I am ever yours.

A Note.—Having made many enquiries about the authenticity of these Fragments, I have got a letter from Mr. David Hume, the historian, which is more satisfactory than anything I have yet met with on that subject : he says,—

' Certain it is that these poems are in everybody's mouth in the Highlands—have been handed down from father to son—and are of an age beyond all memory and tradition. Adam Smith, the celebrated Professor in Glasgow, told me that the piper of the Argyleshire militia repeated to him all those which Mr. Macpherson has translated, and many more of equal beauty. Major Mackay (Lord Rae's brother) told me that he remembers them perfectly well ; as likewise did the Laird of Macfarline (the greatest anti-quarian we have in this country), and who insists strongly on the historical truth, as well as the poetical beauty, of these productions. I could add the Laird and Lady Macleod, with many more that live in different parts of the Highlands, very remote from each other, and could only be acquainted with what had become (in a manner) national works. There is a country-surgeon in Lochaber, who has by heart the entire epic poem mentioned by Mr. Macpherson in his Preface, and, as he is old, is perhaps the only person living that knows it all, and has never committed it to writing. We are in the more haste to recover a monument which will certainly be regarded as a curiosity in the republic of letters. We have therefore set about a subscription of a guinea or two guineas a-piece in order to enable Mr. Macpherson to undertake a mission into the Highlands to recover this poem and other fragments of antiquity.'

I forgot to mention to you that the names of Fingal, Ossian, Oscar, etc., are still given in the Highlands to large mastiffs, as we give to ours the names of Cæsar, Pompey, Hector, etc.

127. To WHARTON

London. Oct: 21. 1760.

DEAR DOCTOR,—Don't be afraid of me: I will not come, till you tell me, I may: though I long very much to see you. I hear, you have let your hair grow, & visit none of your neighbouring gentry, two (I should think) capital crimes in that county, and indeed in all counties. I hear too (& rejoice) that you have recover'd your hearing. I have nothing equally important to tell you of myself, but that I have not had the Gout, since I saw you: yet don't let me brag; the winter is but just begun.

I have pass'd a part of the summer on a charming hill near Henley with the Thames running at my foot; but in the company of a pack of Women, that wore my spirits, tho' not their own. the rest of the season I was at Cambridge in a duller, & more congenial, situation. did I tell you, that our friend Chapman, a week before he died, eat five huge mackerel (fat and full of roe) at one dinner, wch produced an indigestion: but on Trinity-Sunday he finish'd himself with the best part of a large Turbot, wch he carried to his grave, poor Man! he never held up his head after. from Cambridge I am come hither, yet am going into Kent for a fortnight, or so. you astonish me in wondering, that my Lady C: left me nothing. for my part I wonder'd to find she had given me 20£ for a ring; as much as she gave to several of her own Nieces. The

World said before her death, that M^rs Sp: and I had shut ourselves up with her in order to make her Will, & that afterwards we were to be married.

There is a second Edition of the Scotch Fragments, yet very few admire them, & almost all take them for fictions. I have a letter from D: Hume, the Historian, that asserts them to be genuine, & cites the names of several People (that know both languages) who have heard them current in the mouths of Pipers & other illiterate persons in various & distant parts of the Highlands. there is a subscription for Mr Macpherson, wch will enable him to undertake a mission among the Mountaineers, & pick up all the scattered remnants of old poetry. he is certainly an admirable Judge ; if his *learned* Friends do not pervert or over-rule his taste.

Mason is here in Town, but so dissipated with his duties at Sion-Hill, or his attention to the Beaux Arts, that I see but little of him. the last spring (for the first time) there was an Exhibition in a public room of pictures, sculptures, engravings, &c. : sent in by all the Artists in imitation of what has been long practised at Paris. among the rest there is a Mr Sandby, who excells in Landscape, with figures, Views of Buildings, Ruins, &c : & has been much employed by the Duke, Ld Harcourt, Ld Scarborough, & others. hitherto he has dealt in wash'd Drawings & Water-Colours, but has of late only practised in oil. he (& Mason together) have cook'd up a great picture of M: Snowdon, in wch the Bard & Edward the first make their appearance ; and this is to be his *Exhibition-Picture* for next year, but (till then) it is a sort of secret.

The great Expedition takes up every body's thoughts. there is such a train of artillery on board, as never was seen before during this war. some talk of Brest, others of Rochefort. if the wind (wch is very high) does not blow it away, I do believe, it will succeed, for the French seem in a miserable way.

The Duke is well-recover'd of his paralytick attack, tho' it is still visible in his face, when he speaks. it has been occasioned by the long intermission of his usual violent exercises, for he can not ride, or walk much now on account of a dropsy confined *to a certain part*, and not dangerous in itself. yet he appears at New-Market, but in his Chaise.

Mason and Mr Brown send their best services. Dr Heberden enquires *kindly* after you, & has his good dinners as usual. Adieu, dear S^r, & present my compliments to Mrs Wharton.—I am ever

Truly Yours
TG:

128. To the Rev. James Brown

October 25, 1760.

Dear Sir,—You will wonder at another letter so soon; it is only to tell you what you will probably hear before this letter reaches you.

The King is dead. He rose this morning about six (his usual early hour) in perfect health, and had his chocolate between seven and eight. An unaccountable noise was heard in his chamber; they ran in, and found him lying on the floor. He was directly bled, and a few drops came from him, but he instantly expired.

This event happens at an unlucky time, but (I should think) will make little alteration in public measures.

I am rather glad of the alteration with regard to Chambers, for a reason which you will guess at.

My service to Pa. I will write to him soon, and long to see his manuscripts, and blue books, and precipices. Adieu.—I am yours, T. G.

129. To Mason

London, Jan. 22, 1761.

Dear Mason,—I am delighted with Frederic Hervey and letter, and envy you his friendship, for the foundation of it (I am persuaded) was pure friendship, as far as his idea of the thing extended; and if one could see his little heart one should find no vanity there for over-reaching you and artfully gilding so dirty a pile,

but only a degree of self-applause for having done one
of the genteelest and handsomest things in the world.
I long to see the originals and (if you have any gratitude) you will publish them in your first volume.
Alas! there was a time when he was my friend, and
there was a time (he owned) when he had been my
greatest enemy; why did I lose both one and the
other of these advantages, when at present I could
be so happy with either, I care not which? Tell him,
he may take his choice; it is not from interest I say
this, though I know he will some time or other be Earl
of Bristol, but purely because I have long been without
a knave and fool of my own. Here is a bishopric
(St. David's) vacant, can I anyhow serve him? I hear
Dr. Ayscough and Dean Squire are his competitors.
God knows who will go to Ireland; it ought to be
somebody, for there is a prodigious to-do there; the
cause I have been told, but, as I did not understand
or attend to it, no wonder if I forgot it; it is somewhat
about a money-bill, perhaps you may know. The
Lords Justices absolutely refuse to comply with what
the Government here do insist upon, and even offer
to resign their posts; in the mean time none of the
pensions on that establishment are paid. Nevertheless
two such pensions have been bestowed within this
few weeks, one on your friend Mrs. Anne Pitt (of 500*l.*
a year), which she asked, and Lord B. got it done
immediately; she keeps her place with it: the other
(of 400*l.*) to Lady Harry Beauclerk, whose husband
died suddenly, and left her with six or seven children
very poorly provided for; the grant was sent her
without being asked at all by herself, or any friend.
I have done with my news, because I am told that
there is an express just set out for Yorkshire, whom
you are to meet on the road. I hope you will not fail
to inform him who is to be his First Chaplain; perhaps
you will think it a piece of treachery to do so, or perhaps
you will leave the thing to itself, in order to make an
experiment.

I cannot pity you; *au contraire*, I wish I had been

at Aston when I was foolish enough to go through the six volumes of the Nouvelle Heloise. All that I can say for myself is, that I was confined at home for three weeks by a severe cold, and had nothing better to do. There is no one event in it that might not happen any day of the week (separately taken), in any private family : yet these events are so put together that the series of them are more absurd and more improbable than Amadis de Gaul. The *dramatis personœ* (as the author says) are all of them good characters ; I am sorry to hear it, for had they been all hanged at the end of the third volume nobody (I believe) would have cared. In short, I went on and on in hopes of finding some wonderful *dénouement* that would set all right, and bring something like nature and interest out of absurdity and insipidity ; no such thing, it grows worse and worse, and (if it be Rousseau, which is not doubted) is the strongest instance I ever saw that a very extraordinary man may entirely mistake his own talents. By the motto and preface it appears to be his own story, or something similar to it.

The Opera House is crowded this year like any ordinary theatre. Elisi is finer than anything that has been here in your memory, yet, as I suspect, has been finer than he is. He appears to be near forty, a little pot-bellied and thick-shouldered, otherwise no bad figure ; his action proper, and not ungraceful. We have heard nothing, since I remember operas, but eternal passages, divisions, and flights of execution ; of these he has absolutely none whether merely from judgment, or a little from age, I will not affirm. His point is expression, and to that all the graces and ornaments he inserts (which are few and short), are evidently directed. He goes higher (they say) than Farinelli, but then this celestial note you do not hear above once in a whole opera, and he falls from this altitude at once to the mellowest, softest, strongest tones (about the middle of his compass) that can be heard. The Mattei (I assure you) is much improved by his example, and by her great success this winter.

But then the Burlettas and the Paganina. I have not been so pleased with anything these many years; she too is fat and about forty, yet handsome withal, and has a face that speaks the language of all nations. She has not the invention, the fire, and the variety of action, that the Spiletta had; yet she is light, agile, ever in motion, and above all graceful; but then her voice, her ear, her taste in singing: Good God!—as Mr. Richardson the painter says. Pray ask my Lord, for I think I have seen him there once or twice, as much pleased as I was.

I have long thought of reading Jeremy Taylor, for I am persuaded that chopping logic in the pulpit, as our divines have done ever since the Revolution, is not the thing; but that imagination and warmth of expression are in their place there as much as on the stage, moderated however, and chastised a little by the purity and severity of religion.

I send you my receipt for *caviche* (Heaven knows against my conscience). Pray, doctor, will the weakness of one's appetite justify the use of provocatives? In a few years (I suppose) you will desire my receipt for tincture of cantharides? I do this the more unwillingly, because I am sensible that any man is rich enough to be an epicure when he has nobody to entertain but himself. Adieu.

I am, *à jamais*, yours.

130. To Wharton

London: Jan. 31. 1761.

MY DEAR DOCTOR,—You seem to forget me: if it were for any other reason, than that you are very busy, that is, very happy, I should not so easily pass it over.

I send you a Swedish & English Calendar. the first column is by Berger, a Disciple of Linnæus; the 2ᵈ by Mʳ Stillingfleet, the 3ᵈ (very imperfect indeed) by me. you are to observe, as you tend your plantations & take your walks, how the Spring advances in the North & whether Old-Park most resembles Upsal, or Stratton. this latter has on one side a barren black heath, on

the other a light sandy loam ; all the country about
it is a dead flat. you see, it is necessary you should
know the situation (I do not mean any reflection upon
any body's place) & this is Mr. Stillingfleet's descrip-
tion of his Friend Mr Marsham's Seat, to wch in summer
he retires, & botanises. I have lately made an acquaint-
ance with this Philosopher, who lives in a garret here
in the winter, that he may support some near relations,
who depend upon him. he is always employ'd, and
always chearful, and seems to me a very worthy honest
Man. His present scheme is to send some Persons
properly qualified to reside a year or two in Attica
to make themselves acquainted with the climate,
productions, & natural history of the country, that
we may understand Aristotle & Theophrastus, &c:
who have been heathen-Greek to us for so many ages.
this he has got proposed to Ld Bute, who is no unlikely
person to put it in execution, being himself a Botanist,
and having now in the press a new System of Botany
of his own writing in several volumes, the profits of
which he gives to Dr Hill (the Inspector) who has got
the place of Master-Gardiner at Kensington, reckon'd
worth near 2000£ a-year. there is an odd thing for you !

One hears nothing of the K: ; but what gives one
the best opinion of him imaginable : I hope, it may
hold. the R:F: run loose about the world, & people
do not know how to treat them, nor they how to be
treated. they visit and are visited : some come to the
Street-door to receive them, & that, they say, is too
much : other to the head of the stairs, & that they
think too little. no body sits down with them, not
even in their own house, unless at a card-table, so
the world are like to grow very weary of the honour.
None but the D: of Y: enjoy themselves (you know, he
always did) but the world seems weary of this honour
too, for a different reason. I have just heard no bad
story of him. when he was at Southampton in the
summer, there was a Clergyman in the neighbourhood
with two very handsome daughters. he had soon wind
of them, and drop'd in for some reason or other, came

again & again, and grew familiar enough to eat a bone of their mutton. at last he said to the father, Miss—— leads a mighty confined life here always at home, why can't you let one of them go, and take an airing now and then with me in my chaise ? Ah ! S^r (says the Parson) do but look at them, a couple of hale fresh-coloured hearty Wenches ! they need no airing, they are well enough ; but there is their Mother, poor Woman, has been in a declining way many years. if your R: H: would give her an airing now & then, it would be doing us a great kindness indeed !

You see, old Wortley-Montague is dead at last at 83. it was not mere avarice, & its companion, absti-nence, that kept him alive so long. he every day drank (I think it was) half a pint of Tokay, wch he imported himself from Hungary in greater quantity than he could use, and sold the Overplus for any price he chose to set upon it. he has left better than half a million of money : to Lady Mary 1200£ a-year, in case she gives up her pretensions to dowry ; and if not, it comes to his Son. to the same son 1000£ per an: for life only, & after him to his Daughter, Lady Bute. (now this son is about 80,000£ in debt) to all Lady Bute's children, which are eleven, 2000£ a-piece. *all the remainder* to Lady Bute, & after her to her second Son, who takes the name of Wortley, & (if he fail) to the next in order ; & after all these & their children to Ld Sandwich, to whom *in-present* he leaves some old Manuscripts. now I must tell you a story of Lady Mary. as she was on her travels, she had occasion to go somewhere by sea, & (to save charges) got a passage on Board a Man of War : the ship was (I think) Commodore Barnet's. when he had landed her, she told him, she knew she was not to offer to pay for her passage, but in con-sideration of his many civilities intreated him to wear a ring for her sake, and press'd him to accept it, wch he did. it was an emerald of remarkable size and beauty. some time after, as he wore it, some Friend was admiring it, & asking how he came by it. when he heard from whom it came, he laugh'd & desired him to

shew it to a Jeweller, whom he knew. the man was sent
for: he unset it; it was a paste not worth 40 shillings.

The Ministry are much out of joint. M^r P: much
out of humour, his popularity tottering, chiefly
occasion'd by a Pamphlet against the German War,
written by that *squeaking* acquaintance of ours, Mr.
Mauduit: it has had a vast run. The Irish are very intractable, even the L^ds J:^s themselves; great difficulties
about who shall be sent over to tame them: my L^d H:^ss
again named, but (I am told) has refused it. everybody
waits for a new Parliament to settle their ideas.

I have had no gout, since you went: I will not
brag, lest it return with redoubled violence. I am very
foolish, & do nothing to mark, that I ever was: I am
going to C:^ge to take the *fresh air* this fine winter for
a month or so. we have had snow one day this winter,
but it did not lie: it was several months ago. The
18th of Jan: I took a walk to *Kentish-Town*, wind
N: W., bright & frosty. Therm: at Noon was at 42. the
grass remarkably green and flourishing. I observed, on
dry banks facing the south that Chickweed, Dandelion,
Groundsel, Red Archangel, & Shepherd's Purse were
beginning to flower. this is all I know of the Country.

My best compliments to Mrs Wharton. I hear her
butter is the best in the Bishoprick, and that even
Deborah has learn'd to spin. I rejoice you are all in
health, but why are you deaf: & blind too, or you
could not vote for F: V:! I have abundance more to
say, but my paper won't hear of it. Adieu!

1755

	UPSAL IN SWEDEN, lat. 59° 51½"	STRATTON IN NORFOLK, lat. 52° 45'	CAMBRIDGE
Hasel begins to f.	12 April	23 Jan.	——
Snow-drop F. .	13 April	26 Jan.	4 Feb.
(White Wagtail) appears	13 April	12 Feb.	3 Feb.
Violets F.	3 May	28 Mar.	28 Mar.
Snow-drop goes off			——
Apricot f.		1 April	——

	UPSAL IN SWEDEN, lat. 59° 51½"	STRATTON IN NORFOLK, lat. 52° 45"	CAMBRIDGE
Elm F.	8 May	1 April	——
(Swallow returns)	9 May	6 April	——
(Cuckoo heard)	12 May	17 April	——
(Nightingale sings)	15 May	9 April	——
Birch L.	13 May	1 April	——
Alder L.	14 May	7 April	——
Bramble L.	7 May	3 April	——
Elm L.	15 May	10 April	16 April
Hawthorn L.	15 May	.	10 April
Acacia L.	15 May	12 April	——
Lime L.	21 May	12 April	16 April
Aspen L.	20 May	26 April	——
Sycamore L.	.	13 April	——
White Poplar L.	.	17 April	——
Beech L.	.	21 April	——
Chestnut & Maple L.	.	18 April	18 April
Oak L.	20 May	18 April	18 April
Ash L.	21 May	22 April	——
Fig L.	.	21 April	24 April
Horse Chestnut F.	.	12 May	12 May
Mulberry L.	.	14 May	——
Crab & Apple f.	2 June	23 April	22 April
Cherry f.	28 May	18 April	17 April
Lilac f.	8 June	27 April	24 April
Hawthorn f.	17 June	10 May	12 May
Plumb tree f.	28 May	16 April	——
Lilly of yᵉ Valley F.	30 May	3 May	——
Broom F.	.	24 April	——
Mulberry L.	.	14 May	——
Elder f.	29 June	25 April	——
Lady-Smock f.	28 May	18 April	——
Pea & Bean f.	.	29 April	——
Strawberries ripe	26 June	9 July	16 June
Cherries	7 July	(on Walls)	25 June
Currants	9 July	30 June	4 July
Hay cut	7 July	(near Lond:)	18 May
Rye	4 Aug.	(at Stoke)	19 June
Wheat	.	21 Aug. (latest)	15 Sept.
Barley	16 Aug.	3 Aug.	4 Sept.
(Cuckoo silent)	15 July	end of July	

	UPSAL IN SWEDEN, lat. 59° 51½″	STRATTON IN NORFOLK, lat. 52° 45″	CAMBRIDGE
(Swallow gone) .	17 Sept.	. 21 Sept.	. 28 Sept.
Birch, Elm, Syco- more, Lime, change colour	} 22 Sept.	. 14 Sept.	——
Ash drops its leaves	6 Octob:	. 9 Octob:	. 5 Oct.
Elm stripped . .	7 Octob:	. . .	——
Lime falls .	12 Octob:	. . .	——
Hasel stripped .	17 Octob:	. . .	——

N.B.—*l:* stands for *opening its leaves, L.* for *in full leaf.*
f: for beginning to flower, *F:* for full bloom.
the summer flowers, especially such as blow about the
solstice, I take no notice of, as they blow at the same time
in Sweden and in England, at least the difference is only
a day or two.

Observe, from this calendar it appears, that there
is a wonderful difference between the earlier Phæno-
mena of the Spring in Sweden & in England, no less
than 78 days in the flowering of the Snow-Drop, 61
days in the appearance of the Wagtail, 62 days in the
bloom of the Lilac, 43 days in the leafing of the Oak,
40 days in the blooming of the Cherry-tree, 36 days
in the singing of the Nightingale, 33 in the return of
the Swallow, 25 in that of the Cuckow, & so on. yet
the summer flowers nearly keep time alike in both
climates, the Harvest differs not a fortnight, some of
the Fruits only 9 days ; nay, strawberries come earlier
there by 13 days, than with us. The Swallow stays
with us only 4 days longer than with them, and the
Ashtree begins to lose its leaves within 3 days of the
same time. these differences, & these uniformities
I know not how to account for.

Mr Stillingfleet's Kalendar goes no farther than Oct:
26 ; but I observed, that, on Dec: 2, many of our Rose
trees had put out new leaves, and the Laurustine,
Polyanthus, single yellow, & bloody Wall flowers,
Cytisus, and scarlet Geraniums were still in flower.

Jan: 15. 1756, the Honeysuckles were in leaf, and
single Hepatica & Snowdrop in flower.

As to the noise of Birds, M^r St: marks their times thus in Norfolk.

4 Feb:	Woodlark singing.
12 D°	Rooks pair.
16 Feb:	Thrush sings.
D°	Chaffinch sings.
22 D°	Partridges pair.
2 March.	Rooks build.
5 D°	Ring Dove cooes.
14 April.	Bittern bumps.
16 D°	Redstart returns.
28 D°	Blackcap sings.
D°	Whitethroat seen.
5 June	Goatsucker (or Fern-Owl), heard in the evening. After the end of June most birds are silent for a time, probably the moulting-season; only the Goldfinch, Yellow Hammer, & Crested Wren are heard to chirp.
7 Aug:	Nuthatch chatters.
14 D°	Stone Curlew whistles at night.
15 D°	Young Owls heard in the evening.
17 D°	Goatsucker no longer heard.
26 D°	Robins singing.
16 Sept:	Chaffinch chirping.
25 D°	Woodlark sings, and Fieldfares arrive.
27 D°	Black-bird sings.
29 Aug.	Thrush sings.
2 Octob:	Royston-Crow comes.
10 D°	Woodlark in full song.
D°	Ringdove cooes.
22 D°	Woodcock returns.
24 D°	Skylark sings.

I add the order of several fruits ripening at Stoke, that year.

Hautboy-Strawberry	25 June.
Wall Duke Cherry	D°
Early Apricot	D°
Black-heart Cherry	2 July
Raspberry	4 D°
Gooseberry	15 D°
Masculine Apricot	D°
Black Fig	30 D°

Muscle					
Orleans	} Plumb }	.	.	.	18 Aug.
Green Gage					
Filbert		.	.	.	,,
Nectarine					
Newingt: Peach	}	.	.	.	4 Sept:
Morella Cherry					
Mulberry	}	.	.	.	18 D°
Walnut					
Melon					
Burgamot-Pear	}	.	.	.	25 D°
Black Muscadine Grape					
Nectarine over		.	.	.	4 Sept:
White Muscad: Grape		.	.	.	12 Oct:

131. To the Rev. James Brown

London. February 9. 1761.

DEAR S^r,—If I have not sooner made answer to your kind enquiries, it has been owing to the uncertainty I was under as to my own motions. now at last, I perceive, I must stay here till March and part of April are over, so I have accommodated myself to it, and perhaps it may be better to come, when your codlin hedge is in bloom than at this dull season. my cold, which Mr. Bickham told you of, kept me at home above three weeks, being at first accompanied with a slight fever: but at present I am marvellous: not a word of the gout yet; but don't say a word; if you do, it will come. a fortnight ago I had two sheets from Mr. Pitt dated Genoa, Dec: 23; he had been thirty days in going from Barcelona thither, a passage often made in four; he spends the winter with Sr Richard Lyttelton, and hopes to pass the end of the Carnaval at Milan with Lord Strathmore, who has been ill at Turin, but is now quite recover'd. He does not speak with transport of Andalusia (I mean of the Country, for he describes only that in generall, and refers for particulars to our meeting); it wants verdure, & wood, and hands to cultivate it: but Valencia and Murcia (he says) are one continued garden, a shady scene of

cultivated lands, interspersed with cottages of reed,
and water'd by a thousand artificial rills. a like spirit
of industry appears in Catalonia. he has written to
Pa: also, I suppose, to the same purpose.

The only remarkable thing I have to tell you is old
Wortley's Will, and that perhaps you know already.
he died worth 600,000£. this is the least I have heard,
and perhaps the truest ; but Lord J : and Mr Montagu
tell me to-day, it is above a Million, & that he had
near 800,000£ in Mortgages only. He gives to his
Son (who is 50,000£ in debt) 1000£ a year for life only.
to his Wife, Lady Mary, (if she does not claim her
dower) 1200£ a year : otherwise this to go to his son
for life, and after him to Lady Bute, his Daughter.
To all Lady Bute's Children, wch are eleven, 2000£
a-piece. to Lady Bute for her life *all the remainder*
(no notice of my Lord) and after her to her second
Son, who takes the name of Wortley, and so to all
the Sons, & (I believe) Daughters too in their order,
& if they all die without issue, to Ld Sandwich, to
whom at present he gives some old Manuscripts about
the Montagu family.

And now I must tell you a little story about Lady Mary
wch I heard lately. upon her travels (to save charges),
she got a passage in the Mediterranean, on board a
Man of War, I think it was Commodore Barnet. when
he had landed him safe she told him, she knew she was
not to offer him money, but intreated him to accept
of a ring in memory of her, w^{ch} (as she pressed him)
he accepted : it was a very large emerald. some time
after, a friend of his taking notice of its beauty, he told
him, how he came by it : the Man smiled, & desired
him to shew it to a Jeweller. he did so ; it was unset
before him, and proved a Paste worth 40 Shillings.

And now I am telling stories, I will tell you another
nothing at all to the purpose, nor relating to anybody
I have been talking of.

In the year 1688 my Lord Peterborough had a great
mind to be well with Lady Sandwich (Mrs. Bonfoy's
old friend). there was a Woman, who kept a great

Coffee-house in Pall-Mall, & she had a miraculous
Canary-Bird, that piped twenty tunes. Lady S: was
fond of such things, had heard of, & seen the bird.
Lord P: came to the Woman, and offered her a large
sum of money for it ; but she was rich, & proud of it,
and would not part with it for love or money. however
he watch'd the bird narrowly, observed all its marks
and features, went and bought just such another,
sauntered into the Coffee-room, took his oportunity
when no one was by, slipped the wrong bird into the
cage, & the right into his pocket, & went off undiscover'd to make my L^y Sandwich happy. this was
just about the time of the Revolution ; & a good while
after, going into the same Coffee-house again he saw
his bird there, & said, well, I reckon, you would give
your ears now, that you had taken my money. money !
(says the Woman) no, nor ten times that money now ;
dear little Creature ; for, if your L^p will believe me
(as I am a Christian it is true,) it has moped & moped,
and never once opened its pretty lips, since the day
that the *poor king* went away !

Adieu, Old Pa: (spite of his misfortunes) talks of
coming to Town this spring : could not you come too ?
My service to Mr Lyon.

132. To Wharton

Dear Doctor,—When I received your letter I was
still detained in Town : but am now at last got to
Cambridge. I applied immediately to Dr Ashton
(who was nearest at hand) for information as to the
expenses of Eton without naming any one's name.
He returned me the *civilest* of answers, & that if the
boy was to be on the foundation, I had no more to
do but send him to him, and the business should be
done. as to the charges, he was going to Eton, &
would send me an account from thence ; wch he did
accordingly on Sunday last, & here it is enclosed with
his second letter. You will easily conceive, that there
must be additional expences, that can be reduced to

no rules, as pocket-money, cloths, books, &c : & wch are left to a Father's own discretion.

My notion is, that your Nephew being an only Son, & rather of a delicate constitution, ought not to be exposed to the hardships of the College. I know, that the expence in that way is much lessen'd ; but your Brother has but one Son, & can afford to breed him an Oppidant. I know, that a Colleger is sooner form'd to scuffle in the world, that is, by drubbing & tyranny is made more hardy or more cunning, but these in my eyes are no such desirable acquisitions : I know too, that a certain (or very probable) provision for life is a thing to be wish'd : but you must remember, what a thing a fellow of King's is. in short you will judge for yourselves. if you accept my *good Friend's* offer, I will proceed accordingly : if not, we will thank him, & willingly let him recommend to us a cheap boarding-house, not disdaining his protection & encouragement, if it can be of any little use to your Nephew. He has married one of Amyand's Sisters with 12,000£: (I suppose you know her ; she is an enchanting object !), and he is settled in the Preachership of Lincolns-Inn.

Sure Mr Jon: or some one has told you, how your *good Friend*, Mr. L: has been horsewhip'd, trampled, bruised, and p——d upon, by a Mrs Mackenzie, a sturdy Scotch Woman. it was done in an Inn-yard at Hampstead in the face of day, & he has put her in the Crown-Office. it is very true. I will not delay this letter to tell you any more stories. Adieu ! I am ever

Yours
T: G:

Pembroke-Hall June 23 1761.

Mr. Brown (the *petit bon-homme*) joins his compliments to mine, & presents them to you and Mrs. Wharton.

I have been dreadfully disappointed in Rousseau's Heloïse : but Mason admires it.

133. To Mason

August 1761.

DEAR MASON,—Be assured your York canon never will die, so the better the thing is in value the worse for you. The true way to immortality is to get you nominated one's successor. Age and diseases vanish at your name, fevers turn to radical heat, and fistulas to issues. It is a judgment that waits on your insatiable avarice. You could not let the poor old man die at his ease when he was about it; and all his family, I suppose, are cursing you for it.

I should think your motions, if you are not perverse, might be so contrived as to bring you hither for a week or two in your way to the Coronation, and then we may go together to town, where I must be early in September. Do, and then I will help you to write a . . . sermon on this happy occasion. Our friend Jeremy Bickham is going off to a living (better than £400 a-year) somewhere in the neighbourhood of Mr. Hurd; and his old flame, that he has nursed so many years, goes with him. I tell you this to make you pine.

I wrote to Lord John on his recovery, and he answers me very chearfully, as if his illness had been but slight, and the pleurisy were no more than a hole in one's stocking. He got it, he says, not by scampering, and racketing, and heating his blood, as I had supposed, but by going with ladies to Vauxhall. He is the picture (and pray so tell him if you see him) of an old alderman that I knew, who, after living forty years on the fat of the land (not milk and honey, but arrack-punch and venison), and losing his great toe with a mortification, said to the last that he owed it to two grapes which he ate one day after dinner. He felt them lie cold at his stomach the minute they were down.

Mr. Montagu (as I guess at your instigation) has earnestly desired me to write some lines to be put on a monument, which he means to erect at Belleisle. It is a task I do not love, knowing Sir W. Williams so slightly as I did; but he is so friendly a person, and his affliction seemed to me so real, that I could not refuse him. I have sent him the following verses, which I neither like myself, nor will he, I doubt: however, I have showed him that I wished to oblige him. Tell me your real opinion :—

> Here foremost in the dang'rous paths of fame,
>   Young Williams fought for England's fair renown ;
> His mind each muse, each grace adorn'd his frame,
>   Nor envy dared to view him with a frown.
> At Aix uncall'd his maiden sword he drew,
>   There first in blood his infant glory seal'd ;
> From fortune, pleasure, science, love, he flew,
>   And scorn'd repose when Britain took the field.
> With eyes of flame and cool intrepid breast,
>   Victor he stood on Belleisle's rocky steeps ;
> Ah gallant youth ! this marble tells the rest,
>   Where melancholy friendship bends and weeps.

Three words below to say who set up the monument.

134. To the Rev. James Brown

London, September 24, 1761.

DEAR SIR,—I set out at half an hour past four in the morning for the Coronation, and (in the midst of perils and dangers) arrived very safe at my Lord Chamberlain's box in Westminster Hall. It was on the left hand of the throne, over that appropriated to the foreign ministers. Opposite to us was the box of the Earl Marshal and other great officers ; and below it that of the princess and younger part of the royal family. Next them was the royal side-board. Then below the steps of the *haut pas* were the tables of the nobility, on each side quite to the door ; behind them boxes for the sideboards ; over these other galleries for the peers' tickets ; and still higher the boxes of the Auditor, the Board of Green Cloth, etc. All these thronged with people head above head, all dressed ; and the women with their jewels on. In front of the throne was a *triomphe* of foliage and flowers resembling nature, placed on the royal table, and rising as high as the canopy itself. The several bodies that were to form the procession issued from behind the throne gradually and in order, and, proceeding down the steps, were ranged on either side of hall. All the privy councillors that are commoners (I think) were there, except Mr. Pitt, mightily dressed in rich stuffs of gold and colours, with long flowing wigs, some of them comical figures enough. The Knights of the Bath, with their high plumage, were very ornamental. Of the Scotch peers or peeresses that you see in the list very few walked, and of the English dowagers as few, though many of them were in town, and among the spectators. The noblest and most graceful figures among the ladies were the Marchioness of Kildare (as Viscountess Leinster), Viscountess Spencer, Countesses of Harrington, Pembroke, and Strafford, and the Duchess of Richmond. Of the older sort (for there is a grace that belongs to age too), the Countess of Westmoreland, Countess of Albemarle, and Duchess of Queensberry. I should mention too the odd and extraordinary appearances. They were the Viscountess Say and Sele, Countesses of Portsmouth and another that I do not name, because she is said to be an extraordinary good woman, Countess of Harcourt, and Duchess of St. Albans. Of the men doubtless the noblest and most striking figure was the Earl of Errol, and after him the Dukes of Ancaster, Richmond, Marlborough, Kingston, Earl of Northampton, Pomfret, Viscount Weymouth, etc. The men were—the Earl Talbot (most in sight of anybody), Earls of Delaware and Macclesfield, Lords Montford and Melcombe ; all these I beheld at great leisure. Then the princess and royal family entered their box. The Queen and then the King took their places in their chairs of state, glittering with jewels, for the hire of which, beside all his own, he paid £9000 ; and the dean and chapter (who had been waiting without doors a full hour and half) brought up the regalia, which the Duke of Ancaster received and placed on the table. Here ensued great confusion in the delivering them out to the lords who were appointed to bear them; the heralds were stupid; the great officers knew nothing of what they were doing. The Bishop of Rochester would have dropped the crown if it had not been pinned to the cushion, and the king was often obliged to call out, and set matters right; but the sword of state had been entirely forgot, so Lord Huntingdon was forced to carry the lord mayor's great two-handed sword instead of it. This made it later than ordinary before they got under their canopies and set forward. I should have told you that the old Bishop of Lincoln, with his stick, went doddling by the side of the Queen, and the Bishop of Chester had the pleasure of bearing the gold paten. When they were gone, we went down to dinner, for there were three rooms below, where the Duke of Devonshire was so good as to feed us with great cold sirloins of beef, legs of mutton, fillets of veal, and other substantial viands and liquors, which we devoured all higgledy-piggledy, like porters; after which every one scrambled up again, and seated themselves. The tables were now spread, the cold viands eat, and on the king's table and sideboard a great show of gold plate, and a dessert representing Parnassus, with abundance of figures of Muses, Arts, etc., designed by Lord Talbot. This was so high that those at the end of the hall could see neither king nor queen at supper. When they returned it was so dark that the people without doors scarce saw anything of the procession, and as the hall had then no other light than two long ranges of candles at each of the peers' tables, we saw almost as little as they, only one perceived the lords and ladies sidling in and taking their places to dine; but the instant the queen's canopy entered, fire was given to all the lustres at once by trains of prepared flax, that reached from one to the other. To me it seemed an interval of not half a minute before the whole was in a blaze of splendour. It is true that for that half minute it rained fire upon the heads of all the spectators (the flax falling in large flakes); and the ladies, Queen and all, were in no small terror, but no mischief ensued. It was out as soon as it fell, and the most magnificent spectacle I ever beheld remained. The King (bowing to the lords as he passed) with his crown on his head, and the sceptre and orb in his hands, took his place with great majesty and grace. So did the Queen, with her crown, sceptre, and rod. Then supper was served in gold plate. The Earl Talbot, Duke of Bedford, and Earl of Effingham, in their robes, all three on horseback, prancing and curveting like the hobby-horses in the Rehearsal, ushered in the courses to the foot of the haut-pas. Between the courses the Champion performed his part with applause. The Earl of Denbigh carved for the King, the Earl of Holdernesse for the Queen. They both eat like farmers. At the board's end, on the right, supped the Dukes of York and Cumberland; on the left Lady Augusta; all of them very rich in jewels. The maple cups, the wafers, the faulcons, etc., were brought up and presented in form; three persons were knighted; and before ten the King and Queen retired. Then I got a scrap of supper, and at one o'clock I walked home. So much for the spectacle, which in magnificence surpassed everything I have seen. Next I must tell you that the Barons of the Cinque Ports, who by ancient right should dine at a table on the haut-pas, at the right hand of the throne, found that no provision at all had been made for them, and, representing their case to Earl Talbot, he told them, ' Gentlemen, if you speak to me as High Steward, I must tell you there was no room for you; if as Lord Talbot, I am ready to give you satisfaction in any way you think fit.' They are several of them gentlemen of the best families; so this has bred ill blood. In the next place, the City of London found they had no table neither; but Beckford bullied my Lord High Steward till he was forced to give them that intended for the Knights of the Bath, and instead of it they dined at the entertainment prepared for the great officers. Thirdly. Bussy was not at the ceremony. He is just setting out for France. Spain has supplied them with money, and is picking a quarrel with us about the fishery and the logwood. Mr. Pitt says so much the better, and was for recalling Lord Bristol directly; however, a flat denial has been *returned* to their pretensions. When you have read this send it to Pa[lgrave].

135. To Wharton

Pemb: Coll: Jan: 1761 [2].

DEAR DOCTOR,—The best piece of news I have to send you is, that Mason is Residentiary of York, wch is worth near 200£ a year: he owes it to our friend M^r F: Montagu, who is Brother-in-Law to Dean Fountayne. the Precentorship (worth as much more) being vacant at the same time, L^d H: has obtain'd that too for him: but for this he must come and kiss hands; & as the ceremony is not yet over, we do not proclaim it aloud for the present. he now (I think) may wait for Mr Hutton's exit with great patience, and shut his insatiable repining mouth. I hope to see him here in his way to Town.

I pity your Brother, & have little hope left of his Wife's recovery: tho' I have been told that Dr Lowth's, after she had continued for some years in that condition, was perfectly restored. it may be worth while to enquire in what method she was treated. the papers were to have been sent to Boswel-Court the week after I left London to be seen before they were pack'd up. Mr Jonathan is perhaps unable to attend to it, but doubtless you have order'd somebody to hasten Bromwich, & see that the sorts are right. I shall not be at London till the middle of March. My old Friend Miss Speed has done what the World calls a very foolish thing. she has married the Baron de la Peyriere, Son to the Sardinian Minister, the Comte de Viry. He is about 28 years old (ten years younger than herself) but looks nearer 40. this is not the effect of debauchery, for he is a very sober Man; good natured & honest, & no Conjurer. the estate of the family is about 4000£ a-year. The Castle of Viry is in Savoy a

few miles from Geneva, commanding a fine view of
the Lake. what she has done with her money, I know
not: but (I suspect) kept it to herself. her religion
she need not change, but she must never expect to be
well-received at that Court, till she does; & I do not
think she will make quite a *Julie* in the country.

The Heloïse cruelly disappointed me, but it has its
Partisans, among wch are Mason and Mr Hurd. for
me, I admire nothing but Fingal (I conclude, you have
read it; if not, Stonhewer can lend it you), yet I remain
still in doubt about the authenticity of those
poems, though inclining rather to believe them genuine
in spite of the World. whether they are the inventions
of antiquity, or of a modern Scotchman, either case
is to me alike unaccountable. je m'y pers.

I take no joy in the Spanish War, being too old to
privateer, & too poor to buy stock; nor do I hope
for a good end of any war, as it will be now probably
conducted. oh that foolishest of Great Men, that
sold his inestimable diamond for a paltry peerage &
pension: the very night it happen'd was I swearing,
that it was a damn'd lie, & never could be: but it was
for want of reading Thomas a Kempis, who knew
mankind so much better, than I.

Young Pitt (whom I believe you have heard me
mention) is return'd to England: from him I hope to
get much information concerning Spain, which nobody
has seen: he is no bad Observer. I saw a man yesterday, who has been atop of M: Ætna, and seen the ruins
of a temple at Agrigentum, whose Columns (when
standing) were 96 feet in height: a moderate Man
might hide himself in one of the flutings. by the way
there is a Mr Phelps (now gone secretary with the
Embassy to Turin) who has been all over Sicily, &
means to give us an account of its remains. there are
two more volumes of Buffon (the 9th & 10th) arrived
in England; & the two last Maps of D'anville's Europe.
One Mr Needham, tutor to a Ld Gormanstown now on
his travels, has made a strange discovery. he saw
a figure of Isis at Turin, on whose back was a pilaster

of antique characters, not hieroglyphicks, but such as are sometimes seen on Egyptian statues. when he came to Rome, in the Vatican Library he was shew'd a Glossary of the ancient Chinese tongue. he was struck with the similitude of the characters, & on comparing them with an exact copy he had of the inscription, found that he could read it, and that it signified, This Statue of Isis is copied from another, in such a City : the original is so many measures in height, & so many in breadth. if this be true, it may open many new things to us. Deguignes some time ago wrote a dissertation to prove, that China was peopled from Egypt.

I still flatter myself with the notion of seeing you in Summer ; but God knows, how it will be. I am persuading Mr Brown to make a visit to Lady Strathmore (who has often invited him) & then you will see him too : he is at present not very well, having something of the Sciatica, which hangs about him. present my best services to Mrs Wharton, I am ever

Truly Yours
T G:

P:S: the Q: is said here to be ill, & to spit blood : she is not with child, I am afraid.

136. GRAY TO WALPOLE

Sunday, February 28, 1762.

I return you my best thanks for the copy of your book, which you sent me, and have not at all lessened my opinion of it since I read it in print, though the press has in general a bad effect on the complection of one's works. The engravings look, as you say, better than I had expected, yet not altogether so well as I could wish. I rejoice in the good dispositions of our court, and in the propriety of their application to you : the work is a thing so much to be wished ; has so near a connection with the turn of your studies and of your curiosity ; and might find such ample materials among your hoards and in your head; that it will be a sin if you let it drop and come to nothing, or worse than nothing, for want of your assistance. The historical part should be in the manner of Henault, a mere abridgement, a series of facts selected with judgment, that may serve as a clue to lead the mind along in the midst of those ruins and scattered monuments of art, that time has spared. This would be sufficient, and better than Montfaucon's more diffuse narrative. Such a work (I have heard) Mr. Burke is now employed about, which though not intended for this purpose might be applied perhaps to this use. Then at the end of each reign should come a dissertation explanatory of the plates, and pointing out the turn of thought, the customs, ceremonials, arms, dresses, luxury, and private life, with the improvement or decline of the arts during that period. This you must do yourself, beside taking upon you the superintendence, direction, and choice of materials. As to the expense, that must be the king's own entirely, and he must give the book to foreign ministers and people of note; for it is obvious no private man can undertake such a thing without a subscription, and no gentleman will care for such an expedient; and a gentleman it should be, because he must have easy access to archives, cabinets, and collections of all sorts. I protest I do not think it impossible but they may give into such a scheme: they approve the design, they wish to encourage the arts and to be magnificent, and they have no Versailles or Herculaneum.

I hope to see you toward the end of March. If you bestow a line on me, pray tell me whether the baronne de la Peyriere is gone to her castle of Viry; and whether Fingal be discovered or shrewdly suspected to be a forgery. Adieu!

I am yours ever,

T. GRAY.

137. To Mason

Cambridge, March 17, 1762.

DEAR DOCTOR,—I send your reverence the lesson, which is pure good-nature on my part, knowing already, as I do, that you do not like it. No sooner do people feel their income increase than they want amusement. Why, what need have you of any other than to sit like a Japanese divinity with your hands folded on your fat belly, wrapped and, as it were, annihilated in the contemplation of your own *copuses* and revenues ? The pentagrapher is gone to town, so you have nothing to do but to go and multiply in your own vulgar way ; only don't fall to work and forget to say grace.

The laureate has honoured me (as a friend of yours, for I know no other reason) with his new play and his ' Charge to the Poets ' : the first very middling ; the second I am pleased with, chiefly with the sense, and sometimes with the verse and expression ; and yet the best thing he ever wrote was that ' Elegy against Friendship ' you once shewed me, where the sense was detestable ; so that you see it is not at all necessary a poet should be a good sort of man—no, not even in his writings. Bob Lloyd has published his works in a just quarto volume, containing, among other things, a Latin translation of my Elegy ; an epistle, in which is a very serious compliment to me by name, particularly on my Pindaric accomplishments ; and the very two odes you saw before, in which we were abused, and a note to say they were written in concert with his friend Mr. Colman ; so little value have poets for themselves, especially when they would make up a just volume. Mr. Delap is here, and has brought his cub to Trinity. He has picked up again purely since his misfortune, and is fat and well, all but a few bowels. He says Mrs. Pritchard spoilt his *Hecuba* with sobbing so much, and that she was really so moved that she fell in fits behind the scenes. I much like Dr. Lowth's Grammar ; it is concise, clear, and elegant. He has selected his solecisms from all the best writers of our tongue. I hear Mr. Hurd is seriously writing against Fingal, by the instigation of the devil and the bishop. Can it be true ? I have exhausted all my literary news, and I have no other. Adieu.—I am truly yours,

T. G.

Mr. Brown has got a cap, and hopes for a suitable hood. You must write a line to tell him how to send them. I go to town on Monday, but direct to me here.

138. To Wharton

Dear Doctor,—I have no other apprehension, if I should come into the North, than that of somehow incommoding you and your family ; & yet I believe, my strong inclination to see you and your Carthage will prevail over so reasonable an apprehension. as to all the inconveniences, that regard myself, & wch you are so kindly providing against, I set them at nought. however you shall know of my motions before I stir.

You are not to take this for a letter : it is a message, that I am forced to send. there is a Mr. Thomas Hornsby, an Apothecary at Durham, who makes a sort of Lozenges, said to be good in a gouty cough, and indigestions. A relation of mine, a poor girl, who is exceedingly ill, having had some of these from the Abdy-family (whose stock is nearly exhausted) fancies they do her great service. I therefore must beg you would send to Mr. Hornsby, & let him put up a quarter of a pound in as little compass as he can, & send it to the Post-Master (directed to Mrs Antrobus, Post-Mistress at Cambridge), & let him put it in the mail. the sooner this can be done the better, & you will oblige me & the patient.

I am sorry, you are forced to complain of this untoward suffocating season : but who has escaped without illness ? for me I have felt neither cold nor fever : but I have had two slight attacks of the Gout after near three years intermission : it is well, if I escape so.

Adieu, Dear Doct^r. My best services to Mrs. Wharton. I am ever truly yours,

T: GRAY.

June 4. 1762. Pemb: Hall.

I am just return'd hither from London, where I have been these two months.

139. TO JOHN CHUTE

MY DEAR S^R,—I was yesterday told, that Turner (the Professor of Modern History here) was dead in London. if it be true; I conclude it is now too late to begin asking for it: but we had (if you remember) some conversation on that Head at Twickenham; & as you have probably found some Opportunity to mention it to M^r W: since, I would gladly know his Thoughts about it. What he can do, he only can tell us: what he will do, if he can, is with me no Question. if he could find a proper channel; I certainly might ask it with as much, or more Propriety, than any one in this Place. if any thing more were done, it should be as private as possible; for if the People, who have any Sway here, could prevent it, I think they would most zealously. I am not sorry for writing you a little interested Letter: perhaps it is a Stratagem; the only one I had left, to provoke an Answer from you, & revive our—Correspondence, shall I call it? there are many particulars relating to you, that have long interested me more than twenty Matters of this Sort, but you have had no Regard for my Curiosity; & yet it is something, that deserves a better Name! I don't so much as know your Direction, or that of Mr Whithed. Adieu! I am ever

Yours

T GRAY.

140. TO WHARTON

DEAR DOCTOR,—I feel very ungrateful every day, that I continue silent, & yet I do not write to you: but now the pen is in my hand, and I am in for it. when I left you, in spite of the rain I went out of my way to Richmond, and made a shift to see the Castle, & look down upon the valley, through which the Swale winds: that was all the weather would permit. at Rippon I visited the Church, which we had neglected before, with some pleasure, and saw the Ure full to its brink & very inclinable to overflow. some faint gleams of sunshine gave me an opportunity of walking over Studley, and descending into the ruins of Fountain's Abbey, which I examined with attention. I pass'd over the ugly moor of Harrowgate, made a bow to the Queen's-Head, and got late at night to Leedes: here the rain was so perverse I could scarce see the Town, much less go to Kirkstall-Abbey, wᶜʰ was my intention; so I proceeded to Wakefield, & Wentworth Castle. here the Sun again indulged me, and open'd as beautiful a scene of rich & cultivated country, as (I am told) Yorkshire affords. the water is all artificial, but with an air of nature; much wood; a very good house in the Q: Anne style, wᶜʰ was now new-fronting in a far better taste by the present Earl; many pictures not worth a farthing, & a castle built only for a plaything on the top of the hill as a point of view, & to command a noble prospect. I went on to Sheffield, liked the situation in a valley by a pretty river's side, surrounded with charming hills: saw the handsome parish-church with the chappel & monuments of the Talbots. then I entered the Peak, a countrey beyond comparison uglier than any other I have seen in England, black, tedious, barren, & not mountainous enough to please one with its horrors. this is mitigated, since you were there, by a road like a bowling-green, which soon brought me to Chatsworth. The house has the air of a Palace, the hills rising on three of its sides shut out the view of its dreary neighbourhood, & are covered with wood to their tops: the front opens to the Derwent winding thro' the valley, which, by the art of Mʳ Brown is now always visible & full to its brim. for heretofore it could not well be seen (but in rainy seasons) from the windows. a handsome bridge is lately thrown over it, & the stables taken away, wch stood full in view between the house & the river. the prospect opens here to a wider tract of country terminated by more distant hills: this scene is yet in its infancy, the objects are thinly scatter'd, & the clumps and plantations lately made, but it promises well in time. within doors the furniture corresponds to the stateliness of the appartments, fine tapestry, marble doorcases with fruit, flowers, & foliage, excellently done by Old Cibber's Father, windows of plate glass in gilded frames, & such a profusion of Gibbons' best carving in wood, viz. Dead-Game, fish, shells, flowers, &c: as I never saw anywhere. the cielings and staircases all painted by Verrio or Laguerre, in their usual sprawling way, & no other pictures, but in one room 8 or 10 portraits, some of them very good, of James & Charles the first's time. the gardens are small, & in the French style; with water-works, particularly a grand Cascade of steps, & a *Temple d'eaux* at the head of it. from thence I went to Hardwick. one would think Mary Queen of Scots, was but just walked down into the Park with her guard for half-an-hour. her Gallery, her room of audience, her anti-chamber, with the very canopies, chair of state, footstool, Lit-de-repos, Oratory, carpets, & hangings, just as she left them. a little tatter'd indeed, but the more venerable; & all preserved with religious care, & paper'd up in winter. the park & country are just like Hertfordshire. I went by Chesterfield & Mansfield to revisit my old friend the Trent at Nottingham, where I passed 2 or 3 days, & from thence took stage-coach to London.

When I arrived there, I found Professor Turner had been dead above a fortnight, & being cocker'd and spirited up by some friends (tho' it was rather of the latest) I got my name suggested to L^d B:. you may easily imagine who undertook it, and indeed he did it with zeal. I received my answer very soon, wch was what you may easily imagine, but joined with great professions of *his desire to serve me* on any future occasion, & many more fine words, that I pass over, not out of modesty, but for another reason. so you see I have made my fortune, like S^r F^r: Wronghead. this *nothing* is a profound secret, and no one here suspects it even now: today I hear, that Delaval has got it, but we are not yet certain: next to myself I wish'd for him.

You see we have made a peace. I shall be silent about it, because if I say anything antiministerial, you will tell me, you know the reason; & if I approve it, you will tell me, I have expectations still. all I know is, that the D: of Newcastle & Ld Hardwick both say, it is an excellent Peace; & only Mr Pitt calls it inglorious and insidious.

I had a little Gout twice, while I was in Town, which confined me some time: yet I bespoke your chairs. they are what is call'd *Rout-chairs*, but as they are to be a little better in shape & materials than ordinary, will come to about 6s. 9d. a chair. I desired your Brother to judge, how he perform'd, & the first, that was made, was to be sent him to see.

My best respects attend Mrs Wharton, who I suppose, receives them in bed. how does she doe? My compliments to Miss. I am ever truly

Yours

Cambridge, Dec: 4, 1762.
Mason is in Yorkshire now, but I miss'd of him.

141. To Mason

Cambridge, December 21, 1762.

DEAR MASON,—As to my pardon, for which you supplicate, you know too well how easily it is obtained without any reason at all; but now I have a very good one, as I have read the third book of the *Ghost*, where Churchill has so mumbled Mr. Whitehead, to whom you owe all your principles (see the unpublished elegy de Amicitia), that it would be base in me to demand any farther satisfaction. This only I shall add, that I would rather steal the Laureate's verses than his sentiments.

I am sorry for the disagreeable event you mention, which I learnt by mere accident from Mr. Curtall in a coffee-house. I do not doubt it must have taken up a good deal of your thoughts and time, and should wish to know whether there are any hopes of the poor fellow's recovery.

We have received your poetical packet and delivered them to the several parties. The sentiments we do not remark, as we can find nothing within ourselves congenial to them : for the expression, we hint (but in a low, timid voice) that there is a want of strength and spirit ; in short, they are nothing like the choruses in *Elfrida*, only the lines that relate to Lady C——'s beauty have made a deep impression upon us ; we get them by heart and apply them to our sempstresses and bedmakers. this is (I think) the sum and substance of our reflections here ; only Mrs. Rutherford observes that there is great delicacy and tenderness in the manner of treating so frail a character as that of Lady C——, and that you have found a way to reconcile contempt and compassion : these might not be her words, but this was the sense of them ; I don't believe she had it from the doctor.

I rejoice (in a weakly way you may be sure, as I have not seen him some years, and am in so different a way of life), but I rejoice to hear of any accession to Mr. Hurd's fortune, as I do not believe he will be anything the worse for it. Forester (whom I perceive you can still remember) is removed from Easton to a better living by his patron Lord Maynard, on purpose to get rid of him ; for Easton is his own parish, and he was sick to death of his company. He is now seated just by his brother Pulter, and they are mortal foes.

Mr. Brockett has got old Turner's professorship, and Delaval has lost it. When we meet I have something to tell you on this subject. I hope to continue here till March ; if not, I shall inform you. How does the peace agree with you ? Adieu.—I am ever yours.

142. To the Rev. James Brown

February 17, 1763.

You will make my best acknowledgments to Mr. Howe, who not content to rank me in the number of his friends, is so polite as to make excuses for having done me that honour.

I *was not born so far from the sun* as to be ignorant of Count Algarotti's name and reputation; nor am I so far advanced in years or in philosophy, as not to feel the warmth of his approbation. The Odes in question, as their motto shews, were meant to be *vocal to the intelligent alone.* How few *they* were in my own country, Mr. Howe can testify; and yet my ambition was terminated by that small circle. I have good reason to be proud, if my voice has reached the ear and apprehension of a stranger distinguished as one of the best judges in Europe.

I am equally pleased with the just applause he bestows on Mr. Mason, and particularly on his *Caractacus,* which is the work of a Man: whereas the *Elfrida* is only that of a boy, a promising boy indeed, and of no common genius: yet this is the popular performance with us, and the other little known in comparison.

Neither Count Algarotti, nor Mr. Howe (I believe) have heard of *Ossian, the son of Fingal.* If Mr. Howe were not upon the wing, and on his way homewards, I would send it to him in Italy. He would there see, that Imagination dwelt many hundred years ago in all her pomp on the cold and barren mountains of Scotland. The truth (I believe) is that without any respect of climates she reigns in all nascent societies of men, where the necessities of life force every one to think and act much for himself. Adieu!

143. To the Rev. William Mason

1763.

Dear Mason,—As I have no more received my little thing than you have yours, though they were sent by the Beverley, Captain Allen, I have returned no answer yet ; but I must soon, and that in plain English, and so should you too. In the meantime I borrowed and read them. That on the Opera is a good clever dissertation, dedicated to Guglielmo Pitt ; the other (Il Congresso di Citera), in poetical prose, describes the negociation of three ambassadresses sent by England, France, and Italy to the Court of Cupid, to lay before him the state of his empire in the three nations ; and is not contemptible neither in its kind ; so pray be civil to the count and Signor Howe.

I think it may be time enough to send poor Smart the money you have been so kind to collect for him when he has dropped his lawsuit, which I do not doubt must go against him if he pursues it. Gordon (who lives here) knows and interests himself about him ; from him I shall probably know if he can be persuaded to drop his design. There is a Mr. Anguish in town (with whom I fancy you were once acquainted) ; he probably can best inform you of his condition and motions, for I hear he continues to be very friendly to him.

When you speak of Mr. Bedingfield, you have always a dash of gall that shows your unforgiving temper, only because it was to my great chair he made the first visit. For this cause you refused the snuff-box (which to punish you I shall accept myself), and for this cause you obstinately adhere to the Church of England.

I like your Sonnet better than most dedications ; it is simple and natural. The best line in it is :—

So, to deceive my solitary days, &c.

There are an expression or two that *break the repose of* it by looking common and overworn : ' sequestered shade,' ' woodbine sprays,' ' selected lays ; ' I dare not mention ' lettered ease.' ' Life's vain vision ' does not pronounce well. Bating these, it looks in earnest, and as if you could live at Aston, which is not true ; but that is not my affair.

I have got a mass of Pergolesi, which is all divinity ;

but it was lent me, or you should have it by all means. Send for six lessons for the pianoforte or harpsichord of Carlo Bach, not the Opera Bach, but his brother. To my fancy they are charming, and in the best Italian style. Mr. Neville and the old musicians here do not like them, but to me they speak not only music, but passion. I cannot play them, though they are not hard; yet I make a smattering that serves ' to deceive my solitary days; ' and I figure to myself that I hear you touch them triumphantly. Adieu! I should like to hear from you.

The Petit Bon sends his love to you. All the rest (but Dr. May and the master) are dead or married.

144. To Wharton

Dear Doctor,—You may well wonder at my long taciturnity: I wonder too, and know not what cause to assign, for it is certain, I think of you daily. I believe, it is owing to the nothingness of my history, for except six weeks that I passed in Town towards the end of Spring, and a little jaunt to Epsom & Box-hill, I have been here time out of mind in a place, where no events grow, tho' we preserve those of former days by way of *Hortus Siccus* in our libraries. my slumbers were disturbed the other day by an unexpected visit from Mr. W: who dined with me, seemed mighty happy for the time he stay'd, & said he could like to live here : but hurried home in the evening to his new Gallery, wch is all Gothicism, & gold, & crimson, & looking-glass. He has purchased at an auction in Suffolk ebony-chairs & old moveables enough to load a waggon.

Mason and I have received letters from Count Algarotti, Chambellan de sa Majeste le Roi de Prusse, with observations, (that is panegyrics) on our Tragedies & our Odes, and a present of certain Italian Dissertations wch he has lately publish'd on the state of Painting and Musick. one of them is dedicated to Mr. Pitt, whom he styles—*Uomo immortale, e Restitutore d' Inghilterra, Amico del gran Federigo.*

I was in town, when Mr Middleton died, & immediately got all the information I could (first from St:^r and then from your Brother) of the dispositions he had made. I suppose, they are as good as you expected, & tho' the prospect is but small, that you should enjoy the benefit of them in your own person, yet that is not impossible ; & your Son (I think) stands a very good chance, wch cannot chuse but open an agreeable prospect to you, in wch I take a part, & congratulate you both upon it. I doubt you have not read Rousseau's *Émile* : everybody that has children, should read it more than once, for tho' it abounds with his usual glorious absurdity, tho' his general scheme of education be an impracticable chimera : yet there are a thousand lights struck out, a thousand important truths better express'd than ever they were before, that may be of service to the wisest Man. particularly I think he has observed children with more attention & knows their meaning & the working of their little passions better than any other Writer. As to his religious discussions, wch have alarmed the world, and engaged their thoughts more than any other part of his book, I set them all at nought, & wish they had been omitted. Mrs Jonathan told me, you begun your evening-prayer as soon as I was gone, & that it had a great effect upon the congregation : I hope you have not grown weary of it, nor lay it aside, when company comes. poor Mrs. Bonfoy (who taught me to pray) is dead. She struggled near a week against the Iliac Passion (I fear) in great torture with all her senses about her, and with much resolution took leave of her physician some days before she expired, & would suffer no one to see her afterwards but common Servants.

You describe Winston *con tanto amore*, that I take it amiss I was not suffer'd to see it, and want to be buried there too. but enough of death ! I have forgot to tell you that Dr. Long has had an audience of the K: & Queen an hour long at Buckingham House. his errand was to present them with a Lyricord (such a one !)

of his own making, & a glass-sphere : he had long been solliciting this honour, wch Ld Bute at last procured him, & he is very happy. the K: told him, he bid fair for a century of life at least ; ask'd him, whether he preach'd ; why he did not write verses in the Cambridge collection ; & what not ? The Q. spoke French to him, & ask'd, how he liked Handel ?

And I ask you, how you like the present times ? whether you had not rather be a Printer's Devil, than a Secretary of State ? you are to expect (I hear) a new Ministry, composed of the Earl of Shelburne, Mr Rigby, Duke & Dutchess of Bedford, Earl Gower, &c., which doubtless will give universal satisfaction. the great Ld Holland, who is at Paris, being lately asked by a young Man, who was returning home, whether he had any commands in England, made no reply but by shrugging up his shoulders, & fetching a deep sigh.

I kept an exact account of Heat and Cold in the Spring here : the sum & substance of wch is, that (at 9 in the morning) on the 18th of January, the Therm: was at 31, & the small birds were so tame you might take them up with your hand. this was the greatest cold. on the 15th of April it was at 58, & the same afternoon at 65, wch was the greatest heat from Jan: 1 to May 1st.

Feb. 3. Snowdrops flower'd.
    12. Crocus & Hepatica fl: the snow then lieing, & Therm: at 45.
    18. Chaffinch sings. Bees appear.
    21. White butterfly abroad.
    25. Gnats flie. & large flies. Mezereon fl:
    27. Honeysuckle and Gooseberry unfold their leaves.
March 1. Violet flowers (in the garden). Rose opens its leaf.
    3. Daffodil & single hyacinth fl: Spider spins.
    5. Thrush singing.
    6. Elder in leaf: currant and Weeping Willow in l:
    8. Apricot blows. Sky-Lark singing.
    11. Wind very high at S:E:, wch continued with hard frost.

16. Frost gone.
18. Apricot in full bloom.
19. Almond flowers. Lilac, Barberry, & Gelder-rose in leaf.

April 2. Standard-Abricot, & Wall-Pears flower. Quince, Apple, and Sweet-briar, in leaf. Currant flowers. Dutch-Elm opens its leaf.

4. Plumb in leaf.
5. Crown Imperial fl:
6. Plumb flowers; Hawthorn, Horse-Chesnut, Mountain-Ash, in leaf.
9. Lime-tree in leaf. Jonquil & single Anemone flower. Lady-birds seen.
11. Cowslip flowers, & Auricula. Swallow appears. young Rooks caw in the nest.
14. Red-Start appears. Cherries in full bloom.
15. Frontignac Vine in leaf. Double Wall-flower blows.
16. Nightingale sings. Apple blossoms.
19. Chaffinch and Red-Start sit on their eggs.
20. Elm, Willow, and Ash, in flower (with the Black-thorn) Hawthorn in full leaf.
21. Sycomore quite green. Oak puts out.

Pray present my respects to M^{rs} & Miss Wharton. I am ever

Sincerely Yours.

Pembroke, Aug: 5, 1763.

We have nothing but rain & thunder of late.

145. To Count Algarotti
Cambridge, September 9, 1763.

Sir,—I received some time since the unexpected honour of a Letter from you, and the promise of a pleasure, which, till of late I had not the opportunity of enjoying. Forgive me if I make my acknowledg-ments in my native tongue, as I see it is perfectly familiar to you, and I (though not unacquainted with the writings of Italy) should from disuse speak its language with an ill grace, and with still more constraint to one, who possesses it in all its strength and purity.

I see with great satisfaction your efforts to reunite

the congenial arts of poetry, music and the dance, which with the assistance of painting and architecture, regulated by taste, and supported by magnificence and power, might form the noblest scene, and bestow the sublimest pleasure, that the imagination can conceive. But who shall realise these delightful visions? There is, I own, one Prince in Europe, that wants neither the will, the spirit, nor the ability: but can he call up Milton from his grave, can he re-animate Marcello, or bid the Barberina or the Sallé move again? can he (as much a king as he is) govern an Italian *Virtuosa*, destroy her caprice and impertinence, without hurting her talents, or command those unmeaning graces and tricks of voice to be silent, that have gained her the adoration of her own country?

One cause, that so long has hindered, and (I fear) will hinder that happy union, which you propose, seems to be this: that poetry (which, as you allow, must lead the way, and direct the operation of the subordinate arts) implies at least a liberal education, a degree of literature, and various knowledge, whereas the others (with a few exceptions) are in the hands of slaves and mercenaries, I mean, of people without education, who, though neither destitute of genius, nor insensible to fame, must yet make gain their principal end, and subject themselves to the prevailing taste of those, whose fortune only distinguishes them from the multitude.

I cannot help telling you, that eight or ten years ago, I was a witness to the power of your comic music. —There was a little troop of Buffi, that exhibited a Burletta in London, not in the Opera House, where the audience is chiefly of the better sort, but on one of the common Theatres full of all kinds of people and (I believe) the fuller from that natural aversion we bear to foreigners: their looks and their noise made it evident, they did not come thither to hear; and on similar occasions I have known candles lighted, broken bottles, and pen knives flung on the stage, the benches torn up, the scenes hurried into the street and set on fire. The curtain drew up, the music was of Cocchi, with a few airs of Pergolesi interspersed. The singers were (as usual) deplorable, but there was one girl (she called herself the Niccolina) with little voice and less beauty; but with the utmost justness of ear, the strongest expression of countenance, the most speaking eyes, the greatest vivacity and variety of gesture. Her first appearance instantly fixed their attention; the tumult sunk at once, or if any murmur rose, it was hushed by a general cry for silence. Her first air ravished everybody; they forgot their prejudices, they forgot, that they did not understand a word of the language; they entered into all the humour of the part, made her repeat all her songs, and continued their transports, their laughter, and applause to the end of the piece. Within these three last years the Paganini and Amici have met with almost the same applause once a week from a politer audience on the Opera stage. The truth is, the Opera itself, though supported there at a great expence for so many years, has rather maintained itself by the admiration bestowed on a few particular voices, or the borrowed taste of a few men of condition, that have learned in Italy how to admire, than by any genuine love we bear to the best Italian music: nor have we yet got any style of our own, and this I attribute in great measure to the language, which in spite of its energy, plenty, and the crowd of excellent writers this nation has produced, does yet (I am sorry to say it) retain too much of its barbarous original to adapt itself to musical composition. I by no means wish to have been born anything but an Englishman; yet I should rejoice to exchange tongues with Italy.

Why this nation has made no advances hitherto in painting and sculpture is hard to say. The fact is undeniable, and we have the vanity to apologise for ourselves, as Virgil did for the Romans, *Excudent alii*, etc. It is sure, that architecture had introduced itself in the reign of the unfortunate Charles I. and Inigo Jones has left us some few monuments of his

skill, that shew him capable of greater things. Charles
had not only a love for the beautiful arts, but some
taste in them. The confusion that soon followed,
swept away his magnificent collection ; the artists
were dispersed, or ruined, and the arts disregarded
till very lately. The young monarch now on the throne
is said to esteem and understand them. I wish he
may have the leisure to cultivate and the skill to
encourage them with due regard to merit, otherwise
it is better to neglect them. You, Sir, have pointed
out the true sources, and the best examples to your
countrymen. They have nothing to do, but to be what
they once were ; and yet perhaps it is more difficult
to restore good taste to a nation, that has degenerated,
than to introduce it in one, where as yet it has never
flourished. You are generous enough to wish, and
sanguine enough to foresee, that it shall one day
flourish in England. I too must wish, but can hardly
extend my hopes so far. It is well for us that you do
not see our public exhibitions.—But our artists are
yet in their infancy, and therefore I will not absolutely
despair.

I owe to Mr. How the honour I have of conversing
with Count Algarotti, and it seems as if I meant to
indulge myself in the opportunity : but I have done.
Sir, I will only add, that I am proud of your approbation, having no relish for any other fame than what is
conferred by the few real judges, that are so thinly
scattered over the face of the earth. I am, Sir, with
great respect, your most obliged humble Servant,

T. GRAY.

A. S. E. Il Conte Fransisco Algarotti, Ciambellan di
S. M. il Ré di Prussia, etc. etc. Italia, Bologna.

146. To WHARTON

Feb: 21. 1764.

DEAR DOCTOR,—If the ill-news be true, wᶜʰ your
last letter to Mʳ Brown makes very probable, I am
heartily sorry for the loss you have had of poor Mʳ R:

Wharton, as I am sure you cannot but feel it very sensibly in many respects.

I have indeed been very remiss in writing to you, nor can alledge any other excuse for it but the lowness of spirits, which takes from me the power of doing everything I ought: this is not altogether without cause, for ever since I went last to Town, in the beginning of November I have suffer'd a good deal from a *complaint*, wch I have often mention'd to you, and which is now grown almost constant. I have left off wine, eat less than common, have made use of the common applications in such cases, & am now taking soap: yet find no essential amendment in myself, so that I have but an uncomfortable prospect before me, even if things remain as they are: but (I own) what I apprehend, is still worse.

Mason has pass'd three weeks here with me in his way to Town. the general report was, that he was going to be married out of hand: but I find it was only a faint sort of tendency that way, that may or may not come to something of maturity just as the season of the year shall incline him. the best I can tell you of her is, that she is no fine lady, and the worst, that her fortune is not large. now you know it might have been a fine lady with no money at all. He still talks of visiting Old-Park before he is tied down to his Summer-Residence.

This silly dirty Place has had all its thoughts taken up with chusing a new High-Steward, and had not Ld Hardwick surprisingly & to the shame of the faculty recover'd by a Quack-medicine, I believe in my conscience the noble Earl of Sandwich had been chosen, tho' (let me do them the justice to say) not without a considerable opposition. His principal Agents are Dr Brook of St. John's, Mr Brocket, & Dr Long, whose old Tory notions, that had long lain by neglected & forgotten, are brought out again & furbish'd for present use, tho' rusty & out of joint, like his own Spheres and Orreries. their crests are much fallen, & countenances lengthen'd by the transactions of last week, for the Ministry on Tuesday last (after sitting till near eight in the morning) carried a small point by a majority of only 40, & on another previous division by one of 10 only ; and on Friday last (at five in the morning) there were 220 to 234, & by this the court only obtained to adjourn the debate for four months, & not to get any declaration in favour of their measures. if they hold their ground many weeks after this, I shall wonder : but the new reign has already produced many wonders. the other House I hear, will soon take in hand a book lately publish'd by some scoundrel Lawyer on the Prerogative, in which is scraped together all the flattery & blasphemy of our old Law-books in honour of Kings. I presume, it is understood, that the court will support the cause of this impudent Scribbler. there is another impudent Fellow of the same profession, but somewhat more conspicuous by his place (a Friend of yours, with whom I sup'd at your house ten or eleven years ago) that has gain'd to himself the most general & universal detestation of any Man perhaps in this age. I congratulate you on your acquaintance with him.

Mr Brown is preparing your grafts, wch are to be sent about a week hence, for that is the proper time : but as your parcels used to be carried to your Brother's, we are afraid they may be neglected there in the present confusion. if you think so, you will direct him forthwith to whom he may address them.

Pray tell me (when you are at leisure) all the transactions & improvements of Old-Park, that I may rectify and model my Ideas accordingly. what has become of you in these inundations, that have drowned us all, & in this hot and unseasonable winter ? Present my respects to Mrs Wharton, and my compliments to Miss. how do the little family do ? I am ever sincerely yours.

147. To Wharton

Cambr: July 10, 1764.

My Dear Doctor,—I do remember and shall ever remember, as I ought, your extreme kindness in offering to be present, & to assist me in the *perilous hour*.

when I received your letter, I was pleased to find, I had done everything almost, that you advised. The fault lay in deferring matters too long. upon inspection they found no reason to apprehend a Fistula, but the piles only in an extreme degree, that threaten'd mortification. 9 or 10 strokes of the lancet, and the application of a caustic, with fomentations innumerable I suffered manfully : indeed the pain in idea is much greater than in reality, & now I am glad, I know it. it is certain, I am better at present, than I had been in at least a year before the operation. I should tell you, that for some days before I submitted to it, I had taken soap in large quantities, & for aught I know the inflammation might be rather increased by it. Dr. Whytt (I remember) speaking of the use of Limewater and Soap, says, that if the Patient be subject to the piles, he must omitt the latter. towards the end of my confinement, during w^{ch} (you may believe) I lived on nothing, came the Gout in one foot, *but* so tame you might have stroked it ; such a *Minikin*, you might have play'd with it. in 3 or 4 days it disappear'd.

It was true, as Stonhewer told you, that I had a great tendency towards Old-Park & Hart-le-pool : but on prudent consideration I find, I cannot well afford it, & must defer that pleasure to another summer. The Minikin and I act upon the same principles : she cannot be a river, nor I a traveller, without money. If we had but a *head*, we should both of us make a figure in the world.

Mason does not seem very impatient, for he writes word, that he is busy in modelling antique vases in clay, & in reading a course of ecclesiastical History, when I expected *consummation*, & was praying heaven to give him a good and gentle Gouverness : no Man wants such a thing more in all senses ; but his greatest wants do not make him move a foot the faster, nor has he properly speaking anything one can call a passion about him, except a little malice and revenge.

Our election here is in Westminster-Hall : but it is

not likely that any great matter can be done in it till Michaelmas Term next. in the meantime Ld Sandwich & his friends do what they can to keep up an interest & a bustle. here is a poor Scribler, that he hires to write a weekly paper called the *Scrutator*, who by abuse of characters does all in his power to provoke people : but can not so much as get himself answer'd. I could not find any one in Town, that ever heard of it (tho' the subject is well known there), & if anybody saw its name in the advertisements, I believe, they only took it for a *Scrutore* to be sold. the Nation is in the same hands as the University, & really does not make so manful a resistance. grumble indeed every one does, but since Wilkes's affair they fall off their metal, & seem to shrink under the brazen hand of Norton & his colleagues. I hear there will be no parliament till after Christmas. if the French should be so unwise as to suffer the Spanish Court to go on in their present measures (for they refuse to pay the ransom of Manilla, & have driven away our Logwoodcutters already) down go their friends the Ministry, & all the schemes of Right Divine & Prerogative ; and this is perhaps the best chance we have. are you not struck with the great similarity there is between the first years of Charles the first, and the present times ? who would have thought it possible five years ago ?

That old rogue Ld Bath is dead at last. I understood the contest for his spoils lay between your noble Friend at Raby and Mr Coleman, the Comick Poet, but whether they are fallen to either of them I have not heard as yet. pray what is the policy of that castle ? the elder Brother lives more than usual in the country, as if he were not in the best humour with his Friends at Court, and the younger has been at times an Orator in the opposition ? have they been disobliged, or do they fear to disoblige their former friends, who may come into play again ?

Two more volumes of Buffon are come over : I mention them in case you chuse to have them. I know of nothing else, except half a dozen new works of that inexhaustible, eternal, entertaining Scribler Voltaire, who at last (I fear) will go to heaven, for to him entirely it is owing, that the king of France & his council have review'd & set aside the decision of the parliament of Thoulouse in the affair of Calas. the poor man, 'tis true, has been broke on the wheel long ago : but his Widow and wretched family may have some reparation & his Murtherers may smart a little for it. You see a Scribler may be of some use in the world !

If you see Stonhewer at his return from Buxton, be so good to tell him, that there will be only 200 copies of Ld Herbert's Life printed, half of which are for Ld Powis, & the rest will be given away only. if I happen to have two (wch I do not expect) he shall have one of them.

Ah ! poor James Lyon !—how do the—Family bear it ? my best respects to the Lady of Old-Park (the Dutchess I should say) & Lady Mary, &c. I hope they are all well. are M^r and Mrs Jonathan with you ? do you say your prayers o' nights ? Adieu, I am ever,

Yours

T.G.

Mr. Brown, who is quite well, presents his humble Service. he would wish to come to-morrow, only he thinks it impossible ; and does not believe any body did ever really go so far.

To Dr Thomas Wharton Old-Park near Durham.

148. To the Rev. James Brown

Southampton, at Mr. Vining's
Plumber, in High Street. . . . . .
Monday.

Dear Sir,—I received your letter before I left London, and sit down to write to you, after the finest walk in the finest day that ever shone to Netley Abbey —my old friend, with whom I longed to renew my acquaintance. My ferryman (for one passes over a little arm of the sea about half a mile) assured me he

would not go near it in the night-time for all the world,
tho' he knew much money had been found there. The
sun was 'all too glaring and too full of gauds' for
such a scene, wch ought to be visited only in the dusk
of the evening. It stands in a little quiet valley, w^ch
gradually rises behind the ruins into a half-circle
crowned with thick wood. Before it, on a descent,
is a thicket of oaks, that serves to veil it from the broad
day and from profane eyes, only leaving a peep on
both sides, where the sea appears glittering thro' the
shade, and vessels, with their white-sails, that glide
across and are lost again. Concealed behind the thicket
stands a little Castle (also in ruins), immediately on
the shore, that commands a view over an expanse of
sea clear and smooth as glass (when I saw it), with
Southampton and several villages three miles off to
the right, Calshot Castle at seven miles' distance, and
the high lands of the Isle of Wight to the left, and in
front the deep shades of the New Forest distinctly
seen, because the water is no more than three miles
over. The abbey was never very large. The shell of
its church is almost entire, but the pillars of the aisles
are gone, and the roof has tumbled in ; yet some little
of it is left in the transept, where the ivy has forced
its way thro', and hangs flaunting down among the
fretted ornament and escutcheons of the Benefactors.
Much of the lodgings and offices are also standing,
but all is overgrown with trees and bushes, and mantled
here and there with ivy, that mounts over the battlements.

In my way I saw Winchester Cathedral again with
pleasure, and supped with Dr. Balguy, who, I perceive,
means to govern the Chapter. They give £200 a year
to the Poor of the City : his present scheme is to take
away this, for it is only an encouragement to laziness.
But what do they mean to do with it ? That indeed,
I omitted to enquire, because I thought I knew. I saw
St. Cross, too, the almshouse of Noble Poverty (so it
was called), founded by Henry de Blois and Cardinal
Beaufort. It maintains nine decayed footmen, and

a master (Chancellor Hoadly), who has £800 a-year out of it.

This place is still full of Bathers. I know not a soul, nor have once been at the rooms. The walks all round it are delicious, and so is the weather. Lodgings very dear, and fish very cheap. Here is no coffee-house, no bookseller, no pastrycook ; but here is the Duke of Chandos. I defer my politics. My service to Mr. Talbot, Gould, etc., and to Mr. Howe, if with you.— Adieu.

149. To the Rev. James Brown

Southampton, October 13, 1764.

Dear Sir,—Since I have been here, I have received from you, and by your means, five letters. That from Pa. I could wish you had opened, as I know you, by your good will, would have done. The sun of it is, that he is at Geneva, with the Rhone tumbling its blue and green tide directly under his window. That he has passed a fortnight in the Pays de Vaud, and the Cantons of Berne, Fribourg, and Soleure, and returned by the lake of Neufchâtel. That the whole country, and particularly the last-named, appeared to him astonishingly beautiful. He inquired much after Rousseau, but did not meet with him ; his residence is at Moitier au Travers, about four leagues from Neufchâtel, where he lives in great plenty, the booksellers at the Hague being his bank, and ready to answer any sum he draws for. It is amazing what he got by his last two books. He is often flying about from village to village ; generally wears a sort of Armenian dress, and passed for a kind of misanthrope, but is held in great veneration by the people.

He says, he saw all the matters that come in course in France, and was greatly disappointed. The only thing he mentions is the church at Amiens, which was really fine. They set out in a few days (his date is 19th September), and go by Chambery to Turin, from whence he will write to you. His letter, he says, is not worth the postage; but it is the abundance and not the want of matter that makes it so poor.

After this what shall I say to you of my Lilliputian travels? On Monday I think to see Salisbury, and to be sure Wilton, and Amesbury, and Stonehenge. This will take up three days, and then I come back hither, and think to be in London on Saturday or Monday after, for the weather grows untoward, and the sea (that is, the little miniature of it, Southampton River) rages horribly, and looks as if it would eat one, else I should have gone to Lymington and Christchurch, and called upon Mr. Mansfield in the New Forest, to see the bow that killed William Rufus, which he pretends to possess. Say not a word of Andover. My Lord Delawar has erected a little monument over the spot where, according to ancient tradition, that king was slain, and another in God's House Chapel, where the Earl of Cambridge, Lord Scroop, and Sir Thomas Grey, were interred by Henry V. after he had cut off their heads. It is in this town, and now the French Church. Here lives Dr. Saint André, famous for the affair of the Rabbit-Woman, and for marrying Lady Betty Molyneux after they had disposed of her first husband. She died not long since in the odour of sanctity. He is 80 years old and is now building a palazzino here hard by, in a delightful spot called Bellevue, and has lately produced a natural son to inherit it. What do you say to poor Iwan, and the last Russ manifesto? Will nobody kill me that dragoness? Must we wait till her son does it himself?

Mr. Stonhewer has been at Glamis. He tells me no news. He only confutes a piece of news I sent him, which I am glad to hear is a lie. I must tell you a small anecdote I just hear, that delights me. Sir F. Norton has a mother living at a town in Yorkshire, in a very indifferent lodging. A good house was to be sold there the other day. He thought in decency he ought to appear willing to buy it for her. When the people to whom it belongs imagined that everything was agreed on, he insisted on having two pictures as fixtures, which they value at £60, so Mrs. Norton lives where she did.

I am sorry for the Duke of Devonshire. The cause, I fear, is losing ground, and I know the person (where Mr. T. has lately been) looked upon all as gone, if this event should happen. Adieu. When I get to town I shall pick up something to tell you.—I am ever yours.

I know nothing of Mason, but that he is well.

Southampton, at Mr. Vining's, plumber, in High Street.

150. To Norton Nicholls

Monday 19 Nov: 1764.

S^r,—I received your letter at Southampton, & as I would wish to treat every body according to their own rule & measure of good-breeding, have against my inclination waited till now, before I answer'd it, purely out of fear & respect, & an ingenuous diffidence of my own abilities. if you will not take this as an excuse, accept it at least as a well-turn'd period, wch is always my principal concern.

So I proceed to tell you, that my health is much improved by the sea : not that I drank it, or bathed in it, as the *common people* do : no ! I only walk'd by it, & look'd upon it. the climate is remarkably mild, even in Octob: and November. no snow has been seen to lie there for these 30 years past, the myrtles grow in the ground against the houses, and Guernsey-Lillies bloom in every window. the Town, clean & well built, surrounded by its old stone-walls with their towers & gateways, stands at the point of a peninsula, & opens full south to an arm of the sea, wch having form'd two beautiful bays on each hand of it stretches away in direct view till it joins the British Channel. it is skirted on either side with gently-rising grounds cloath'd with thick wood, & directly cross its mouth rise the high lands of the Isle of Wight at distance, but distinctly seen. in the bosom of the woods (conceal'd from profane eyes) lie hid the ruins of Netteley-

abbey. there may be richer and greater houses of
religion, but the Abbot is content with his situation.
see there, at the top of that hanging meadow under
the shade of those old trees, that bend into a half-
circle about it, he is walking slowly (good Man!) &
bidding his beads for the souls of his Benefactors,
interr'd in that venerable pile, that lies beneath him.
Beyond it (the meadow still descending) nods a thicket
of oaks, that mask the building, and have excluded
a view too garish, & too luxuriant for a holy eye, only
on either hand they leave an opening to the blew
glittering sea. did not you observe how, as that white
sail shot by and was lost, he turn'd and cross'd himself,
to drive the Tempter from him, that had thrown that
distraction in his way. I should tell you, that the
Ferryman, who row'd me, a lusty young Fellow, told
me, that he would not for all the world pass a night
at the Abbey, (there were such things seen near it,)
tho' there was a power of money hid there. from
thence I went to Salisbury, Wilton, & Stone-Henge,
but of these things I say no more: they will be
publish'd at the University-Press.

I have been at London this month, that tiresome
dull place! where all people under thirty find so much
amusement. the Opera, with Manzuoli in it opens
on Saturday, and I go to C: the Wednesday preceding.
the Ministry are all together by the ears, so are the
Opposition: the only doubt is wch will be the
weakest: I am afraid I know. the sentence of Alma-
Mater, of the North-Briton, & of D'Eon are defer'd.
in the meantime, Du-Vergy, the Adventurer who
enraged D'Eon almost to madness, & has been in jail
(for debt) ever since December last, having regain'd
his liberty by the help (he says) of his countrymen,
declares upon oath, that he was sent from France with
a half promise of being declared Secretary to the
Embassy, that he might *se servir de son epée*, if occasion
were, against D'Eon, or at least urge him to do something, that might for ever disgrace him. He gives
a detail of all his private conversations with G: & others

on this head. Mons: de G: is (I hear) much troubled, declares the whole a lye, but what is he to do ? must he have another *Plaidoyer* in our Courts against this Scoundrel ? and indeed from his own narrative he appears to be no better, though it is interlarded with fine French sentiment about justice, & virtue, & honour, and such like.

I had prepared a finer period than the other to finish with, but, d—mn it ! I have somehow mislaid it among my papers. you shall certainly have it next summer. how can people subscribe such a devil of a name (I warrant), you call it a *christian*-name, to their letters as you do ? I always thought at times I had a small matter of aversion for you mechanically arising in me, & doubtless this was the reason. fie, fie, put on a white satten-mantle, and be carried to church again. however, I forgive you, for your Ripponhistory's sake. Adieu ! I shall almost be glad to see you again. TG:

Your friend Dr. M: came very kindly to see me, as soon as he had taken possession of his new Mastership, and return'd me his thanks for my civilities to you. so never say any more on that head. you see I am paid.

151. To Walpole

I have received the C. of O:, & return you my thanks for it. it engages our attention here, makes some of us cry a little, & all in general afraid to go to bed o' nights. we take it for a translation, & should believe it to be a true story, if it were not for St Nicholas.

When your pen was in your hand, you might have been a little more communicative : for, tho' disposed enough to believe the Opposition rather consumptive, I am entirely ignorant of all the symptoms. even what the Yorks have been doing for themselves, or attempting to do, is to me a secret. your canonical book I have been reading with great satisfaction. he speaketh as one having authority. if Englishmen have any feeling left, methinks they must feel now ; & if the

Ministry have any feeling (whom no body will suspect of insensibility) they must cut off the Author's ears, for it is in all the forms a most wicked libel. is the old Man, & the Lawyer put on, or is it real ? or has some real Lawyer furnish'd a good part of the materials, & another Person employ'd them ? this I guess, for there is an uncouthness of diction in the beginning, wch is not supported throughout, though it now & then occurs again, as if the Writer was weary of supporting the character he had assumed, when the subject had warmed him beyond dissimulation.

Rousseau's letters I am reading heavily, heavily ! he justifies himself, till he convinces me, that he deserved to be burnt, at least that his book did. I am not got thro' him, & you never will. Voltaire I detest, & have not seen his book : I shall in good time. You surprise me, when you talk of going in February : pray, does all the Minority go too ? I hope, you have a *reason. desperare de republicâ* is a deadly sin in politicks.

Adieu ! I will not take my leave of you, for (you perceive) this letter means to beg another, when you can spare a little.

[Cambridge] Sunday. Dec: 30. 1764.

To The Honble Horace Walpole in Arlington Street London

152. To Mason

Cambridge, Thursday, 1765.

DEAR MR. MASON,—As you are alone and not quite well, I do feel a little sort of (I am almost ashamed to speak it) tenderness for you, but then I comfort myself with the thought that it does not proceed from any remnant of old inclination or kindness that I have for you. That, you must allow, would be folly, as our places of abode are so distant, and our occupations and pursuits so different. But the true cause is, that I am pretty lonely too, and besides have a complaint in my eyes that possibly may end in blindness. It consists in not being able to read at all with one eye, and having very often the *muscæ volitantes* before the other. I may be allowed therefore to think a little of you and Delaval, without any disparagement to my knowledge of mankind and of human nature.

The match you talk of is no more consummated than your own, and Kitty is still a maid for the Doctor, so that he wants the requisite thing, and yet, I'll be sworn, his happiness is very little impaired. I take broiled salmon to be a dish much more necessary at your table than his. I had heard in town (as you have) that they were married; and longed to go to Spilsby and make them a visit; but here I learn it is not true yet, whatever it may be. I read and liked the Epigram as it was printed, and do insist it is better without the last lines, not that the thought is amiss, but because the same rhyme is repeated, and the sting is not in the epigrammatic style; I mean, not easy and familiar. In a satire it might do very well. Mr. Churchill is dead indeed, drowned in a butt of claret, which was tapped on the meeting of the Friends at Boulogne. He made an excellent end, as his executor Humphrey Cotes testifies. I did not write any of the elegies, being busy in writing the *Temple of Tragedy*. Send for it forthwith, for you are highly interested in it. If I had not owned the thing, perhaps you might have gone and taken it for the Reverend Mr. Langhorne's. It is divine. I have not read the *Philosophic Dictionary*. I can stay with great patience for anything that comes from Voltaire. They tell me it is frippery, and blasphemy, and wit. I could have forgiven myself if I had not read Rousseau's *Letters*. Always excepting the *Contract Social*, it is the dullest performance he ever published. It is a weak attempt to separate the miracles from the morality of the Gospel. The latter he would have you think he believes was sent from God, and the former he very explicitly takes for an imposture. This is in order to prove the cruelty and injustice of the State of Geneva in burning his *Émile*. The latter part of his book is to shew the abuses that have crept into the constitution of his country, which point (if you are concerned about it) he makes out very well, and his intention in this is plainly to raise a tumult in the city, and to be revenged on the *Petit Conseil*, who condemned his writings to the flames.

Cambridge itself is fruitful enough of events to furnish out many paragraphs in my Gazette. The most important is, that Frog Walker is dead; his last words were (as the nurses sat by him and said, ' Ah! poor gentleman, he is going!'); ' Going, going! where am I going? I'm sure I know no more than the man in the moon.' Doctor Ridlington has been given over with a dropsy these ten weeks. He refused all tapping and scarifying, but obeyed other directions, till, finding all was over, he prescribed to himself a boiled chicken entire, and five quarts of small beer. After this he brought up great quantities of blood, the swelling and suffocation, and all signs of water disappeared, his spirits returned, and, except extreme weakness, he is recovered. Everybody has ceased to enquire after him, and, as he would not die when he should, they are resolved to proceed as if he were dead and buried. Dr. Newcome is dead. For six weeks or more before his death he was distracted, not childish, but really raving. For the last three weeks he took no nourishment but by force. Miss Kirke and the younger Beadon are executors and residuary legatees. I believe, he left about £10,000, but there are many legacies. Had I a pen of adamant, I could not describe the business, the agitation, the tempest, the University is in about the Margaret Professorship. Only D.D.'s and B.D.'s have votes, so that there are acts upon acts. The bell is eternally tolling, as in time of pestilence, and nobody knows whose turn it may be next. The candidates are Dr. Law and Z. Brooke and my Lord Sandwich. The day is Saturday next. But alas! what is this to the warm region of Saint John's? It is like Lisbon on the day of the earthquake; it is like the fire of London. I can hear and smell it hither. Here too appears the furious Zachary; but his forces are but three or four men. Here towers Doctor Rutherforth, himself an host, and he has about three champions. There Skinner, with his powerful oratory, and the decent Mr. Alvis, with their several invisible squadrons : Ogden and Gunning each fighting for himself, and disdaining the assistance of others. But see, where Frampton [? rages], with his 17 votes, and on his buckler glitters the formidable name of Sandwich, at which fiends tremble. Last of all comes, with his mines and countermines, and old Newcastle at his back, the irresistible force of Powell. 23 are a majority, and he has already 22½. If it lapses to the Seniors he has it ; if it lapses to the Visitor he has it. In short, as we all believe it, he has it every way. I know you are overjoyed, especially for that he has the Newcastle interest. I have had a very civil visit of two hours from Archimage, busy as he is ; for you know I inherit all your old acquaintance, as I do all Delaval's old distempers. I visited Dr. Balguy the other day at Winchester, and he me at Southampton. We are as great as two peas. The day of election at Saint John's is Friday se'nnight.

Mr. Brown is well, and has forgot you. Mr. Nicholls is profuse of his thanks to me for your civilities to him at York, of which, God knows, I knew no more than the man in the moon. Adieu.

153. To Mason

Pembroke Hall, Saturday, 1765 [? 1763].

DEAR MASON,—I rejoice ; but has she common sense ? Is she a gentlewoman ? Has she money ? Has she a nose ? I know she sings a little, and twiddles on the harpsichord, hammers at sentiment, and puts herself in an attitude, admires a cast in the eye, and can say *Elfrida* by heart. But these are only the virtues of a maid. Do let her have some wife-like qualities, and a double portion of prudence, as she will have not only herself to govern, but you also, and that with an absolute sway. Your friends, I doubt not, will suffer for it. However, we are very happy, and have no other wish than to see you settled in the world. We

beg you would not stand fiddling about it, but be
married forthwith, and then take chaise, and come . . .
all the way to Cambridge to be touched by Mr. Brown,
and so to London, where, to be sure, she must pass the
first winter. If good reasons (and not your own nor
her coquetry) forbid this, yet come hither yourself,
for our copuses and Welsh rabbits are impatient for you.

I sent your letter to Algarotti directly. My Coserella
came a long while ago from Mr. Holles, I suppose, who
sent me, without a name, a set of his engravings, when
I was last in town ; which, I reckon, is what you mean
by your fine presents. The *Congresso di Citera* was not
one of the books. That was my mistake. I like his
treatises very well.

I hope in God the dedicatorial sonnet has not staid
for me. I object nothing to the second line, but like
it the better for Milton, and with him too I would
read *in penult.* (give me a shilling) ' his ghastly
smile,' etc. But if you won't put it in, then read
' wonted smile,' and a little before ' secure from
envy.' I see nothing to alter. What I said was the
best line still. Do come hither, and I will read and
criticise ' your amorous ditties all a winter's day.'
Adieu, I am truly yours. I hope her hair is not red
though. I have been abroad, or I had wrote sooner.

154. To Wharton

Cambr: 29 Apr: 1765.

DEAR DOCTOR,—I have lately heard, that you have
been very ill, & that in the midst of your illness your
poor sister Ettrick was obliged to fly from her Perse-
cutor, & put herself under your protection. pray
inform me, as soon as you can, of the state of your
health in the first place ; & next, how you have been
able to secure a poor frighted Woman from the brutality
of such a husband, wch under our excellent constitution
(I take it) is rather a more difficult thing, than it would
be in Turkey.

For me, I passed the latter part of the last autumn

at Southampton all alone (for I went to no rooms, nor
saw any company, as they call it) in a most beautiful
country, & very gentle climate. the air and the walks
agreed with me wonderfully, the sea-water I scarce
tried (as the winter approached) enough to say, whether
it would suit me, or not. some time after I return'd
hither, came the gout in both feet successively, very
gentle as to pain, but it left a weakness & sense of
lassitude behind it, that even yet is not wholly dissipated. I have a great propensity to Hartlepool this
summer, it is in your neighbourhood, & that is to make
up for climate & for trees. the sea, the turf, & the
rocks, I remember, have merit enough of their own.
Mr Brown is so invincibly attach'd to his duties of
Treasurer and Tutor, & I know not what, that I give
up all hopes of bringing him with me : nor do I (till
I have been at London) speak determinately as to
myself : perhaps I may find good reasons (against my
inclination) to change my mind.

Your Mother, the University, has succeeded in her
great cause against the Secretary of State. Ld Hardwick is declared duly elected by a majority of one
voice. all the Judges of the King's-bench took occasion
to declare their opinion in set speeches on the question ;
I suppose, in order to gain a little popularity, for
whatever seems against Ld S:, must be popular. Ld
Mansfield was express on two points, that the Universities were not subject to any Royal Visitations, but
might always apply to & receive redress from his Maj:s
Courts of Justice ; & that they were bound by no
statutes, but such as they themselves had thought
fit to receive. these things are doubtless of far more
consequence to them than the cause in question, for
wch I am the less concern'd, because I do believe the
two Pretenders had (privately) agreed the matter
beforehand, for the House of Yorke have undoubtedly
been long making up to the Court. I should tell you,
that Dr. Long's Affidavit was only begun to be read,
& laid aside as of no consequence. I suppose you know
by this time, that our Friend the B: of Ch: was the

private Embassador of Ld Sandwich to this place,
& made proposals in his name. he also was present
on the side of that worthy Nobleman at the remarkable
interview with Mr Charles Yorke. it is certain he
refused the Archb:^k of Armagh ; but why, I cannot
yet learn : some say, because they intended to quarter
so many pensions upon it : others, because they would
keep to themselves the disposal of all the preferments.
but neither of these seem to be sufficient reasons. it
is sure, he wrote circular letters to his friends to
acquaint them of this refusal, & that he was snub'd
for doing so. whereas B^p Newton, to whom it was first
offer'd, made a great secret of it, as a good Courtier
should do. now I am talking of Bishops, I must tell
you, that not long ago B:^p Warburton in a sermon at
Court asserted, that all preferments were bestowed
on the most illiterate & worthless objects, & in speaking
turned himself about & stared directly at the B^p. of
London. he added, that if any one arose distinguish'd
for merit and learning, there was a combination of
dunces to keep him down. I need not tell you, that
he expected the B^p of London himself, when Terrick
got it. So ends my ecclesiastical history.

Our friend, the Precentor, who has so long been in
a *mariturient* way, is not yet married, and I doubt, it
is all gone off. I dare not ask about it, but if I go northward, shall take him in my way, and see, whether he
will tell me. Present my best compliments to Mrs.
Wharton, & Miss. I have no idea of the family at
present, & expect to see a multitude of little new faces,
that know not Joseph.—Adieu ! dear S^r, I am ever

Most sincerely Yours

TG:

I hear, you are well again : but pray tell me, how well.

155. To the Rev. James Brown

London, Tuesday night, 1765.

Dear Sir,—I hope to be with you by Thursday or
Friday se'nnight. You will hardly go before that
time out of college ; but if you do, the writings will

be as safe in your drawers as in mine. You have heard so much news from the party that were going to Scotland, that it would be a vain thing for me to talk about it. I can only add, that you will shortly hear, I think, of a great change of affairs, which, whenever I come to town, always follows. To-day I met with a report that Mr. Pitt lies dangerously ill; but I hope, and rather believe, it is not true. When he is gone all is gone, and England will be old England again, such as, before his administration, it always was ever since we were born.

I went to-day to Becket's to look at the last volume of SEBA. It comes unbound to four guineas and a half, and contains all the insects of that collection (which are exceedingly numerous), and some plates of fossils. The graving, as usual, very unequal, and the descriptions as poor as ever. As you have the rest, I conclude you must have this, which completes the work, and contains the index.

Are you not glad of the Carlisle history? Walking yesterday in the Windsor Park, I met the brother of the disgraced party, and walked two hours with him. I had a vast inclination to wish him joy, but did not dare. Adieu.—I am ever yours,

T. G.

156. To MASON

Jermyn Street, May 23 [1765].

DEAR MASON,—In my way into the remote parts of the north, I mean to make you a visit at York; probably you will see me there on Wednesday next in the evening. It is your business to consider whether you have a house and a tea for me, for I shall stay there a week perhaps, if you continue agreeable so long. I have been in town this month, every day teeming with prodigies. I suppose you receive expresses every three hours, and therefore I pass over the Regency Bill, the weavers' petition, the siege of Bedford House, the riot on Ludgate Hill, the royal embassy to Hayes, the *carte blanche* refused with disdain, the subversion of the ministry, which fights to the last gasp, and after-

wards like the man *che combattea e era morto*, and yet
stands upon its legs and spits in its master's face to
this day because nobody will deign to take its place ;
the House of Commons standing at gaze with its hands
before it ; the House of Lords bullying the justices of
peace, and fining the printers ; the King——, etc. etc.
The rest is left to oral tradition. Adieu !

157. To Mason

July 16, 1765.

WILLIAM SHAKESPEARE to Mrs. ANNE, Regular
Servant to the Rev. Mr. PRECENTOR, of York.

A moment's patience, gentle Mistris Anne
　(But stint your clack for Sweet St. Charitie) :
'Tis Willey begs, once a right proper man,
　Though now a book, and interleav'd you see.
Much have I borne from canker'd critic's spite,
　From fumbling baronets, and poets small,
Pert barristers, and parsons nothing bright :
　But what awaits me now is worst of all.
'Tis true, our master's temper natural
　Was fashion'd fair in meek and dove-like guise ;
But may not honey's self be turn'd to gall
　By residence, by marriage, and sore eyes ?
If then he wreak on me his wicked will,
　Steal to his closet at the hour of prayer ;
And (when thou hear'st the organ piping shrill)
　Grease his best pen, and all he scribbles, tear.
Better to bottom tarts and cheesecakes nice,
　Better the roast meat from the fire to save,
Better be twisted into caps for spice,
　Than thus be patch'd and cobbled in one's grave.
So York shall taste what Clouet never knew,
　So from our works sublimer fumes shall rise ;
While Nancy earns the praise to Shakespeare due,
　For glorious puddings and immortal pies.

Tell me if you do not like this, and I will send you a
worse. I rejoice to hear your eyes are better, as much
as if they were my own ; but the cure will never be
lasting without a little sea. I have been for two days

at Hartlepool to taste the waters, and do assure you nothing can be salter, and bitterer, and nastier, and better for you. They have a most antiscorbutic flavour. I am delighted with the place. There are the finest walks, and rocks, and caverns, and dried fishes, and all manner of small inconveniences a man can wish. I am going again this week, so wait your commands.

Dr. Wharton would be quite happy to see you at Old Park. If you should have kindness and resignation enough to come, you must get to Darlington, then turn off the great road to Merrington, then inquire the way to Spennymoor House, where they will direct you hither. Adieu, I am ever yours,   T. G.

158. To WHARTON

DEAR DOCTOR,—I deferr'd writing to you, till I had seen a little more of this countrey, than you yourself had seen, and now being just return'd from an excursion, wch I & the Major have been making, into the High-lands, I sit down to tell you all about it : but first I must return to my journey hither, on wch I shall be very short, partly because you know the way as far as Edinburgh, & partly, that there was not a great deal worth remarking. the first night we pass'd at Tweedmouth (77 miles), the next at Edinburgh (53 m:), where L^d S: left the Major and me, to go to Lenox-love (Ld Brantyre's) where his Aunt lives. So that afternoon & all next day I had leisure to visit the Castle, Holy-Rood-House, Heriot's Hospital, Arthur's-Seat, &c : and am not sorry to have seen that most picturesque (at a distance) & nastiest (when near) of all capital Cities. I sup'd with Dr Robertson and other Literati, & the next morning L^d S: came for us. we cross'd at the Queen's Ferry in a four-oared yawl without a sail, & were toss'd about rather more than I should wish to hazard again. lay at Perth, a large *Scotch* Town with much wood about it on the banks of the Tay, a very noble river. next morning ferried over it, and came by dinner time to Glamis, being (from

Edinburgh) 67 miles, wch makes in all from Hetton
197 m:. The Castle stands in Strathmore (i:e: the
Great Vally), wch winds about from Stonehaven on
the East-Coast of Kincairdinshire obliquely as far as
Stirling near 100 miles in length, and from 7 to 10
miles in breadth, cultivated everywhere to the foot of
the Hills on either hand with oats or bere-barley,
except where the soil is mere peat-earth (black as a
coal) or barren sand cover'd only with broom & heath,
or a short grass fit for sheep. here & there appear just
above ground the huts of the inhabitants, wch they
call Towns, built of & cover'd with turf, & among
them at great distances the Gentlemen's houses with
inclosures & a few trees round them. amidst these our
castle distinguishes itself, the middle part of it rising
proudly out of what seems a great & thick wood of
tall trees with a cluster of hanging towers on the top.
you descend to it gradually from the South through
a double and triple avenue of Scotch Firs, 60 or 70
feet high under three Gateways. this approach is a
full mile long & when you have pass'd the 2^d Gate,
the Firs change to Limes, & another oblique avenue
goes off on either hand toward the Offices. these as
well as all the enclosures, that surround the house,
are border'd with 3 or 4 ranks of sycomores, ashes,
& white poplars of the noblest height, & from 70 to
100 years old. other allies there are that go off at
right angles with the long one, small groves & wall'd
gardens of Earl Patrick's planting, full of broad-leaved
elms, oaks, birch, black-cherry trees, Laburnums, &c:,
all of great stature & size, wch have not till this week
begun to shew the least sense of morning frosts. the
third gate delivers you into a Court with a broad pavement, & grass-plats adorned with statues of the four
Stuart Kings, border'd with old silver-firs & yew-trees
alternately, & opening with an iron palissade on either
side to two square old-fashion'd parterres surrounded
by stone-fruit-walls. the house from the height of
it, the greatness of its mass, the many towers atop,
& the spread of its wings, has really a very singular

& striking appearance, like nothing I ever saw. you
will comprehend something of its shape from the plan
of the 2ᵈ floor, wᶜʰ I enclose. The wings are about
50 feet high, the body (wᶜʰ is the old castle with walls
10 feet thick) is near 100. from the leads I see to the
South of me (just at the end of the avenue), the little
town of Glames, the houses built of stone & slated,
with a neat Kirk & small square Tower (a rarity in
this region) just beyond it rises a beautiful round hill,
& another ridge of a longer form adjacent to it, both
covered with woods of tall fir: beyond them peep
over the black hills of *Sid-law*, over which winds the
road to Dundee. to the North within about seven
miles of me begin to rise the Grampions, hill above hill,
on whose tops 3 weeks ago I could plainly see some
traces of the snow, that fell in May last. To the East
winds away the *Strath*, such as I have before described
it, among the hills, wᶜʰ sink lower and lower, as
they approach the sea. to the West the same valley
(not plain, but broken unequal ground), runs on for
above 20 miles in view: there I see the crags above
Dunkeld, there *Beni-Gloe* & *Beni-More* rise above the
clouds, & there is that *She-khallian*, that spires into
a cone above them all, & lies at least 45 miles (in a
direct line) from this place. Lᵈ S: who is the greatest
farmer in this neighbourhood, is from break of day to
dark night among his husbandmen & labourers; he
has near 2000 acres of land in his own hands, and is
at present employed in building a low wall of 4 miles
long; & in widening the bed of the little river *Deane*,
which runs to S: & S:E: of the house, from about 20
to 50 feet wide, both to prevent inundations, and to
drain the Lake of Forfar. this work will be two years
more in completing; & must be 3 miles in length. all
the Highlanders, that can be got, are employ'd in it;
many of them know no English, & I hear them
singing Erse-songs all day long. the price of labour
is 8 pence a-day; but to such, as will join together
and engage to perform a certain portion in a
limited time, 2 shillings. I must say, that all our

labours seem to prosper, and my L^d has casually found in digging such quantities of shell-marle, as not only fertilize his own grounds, but are disposed of at a good price to all his neighbours. in his nurseries are thousands of oaks, beech, larches, horse-chesnuts, spruce-fir, &c:, thick as they can stand, & whose only fault is, that they are grown tall and vigorous, before he has determined, where to plant them out. the most advantageous spot we have for beauty lies West of the house, where (when the stone walls of the meadows are taken away) the grounds (naturally unequal) will have a very park-like appearance. they are already full of trees, wch need only thinning here & there to break the regularity of their lines, & thro' them winds the *Burn of Glames*, a clear & rapid trout-stream, which joins the R: Deane hard by. pursuing the course of this brook upwards, you come to a narrow sequester'd valley shelter'd from all winds, through wch it runs murmuring among great stones ; on one hand the ground gently rises into a hill, on the other are the rocky banks of the rivulet almost perpendicular, yet covered with syca-more, ash, & fir, that (tho' it seems to have no place or soil to grow in) yet has risen to a good height, and forms a thick shade. you may continue along this gill, & passing by one end of the village & its church for half a mile it leads to an opening between the two hills cover'd with fir-woods, that I mention'd above, thro' wch the stream makes its way, and forms a cascade of 10 or 12 feet over broken rocks. a very little art is necessary to make all this a beautiful scene. the weather till the last week has been in general very fine & warm : we have had no fires till now, & often have sat with the windows open an hour after sunset. now & then a shower has come, & sometimes sudden gusts of wind descend from the mountains that finish as suddenly as they arose : but to-day it blows a hurricane. upon the whole I have been exceedingly lucky in my weather, & particularly in my highland expedition of five days.

We set out then the 11th of Sept : & continuing

along the Strath to the West pass'd through *Megill*,
where is the tomb of *Queen Wanders, that was riven
to dethe by staned-horses for nae gude, that she did.* so
the women there told me, I'm sure. through Cowper
of Angus ; over the river Ila, then over a wide &
dismal heath fit for an assembly of Witches, till we came
to a string of four small lakes in a valley whose deep-
blew waters, & green margin, with a Gentleman's
house or two seated on them in little groves, contrasted
with the black desert, in wch they were inchased. the
ground now grew unequal, the hills more rocky seem'd
to close in upon us, till the road came to the brow of a
steep descent, & (the sun then setting) between two
woods of oak we saw far below us the river Tay come
sweeping along at the bottom of a precipice at least
150 feet deep, clear as glass, full to the brim, & very
rapid in its course. It seem'd to issue out of woods
thick & tall, that rose on either hand, & were overhung
by broken rocky crags of vast height : above them to
the West the tops of higher mountains appear'd, on
which the evening clouds reposed. down by the side
of the river under the thickest shades is seated the
Town of Dunkeld : in the midst of it stands a ruin'd
Cathedral, the towers & shell of the building still entire.
a little beyond it a large house of the Duke of Athol,
with its offices and gardens extends a mile beyond
the town, and as his grounds were interrupted by the
streets and roads he has flung arches of communication across them, that add to the scenery of the place,
wch of itself is built of good white stone, & handsomely
slated, so that no one would take it for a Scotch Town
till they come into it. here we pass'd the night : if
I told you how, you would bless yourself. Next day
we set forward to Taymouth 27 miles farther West,
the road winding through beautiful woods with the
Tay almost always in full view to the right, being here
from 3 to 400 feet over. the Strath-Tay from a mile
to 3 miles or more wide, cover'd with corn & spotted
with groups of people then in the midst of their harvest.
on either hand a vast chain of rocky mountains, that

changed their face & open'd something new every
hundred yards, as the way turn'd, or the clouds pass'd:
in short altogether it was one of the most pleasing
days I have pass'd these many years, & at every step
I wish'd for you. at the close of day, we came to
Balloch, so the place was call'd ; but now for decency
Taymouth, improperly enough, for here it is that the
river issues out of Loch-Tay (a glorious lake 15 miles
long, & 1½ broad), surrounded with prodigious mountains. there on its North Eastern brink impending
over it is the vast hill of Lawers : to the East is that
monstrous creature of God, *She-khallian* (i:e: the
Maiden's Pap), spiring above the clouds. directly
West (beyond the end of the lake), *Beni-More* (the
Great Mountain) rises to a most aweful height, and
looks down on the tomb of Fingal. Ld Braidalbin's
policy (so they call here all such ground as is laid out
for pleasure) takes in about 2000 acres, of wch his house,
offices, & a deer-park about three miles round occupy
the plain or bottom, wch is little above a mile in breadth.
thro' it winds the Tay, which by means of a bridge
I found here to be 156 feet over. his plantations and
woods rise with the ground on either side the vale,
to the very summit of the enormous crags, that over-
hang it. along them on the mountain's side runs a
terrass a mile & ½ long, that overlooks the course of
the river. from several seats and temples perch'd on
particular rocky eminences you command the lake
for many miles in length, wch turns like some huge
river, & loses itself among the mountains, that surround
it. at its eastern extremity, where the river issues
out of it, on a Peninsula my L^d has built a neat little
town & church with a high square tower, & just before
it lies a small round island in the lake covered with
trees, amongst which are the ruins of some little
religious house. trees (by the way) grow here to great
size & beauty. I saw four old chestnuts in the road,
as you enter the park, of vast bulk & height. One
beech tree I measured, that was 16 feet, 7 inches in
the girth, & (I guess) near 80 feet in height. The

Gardiner presented us with peaches, nectarines, &
plums from the stone-walls of the kitchen-garden (for
there are no brick nor hot walls) the peaches were good,
the rest well-tasted, but scarce ripe. we had also
golden-pippens from an espalier (not ripe) & a melon
very well flavour'd and fit to cut. of the house I have
little to say; it is a very good nobleman's house handsomely furnish'd & well-kept, very comfortable to
inhabit, but not worth going far to see. of the Earl's
taste I have not much more to say, it is one of those
noble situations, that Man cannot spoil: it is however
certain, that he has built an inn & a town just where
his principal walks should have been, & in the most
wonderful spot of ground, that perhaps belong to
him. in this inn however we lay, & next day returning
down the river four miles we passed it over a fine bridge,
built at the expense of the Government, and continued
our way to *Logie-Rait*, just below wch in a most charming scene the *Tummel*, wch is here the larger river of the
two, falls into the Tay. we ferried over the Tummel
in order to get into Marshal Wade's road (wch leads
from Dunkeld to Inverness), and continued our way
along it toward the North. the road is excellent, but
dangerous enough in conscience. the river often
running directly under us at the bottom of a precipice
200 feet deep, sometimes masqued indeed by wood,
that finds means to grow where I could not stand:
but very often quite naked & without any defence.
in such places we walked for miles together partly for
fear, and partly to admire the beauty of the country,
wch the beauty of the weather set off to the greatest
advantage. as evening came on, we approached the
Pass of Gillikrankie, where in the year 45 the Hessians
with their Prince at their head stop't short, & refused
to march a foot farther. *Vestibulum ante ipsum,
primisq in faucibus Orci* stands the solitary mansion
of Mr Robinson of Faseley. close by it rises a hill
cover'd with oak, with grotesque masses of rock staring
from among their trunks, like the sullen countenances
of Fingal & all his family frowning on the little mortals

of modern days. from between this hill and the
adjacent mountains pent in a narrow channel, comes
roaring out the river Tummel, and falls headlong down
involved in white foam, wch rises into a mist all round
it.—but my paper is deficient, & I must say nothing
of the Pass itself, the black river Garry, the Blair of
Athol, Mount Beni-Gloe, my return (by another road)
to Dunkeld, the Hermitage, the *Stra-Brann*, & the
Rumbling-Brigg. in short since I saw the Alps, I
have seen nothing sublime till now. in about a week
I shall set forward by the Stirling-road on my return
all alone. pray for me, till I see you, for I dread Edinburgh & the itch ; and expect to find very little in
my way worth the perils I am to endure. my best
compliments to Mrs Wharton and the young Ladies
(including herself) & to Mr. and Mrs. Jonathan if they
are with you. Adieu !—I am ever

Yours

T G:

[In Wharton's hand is added, Glamis, September
1765.]

159. To James Beattie

Glames Castle, October 2, 1765.

I must beg you would present my most grateful
acknowledgments to your society for the public mark
of their esteem, which you say they are disposed to
confer on me, I embrace, with so deep and just a sense
of their goodness, the substance of that honour they
do me, that I hope it may plead my pardon with them
if I do not accept the form. I have been, Sir, for several
years a member of the University of Cambridge, and
formerly (when I had some thoughts of the profession)
took a Bachelor of Laws' degree there ; since that
time, though long qualified by my standing, I have
always neglected to finish my course, and claim my
doctor's degree : judge, therefore, whether it will not
look like a slight, and some sort of contempt, if I
receive the same degree from a Sister University. I
certainly would avoid giving any offence to a set

of men, among whom I have passed so many easy, and I may say, happy hours of my life ; yet shall ever retain in my memory the obligations you have laid me under, and be proud of my connection with the University of Aberdeen.

It is a pleasure to me to find that you are not offended with the liberties I took when you were at Glames ; you took me too literally, if you thought I meant in the least to discourage you in your pursuit of poetry : all I intended to say was, that if either vanity (that is, a general and undistinguishing desire of applause), or interest, or ambition has any place in the breast of a poet, he stands a great chance in these our days of being severely disappointed ; and yet, after all these passions are suppressed, there may remain in the mind of one, ' ingenti perculsus amore ' (and such I take you to be), incitements of a better sort, strong enough to make him write verse all his life, both for his own pleasure and that of all posterity.

I am sorry for the trouble you have had to gratify my curiosity and love of superstition ; yet I heartily thank you. On Monday, Sir, I set forward on my way to England ; where if I can be of any little use to you, or should ever have the good fortune to see you, it will be a particular satisfaction to me. Lord Strathmore and the family here desire me to make their compliments to you.

P.S.—Remember Dryden, and be blind to all his faults.

160. To Mason

1765.

DEAR MASON,—*Res est sacra miser* (says the poet,) but I say it is the happy man that is the sacred thing, and therefore let the profane keep their distance. He is one of Lucretius' gods, supremely blessed in the contemplation of his own felicity, and what has he to do with worshippers ? This, mind, is the first reason why I did not come to York : the second is, that I do not love confinement, and probably by next summer may be permitted to touch whom, and where, and with what I think fit, without giving you any offence : the third and last, and not the least perhaps, is, that the finances were at so low an ebb that I could not exactly do what I wished, but was obliged to come the shortest road to town and recruit them. I do not justly know what your taste in reasons may be, since you altered your condition, but there is the ingenious, the petulant, and the dull ; for you any one would have done, for in my conscience I do not believe you care a half-penny for reasons at present ; so God bless you both, and give ye all ye wish, when ye are restored to the use of your wishes.

I am returned from Scotland charmed with my expedition ; it is of the Highlands I speak ; the Lowlands are worth seeing once, but the mountains are ecstatic, and ought to be visited in pilgrimage once a year. None but those monstrous creatures of God know how to join so much beauty with so much horror. A fig for your poets, painters, gardeners, and clergymen, that have not been among them ; their imagination can be made up of nothing but bowling-greens, flowering shrubs, horse-ponds, Fleet ditches, shell grottoes, and Chinese rails. Then I had so beautiful an autumn, Italy could hardly produce a nobler scene, and this so sweetly contrasted with that perfection of nastiness, and total want of accommodation, that Scotland only can supply. Oh, you would have blessed yourself. I shall certainly go again ; what a pity it is I cannot draw, nor describe, nor ride on horseback.

Stonhewer is the busiest creature upon earth except Mr. Fraser ; they stand pretty tight, for all his Royal Highness. Have you read (oh no, I had forgot) Dr. Lowth's pamphlet against your uncle the Bishop ? Oh, how he works him. I hear he will soon be on the same bench. To-day Mr. Hurd came to see me, but we had not a word of that matter ; he is grown pure and plump, just of the proper breadth for a celebrated town-preacher. There was Dr. Balguy too ; he says Mrs. Mason is very handsome, so you are his friend for ever. Lord Newnham, I hear, has ill health of late ; it is a nervous case, so have a care. How do your eyes do ?

Adieu : my respects to the bride. I would kiss her, but you stand by and pretend it is not the fashion, though I know they do so at Hull.—I am ever yours,

T. G.

161. To Walpole

[London : November, 1765]

At my return from Scotland instead of seeing you I find an empty house, & an uncomfortable account of your situation : that you have been very ill with the gout in both feet, that you have been some time in France for your health, that you have got no farther than Paris, have again been confined there, & are just beginning to go abroad again. at the hazard of being call'd an old woman I will take upon me to desire, when the fit is actually upon you, that you will make no sudden changes in your diet, I do not say in quantity, but in quality. that when you are recovering & the pain is gone, but has left behind it a weakness in the joint, you will not be too indulgent to that weakness : but give yourself so much of motion & exercise, as you can well endure. above all, keep your legs warmer at all times, whether you are well or ill, in bed or up, than you have commonly used to do, & as far as may be, always in the same temperature. the quantity of wine you have commonly used has been so inconsiderable, that I do not believe it ever did, or will hurt you : but if you leave it off, mix a little quantity of spirit, brandy or whatever else is palatable to you, with your water. remember, it is only the wine-drinking nations, that know what the gout is : whereas those, that even indulge themselves in distill'd liquours, as well the laborious & hard-faring people, as the indolent & luxurious, tho' subject to many other disorders, are utter strangers to this. my prescriptions are simple, but they are such as I use myself, who am a Fellow-sufferer with you, about your own age, have (unhappily

L

for me) a better right to this malady than you, begun
to feel it earlier, & yet have hitherto felt it mildly,
& never in my stomach or head. I only say, they are
better than French Nostrums, or People of Qualitie's
receipts. you will do me pleasure (if you are able) in
telling me yourself, how you do, for I have no body but
your Servants to inform me.

I am come back from the Highlands very much the
better for my journey & (what I little expected) very
much pleased with what I have seen. I would send
you *English news*, but that I know, you receive it from
much better hands. they tell me *our* Ministry will
stand upon its legs, tho' they have lost the Duke.
there are three separations I hear talk'd of in the
married world, the Boling:ˢ, the Shelb:ˢ & the Warkw: ;
the last I believe may be true. Adieu ! take care of
yourself ! I am ever

Yours.

To The Honᵇˡᵉ Horace Walpole

162. To WALPOLE

Cambridge, December 13, 1765.

I am very much obliged to you for the detail you
enter into on the subject of your own health : in this
you cannot be too circumstantial for me, who had
received no account of you, but at second hand—such
as, that you were dangerously ill, and therefore went
to France ; that you meant to try a better climate, and
therefore staid at Paris ; that you had relapsed, and
were confined to your bed, and extremely in vogue,
and supped in the best company, and were at all
public diversions. I rejoice to find (improbable as it
seemed) that all the wonderful part of this is strictly
true, and that the serious part has been a little exag-
gerated. This letter I conclude not so much from
your own account of yourself, as from the spirits in
which I see you write ; and long may they continue
to support you ! I mean in a reasonable degree of
elevation : but if (take notice) they are so volatile, so

flippant, as to suggest any of those doctrines of health, which you preach with all the zeal of a French atheist ; at least, if they really do influence your practice ; I utterly renounce them and all their works. They are *evil spirits*, and will lead you to destruction.—You have long built your hopes on temperance, you say, and hardiness. On the first point we are agreed. The second has totally disappointed you, and *therefore* you will persist in it ; by all means. But then be sure to persist too in being young, in stopping the course of time, and making the shadow return back upon your sun-dial. If you find this not so easy, acquiesce with a good grace in my *anilities*, put on your under-stockings of yarn or woollen, even in the night-time. Don't provoke me ! or I shall order you two night-caps (which by the way would do your eyes good), and put a little of any French liqueur into your water : they are nothing but brandy and sugar, and among their various flavours some of them may surely be palatable enough. The pain in your feet I *can* bear ; but I shudder at the sickness in your stomach, and the weakness, that still continues. I conjure you, as you love yourself ; I conjure you by Strawberry, not to trifle with these edge-tools. There is no cure for the gout, when in the stomach, but to throw it into the limbs. There is no relief for the gout in the limbs, but in gentle warmth and gradual perspiration.

I was much entertained with your account of our neighbours. As an Englishman and an Antigallican, I rejoice at their dulness and their nastiness : though I fear we shall come to imitate them in both. Their atheism is a little too much, too shocking to rejoice at. I have been long sick at it in their authors, and hated them for it : but I pity their poor innocent people of fashion. They were bad enough, when they believed every thing !

I have searched where you directed me ; which I could not do sooner, as I was at London when I received your letter, and could not easily find her grace's works. Here they abound in every library.

The print you ask after is the frontispiece to *Nature's pictures drawn by Fancy's pencil*. But lest there should be any mistake, I must tell you, the family are not at dinner, but sitting round a rousing fire and telling stories. The room is just such a one as we lived in at Rheims : I mean as to the glazing and ceiling. The chimney is supported by cariatides : over the mantle-piece the arms of the family. The duke and duchess are crowned with laurel. A servant stands behind him, holding a hat and feather. Another is shutting a window. Diepenbecke delin. & (I think) S. Clouwe sculps. It is a very pretty and curious print, and I thank you for the sight of it. If it ever was a picture, what a picture to have !

I must tell you, that upon cleaning an old picture here at St. John's Lodge, which I always took for a Holbein ; on a ring, which the figure wears, they have found H.H. It has been always called B^D Fisher ; but is plainly a layman, and probably sir Anthony Denny, who was a benefactor to the college.

What is come of your Sevigné-curiosity ? I should be glad of a line now and then, when you have leisure. I wish you well, and am ever

Yours,

T. GRAY.

163. To WHARTON
Pemb: C: March 5, 1766.

DEAR DOCTOR,—I am amazed at myself, when I think I have never wrote to you : to be sure it is the sin of witchcraft or something worse. something indeed might be said for it, had I been married like Mason, who (for the first time since that great event) has just thought fit to tell me, that he never pass'd so happy a winter as the last, and this in spite of his anxieties, which perhaps (he says) might even make a part of his happiness : for his wife is by no means in health, she has a constant cough, yet he is assured her lungs are not affected, & that it is nothing of the consumptive kind. what say you to this case ? may

I flatter him, that breeding will be a cure for this disorder ? If so, I hear she is in a fair way to be well. as
to me I have been neither happy nor miserable : but
in a gentle stupefaction of mind, & very tolerable
health of body hitherto. if they last, I shall not much
complain. the accounts one has lately had from all
parts make me suppose you buried under the snow,
like the old Queen of Denmark. as soon as you are
dug out, I should rejoice to hear your voice from the
battlements of Old-Park. the greatest cold we have
felt here was January 2, Thermom : (in the garden)
at 4 in the afternoon standing at 30 Deg: $\frac{1}{2}$, and the
next day fell a little snow, wch did not lie. it was the
first we had had during the winter. again, Feb: 5
toward night, Therm: was down at 30 D: with a clear
sky ; the snow-drops then beginning to blow in the
garden : next day was a little snow. but on the
11th and 12th fell a deep snow (the weather not very
cold) wch however was melted on ye 15th, & made a
flood in the river. next day the Thrush was singing,
& the Rooks building. at & about London instead
of snow they had heavy rains. on the 19th the red
Hepatica blew, & next day the Primrose. the Crocus
is now in full bloom. so ends my chronicle.

My oracle of state (who now and then utters a little,
as far as he may with discretion) is a very slave and
pack-horse, that never breaths any air better than
that of London, except like an Apprentice, on Sundays
with his Master and Co:. however he is in health,
& a very good Boy. it is strange, the turn that things
have taken. that the late Ministry should negociate
a reconciliation with L^d B:, & that Ld Temple should
join them ; that they should after making their (bad)
apologies be received with a gracious kind of contempt,
& told that his L^{dp}: could enter into no political con-
nections with them : that on the first division on the
American business that happened in the H: of Lords
they should however all join to carry a point against
the Ministry by a majority indeed of four only, but the
D: of Y—k present & making one : that when the

Ministers expostulated in a proper place, they should be seriously assured the K: would support them. that on a division on an insignificant point to try their strength in the House of Commons they should again lose it by 12 majority : that they should persist nevertheless : that Mr Pitt should appear *tanquam e machinâ*, speak for 3 hours & ½, & assert the rights of the Colonies in their greatest latitude : that the Minister should profess himself ready to act with & even serve under him : that he should receive such a compliment with coldness, & a sort of derision : that Norton should move to send him to the Tower : that when the great questions came on, the Min^y: should always carry their point at one, two, three in the morning by majorities of 110 & 170 (Mr Pitt entirely concurring with them, & the Tories, People of the Court, & many Placemen, even L^d G: Sackville, constantly voting against them) all these events are unaccountable on any principles of common-sense.—I attribute much of the singular part to the interposition of *Women*, as rash as they are foolish. on Monday (I do not doubt, tho' as yet I do not certainly know it) the Bill to repeal the Stamp-act went thro', that House, & to-day it is before the Lords, who surely will not venture to throw it out. oh, that they would !—but after this important business is well over, there must be an eclaircissement : some amends must be made, & some gracious condescensions insisted on, or else who would go on, that really means to serve his country ! The D: of Bedford & Ld Temple were gone down to their villas, & I believe are not likely to come back. Ld Chesterfield, who had not been for many years at the House, came the other day to qualify himself in order to leave a proxy, that should vote with the Ministry. somebody (I thought) made no bad application of those lines in Virgil L: 6. v: 489

At Danaum proceres, Agamemnoniæq phalanges, &c:

to Mr Pitt's first appearance (for no one expected him) in the House. turn to the place.

Everything is politicks. there are no literary productions worth your notice, at least of our country. the French have finished their great Encyclopedie in 17 Volumes : but there are many flimsey articles very hastily treated, & great incorrectness of the Press. there are now 13 V: of Buffon's Natural History, & he is not come to the Monkies yet, who are a very numerous people. the Life of Petrarch has entertain'd me : it is not well written, but very curious & laid together from his own letters & the original writings of the 14th Century. So that it takes in much of the history of those obscure times, & the characters of many remarkable persons. there are 2 vols: 4to, and another (unpublish'd yet) that will compleat it.

Mr W: writes me now & then a long and lively letter from Paris, to which place he went the last Summer with the gout upon him sometimes in his limbs, often in his stomach and head. he has got somehow well (not by means of the climate, one would think) goes to all public places, sees all the best company and is very much in fashion. he says, he sunk like Queen Eleanor at Charing-Cross, & has risen again at Paris. he returns again in April : but his health is certainly in a deplorable state. Mad: de la Perriere is come over from the Hague to be Ministress at London. Her Father-in-law Viry is now first Minister at Turin. I sate a morning with her before I left London. She is a prodigious fine Lady, & a Catholick (though she did not expressly own it to me) not fatter than she was : she had a cage of foreign birds and a piping Bullfinch at her elbow, two little Dogs on a cushion in her lap, a Cockatoo on her shoulder, & a slight [?] suspicion of Rouge on her cheeks. They were all exceeding glad to see me, and I them.

Pray tell me the history of your winter, & present my respects to Mrs Wharton. I hope Miss Wharton & Miss Peggy with the assistance of Sister Betty make a great progress in Natural History : recommend me to all their good graces, & believe me ever

Truly Yours

If you chance to see or send to M^r and Mrs Leighton, I will trouble you to make my compliments : I have never received the box of shells, tho' possibly it may wait for me at Mr Jonathan's in Town, where I shall be in April. Mr Brown is well & desires to be remembered to you & Mrs Wharton. I have just heard, there are like to be warm debates in the house of Lords, but that the Ministry will undoubtedly carry it in spite of them all. They say Ld Cambden will soon be Chancellour.

Addressed to Wharton at Old Park, near Darlington, Durham.

164. To Norton Nicholls

Pemb. Hall, August 26, 1766.

Dear Sir,—It is long since, that I heard you were gone in hast into Yorkshire on account of your Mother's illness, and the same letter informed me that she was recovered ; otherwise I had then wrote to you, only to beg you would take care of her, and to inform you that I had discovered a thing very little known, wch is, that in one's whole life one never can have any more than a single Mother. You may think this is obvious, and (what you call) a trite observation. You are a green Gossling ! I was at the same age (very near) as wise as you, and yet I never discovered this (with full evidence and conviction, I mean) till it was too late. it is 13 years ago, and seems but yesterday, and every day I live it sinks deeper into my heart. many a corollary could I draw from this axiom for your use (not for my own) but I will leave you the merit of doing it yourself. pray tell me how your own health is. I conclude it perfect, as I hear you offered yourself for a guide to Mr. Palgrave into the Sierra-Morena of Yorkshire. for me, I passed the end of May and all June in Kent not disagreeably ; the country is all a garden, gay, rich, and fruitful, and (from the rainy season) had preserved, till I left it, all that emerald verdure, wch commonly one only sees for the first fortnight of the spring. in the west part of it from every eminence the eye catches some long winding reach of the Thames or Medway with all their navigation. in the east the sea breaks in upon you, and mixes its white transient sails and glittering blue expanse with the deeper and brighter greens of the woods and corn. this last sentence is so fine, I am quite ashamed : but, no matter ! you must translate it into prose. Palgrave, if he heard it, would cover his face with his pudding sleeve. I went to Margate for a day : one would think, it was Bartholomew fair that had flown down : From Smithfield to Kent in the London machine—like my Lady Stuffdamask (to be sure you have read the New Bath Guide, the most fashionable of books) so then I did *not* go to Kingsgate, because it belonged to my Ld Holland : but to Ramsgate I did, & so to Sandwich and Deal and Dover and Folkstone and Hithe all along the coast very delightful. I do not tell you of the great and small beasts, and creeping things innumerable that I met with, because you do not suspect, that this world is inhabited by anything but Men and Women, and Clergy, and such two-legged cattle. now I am here again very disconsolate and all alone : even Mr Brown is gone, and the cares of this world are coming thick upon me, I do not mean Children. you, I hope are better off, riding and walking with Mr Aislaby, singing Duets with my cousin Fanny, improving with Mr Weddell, conversing with Mr Harry Duncomb. I must not wish for you here : besides I am going to town at Michaelmas, by no means for amusement. Do you remember, how we are to go into Wales next year ? well !—Adieu, I am Sincerely yours.

TG :

P.S.—Pray how does poor Temple find himself in his new situation ? Is L^d L: as good as his letters were ? What is come of the Father and Brother ? Have you seen Mason ?

165. To Wharton

DEAR DOCTOR,—Whatever my pen may do, I am sure my thoughts expatiate no where oftener or with more pleasure, than to Old-Park. I hope you have made my peace with Miss Deborah. it is certain, whether her name were in my letter or not, she was as present to my memory, as the rest of the little family, & I desire you would present her with two kisses in my name, & one a piece to all the others : for I shall take the liberty to kiss them all (great & small) as you are to be my proxy.

In spite of the rain, wch I think continued with very short intervals till the beginning of this month, & quite effaced the summer from the year, I made a shift to pass May & June not disagreeably in Kent. I was surprised at the beauty of the road to Canterbury, which (I know not why) had not struck me in the same manner before. the whole country is a rich and well-cultivated garden, orchards, cherry-grounds, hop-gardens, intermix'd with corn & frequent villages, gentle risings cover'd with wood, and everywhere the Thames and Medway breaking in upon the Landscape with all their navigation. it was indeed owing to the bad weather, that the whole scene was dress'd in that tender emerald-green, wch one usually sees only for a fortnight in the opening of spring, & this continued till I left the country. My residence was eight miles east of Canterbury in a little quiet valley on the skirts of Barhamdown. in these parts the whole soil is chalk, and whenever it holds up, in half an hour it is dry enough to walk out. I took the opportunity of three or four days fine weather to go into the Isle of Thanet, saw Margate (wch is Bartholomew-Fair by the sea side), Ramsgate, & other places there, and so came by Sandwich, Deal, Dover, Folkstone, & Hithe, back again. the coast is not like Hartlepool : there are no rocks, but only chalky cliffs of no great height, till you come to Dover. there indeed they are noble & picturesque, and the opposite coasts of France begin

to bound your view, wch was left before to range unlimited by anything but the horizon : yet it is by no
means a *shipless* sea, but everywhere peopled with
white sails & vessels of all sizes in motion ; and take
notice (except in the Isle, wch is all corn-fields, and
has very little inclosure) there are in all places hedge-
rows & tall trees even within a few yards of the beach,
particularly Hithe stands on an eminence cover'd
with wood. I shall confess we had fires of a night
(ay, & a day too) several times even in June : but don't
go & take advantage of this, for it was the most untoward year that ever I remember.

Your Friend Rousseau (I doubt) grows tired of M^r
Davenport and Derbyshire. he has picked a quarrel
with David Hume & writes him letters of 14 pages
Folio upbraiding him of all his *noirceurs.* take one
only as a specimen, he says, that at Calais they chanced
to sleep in the same room together, & that he overheard
David talking in his sleep, and saying, *Ah ! Je le tiens,
ce Jean-Jacques là.* In short (I fear) for want of
persecution & admiration (for these are real complaints)
he will go back to the Continent.

What shall I say to you about the Ministry ? I am
as angry as a Common-council Man of London about
my Ld Chatham : but a little more patient, & will hold
my tongue till the end of the year. in the mean time I
do mutter in secret & to you, that to quit the house
of Commons, his natural strength ; to sap his own
popularity & grandeur (which no one but himself could
have done) by assuming a foolish title ; & to hope that
he could win by it and attach to him a Court, that hate
him & will dismiss him, as soon as ever they dare, was
the weakest thing, that ever was done by so great
a Man. Had it not been for this, I should have rejoiced at the breach between him & Ld Temple, & at
the union between him & the D: of Grafton & Mr Conway : but patience ! we shall see ! St: perhaps is in the
country (for he hoped for a month's leave of absence) and
if you see him, you will learn more than I can tell you.

Mason is at Aston. he is no longer so anxious about

his wife's health, as he was, tho' I find she still has a cough, & moreover I find she is not with child : but he made such a bragging, how could one chuse but believe him.

When I was in town, I marked in my pocket-book the utmost limits & divisions of the two columns in your Thermometer, and asked Mr. Ayscough the Instrument-Maker on Ludgate Hill, what scales they were. he immediately assured me, that one was Fahrenheit's, & shew'd me one exactly so divided. the other he took for Reaumur's, but, as he said there were different scales of his contrivance, he could not exactly tell, wch of them it was. your Brother told me, you wanted to know, who wrote Duke Wharton's life in the Biography : I think, it is chiefly borrowed from a silly book enough call'd *Memoirs of that Duke* : but who put it together there, no one can inform me. the only person certainly known to write in that vile collection (I mean these latter volumes) is Dr Nicholls, who was expell'd here for stealing books.

Have you read the *New Bath-Guide* ? it is the only thing in fashion, & is a new & original kind of humour. Miss Prue's Conversion I doubt you will paste down, as S^r W: St Quintyn did, before he carried it to his daughter. Yet I remember you all read *Crazy Tales* without pasting. Buffon's first collection of Monkies are come out (it makes the 14th volume) something, but not much, to my edification : for he is pretty well acquainted with their persons, but not with their manners.

I shall be glad to hear, how far Mrs Ettrick has succeeded, & when you see an end to her troubles. my best respects to Mrs. Wharton, & compliments to all your family : I will not name them, least I should afront any body. Adieu, dear S^r,

I am most sincerely yours,

TG:

August 26, 1766, Pembroke College.

Mr. Brown is gone to see his Brother near Margate. When is Ld Str: to be married ? If M^r and Mrs Jonathan are with you, I desire my compliments.

166. To Mason

[August 1766.]

DEAR MASON,—I rejoice to find you are both in health, and that one or other of you at least can have your teeming time : you are wise as a serpent, but the devil of a dove, in timing both your satire and your compliments. When a man stands on the very verge of dissolution, with all his unblushing honours thick upon him ; when the gout has nipped him in the bud and blasted all his hopes at least for one winter, then come you buzzing about his nose, and strike your sting deep into the reddest, angriest part of his toe ; which will surely mortify. When another has been weak enough in the plenitude of power to disarm himself of his popularity, and to conciliate a court that naturally hates him, submits to be decked in their trappings and fondle their lap-dogs, then come you to lull him with your gentlest hum, recalling his good deeds, and hoping what I (with all my old partialities) scarce should dare to hope, if I had but any one else to put my trust in. Let you alone, where spite and interest are in view : ay, ay, Mrs. M. (I see) will be a bishopess.

Well, I transcribed your wickedness in a print hand, and sent it by last Sunday's post to Dr. Gisborne, with your orders about it, for I had heard St[onehewer] say that he hoped for a month's respite to go into the North, and did not know but he might be gone. G. was to send me word he had received it, but has not yet done so, and (Lord bless me) who knows but he may be gone into Derbyshire, and the Ode gone after him ; if so, mind I am innocent, and meant for the best. I liked it vastly, and thought it very well turned and easy, especially the diabolical part of it. I fear it will not keep, and would have wished the public might have eat it fresh ; but, if any untoward accident should delay it, it will be still better than most things that appear at their table.

I shall finish where you begun, with my apology. You say you have neglected me, and (to make it relish the better) with many others : for my part I have not neglected you, but I have always considered the happy, that is, new-married people, as too sacred or too profane a thing to be approached by me ; when the year is over, I have no longer any respect or aversion for them.

Adieu : I am in no spirits, and perplexed besides with many little cares, but always sincerely yours,

T. G.

P.S.—My best respects to " Madam in her grogram gown." I have long since heard that you were out of pain with regard to her health. Mr. Brown is gone to see his brother near Margate.

167. To Norton Nicholls

My dear S^r,—I was absent in Suffolk, & did not receive your melancholy letter till my return hither yesterday : so you must not attribute this delay to me, but to accident. to sympathize with you in such a loss is an easy task for me : but to comfort you not so easy. can I wish to see you unaffected with the sad scene now before your eyes, or with the loss of a person, that thro' a great part of your life has proved himself so kind a Friend to you ? he who best knows our nature (for he made us, what we are) by such afflictions recalls us from our wandering thoughts and idle merriment, from the insolence of youth & prosperity, to serious reflection, to our duty and to himself : nor need we hasten to get rid of these impressions ; Time (by appointment of the same Power) will cure the smart, & in some hearts soon blot out all the traces of sorrow : but such as preserve them longest (for it is left partly in our own power) do perhaps best acquiesce in the will of the Chastiser.

For the consequences of this sudden loss I see them well, & (I think) in a like situation could fortify my mind so as to support them with chearfulness and good hopes, tho' not naturally inclined to see things in their best aspect. your Cousins seem naturally kind and well disposed worthy young People : your Mother &

they will assist one another. you too (when you have time to turn you round) must think seriously of your profession. you know I would have wish'd to see you wear the livery of it long ago. but I will not dwell on this subject at present. to be obliged to those we love and esteem is a pleasure : but to serve and to oblige them is a still greater, & this with independence (no vulgar blessings) are what a Profession at your age may reasonably promise. without it they are hardly attainable. remember, I speak from experience !

Poor Mr. W: is struck with a paralytic disorder. I know it only from the papers, but think it very likely. he may live in this state, incapable of assisting himself, in the hands of servants or relations, that only gape after his spoils, perhaps for years to come. think how many things may befall a man far worse than death. Adieu ! I sincerely wish your happiness, and am

Faithfully yours

TG:

Pemb: C: Sept: 23. 1766.

P:S: I must go soon to London : but if you direct to me here, I shall have your letters. let me know soon, how you go on.

168. TO NORTON NICHOLLS

MY DEAR SR,—I have received a second instance of your kindness & confidence in me. and surely you hazard nothing in trusting me with the whole of your situation. it appears not to me so new, as it does to you. you well know the tenour of my conversation (urged perhaps at times a little farther than you liked) has been intended to prepare you for this event, to familiarize your mind with this spectre that you call by its worst name ; but remember, that *Honesta res est læta paupertas.* I see it with respect, and so will every one, whose poverty is not seated in their mind. there is but one real evil in it (take my word, who know it well) & that is, that you have less the power of assisting others who have not the same resources to support them. it is this consideration that makes me remind you that Ansel is lately dead, a Lay-fellow of your college, that if Dr. M: (whose follies let us pardon, because he has some feeling & means us well) be of little use, & if Dr. H: (another simple Friend of ours, perhaps with less sensibility) cannot serve us in this : yet Dr. R: is not immortal, you have always said to succeed him was not impracticable, I know it would be creditable, I know it would be profitable, I know it would, in lieu of a little drudgery, bring you freedom, that drudgery would with a little use grow easy. in the mean time if any better prospect present itself, there you are ready to take advantage of the opportunity. in short this was always my favourite project, & now more than ever for reasons, that will occur to yourself. in waiting for the accomplishment of it, you will take orders, and if your Uncles are slow in their motions, you will accept a Curacy (for a title will be requisite), not under every body, that offers, but under some gentlemanlike friendly Man, and in a christian country. a profession you must have : why not then accommodate yourself chearfully to its beginnings ; you have youth, you have many kind well-intention'd people belonging to you, many acquaintance of your own, or familie's, that will wish to serve you consider how many have had the same, or greater cause for dejection with none of these resources before their eyes.

I am in Town for a month or more, & wish to hear from you soon. Mr. W: has indeed been dangerously ill with the gout in his stomach, but nothing paralytic, as was said. he is much recovered, and gone to Bath. Adieu, Dear S^r, I am faithfully Yours,   TG.

I will write again soon.

169. To the Rev. James Brown

Jermyn Street, November 18, 1766.

DEAR SIR,—I paid the sum above-mentioned this morning at Gillam's office in Bishopsgate Street. The remittance you will please to pay out of it. I have not time to add all the bad news of the times, but in a few days you shall have some of it ; though the worst of all is just what I cannot write. I am perfectly out of humour, and so will you be.

Mason is here, and has brought his wife, a pretty, modest, innocent, interesting figure, looking like 18, though she is near 28. She does not speak, only whispers, and her cough as troublesome as ever ; yet I have great hopes there is nothing consumptive. She is strong and in good spirits. We were all at the opera together on Saturday last. They desire their loves to you. I have seen Mr. Talbot and Delaval lately. Adieu.—I am ever yours,   T. G.

I cannot find Mons. de la Chalotais in any of the shops. Lord Strathmore, I am told, is to be married here. I know nothing of Pa. but that he was still at Mr. Weddell's a fortnight since. Be so good to tell me you have received this, if you can, by the return of the post.

170. To Mason

Pembroke Hall, January 27, 1767.

DEAR MASON,—Dean Swift says, one never should write to one's friends but in high health and spirits. By the way it is the last thing people in those circumstances usually think of doing. But it is sure, if I were to wait for them, I never should write at all. At present, I have had for these six weeks a something growing in my throat, which nothing does any service to, and which will, I suppose, in due time stop up the passage. I go however about, and the pain is very little. You will say, perhaps, the malady is as little, and the stoppage is in the imagination ; no matter for that. If it is not sufficient to prove want of health (for indeed this is all I ail), it is so much the stronger proof of the want of spirits. So, take it as you please, I carry my point, and shew you that it is very obliging in me to write at all. Indeed, perhaps on your account,

I should not have done it, but, after three such weeks of Lapland weather, I cannot but enquire after Mrs. Mason's health. If she has withstood such a winter and her cough never the worse, she may defy the doctors and all their works. Pray, tell me how she is, for I interest myself for her, not merely on your account, but on her own. These last three mornings have been very vernal and mild. Has she tasted the air of the new year, at least in Hyde Park ?

Mr. Brown will wait on her next week, and touch her. He has been confined to lie on a couch, and under the surgeon's hands ever since the first of January with a broken shin, ill doctored. He has just now got abroad, and obliged to come to town about Monday, on particular business.

Stonhewer was so kind as to tell me the mystery now accomplished, before I received your letter. I rejoice in all his accessions. I wish you would persuade him to take unto him a wife, but do not let her be a fine lady. Adieu. Present my respects and good wishes to Argentile.—I am truly yours,

T. G.

171. To Mason

Sunday, February 15, 1767.

DEAR MASON,—It grieves me to hear the bad account you give of our poor patient's health. I will not trouble you to enquire into the opinions of her physicians ; as you are silent on that head, I doubt you are grown weary of the inutility of their applications. I, you will remember, am at a distance, and cannot judge, but by conjecture, of the progress her disorder seems to make, and particularly of that increasing weakness which seems, indeed, an alarming symptom. I am told that the sea-air is advised as likely to be beneficial, and that Lord Holdernesse offers you the use of Walmer Castle, but that you wait till the spring is more advanced to put this in execution. I think I should by no means delay at all. The air of the coast is at all seasons warmer than that of the inland country. The weather is now mild and open, and (unless the rains increase) fit for travelling. Remember how well she bore the journey to London ; and it is certain that sort of motion, in her case, instead of fatigue, often brings an accession of strength. I have lately seen that coast, and been in Deal Castle, which is very similar in situation to Walmer and many other little neighbouring forts ; no doubt, you may be very well lodged and accommodated there. The scene is delightful in fine weather, but in a stormy day and high wind (and we are but just got so far in the year as the middle of February), exposed to all the rage of the sea and full force of the east wind ; so that, to a person unused to the sea, it may be even dreadful. My idea, therefore, is that you might go at present to Ramsgate, which is sheltered from the north, and opening only to the south and south-east, with a very fine pier to walk on. It is a neat town, seemingly, with very clean houses to lodge in, and one end of it only running down to the shore ; it is at no season much pestered with company, and at present, I suppose, there is nobody there. If you find Mrs. Mason the better for this air and situation (which God send), when May and fine settled weather come in, you will easily remove to Walmer, which at that season will be delightful to her. If—forgive me for supposing the worst, your letter leaves me too much reason to do so, though I hope it was only the effect of a melancholy imagination —if it should be necessary to meet the spring in a milder climate than ours is, you are very near Dover, and perhaps this expedient (if she grow very visibly worse) may be preferable to all others, and ought not to be deferred : it is usually too long delayed.

There are a few words in your letter that make me believe you wish I were in town. I know myself how little one like me is formed to support the spirits of another, or give him consolation ; one that always sees things in their most gloomy aspect. However, be assured I should not have left London while you were in it, if I could well have afforded to stay there till the beginning of April, when I am usually there. This, however, shall be no hindrance, if you tell me it would signify anything to you that I should come sooner. Adieu: you (both of you) have my best and sincerest good wishes.—I am ever yours,

T. G.

P.S.—Remember, if you go into Kent, that W. Robinson lives at Denton (eight miles from Dover); perhaps he and his wife might be of some little use to you. Him you know; and for her, she is a very good-humoured, cheerful woman, that (I dare swear) would give any kind of assistance in her power: remember, too, to take whatever medicines you use with you from London. A country apothecary's shop is a terrible thing.

My respects to Dr. Gisborne, and love to Stonhewer. When you have leisure and inclination, I should be very glad to hear from you. Need I repeat my kindest good wishes to Mrs. Mason.

172. To Mason

March 28, 1767.

My Dear Mason,—I break in upon you at a moment when we least of all are permitted to disturb our friends, only to say that you are daily and hourly present to my thoughts. If the worst be not yet passed, you will neglect and pardon me; but if the last struggle be over, if the poor object of your long anxieties be no longer sensible to your kindness, or to her own sufferings, allow me (at least in idea, for what could I do were I present more than this), to sit by you in silence, and pity from my heart, not her who is at rest, but you who lose her. May He who made us, the Master of our pleasures and of our pains, preserve and support you. Adieu!

I have long understood how little you had to hope.

173. To the Rev. James Brown

[Jermyn Street,
probably, last week in May, 1767.]

How do you do, good Mr. Brown ? Do your inclinations begin to draw northward, as mine do, and may I take you a place soon ? I wait but for an answer from Mason how to regulate our journey, which I should hope may take place in a little more than a week. I shall write a line again to settle the exact day, but you may now tell me whether you will come to town, or be taken up at Buckden, or thirdly, whether you will go in a chaise with me by short journeys, and see places in our way. I dined yesterday on Richmond Hill, after seeing Chiswick, and Strawberry, and Sion ; and be assured the face of the country looks an emerald, if you love jewels.

The Westminster Theatre is like to come to a sudden end. The manager will soon embark for Italy without Callista. The reason is a speech, which his success in Lothario emboldened him to make the other day in a greater theatre. It was on the subject of America, and added so much strength to the opposition, that they came within six of the majority. He did not vote, however, though his two brothers did, and, like good boys, with the ministry. For this he has been rattled on both sides of his ears, and forbid to appear there any more. The Houses wait with impatience the conclusion of the East India business to rise. The E. of Chatham is mending slowly in his health, but sees nobody on business yet, nor has he since he came from Marlborough : yet he goes out daily for an airing.

I have seen his lordship of Cloyne often. He is very jolly, and we devoured four raspberry-puffs together in Cranbourn-alley standing at a pastrycook's shop in the street ; but he is gone, and Heaven knows when we shall eat any more.

Rousseau you see is gone too. I read his letter to my Lord Chancellor from Spalding, and hear he has written another long one to Mr. Conway from Dover, begging he might no longer be detained here. He retains his pension. The whole seems madness increasing upon him. There is a most bitter satire on him and his Madlle. le Vasseur, written by Voltaire, and called *Guerre de Geneve*. Adieu, and let me hear from you.

I am ever yours,

T. G.

How do our Elmsted friends ? Are they married yet ? Old Pa. is here, and talks of writing soon to you.

174. To the Rev. James Brown

Jermyn Street, June 2, 1767.

DEAR SIR,—Where are you ? for I wrote to you last week to know how soon we should set out, and how we should go. Mason writes to-day, he will expect us at Aston in Whitsun-week ; and has ordered all his lilacs and roses to be in flower. What can you be doing? And so as I said, shall we go in the Newcastle post-coach or the York coach ? Will you choose to come to town or be taken up on the way ? Or will you go all the way to Bantry in a chaise with me and see sights ? Answer me speedily. In return I will tell you that you will soon hear great news ; but whether good or bad is hard to say ; therefore I shall prudently tell you nothing more. Adieu.—I am ever yours,

T. G.

Old Pa. is still here, going to Ranelagh and the Opera. Lady Strathmore is with child, and not very well, as I hear.

175. To Wharton

Sunday, 21 June, 1767, Aston.

DEAR DOCTOR,—Here we are, Mr Brown & I, in a wilderness of sweets, an Elysium among the coal-pits, a terrestrial heaven. mind, it is not I, but Mason, that says all this, & bids me tell it you. tomorrow we visit Dovedale & the Wonders of the Peak, the Monday following we go to York to reside & two or

three days after set out for Old-Park, where I shall
remain upon your hands; & Mr Brown about the
time of Durham-races must go on to Gibside, & for
ought I know to Glamis: Mason remains tied down
to his Minster for half a year. he & M^r B: desire their
best compliments to you & Mrs Wharton. Adieu!

I am ever Yours,

T. GRAY

Mr. Brown owns the pleasantest day he ever past
was yesterday at Roche-Abbey. it is indeed divine.

176. TO MASON

Old Park, September 11, 1767.

DEAR MASON,—I admire you as the pink of perver-
sity. How did I know about York races, and how
could I be more explicit about our journey? The
truth is, I was only too explicit by half, for we did not
set out in earnest till the 29th of August, being delayed,
partly by the bad weather, and partly by your cousin,
my Lord Perrot, and his assizes, whose train we were
afraid to overtake, and still more afraid of being over-
taken by it. At last then we went in the sun and dust
broiling to Newcastle, and so by the military road to
Hexham at night, where it began to rain, and continued
like fury, with very short intervals, all the rest of our
way. So we got to Carlisle, passed a day there in
raining and seeing delights. Next day got to Penrith
—more delights; the next dined and lay at Keswick;
could not go a mile to see anything. Dr. Wharton
taken ill in the night with an asthma. Went on,
however, over stupendous hills to Cockermouth. Here
the Doctor grew still worse in the night, so we came
peppering and raining back through Keswick to
Penrith. Next day lay at Brough, grew better, raining
still, and so over Stonemoor home. September 5.—In
a heavy thunder-shower. Now you will think from
this detail, which is literally true, that we had better
have staid at home. No such thing; I am charmed
with my journey, and the Doctor dreams of nothing

but Skiddaw, and both of us vow to go again the first opportunity. I carried Mr. Brown to Gibside the 11th of August, and took a receipt for him; they did not set out for Scotland till the 1st of September, and as yet I have not heard from him.

If you are not too much afflicted for the loss of Charles Townshend, now is your time to come and see us. In spite of your coquetry, we still wish of all things to see you, and (bating that vice, and a few more little faults) have a good opinion of you, only we are afraid you have a bad heart. I have known purse-proud people often complain of their poverty, which is meant as an insult upon the real poor. How dare you practise this upon me? Do not I know little Clough? Here is a fuss indeed about a poor three-score miles. Don't I go galloping five hundred, when-ever I please? Have done with your tricks, and come to Old Park, for the peaches and grapes send forth a good smell, and the voice of the robin is heard in our land. My services to Mr. Alderson, for he is a good creature. But I forget, you are at York again. Adieu!

I am, ever yours,

T. G.

The Doctor presents his compliments to you with great cordiality, and desires your assistance. One of his daughters has some turn for drawing, and he would wish her a little instructed in the practice. If you have any professor of the art at York, that would think it worth his while to pass about six weeks here, he would be glad to receive him. His conditions he would learn from you. If he have any merit in his art, doubtless so much the better. But above all he must be elderly, and if ugly and ill-made so much the more acceptable. The reasons we leave to your prudence.

177. To the Rev. Norton Nicholls

Jermyn-Street. 5 Nov: 1767.

DEAR S^R,—I am come, & shall rejoice to congratulate you face to face on your good luck, wch is wonderful in my eyes: I hope there are no rubs in the way to

prevent my seeing you snug in the rectory, surrounded
with fat pigs & stubble-geese, and Madam in her
grogram gown doing the honours of Lovingland, at
the head of your table.

I have much to say, so much that I shall say no more :
but come quickly, if the main chance will suffer you,
or I will know the reason why. Adieu !—I am sincerely
Yours

TG:

178. To James Beattie

Pembroke Hall, December 24, 1767.

Since I had the pleasure of receiving your last
letter, which did not reach me till I had left the North,
and was come to London, I have been confined to my
room with a fit of the gout : now I am recovered and
in quiet at Cambridge, I take up my pen to thank you
for your very friendly offers, which have so much the
air of frankness and real good meaning, that were my
body as tractable and easy of conveyance as my mind,
you would see me to-morrow in the chamber you have
so hospitably laid out for me at Aberdeen. But, alas !
I am a summer-bird, and can only sit drooping till
the sun returns : even then too my wings may chance
to be clipped, and little in plight for so distant an
excursion.

The proposal you make me, about printing at Glasgow what little I have ever written, does me honour.
I leave my reputation in that part of the kingdom to
your care ; and only desire you would not let your
partiality to me and mine mislead you. If you persist
in your design, Mr. Foulis certainly ought to be
acquainted with what I am now going to tell you.
When I was in London the last spring, Dodsley, the
bookseller, asked my leave to reprint, in a smaller
form, all I ever published ; to which I consented :
and added, that I would send him a few explanatory
notes ; and if he would omit entirely the *Long Story*
(which was never meant for the public, and only
suffered to appear in that pompous edition because

of Mr. Bentley's designs, which were not intelligible
without it), I promised to send him something else to
print instead of it, lest the bulk of so small a volume
should be reduced to nothing at all. Now it is very
certain that I had rather see them printed at Glasgow
(especially as you will condescend to revise the press)
than at London; but I know not how to retract my
promise to Dodsley. By the way, you perhaps may
imagine that I have some kind of interest in this
publication; but the truth is, I have none whatever.
The expense is his, and so is the profit, if there be any.
I therefore told him the other day, in general terms,
that I heard there would be an edition put out in
Scotland by a friend of mine, whom I could not refuse;
and that, if so, I would send thither a copy of the same
notes and additions that I had promised to send to
him. This did not seem at all to cool his courage;
Mr. Foulis must therefore judge for himself, whether
he thinks it worth while to print what is going to be
printed also at London. If he does I will send him
(in a packet to you) the same things I shall send to
Dodsley. They are imitations of two pieces of old
Norwegian poetry, in which there was a wild spirit
that struck me; but for my paraphrases I cannot say
much; you will judge. The rest are nothing but a
few parallel passages, and small notes just to explain
what people said at the time was wrapped in total
darkness. You will please to tell me, as soon as you
can conveniently, what Mr. Foulis says on this head;
that (if he drops the design) I may save myself and you
the trouble of this packet. I ask your pardon for
talking so long about it; a little more and my letter
would be as big as all my works.

I have read, with much pleasure, an Ode of yours
(in which you have done me the honour to adopt a
measure that I have used) on Lord Hay's birth-day.
Though I do not love panegyric, I cannot but applaud
this, for there is nothing mean in it. The diction is
easy and noble, the texture of the thoughts lyric, and
the versification harmonious. The few expressions I

object to are . . . These, indeed, are minutiæ ; but they weigh for something, as half a grain makes a difference in the value of a diamond.

179. To Wharton

DEAR DOCTOR,—Many and various maladies have I labour'd under, since I left the north, but none of them (thanks to my summer expedition) *jusqu' a mourir.* the gout came regularly, while I was in town, first in one, then in the other foot, but so tame you might have stroked it. since I got hither, *another* of my troublesome companions for life has confined me to my room, but abstinence has (I believe) got the better of that too, and to-morrow I go abroad again. I sent to your brother, before I left London, the *maps* you wanted, the *Decouvertes des Russes, Voyage de Gmelin* en Siberie, Mr. Clerke of Chichester *on the Saxon coins,* Lee's *Linnœan Dictionary, Verrall's Cookery,* & something else that I have forgot. as to Hudson's *Flora Anglica* it is not to be had, being out of print : a new and more correct edition is soon expected. Willoughby's book of *fishes* was never publish'd in English, so would not answer your end. That of *Birds* is indeed in English, but not to be had in the shops & sells at auctions from 30 to 40 shillings, so I did not buy it without farther orders. I hope this cargo is safe arrived ; and another little one, that I sent to Miss Wharton & Miss Peggy, directed to the former, to be left at Mr Tho: Wilkinson's in Durham : this went by the Newcastle Waggon about 6th of Dec:, & contained twelve Tower-roots, viz : 3 Soleil d'or Narcissus, 2 White Italian do: (*N:B:* of the double white & yellow Italian there are none to be had this year) 2 Pileus Cardinalis, red ; 1 Kroon-vogel, 1 Degeraad, double White ; 1 Belle Grisdelin. 1 Hermaphrodite, & 1 Incomparable, double blew ; Hyacinths. for these you must get glasses from Newcastle. in the same box was a pocket Lens, wch Miss Wh: (if she pleased) was to give to Aunt Middleton, who wanted such a thing.

I desire to know, what you thought of Mason's plans for your ground (wch makes so pretty a figure on paper) ; & whether *Summers* came to Old-Park to advise about planting. he is a very intelligent modest young Man, and might be of great use there. has Miss Wharton served her time yet as a Bride-maid ? I hope it may prove a good omen to her ! does Miss Peggy rival Claude Lorraine yet, & when does she go to York ? do Debo and Betty tend their Chrysalises, & their samplers ? Is Kee's mouth as pretty as ever ? does Robin read like a Doctor, dance like a Fairy, and bow like a Courtier ? Does Dicky kick up his heels, & study Geography ? please to answer me as to all these particulars. my Thermometer presents her compliments to her country-sister, & proposes now to open a correspondence with her. she lives against a pale in the garden with her back to the East at 9 o'clock in the morning precisely : at any other hour she is not visible, unless upon some great occasion. I was in London from 3 Nov: to 14 Dec:, during wch time the weather was commonly open, damp, & mild, with the wind in the West, veering either to N: or S:. on the last mention'd day I found some Brambles & Fever-few yet flowering in the hedges, & in gardens the double Chrysanthemum, double Chamomile, Borage, Stocks, & single Wall-flowers. these were all cut off on the 24th by an E: wind & hard frost, Therm: at 31. next day & today it was at 30. on the 26th a little snow fell, wch still lies & freezes.

Our Ministry has taken in some odd Coadjutors not much to its credit or strength. it appear'd from the first day that the Parliament met, that the Opposition were all to pieces among themselves, & soon after the Duke of Bedford civilly declared to Mr Grenville, that he had the highest opinion of his abilities : but as it was contrary to his principles to keep up a constant opposition to the K^s: measures, he must not wonder, if his Friends should drop the plan they had for some time been pursuing. accordingly he made his terms, four or five of them were directly to be provided for :

the rest were to wait till there was room. Ld Shelburne (the Sec^y:), & Mr Cook (Joint-Paymaster) were to have gone out, but Ld Chatham insisted on their staying in (it is said) & prevail'd. Mr Conway retires, & is to have the army, when Ld Ligonier dies : this is voluntary, I imagine. Ld Northington goes off with his pension. Ld Weymouth, & Earl Gower supply their places. Mr Thynne is Master of ye Household. Ld Sandwich, Joint-Postmaster (Ld Hillsborough being created Secretary of State for America) Rigby is the other, that must come in (to what place I know not) & conduct, I suppose, the House of Commons. how much better and nobler would it have been to have left all these Beggars in the lurch ? indeed what could be said against it, as all that could oppose the Ministry were already broke into three parts, & one of them had declared publickly against the other two ? I conclude the Rockingham-party will at last prevail, as they have some character and credit with the people still left.

Adieu, my dear S^r. you have had, I hope, no returns of your asthma, since you lay in your own bed. my best respects to Mrs Wharton, & love to all the family. I am ever

Yours
TG:

Dec. 28: 1767. Pemb: Coll:
Shall I write out, & send you, what Leland says of your neighbourhood ? it is nothing but short notes taken in his journey : but that journey was towards the end of Henry 8^{th's} reign just after the dissolution of Monasteries, wch makes it valuable.

SPECIMEN

From St Andre's Akeland to Raby Castel 5 miles, part by arrable, but more by pastures, & morisch hilly ground, baren of wood. Raby is the largest Castel of Logginges in al the North-cuntery, & is of a strong building : but not set ether on hil, or very strong ground. as I enterid by a causey into it there was a little stagne on the right hond, and in the first area were but two toures, one at eche end, as Entres, & no other buildid. yn the 2ᵈ area, as an Entring, was a great Gate of iren with a Tour, & 2 or 3 mo on the right hond. then were al the chief Toures of the 3ᵈ Court, as in the hart of the castel. The Haul, & al the Houses of Offices be large & steady; & in the haul I saw an incredible great beame of an Hart. the great Chaumber was exceeding large, but now it is false-rofid, and devidid into 2 or 3 Partes. I saw ther a litle chaumber, wherein was in windows of colorid glass al the petigre of yᵉ Nevilles, &c:

180. To Mason

Pembroke College, January 8, 1768.

DEAR MASON,—I did not write to you—that's to be sure; but then, consider, I had the gout great part of the time that I passed in town, and ever since I came thither I have been confined to my room; and besides, you know, you were at Aston, and did not much care. As to Monsieur de la Harpe, he is not to be had at any of the shops, and, they say, never was in England. What I saw and liked of his must have been in some bibliothèque or journal that I had borrowed.

Here are, or have been, or will be, all your old and new friends in constant expectation of you at Cambridge; yet Christmas is past, and no Scroddles appears.

Weddell attends your call, and Palgrave proud,
[? Stonhewer the lewd], and Delaval the loud.
For thee does Powell squeeze, and Marriot sputter,
And Glyn cut phizzes, and Tom Neville stutter.
Brown sees thee sitting on his nose's tip,
The Widow feels thee in her aching hip,
For thee fat Nanny sighs, and handy Nelly,
And Balguy with a bishop in his belly.

It is true of the two archdeacons. The latter is now here, but goes on Monday. The former comes to take his degree in February. The rector writes to ask whether you are come, that he may do the same. As to Johnny, here he is, divided between the thoughts of . . . and marriage. Delaval only waits for a little entreaty. The master, the doctor, the poet, and the president, are very pressing and warm, but none so warm as the coffee-house and I. Come then away. This is no season for planting, and Lord Richard will grow as well without your cultivation as with it ; at least let us know what we are to hope for, and when, if it be only for the satisfaction of the methodist singing-man your landlord.

You will finish your *opus magnum* here so clever, and your series of historical tragedies, with your books (that nobody reads) all round you ; and your critic at hand, who never cares a farthing, that I must say for him, whether you follow his opinions or not ; and your hypercritics, that nobody, not even themselves, understands, though you think you do. I am sorry to tell you Saint John's Garden is quite at a stand ; perhaps you in person may set it going. If not, here is Mr. Brown's little garden cries aloud to be laid out (it is in a wretched state, to be sure, and without any taste). You shall have unlimited authority over it, and I will take upon me the whole expense. Will you not come ? I know you will. Adieu, I am ever yours,

T. G.

181. To William Taylor Howe

Cambridge, Pembroke College,
January 12, 1768.

Sir,—You perceive by Mr. Brown's letter, that I passed all the summer in the North of England, went from thence to London, and did not arrive here till the middle of December, where I found your parcel. Since that time I have been generally confined to my room, and besides I was willing to go through the eight volumes, before I returned you an answer. This must be my excuse to you, for only doing now, what in mere civility I ought to have done long ago. First I must condole with you, that so neat an edition should swarm in almost every page with errors of the press, not only in notes and citations from Greek, French, and English authors, but in the Italian text itself, greatly to the disreputation of the Leghorn publishers. This is the only reason (I think), that could make an edition in England necessary. But I doubt you would not find the matter much mended here; our presses, as they improve in beauty, declining daily in accuracy; besides you would find the expense very considerable, and the sale in no proportion to it, as in reality, it is but few people in England, that read currently and with pleasure the Italian tongue; and the fine old editions of their capital writers are sold in London for a lower price, than they bear in Italy. An English translation I can by no means advise. The justness of thought and good sense might remain; but the graces of elocution (which make a great part of Algarotti's merit) would be entirely lost, and that merely from the very different genius and complexion of the two languages.

I rather think these volumes should be handsomely bound, before they are put into the library: they bind very neatly here; and if you approve it, Mr. Brown will order it to be done. Doubtless there can be no impropriety in making the same present to the University, nor need you at all to fear for the reputation of your friend: he has merit enough to recommend him in any country, a tincture of various sorts of knowledge; an acquaintance with all the beautiful arts; an easy command, a precision, warmth, and richness of expression, and a judgement, that is rarely mistaken, on any subject to which he applies it. Of the dialogues I have formerly told you my thoughts. The essays and letters (many of them entirely new to me) *on the arts*, are curious and entertaining; those on other subjects (even where the thoughts are not new to me, but borrowed from his various reading and conversation) often better put, and better expressed than in the originals. I rejoice, when I see Machiavel defended or illustrated, who to me appears one of the wisest men that any nation in any age has produced. Most of the other discourses military or political are well worth reading, though that on Kouli-Khan was a mere jeu-d'esprit, a sort of historical exercise. The letters from Russia I have read before with pleasure, particularly the narrative of Munich's and Lascy's campaigns. The detached thoughts are often new and just ; but there should have been a revisal of them, as they are often to be found in his letters repeated in the very same words. Some too of the familiar letters might have been spared. The *Congress of Cythera* I had seen, and liked before, the *Giudicio d'Amore* is an addition rather inferior to it. The verses are not equal to the prose, but they are above mediocrity.

I shall be glad to hear your health is improved, and that you have thoughts of favouring us with your company here. I am, Sir, your most obedient humble servant,   THOS. GRAY.

182. To James Beattie

Pembroke Hall, February 1, 1768.

I am almost sorry to have raised any degree of impatience in you, because I can by no means satisfy it. The sole reason I have to publish these few additions now, is to make up (in both) for the omission of that *Long Story* ; and as to the notes, I do it out of spite, because the public did not understand the two Odes (which I have called Pindaric) ; though the first was not very dark, and the second alluded to a few common facts to be found in any sixpenny history of England, by way of question and answer, for the use of children. The parallel passages I insert out of justice to those writers from whom I happened to take the hint of any line, as far as I can recollect.

I rejoice to be in the hands of Mr. Foulis, who has the laudable ambition of surpassing his predecessors, the *Etiennes* and the *Elzevirs*, as well in literature, as in the proper art of his profession : he surprises me in mentioning a Lady, after whom I have been inquiring these fourteen years in vain. When the two Odes were first published, I sent them to her ; but as I was forced to direct them very much at random, probably they never came to her hands. When the present edition comes out, I beg of Mr. Foulis to offer her a copy, in my name, with my respects and grateful remembrances ; he will send another to you, Sir, and a third to Lord Gray, if he will do me the honour of accepting it. These are all the presents I pretend to make (for I would have it considered only as a new edition of an old book) ; after this if he pleases to send me one or two, I shall think myself obliged to him. I cannot advise him to print a great number ; especially as Dodsley has it in its power to print as many as he pleases, though I desire him not to do so.

You are very good to me in taking this trouble upon you : all I can say is, that I shall be happy to return it in kind, whenever you will give me the opportunity.

183. To Norton Nicholls

28 Jan: 1768. P: Coll:

Dear S^r,—I and mine are safe, & well, but the chambers opposite to me (Mr. Lyon's) wch were getting ready for Mason, are destroy'd. Mr. Brown was in more immediate danger than I ; but he too is well, and has lost nothing. we owe it to Methodism, that any part (at least of that wing) was preserved : for two Saints, who had been till very late at their nocturnal devotions, & were just in bed, gave the first alarm to the college & the town. We had very speedy and excellent assistance of engines and men, and are quit for the fright, except the damage above-mention'd. I assure you it is not amusing to be waked between 2 & 3 in the morning, and to hear, Don't be frighted, S^r ! but the college is all of a fire.

I have not yet return'd the letters you sent me by the fly, not thinking it necessary to do so immediately ; but very soon you shall have them. Mason came two

days after the fire, and will stay some time. Adieu !
I am sincerely
                    Yours

                                        TG:
   I do not see what you can do. everything depends
on their first meeting at Mam-head, & that is now
over. I am afraid everything will go wrong. it is
sure, your last letter could do no hurt.

184. To Walpole

Feb. 14, 1768. Pembroke College.

   I received the book you were so good to send
me, and have read it again (indeed I could hardly
be said to have read it before) with attention and with
pleasure. Your second edition is so rapid in its progress, that it will now hardly answer any purpose to
tell you either my own objections, or those of other
people. Certain it is, that you are universally read
here ; but what *we* think, is not so easy to come at.
We stay as usual to see the success, to learn the judgment of the town, to be directed in our opinions by
those of more competent judges. If they like you,
we shall ; if any one of name write against you, we
give you up : for we are modest and diffident of ourselves, and not without reason. History in particular
is not our *fort* ; for (the truth is) we read only modern
books and the pamphlets of the day. I have heard it
objected, that you raise doubts and difficulties, and do
not satisfy them by telling us what was *really* the case.
I have heard you charged with disrespect to the king
of Prussia ; and above all to king William, and the
revolution. These are seriously the most sensible
things I have heard said, and all that I recollect. If
you please to justify yourself, you may.
   My own objections are little more essential : they
relate chiefly to inaccuracies of style, which either
debase the expression or obscure the meaning. I could
point out several small particulars of this kind, and
will do so, if you think it can serve any purpose after

publication. When I hear you read, they often escape me, partly because I am attending to the subject, and partly because from habit I understand you where a stranger might often be at a loss.

As to your arguments, most of the principal parts are made out with a clearness and evidence that no one would expect where materials are so scarce. Yet I still suspect Richard of the murder of Henry VI. The chronicler of Croyland charges it full on him, though without a name or any mention of circumstances. The interests of Edward were the interests of Richard too, though the throne were not then in view; and that Henry still stood in their way, they might well imagine, because, though deposed and imprisoned once before, he had regained his liberty, and his crown; and was still adored by the people. I should think, from the word *tyranni*, the passage was written after Richard had assumed the crown: but, if it was earlier, does not the bare imputation imply very early suspicions at least of Richard's bloody nature, especially in the mouth of a person that was no enemy to the house of York, nor friend to that of Beaufort?

That the duchess of Burgundy, to try the temper of the nation, should set up a false pretender to the throne (when she had the true duke of York in her hands), and that the queen-mother (knowing her son was alive) should countenance that design, is a piece of policy utterly incomprehensible; being the most likely means to ruin their own scheme, and throw a just suspicion of fraud and falsehood on the cause of truth, which Henry could not fail to seize and turn to his own advantage.

Mr. Hume's first query, as far as relates to the queen-mother, will still have some weight. Is it probable, she should give her eldest daughter to Henry, and invite him to claim the crown, unless she had been sure that her sons were then dead? As to her seeming consent to the match between Elizabeth and Richard, she and her daughters were in his power, which appeared

now well fixed, his enemies' designs within the kingdom
being every where defeated, and Henry unable to raise
any considerable force abroad. She was timorous and
hopeless ; or she might dissemble, in order to cover
her secret dealings with Richmond : and if this were
the case, she hazarded little, supposing Richard to
dissemble too, and never to have thought seriously
of marrying his niece.

Another unaccountable thing is, that Richard, a
prince of the house of York, undoubtedly brave, clear-
sighted, artful, attentive to business ; of boundless
generosity, as appears from his grants ; just and
merciful, as his laws and his pardons seem to testify ;
having subdued the queen and her hated faction, and
been called first to the protectorship and then to the
crown by the body of the nobility and by the parliament ; with the common people to friend (as Carte
often asserts), and having nothing against him but the
illegitimate family of his brother Edward, and the
attainted house of Clarence (both of them within his
power) ;—that such a man should see within a few
months Buckingham, his best friend, and almost all
the southern and western counties on one day in arms
against him ; that, having seen all these insurrections
come to nothing, he should march with a gallant army
against a handful of needy adventurers, led by a
fugitive, who had not the shadow of a title, nor any
virtues to recommend him, nor any foreign strength
to depend on ; that he should be betrayed by almost
all his troops, and fall a sacrifice ;—all this is to me
utterly improbable, and I do not ever expect to see it
accounted for.

I take this opportunity to tell you, that Algarotti
(as I see in the new edition of his works printed at
Leghorn) being employed to buy pictures for the
king of Poland, purchased among others the famous
Holbein, that was at Venice. It don't appear that he
knew any thing of your book : yet he calls it *the consul
Meyer and his family*, as if it were then known to be
so in that city.

A young man here, who is a diligent reader of books, an antiquary, and a painter, informs me, that at the Red-lion inn at Newmarket is a piece of tapestry containing the very design of your marriage of Henry the sixth, only with several more figures in it, both men and women; that he would have bought it of the people, but they refused to part with it.

Mr. Mason, who is here, desires to present his respects to you. He says, that to efface from our annals the history of any tyrant is to do an essential injury to mankind: but he forgives it, because you have shown Henry the seventh to be a greater devil than Richard.

Pray do not be out of humour. When you first commenced an author, you exposed yourself to pit, box and gallery. Any coxcomb in the world may come in and hiss, if he pleases; aye, and (what is almost as bad) clap too, and you cannot hinder him. I saw a little squib fired at you in a newspaper by some of the *house of York*, for speaking lightly of chancellors. Adieu!

I am ever yours,

T. GRAY.

185. TO WALPOLE

Pembroke-college, Feb. 25, 1768.

To your friendly accusation, I am glad I can plead not guilty with a safe conscience. Dodsley told me in the spring that the plates from Mr. Bentley's designs were worn out, and he wanted to have them copied and reduced to a smaller scale for a new edition. I dissuaded him from so silly an expense, and desired he would put in no ornaments at all. The *Long Story* was to be totally omitted, as its only use (that of explaining the prints) was gone: but to supply the place of it in bulk, lest *my works* should be mistaken for the works of a flea, or a pismire, I promised to send him an equal weight of poetry or prose: so, since my return hither, I put up about two ounces of stuff; viz. The Fatal Sisters, The Descent of Odin (of both which you have copies), a bit of something from the Welch, and certain little notes, partly from justice (to acknowledge the debt, where I had borrowed any thing), partly from ill temper, just to tell the gentle reader, that Edward I. was not Oliver Cromwell, nor queen Elizabeth the witch of Endor. This is literally all; and with all this I shall be but a shrimp of an author. I gave leave also to print the same thing at Glasgow; but I doubt my packet has miscarried, for I hear nothing of its arrival as yet. To what you say to me so civilly, that I ought to write more, I reply in your own words (like the pamphleteer, who is going to confute you out of your own mouth), What has one to do, when *turned of fifty*, but really to think of finishing? However, I will be candid (for you seem to be so with me), and avow to you, that till fourscore-and-ten, whenever the humour takes me, I will write, because I like it; and because I like myself better when I do so. If I do not write much, it is because I cannot. As you have not this last plea, I see no reason why you should not continue as long as it is agreeable to yourself, and to all such as have any curiosity or judgment in the subjects you choose to treat. By the way let me tell you (while it is fresh) that lord Sandwich, who was lately dining at Cambridge, speaking (as I am told) handsomely of your book, said, it was pity you did not know that his cousin Manchester had a genealogy of the kings, which came down no lower than to Richard III. and at the end of it were two portraits of Richard and his son, in which that king appeared to be a handsome man. I tell you it as I heard it; perhaps you may think it worth enquiring into.

I have looked into Speed and Leslie. It appears very odd, that Speed in the speech he makes for P. Warbeck, addressed to James IV. of Scotland, should three times cite the *manuscript proclamation* of Perkin, then in the hands of Sir Robert Cotton; and yet when he gives us the proclamation afterwards (on occasion of the insurrection in Cornwall) he does not cite any such manuscript. In Casley's Catalogue of the Cotton

Library you may see whether this manuscript proclamation still exists or not: if it does, it may be found at the Musæum. Leslie will give you no satisfaction at all: though no subject of England, he could not write freely on this matter, as the title of Mary his mistress to the crown of England was derived from that of Henry VII. Accordingly, he every where treats Perkin as an impostor; yet drops several little expressions inconsistent with that supposition. He has preserved no proclamation: he only puts a short speech into Perkin's mouth, the substance of which is taken by Speed, and translated in the end of his, which is a good deal longer: the whole matter is treated by Leslie very concisely and superficially. I can easily transcribe it, if you please; but I do not see that it could answer any purpose.

Mr. Boswell's book I was going to recommend to you, when I received your letter: it has pleased and moved me strangely, all (I mean) that relates to Paoli. He is a man born two thousand years after his time! The pamphlet proves what I have always maintained, that any fool may write a most valuable book by chance, if he will only tell us what he heard and saw with veracity. Of Mr. Boswell's truth I have not the least suspicion, because I am sure he could invent nothing of this kind. The true title of this part of his work is, A Dialogue between a Green-goose and a Hero.

I had been told of a manuscript in Benet-library: the inscription of it is *Itinerarium Fratris Simonis Simeonis et Hugonis Illuminatoris*, 1322. Would not one think this should promise something? They were two Franciscan friars that came from Ireland, and passed through Wales to London, to Canterbury, to Dover, and so to France in their way to Jerusalem. All that relates to our own country has been transcribed for me, and (sorry am I to say) signifies not a halfpenny: only this little bit might be inserted in your next edition of the Painters: Ad aliud caput civitatis (Londoniæ) est monasterium nigrorum monachorum nomine West-monasterium, in quo constanter et communiter omnes reges Angliæ sepeliuntur—et eidem monasterio quasi immediatè conjungitur illud famosissimum palatium regis, in quo est illa vulgata camera, in cujus parietibus sunt omnes historiæ bellicæ totius Bibliæ ineffabiliter depictæ, atque in Gallico completissimè et perfectissimè conscriptæ, in non modicâ intuentium admiratione et maximâ regali magnificentiâ.

I have had certain observations on your Royal and Noble Authors given me to send you perhaps about three years ago : last week I found them in a drawer, and (my conscience being troubled) now enclose them to you. I have even forgot whose they are.

I have been also told of a passage in Ph. de Comines, which (if you know) ought not to have been passed over. The book is not at hand at present, and I must conclude my letter. Adieu !

I am ever yours,

T. GRAY.

186. To WALPOLE

Pembroke-hall, March 6, 1768.

Here is sir William Cornwallis, entitled Essayes of certaine Paradoxes. 2d Edit. 1617, Lond.

> King Richard III.
> The French Pockes
> Nothing ⎱ praised.
> Good to be in debt
> Sadnesse
> Julian the Apostate's vertues. ⎰

The title-page will probably suffice you ; but if you would know any more of him, he has read nothing but the common chronicles, and those without attention : for example, speaking of Anne the queen, he says, she was *barren*, of which Richard had often complained to Rotheram. He extenuates the murder of Henry VI. and his son : the first, he says, might be a malicious accusation, for that many did suppose he died of mere melancholy and grief : the latter cannot be proved to be

M 3

the action of Richard (though executed in his presence);
and if it were, he did it out of love to his brother
Edward. He justifies the death of the lords at Pomfret,
from reasons of state, for his own preservation, the
safety of the commonwealth, and the ancient nobility.
The execution of Hastings he excuses from necessity,
from the dishonesty and sensuality of the man: what
was his crime with respect to Richard, he does not
say. Dr. Shaw's sermon was not by the king's command, but to be imputed to the preacher's own ambition: but if it was by order, *to charge his mother with
adultery was a matter of no such great moment, since it
is no wonder in that sex.* Of the murder in the Tower
he doubts; but if it were by his order, the offence was
to God, not to his people; and *how could he demonstrate
his love more amply, than to venture his soul for their
quiet?* Have you enough, pray? You see it is an idle
declamation, the exercise of a school-boy that is to be
bred a statesman.

I have looked in Stowe: to be sure there is no proclamation there. Mr. Hume, I suppose, means *Speed*,
where it is given, how truly I know not; but that he
had seen the original is sure, and seems to quote the
very words of it in the beginning of that speech which
Perkin makes to James IV. and also just afterwards,
where he treats of the Cornish rebellion.

Guthrie, you see, has vented himself in the Critical
Review. His History I never saw, nor is it here, nor
do I know any one that ever saw it. He is a rascal,
but rascals may chance to meet with curious records;
and that commission to sir J. Tyrrell (if it be not a
lye) is such: so is the order for Henry the sixth's
funeral. I would by no means take notice of him,
write what he would. I am glad you have seen the
Manchester-roll.

It is not I that talk of Phil. de Comines; it was
mentioned to me as a thing that looked like a voluntary
omission: but I see you have taken notice of it in the
note to p. 71, though rather too slightly. You have
not observed that the same writer says, c. 55, *Richard*

*tua de sa main, ou fit tuer en sa presence, quelque lieu
apart, ce bon homme le roi Henry.* Another oversight
I think there is at p. 43, where you speak of the *roll
of parliament* and the contract with lady Eleanor
Boteler, as things newly come to light; whereas Speed
has given at large the same roll in his History. Adieu !

I am ever yours,

T. GRAY.

187. To THE REV. JAMES BROWN

Southampton Row, April 27, 1768.

DEAR SIR,—By this time I conclude, you are return'd
to Cambridge : tho' I thought it a long time, before
I heard of you from Thrandeston, and could have wish'd
you had stay'd longer with Palgrave : perhaps you
are in Hertfordshire, however I write at a venture.
I went to Mr. Mann's, and (tho' he is in Town) not
finding him at home, left a note with an account of my
business with him, and my direction. I have had no
message in answer to it : so possibly he has written
to you, and sent the papers. I know not.

Mr. Precentor is still here, and not in haste to depart,
indeed I do not know whether he has not a fit of the
Gout : it is certain, he had a pain yesterday in his foot,
but whether owing to Bechamel and Claret, or to
cutting a corn, was not determined : he is still at
Stonhewer's house, and has not made his journey to
Eton and to Bath yet, tho' he intends to do it.

We have had no mobs, nor illuminations yet, since
I was here. Wilkes's speech you have seen ; the Court
was so surprised at being contemn'd to its face, and
in the face of the World, that the Chief in a manner
forgot the matter in hand, and enter'd into an apology
for his own past conduct, and so (with the rest of his
Assessors) shuffled the matter off, and left the danger to
the officers of the Crown, that is indeed, to the Ministry.
Nobody had ventured, or would venture to serve the
Capias upon him. I cannot assure, it is done yet ;
tho' yesterday I heard it was, and (if so) he comes

again to-day into Court. He professes himself ready to make any submissions to the K., but not to give up his pursuit of L^d. H^x. The Delavals attend very regularly, and take notes of all that passes. His writ of Error on the Outlawry must come to a decision before the House of Lords.

I was not among the Coal-heavers at Shadwell, tho' seven people lost their lives in the fray: [Nor was] I [in] Goodmans Fields where the Bawdy-house was demolish'd. The Ministry (I believe) are but ticklish in their situation: they talk of Greville and his Brother, again. Lord forbid! it must be dreadful necessity indeed, that brings them back. Adieu! I am ever yours,   T. G.

If you are at Cambridge, pray let me know.

188. To Mary Antrobus

July 29, 1768.

Dear Mary,—I thank you for all your intelligence (and the first news I had of poor Brocket's death was from you) and to reward you in part for it, I now shall tell you, that this day, hot as it is, I kissed the King's hand; that my warrant was signed by him last night; that on Wednesday I received a very honourable letter from the D. of Grafton, acquainting me that his majesty had ordered him to offer me this Professorship, and much more, which does me too much credit by half for me to mention it. The Duke adds, *that from private as well as public considerations, he takes the warmest part in approving this measure of the King's.* These are his own words. You see there are princes (or ministers) left in the world, that know how to do things handsomely; for I profess I never asked for it, nor have I seen his Grace before or after this event.

Dr. R. (not forgetting a certain lady of his) is so good to you, and to me, that you may (if you please) shew him my letter. He will not be critical as to the style, and I wish you would send it also to Mr. Brown, for I have not time to write to him by this day's post;

they need not mention this circumstance to others, they may learn it as they can. Adieu!

I receive your letter of July 28 (while I am writing), consult your friends over the way, they are as good as I, and better. All I can say is, the Board have been so often used to the name of Antrobus lately, that I fear they may take your petition not in good part. If you are sure of the kindness or interest of Mr. A. the opportunity should not be lost; but I always a little distrust new friends and new lawyers.

I have found a man, who has brought Mr. Eyres (I think) up to my price, in a hurry; however he defers his final answer till Wednesday next. He shall not have it a shilling lower, I promise; and if he hesitates, I will rise upon him like a fury. Good-night.—I am ever yours.

How could you dream that St[onehewer], or Hinchl[iffe] would ask this for themselves? The only people that ask'd it were Lort, Marriott, Delaval, Jebb, and Peck—, at least I have heard of no more. Delaval always communicated his thoughts to me, knowing I would make no ill use of that knowledge. Lort is a worthy man, and I wish he could have it, or something as good : the rest are nothing.

189. To Mason

August 1 [1768].

DEAR MASON,—Where you are, I know not, but before this can reach you I guess you will be in residence. It is only to tell you that I profess Modern History and languages in a little shop of mine at Cambridge, if you will recommend me any customers. On Sunday Brocket died of a fall from his horse, drunk, I believe, as some say, returning from Hinchinbroke. On Wednesday the Duke of Grafton wrote me a very handsome letter to say that the King offered the vacant place to me, with many more speeches too honourable for me to transcribe. On Friday, at the levee, I kissed his Majesty's hand. What he said I will not tell you,

because everybody that has been at court tells what
the King said to them. It was very gracious, however.
Remember you are to say that the Cabinet Council
all approved of the nomination in a particular manner.
It is hinted to me that I should say this publicly, and
I have been at their several doors to thank them. Now
I have told you all the exterior; the rest, the most
essential, you can easily guess, and how it came about.
Now are you glad or sorry, pray? Adieu.—Yours ever,

T. G., P. M. H. and L.

190. To Norton Nicholls

3 Aug: 1768. Jermyn-Street
(Mr Roberts's).

Dear Sr,—That Mr. Brockett has broke his neck,
you will have seen in the News-papers, and also that
I (your humble servant) have kissed the K:s hand for
his succession. they both are true, but the manner how
you know not; only I can assure you that I had no
hand at all in his fall, and *almost* as little in the second
happy event. He died on the Sunday, on Wednesday
following, his Gr: of Grafton wrote me a very polite
letter to say that his Maj: commanded him to *offer* me
the vacant Professorship, not only as a reward of, &c:
but as a credit to &c: with much more too high for me
to transcribe. *You are to say*, that I owe my nomination to the *whole Cabinet-Council*, and my success to
the king's *particular knowledge* of me. this last he
told me himself, tho' the day was so hot & the ceremony
so embarrassing to me, that I hardly know what he said.

I am commission'd to make you an offer, wch, I have
told him (not the King) you would not accept, long
ago. Mr. Barrett (whom you know) offers to you 100£
a year with meat, drink, washing, chaise, & lodging,
if you will please to accompany him thro' France into
Italy. he has taken such a fancy to you, that I cannot
but do what he desires me, being pleased with him for
it. I know, it will never do, tho' before you grew a rich
fat Rector, I have often wish'd (ay, and fish'd too) for

such an opportunity. no matter! I desire you to write your answer to him yourself as civil, as you think fit, & then let me know the result. that's all. He lives at *Lee near Canterbury*.

Adieu! I am to perish here with heat this fortnight yet, & then to Cambridge. Dr. Marriott (Mr. Vicecan:) came post hither to ask this vacant office on Wednesday last, and went post to carry the news back on Saturday. the rest were Delaval, Lort, Peck, & Jebb. as to Lort, he deserved it, & Delaval is an honest Gentleman: the rest do me no great honour, no more than my Predecessor did: to be sure, my *Dignity* is a little the worse for wear, but mended and wash'd it will do for me. I am very sincerely

Yours,

TG:

191. To James Beattie

Pembroke Hall, October 31, 1768.

It is some time since I received from Mr. Foulis two copies of my poems, one by the hands of Mr. T. Pitt, the other by Mr. Merrill, a bookseller of this town: it is indeed a most beautiful edition, and must certainly do credit both to him and to me: but I fear it will be of no other advantage to him, as Dodsley has contrived to glut the town already with two editions beforehand, one of 1500, and the other of 750, both indeed far inferior to that of Glasgow, but sold at half the price. I must repeat my thanks, Sir, for the trouble you have been pleased to give yourself on my account; and through you I must desire leave to convey my acknowledgments to Mr. Foulis, for the pains and expense he has been at in this publication.

We live at so great a distance, that, perhaps, you may not yet have learned, what, I flatter myself, you will not be displeased to hear: the middle of last summer his Majesty was pleased to appoint me Regius Professor of Modern History in this University; it is the best thing the Crown has to bestow (on a layman) here; the salary is £400 per ann. but what enhances the value of it to me is, that it was bestowed without being asked. The person, who held it before me, died on the Sunday; and on Wednesday following the Duke of Grafton wrote me a letter to say, that the King offered me this office, with many additional expressions of kindness on his Grace's part, to whom I am but little known, and whom I have not seen either before or since he did me this favour. Instances of a benefit so nobly conferred, I believe, are rare; and therefore I tell you of it as a thing that does honour, not only to me, but to the Minister.

As I lived here before from choice, I shall now continue to do so from obligation: if business or curiosity should call you southwards, you will find few friends that will see you with more cordial satisfaction, than, dear Sir, etc.

192. To NORTON NICHOLLS
Nov: 8. 1768. Pemb: Coll:

Not a single word, since we parted at Norwich, & for ought I know, you may be ignorant, how I fell into the jaws of the King of Denmark at Newmarket, & might have stay'd there till this time, had I not met with Mr Vice chancellor and Mr Orator with their Diplomas and speeches, who on their return to Cambridge sent me a chaise from thence, & deliver'd me out of that den of thieves. however, I pass'd a night there; & in the next room, divided from me by a thin partition, was a drunken Parson & his party of pleasure, singing & swearing and breaking all the ten commandments. all that I saw on my way else was the Abbey-Church at Wyndham, to learned eyes a beautiful remnant of antiquity, part of it in the style of Henry the 1st & part in that of Henry the 6th; the wooden fretwork of the north-ile you may copy, when you build the best room of your new Gothick parsonage. it will cost but a trifle.

So now I am going to Town about my business, wch (if I dispatch to my mind) will leave me at rest, & with a tolerably easy temper for one while. I return hither as soon as I can, & give you notice what a sweet humor I am in. Mrs Nicholls and you take advantage of it, come & take possession of the lodge at Trinity-Hall (by the way, I am commission'd to offer it to you by Dr Marriott for that purpose, & you have nothing to do but to thank him for his civilities, and say at what time you intend to make use of them). and so we live in clover, & partake the benefits of a University education together, as of old. Palgrave is return'd from Scotland, and will perhaps be here. Mason too, if he is not married (for such a report there is) may come, and Dr Hallifax is always at your service. Ld Richard Cavendish is come : he is a sensible Boy, awkward & bashful beyond all imagination, & eats a buttock of beef at a meal. I have made him my visit, & we did tolerably well considering. Watson is his publick tutor, and one Winstanley his private: do you know him ?

Marriott has begun a subscription for a Musical Amphitheatre, has appropriated 500£ (Mr. Titley's legacy to the University) to that purpose, & gives 20 Guineas himself. he has drawn a design for the building & has printed an Argument about the Poors-rates, wch he intended to have deliver'd from the Bench, but one of the parties drop'd the cause. he has spoke at the Quarter-Sessions two hours together, and moved the Towns-People to tears, and the University to laughter. at laying down his office too he spoke Latin, and said, *Invidiam, et opinionum de me commenta delebit dies.* he enlarged (wch is never done) on the qualifications of Hinchliffe his Successor, *qui Mores hominum multorum vidit et urbes—qui cum Magnis vixit & placuit.* next day Hinchliffe made his speech, & said not one word (though it is usual) of his Predecessor. I tell you Cambridge News for want of better. they say Rigby is to move for the expulsion of Wilkes from the House. my respects to Mamma. I am

Yours

TG:

Tell me about my Uncle and Aunt : direct to Roberts's, Jermyn-Str :

193. To Norton Nicholls

2 Jan: 1769. Pemb: Coll:

DEAR SR,—Here am I once again, & have sold my estate, & got a thousand guineas, & four score pounds a year for my old Aunt, & a 20£ prize in the lottery, & Lord knows what arrears in the Treasury, and am a rich Fellow enough, go to ; & a Fellow, that hath had losses, & one, that hath two gowns, & every thing handsome about him ! & in a few days I shall have curtains, are you avised of that ; ay, & a mattrass to lie upon.

And there's Dr. Hallifax tells me, there are three or four fellow-commoners got into the lodge. but they will be out in a week's time, & all ready for Mrs Nicholls's reception and yours. so do your pleasures, I invite nobody. And there's Dr Thomas may be Bp of Carlisle, if he pleases ; and (if not) Dr. Powell : and in the first case Dr Ross will be Dean of Ely. and so I am

Yours

TG:

194. To Norton Nicholls

Pemb: Coll: 24 June. 1769.

And so you have a garden of your own, and you plant & transplant, and are dirty & amused ! are not you ashamed of yourself ? why, I have no so such thing, you monster ; nor ever shall be either dirty or amused as long as I live ! my gardens are in the window, like those of a Lodger up three pair of stairs in Petticoat-lane or Camomile-street, & they go to bed regularly under the same roof that I do. dear, how charming it must be to walk out in one's own garding, & sit on a bench in the open air with a fountain, & a leaden statue, & a rolling stone, & an arbour ! have a care of sore-throats tho', and the *agoe*.

Odicle has been rehearsed again and again, and the boys have got scraps by heart : I expect to see it torn piece-meal in the North-Briton, before it is born. the

musick is as good as the words: the former might be
taken for mine, & the latter for Dr. Randal's. if you
will come, you shall see it & sing in it with Mr Norris,
and Mr Clerke, the Clergyman, and Mr Reinholt, and
Miss Thomas, great names at Salisbury & Gloster
musick-meeting, and well-versed in Judas-Maccabæus.
Dr Marriott is to have Ld Sandwich & the Attorney-
General at his Lodge, not to mention foreign Ministers,
who are to lie with Dr Hallifax, or in the stables. Ld
North is at King's, Ld Weymouth at Mrs Arbuthnot's,
they talk of the D: of Bedford, who (I suppose), has
a bed in King's-Chappel. The Archbishop is to be at
Christ's; Bps of London at Clare Hall, of Lincoln at
Dr. Gordon's, of Chester at Peter-House, of Norwich
at Jesus, of St. David's at Caius; of Bangor, at the
Dog and Porridge-pot, Marq: of Granby at Woodyer's.
the Yorkes and Townshends will not come. Soulsby the
Taylor lets his room for 11 guineas the 3 days, Woodyer
aforesaid, for 15. Brotherton asks 20. I have a bed
over the way offered me at 3 half-crowns a night, but
it may be gone, before you come. I believe, all that
are unlett will be cheap, as the time approaches. I
wish it were once over, and immediately I go for a few
days to London, & so (with Mr. Brown) to Aston, tho'
I fear it will rain the whole summer, & Skiddaw will
be invisible & inaccessible to mortals. I forgot to tell
you, that on the Monday (after his Grace has breakfasted on a Divinity-act), twelve Noble-men and
Fellow-commoners are to settle his stomach with
verses made and repeated by themselves. Saturday
next (you know) is the great day, & he goes away on
Monday after this repast.

I have got *De la Lande's* Voyage thro' Italy, in 8
vol:s. he is a member of the Academy of Sciences, &
pretty good to read. I have read an 8vo volume of
Shenstone's letters. poor Man! he was always wishing
for money, for fame, & other distinctions, & his whole
philosophy consisted in living against his will in retirement, and in a place, wch his taste had adorned, but
wch he only enjoy'd when people of note came to see

& commend it. His correspondence is about nothing else but this place & his own writings with two or three neighbouring Clergymen, who wrote verses too.

I will send the Wilton-book directed to Payne for you, tho' I know it will be lost, & then you will say it was not worth above a shilling, wch is a great comfort to me. I have just found the beginning of a letter wch somebody had drop'd : I should rather call it first thoughts for the beginning of a letter, for there are many scratches and corrections. as I cannot use it myself (having got a beginning already of my own) I send it for your use upon some great occasion.

DEAR S^R,—After so long silence the hopes of pardon & prospect of forgiveness might seem entirely extinct or at least very remote, was I not truly sensible of your goodness and candour, wch is the only Asylum that my negligence can fly to : since every apology would prove insufficient to counterballance it, or alleviate my fault. how then shall my deficiency presume to make so bold an attempt, or be able to suffer the hardships of so rough a campaign ? &c: &c: &c: And am Dear S^r,

Kindly Yours
T: G:

. . . respects to Mrs Nicholls.

I do not publish at all, but Alma Mater prints 5 or 600 for the company.

I have nothing more to add about Southampton, than what you have transcribed already in your map-book.

To The Revd Mr Nicholls at Blundeston near Leostoff Suffolk. By Norwich.

195. To James Beattie

Cambridge, July 16, 1769.

The late ceremony of the Duke of Grafton's installation has hindered me from acknowledging sooner the satisfaction your friendly compliment gave me : I thought myself bound in gratitude to his Grace, unasked, to take upon me the task of writing those verses which are usually set to music on this occasion. I do not think them worth sending you, because they are by nature doomed to live but a single day ; or, if their existence is prolonged beyond that date, it is only by means of newspaper parodies, and witless criticisms. This sort of abuse I had reason to expect, but did not think it worth while to avoid.

Mr. Foulis is magnificent in his gratitude : I cannot figure to myself how it can be worth his while to offer me such a present. You can judge better of it than I ; if he does not hurt himself by it, I would accept his Homer with many thanks. I have not got or even seen it.

I could wish to subscribe to his new edition of Milton, and desire to be set down for two copies of the large paper ; but you must inform me where and when I may pay the money.

You have taught me to long for a second letter, and particularly for what you say will make the contents of it. I have nothing to requite it with, but plain and friendly truth ; and that you shall have joined to a zeal for your fame, and a pleasure in your success.

I am now setting forward on a journey towards the North of England : but it will not reach so far as I could wish. I must return hither before Michaelmas, and shall barely have time to visit a few places and a few friends.

196. To Mason

Old Park, Saturday, August 26, 1769.

DEAR MASON,—I received last night your letter, big with another a week older than itself. You might as well have wrote to me from the deserts of Arabia, and desired me to step over and drink a dish of tea with you. This morning I sent to Auckland for a chaise ; the man's answer is that he had a chaise with four horses returned yesterday from Hartlepool, that the road was next to impassable, and so dangerous that he does not think of sending out any other that way, unless the season should change to a long drought. I would have gone by Durham, but am assured that road is rather worse. What can I do? You speak so jauntily, and enter so little into any detail of your own journey, that I conclude you came on horseback from Stockton (which road, however, is little better for carriages). If so, we hope you will ride over to Old Park with Mr. Alderson; there is room for you both, and hearty welcome. The doctor even talks of coming (for he can ride) to invite you on Monday. I wonder how you are accommodated where you are, and what you are doing with Gen. Carey. I would give my ears to get thither, but all depends on the sun. Adieu.

It is twenty miles to Old Park, and the way is by Hart, over Sheraton Moor, and through Trimdon. There is no village else that has a name. Pray write a line by the bearer.

T. GRAY.

197. TO THE REV. JAMES BROWN

Lancaster, October 10, 1769.

DEAR SIR,—I set out on the 29th September, with poor Doctor Wharton, and lay at Brough, but he was seized with a fit of the asthma the same night, and obliged in the morning to return home. I went by Penrith to Keswick, and passed six days there lap'd in Elysium; then came slowly by Ambleside to Kendal, and this day arrived here. I now am projecting to strike across the hills into Yorkshire, by Settle, and so get to Mason's; then, after a few days, I shall move gently towards Cambridge. The weather has favoured all my motions just as I could wish.

I received your letter of 23d September; was glad you deviated a little from the common track, and rejoiced you got well and safe home.—I am, ever yours,

T. G.

198. JOURNAL. 30 SEPT: 1769.

1

W^d at NW.; clouds & sunshine. a mile & $\frac{1}{2}$ from Brough on a hill lay a great army encamp'd. to the left open'd a fine valley with green meadows & hedge rows, a Gentleman's house peeping forth from a grove of old trees. on a nearer approach, appear'd myriads of horses & cattle in the road itself & in all the fields round me, a brisk stream hurrying cross the way, thousands of clean healthy People in their best party-color'd apparel, Farmers & their families, Esquires & their daughters, hastening up from the dales & down the fells on every side, glittering in the sun & pressing forward to join the throng: while the dark hills, on many of whose tops the mists were yet hanging, served as a contrast to this gay & moving scene, which continued for near two miles more along the road, and the crowd (coming towards it) reach'd on as far as Appleby.

On the ascent of the hill above Appleby the thick hanging wood & the long reaches of the Eden (rapid, clear, & full as ever) winding below with views of the Castle & Town gave much employment to the mirror: but the sun was wanting & the sky overcast. oats & barley cut every where, but not carried in. passed Kirby-thore, S^r W: Dalston's house at Acornbank, Whinfield-park, Harthorn-oaks, Countess-pillar, Brougham-Castle, Mr Brown (one of ye six Clerks) his large new house, cross'd the Eden & the Eimot (pronounce *Eeman*) with its green vale, & at 3 o'clock dined with Mrs Buchanan, at *Penrith*, on trout & partridge. in the afternoon walk'd up the Beacon-hill a mile to the top, saw Whinfield and Lowther-parks, & thro' an opening in the bosom of that cluster of mountains, wch the Doctor well remembers, the lake of Ulz-water, with the craggy tops of a hundred nameless hills. these to W: & S:, to the N: a great extent of black & dreary plains, to E: Cross-fell just visible thro' mists & vapours hovering round it.

Oct: 1. W^d at S:W: a gray autumnal day, air perfectly calm & gentle. Went to see Ulz-water 5 miles distant. soon left the Keswick-road & turn'd to the left thro' shady lanes along the Vale of *Eeman*, which runs rapidly on near the way, rippling over the stones. to the right is *Delmaine*, a large fabrick of pale red stone, with 9 windows in front & 7 on the side built by Mr Hassel, behind it a fine lawn surrounded by woods & a long rocky eminence rising over them. a clear & brisk rivulet runs by the house to join the Eeman, whose course is in sight & at a small distance.

Farther on appears *Hatton St John*, a castle-like old mansion of Mr Huddleston. approach'd *Dunmallert*, a fine pointed hill, cover'd with wood planted by old Mr Hassle beforemention'd, who lives always at home & delights in planting. walk'd over a spungy meadow or two & began to mount this hill thro' a broad & strait green alley among the trees, & with some toil gain'd the summit. from hence saw the Lake opening directly at my feet majestic in its calmness, clear & smooth as a blew mirror with winding shores & low points of land cover'd with green inclosures, white farm-houses looking out among the trees, & cattle feeding. the water is almost every where border'd with cultivated lands gently sloping upwards till they reach the feet of the mountains, wch rise very rude & awful with their broken tops on either hand. directly in front, at better than 3 mile's distance, *Place-Fell*, one of the bravest among them, pushes its bold broad breast into the midst of the Lake & forces it to alter its course, forming first a large bay to the left & then bending to the right.

I descended *Dunmallert* again by a side avenue, that was only not perpendicular, & came to *Barton*-bridge over the *Eeman*, then walking thro' a path in the wood round the bottom of the hill came forth, where the *Eeman* issues out of the lake, & continued my way along it's western shore close to the water, & generally on a level with it. Saw a cormorant flying over it & fishing. . . . (to be continued)

1 Oct: 1769.

2

The figure of Ulz-water nothing resembles that laid down in our maps: it is 9 miles long, & (at widest) under a mile in breadth. after extending itself 3 m: & ½ in a line to S: W: it turns at the foot of *Place-Fell*, almost due West, and is here not twice the breadth of the Thames at London. it is soon again interrupted by the roots of *Helvellyn*, a lofty & very rugged mountain, & spreading again turns off to S: E:, and is lost among the deep recesses of the hills. to this second turning I pursued my way about four miles along its borders beyond a village scatter'd among trees & call'd *Watermalloch*, in a pleasant grave day, perfectly calm & warm, but without a gleam of sunshine: then the sky seeming to thicken, the valley to grow more desolate, & evening drawing on, I return'd by the way I came to *Penrith*.

Oct: 2. W^d at S: E:, sky clearing, *Cross-fell* misty, but the outline of the other hills very distinct. set out at 10 for *Keswick*, by the road we went in 1767. saw *Greystock*-town & castle to the right, wch lie only 3 miles (over the Fells) from *Ulz-water*. pass'd through *Penradock & Threlcot* at the feet of *Saddleback*, whose furrow'd sides were gilt by the noon-day Sun, while its brow appear'd of a sad purple from the shadow of the clouds, as they sail'd slowly by it. the broad & green valley of *Gardies* and *Lowside*, with a swift stream glittering among the cottages & meadows lay to the left; and the much finer (but narrower) valley of St *John's* opening into it. *Hill-top* the large, tho' low, mansion of the Gaskarths, now a Farmhouse, seated on an eminence among woods under a steep fell, was what appear'd the most conspicuous, & beside it a great rock like some antient tower nodding to its fall. pass'd by the side of *Skiddaw* & its cub called *Latterrig*, & saw from an eminence, at two miles distance, the Vale of Elysium in all its verdure, the sun then playing on the bosom of the lake, & lighting up all the mountains with its lustre.

Dined by two o'clock at the Queen's Head, and then straggled out alone to the *Parsonage*, fell down on my back across a dirty lane, with my glass open in one hand, but broke only my knuckles : stay'd nevertheless, & saw the sun set in all its glory.

Oct: 3. Wᵈ at S: E: ; a heavenly day. rose at seven, and walked out under the conduct of my Landlord to *Borrodale*. the grass was cover'd with a hoar-frost, wᶜʰ soon melted, & exhaled in a thin blewish smoke. cross'd the meadows obliquely, catching a diversity of views among the hills over the lake & islands, and changing prospect at every ten paces, left *Cockshut* and *Castle-hill* (wᶜʰ we formerly mounted) behind me, & drew near the foot of *Walla-crag*, whose bare & rocky brow, cut perpendicularly down above 400 feet, as I guess, awefully overlooks the way : our path here tends to the left, & the ground gently rising, & cover'd with a glade of scattering trees & bushes on the very margin of the water, opens both ways the most delicious view, that my eyes ever beheld. behind you are the magnificent heights of *Walla*-crag ; opposite lie the thick hanging woods of Lᵈ *Egremont*, & *Newland*-valley, with green & smiling fields embosom'd in the dark cliffs ; to the left the jaws of *Borrodale*, with that turbulent Chaos of mountain behind mountain roll'd in confusion ; beneath you, & stretching far away to the right, the shining purity of the *Lake*, just ruffled by the breeze enough to shew it is alive, reflecting rocks, woods, fields, & inverted tops of mountains, with the white buildings of *Keswick, Crosthwait*-church, & *Skiddaw* for a back ground at distance. oh Doctor ! I never wish'd more for you ; & pray think, how the glass played its part in such a spot, wᶜʰ is called *Carf-close-reeds* : I chuse to set down these barbarous names, that any body may enquire on the place, & easily find the particular station, that I mean. this scene continues to *Barrow-gate*, & a little farther, passing a brook called *Barrow-beck*, we enter'd *Borrodale*. the crags, named *Lodoor-banks* now begin to impend terribly over your way ; & more terribly, when you hear, that three years since an immense mass of rock tumbled at once from the brow, & bar'd all access to the dale (for this is the only road) till they could work their way thro' it. luckily no one was passing at the time of this fall; but down the side of the mountain, & far into the lake lie dispersed the huge fragments of this ruin in all shapes & in all directions. something farther we turn'd aside into a coppice, ascending a little in front of *Lodoor* water-fall. the height appears to be about 200 feet, the quantity of water not great, tho' (these three days excepted) it had rain'd daily in the hills for near two months before : but then the stream was nobly broken, leaping from rock to rock, & foaming with fury. on one side a towering crag, that spired up to equal, if not overtop, the neighbouring cliffs (this lay all in shade & darkness) on the other hand a rounder broader projecting hill shag'd with wood & illumined by the sun, wch glanced sideways on the upper part of the cataract. the force of the water wearing a deep channel in the ground hurries away to join the lake. we descended again, and passed the stream over a rude bridge. soon after we came under *Gowder-crag*, a hill more formidable to the eye & to the apprehension than that of *Lodoor* ; the rocks atop, deep-cloven perpendicularly by the rains, hanging loose & nodding forwards, seem just starting from their base in shivers : the whole way down & the road on both sides is strew'd with piles of the fragments strangely thrown across each other & of a dreadful bulk. the place reminds one of those passes in the Alps, where the Guides tell you to move on with speed, & say nothing, lest the agitation of the air should loosen the snows above, and bring down a mass, that would over-whelm a caravan. I took their counsel here and hasten'd on in silence.

Non ragioniam di lor ; ma guarda, e passa !

(to be continued).

3

Oct: 3. The hills here are cloth'd all up their steep sides with oak, ash, birch, holly, &c: some of it has been cut 40 years ago, some within these 8 years, yet all is sprung again green, flourishing, & tall for its age, in a place where no soil appears but the staring rock, & where a man could scarce stand upright.

Met a civil young farmer overseeing his reapers (for it is oat-harvest here) who conducted us to a neat white house in the village of Grange, wch is built on a rising ground in the midst of a valley. round it the mountains form an aweful amphitheatre, and thro' it obliquely runs the Darwent clear as glass, and shewing under it's bridge every trout that passes. beside the village rises a round eminence of rock, cover'd entirely with old trees, & over that more proudly towers *Castle-crag*, invested also with wood on its sides, & bearing on its naked top some traces of a fort said to be Roman. by the side of this hill, wch almost blocks up the way, the valley turns to the left & contracts its dimensions, till there is hardly any road but the rocky bed of the river. the wood of the mountains increases & their summits grow loftier to the eye, & of more fantastic forms : among them appear *Eagle's-cliff*, *Dove's-nest*, *Whitedale-pike*, &c: celebrated names in the annals of Keswick. the dale opens about four miles higher till you come to *Sea-Whaite* (where lies the way mounting the hills to the right, that leads to the *Wadd-mines*) all farther access is here barr'd to prying Mortals, only there is a little path winding over the Fells, & for some weeks in the year passable to the Dale's-men ; but the Mountains know well, that these innocent people will not reveal the mysteries of their ancient kingdom, the reign of Chaos & old Night. Only I learn'd, that this dreadful road, dividing again leads one branch to *Ravenglas*, & the other to *Hawkshead*.

For me I went no farther than the Farmer's (better than 4 m: from Keswick) at *Grange*: his mother & he brought us butter. that Siserah would have jump'd at, tho' not in a lordly dish, bowls of milk, thin oaten-cakes, & ale ; & we had carried a cold tongue thither with us. our farmer was himself the Man, that last year plundered the Eagle's eirie : all the dale are up in arms on such an occasion, for they lose abundance of lambs yearly, not to mention hares, partridge, grous, &c: he was let down from the cliff in ropes to the shelf of rock, on wch the nest was built, the people above shouting & hollowing to fright the old birds. wch flew screaming round, but did not dare to attack him. he brought off the eaglet (for there is rarely more than one) & an addle egg. the nest was roundish and more than a yard over, made of twigs twisted together. seldom a year passes but they take the brood or eggs, & sometimes they shoot one, sometimes the other Parent, but the survivor has always found a mate (probably in Ireland) & they breed near the old place. by his description I learn, that this species is the *Erne* (the Vultur *Albicilla* of Linnæus in his last edition, but in yours *Falco Albicilla*) so consult him & Pennant about it.

Walk'd leisurely home the way we came, but saw a new landscape : the features indeed were the same in part, but many new ones were disclosed by the mid-day Sun, and the tints were entirely changed. take notice this was the best or perhaps the only day for going up Skiddaw, but I thought it better employed : it was perfectly serene, & hot as mid-summer.

In the evening walk'd alone down to the Lake by the side of *Crow-Park* after sun-set & saw the solemn colouring of night draw on, the last gleam of sunshine fading away on the hill-tops, the deep serene of the waters, & the long shadows of the mountains thrown across them, till they nearly touched the hithermost shore. at distance heard the murmur of many waterfalls not audible in the day-time. wished for the Moon, but she was *dark to me & silent, hid in her vacant interlunar cave.*

Oct: 4. W^d E:, clouds & sunshine, & in the course of the day a few drops of rain. Walk'd to *Crow-park*, now a rough pasture, once a glade of ancient oaks, whose large roots still remain on the ground, but nothing has sprung from them. if one single tree had remain'd, this would have been an unparallel'd spot, & Smith judged right, when he took his print of the Lake from hence, for it is a gentle eminence, not too high, on the very margin of the water & commanding it from end to end, looking full into the *gorge* of *Borrodale*. I prefer it even to *Cockshut*-hill, wch lies beside it, & to wch I walk'd in the afternoon: It is cover'd with young trees both sown & planted, oak, spruce, scotch-fir, &c:, all wch thrive wonderfully. there is an easy ascent to the top, and the view far preferable to that on Castle-hill (wch you remember) because this is lower and nearer to the Lake: for I find all points, that are much elevated, spoil the beauty of the valley, & make its parts (wch are not large) look poor and diminutive. while I was here, a little shower fell, red clouds came marching up the hills from the east, & part of a bright rainbow seem'd to rise along the side of Castle-hill.

From hence I got to the *Parsonage* a little before Sunset, and saw in my glass a picture, that if I could transmitt to you, & fix it in all the softness of its living colours, would fairly sell for a thousand pounds. this is the sweetest scene I can yet discover in point of pastoral beauty. the rest are in a sublimer style.

(To be continued *without end.*)

P:S: I beg your pardon, but I have no franks. the quill arrived very safe, & doubtless is a very snug and commodious method of travelling, for one of the rarities was alive & hearty, & was three times plunged in spirits, before I could get it to die. you are much improved in observation, for a common eye would certainly take it for a pismire. the place of its birth, form of ye antennae, & abdomen, particularly the long *aculeus* under it, shew it to be a *Cynips* (look among the *Hymenoptera*) not yet compleat, for the 4 wings do not yet appear, that I see. it is not a species described by Linnæus, tho' he mentions others, that breed on the leaves, footstalks, bud, flowers & bark of the Oak. Remember

this year the Wadd-mine had been open'd (which is done once in 5 years) it is taken out in lumps sometimes as big as a man's fist, & will undergo no preparation by fire, not being fusible. when it is pure soft, black, & close-grain'd, it is worth sometimes 30 shillings a pound. there are no Charr ever taken in these lakes, but plenty in Butter-mere-Water, which lies a little way N: of Borrodale, about Martlemas, wch are potted here. they sow chiefly oats & bigg here, wch are now cutting & still on the ground. There is some hay not yet got in. the rains have done much hurt ; yet observe, the soil is so thin and light, that no day has pass'd, in wch I could not walk with ease, & you know, I am no lover of dirt. Their wheat comes from Cockermouth or Penrith. Fell-mutton is now in season for about six weeks; it grows fat on ye mountains, & nearly resembles venison: excellent Pike & Perch (here called *bass*) trout is out of season. partridge in great plenty.

Rec:^t to dress Perch (for Mrs Wharton) Wash, but neither scale, nor gut them. broil till enough ; then pull out the fins, & open them along ye back, take out the bone and all the inwards without breaking them. put in a good lump of butter & salt, clap the sides together, till it melts, & serve very hot. it is excellent. the skin must not be eaten.

At *Keswick* learn'd, that the turn-pike road from thence along the east-side of *Bassingthwait*, or Low-water (which is eight miles) to *Ews-bridge* over Derwent is made in part only, about three miles of it being a cart-road slippery and dangerous, or else narrow and stony lane. the new road from Cockermouth is made (five miles) to *Ews-bridge*, and now carrying on towards *Penrith*.

That the way from *Keswick* to *Ambleside* (eighteen miles) is turnpike not yet compleated by about three miles. the unmade way is thro' narrow country lanes, or rocky road, but nothing dangerous by day-light. it runs mostly thro' deep romantic vallies by the waters of Wiborn at the foot of Helvellyn-Fell, by Grasmere and Ridall. Amble-side is a little Market-town, but

the inns are too mean and unfrequented to lie at. from
thence to *Kendal* is fourteen miles, turnpike-road, but
not quite finish'd; it goes near five miles on the side of
Winander-water with beautiful views, mostly up hill,
but good road, except a small part not yet compleated,
and this is very safe.

From Kendal there is a fine turnpike lately made to
Ulverston (or Ouston) in Furness. it goes by the foot
of Winander-mere-water and over *Penny-bridge* avoid-
ing all the sea-sands, and with many uncommon views
the whole way.

There is also a road not quite finish'd to Kirby-
Lonsdale. from thence it is compleated by *Ingleton* to
Settle in Yorkshire, excellent way.

There is also a turnpike, that goes by *Sedburgh* and
over Cam-hill to Ashrigg in Wensledale.

I learn'd at Kendal, that the *Ulverston* turnpike is
continued a few miles to *Dalton* and there ends: but
that a branch of it (not quite compleated) goes off into
Cumberland to *Ravenglass* and so on along the coast
to Egremont. in this part of it a sand must necessarily
be pass'd, but it is only three or four hundred yards
over, and very safe.

Oct: 8. Left to Keswick & took the Ambleside-road
in a gloomy morning. W^d E: & afterw^{ds} N:E:. about
2 m: from the Town mounted an eminence call'd *Castle-
rigg*, & the sun breaking out discover'd the most
enchanting view I have yet seen of the whole valley
behind me, the two lakes, the river, the mountains all
in their glory ! had almost a mind-to have gone back
again. the road in some little patches is not compleated,
but good country-road through sound, but narrow &
stony lanes, very safe in broad daylight. This is the
case about *Causeway-foot*, & among *Naddle-fells* to
Lanthwaite. the vale you go in has little breadth the
mountains are vast & rocky, the fields little & poor, and
the inhabitants are now making hay, & see not the sun
by two hours in a day so long as at Keswick. came to
the foot of Helvellyn, along which runs an excellent
road, looking down from a little height on *Lee's-water*,

(called also Thirl-meer, or Wiborn-water) and soon descending on its margin. the lake from its depth looks black, (though really as clear as glass) & from the gloom of the vast crags, that scowl over it: it is narrow & about 3 miles long, resembling a river in its course. little shining torrents hurry down the rocks to join it, with not a bush to overshadow them, or cover their march. all is rock & loose stones up to the very brow, wch lies so near your way, that not above half the height of Helvellyn can be seen. (to be continued, but now we have got franks)

Happy new year & many to you all. Hepatica & Mezereon now in flower! I saw Mrs Jonathan, who is much fallen away, & was all in tears for the loss of her Brother's child: she and Miss Wilson desired their compliments. Your Nephew is here & very well; so is Mr Brown, who presents his best wishes.

[*To Wharton.*]

Past by the little chappel of *Wiborn*, out of which the Sunday congregation were then issueing. Past a beck near Dunmailraise and entered Westmoreland a second time ; now begin to see *Helm-crag* distinguished from its rugged neighbours not so much by its height, as by the strange broken outline of its top. like some Gigantic building demolished, and the stones that composed it flung cross each other in wild confusion. just beyond it opens one of the sweetest landscapes that art ever attempted to imitate. the bosom of the mountains spreading here into a broad bason discovers in the midst Grasmere-water ; its margin is hollowed into small bays with bold eminences: some of them rock, some of soft turf that half conceal and vary the figure of the little lake they command. from the shore a low promontory pushes itself far into the water, and on it Stands a white village with the Parish Church rising in the midst of it, hanging enclosures, corn-fields, and meadows green as an emerald with their trees and hedges and cattle fill up the whole space from the edge of the water. just opposite to you is a large farmhouse at the bottom of a steep smooth lawn embosomed in old woods, which climb half way up the mountains side, and discover above them a broken line of crags, that crown the scene. not a single red tile, no flaming Gentleman's house, or garden-walls break in upon the repose of this little unsuspected paradise, but all is peace, rusticity, and happy poverty in its neatest most becoming attire.

The road winds here over Grasmere-hill, whose rocks soon conceal the water from your sight, yet it is continued along behind them, and contracting itself to a river communicates with Ridale-water, another small lake, but of inferior size, and beauty; it seems shallow too, for large patches of reeds appear pretty far within it. into this vale the road descends: on the opposite banks large and ancient woods mount up the hills: and just to the left of our way stands Ridale-hall, the family seat of Sʳ. Mic. Fleming, but now a farm-house, a large old fashioned fabrick surrounded with wood and not much too good for its present destination. Sʳ Michael is now on his travels, and all this timber far and wide belongs to him, I tremble for it when he returns, near the house rises a huge crag called Ridale-head, which is said to command a full view of Wynandermere, and I doubt it not, for within a mile that great lake is visible even from the road, as to going up the crag, one might as well go up Skiddaw.

Came to Ambleside eighteen miles from Keswick, meaning to lie there, but on looking into the best bed-chamber dark and damp as a cellar, grew delicate gave up Wynander-mere in despair, and resolved I would go on to *Kendal* directly 14 miles farther; the road in general fine turnpike but some parts (about 3 miles in all) not made, yet without danger.

Unexpectedly was well rewarded for my determination. the afternoon was fine, and the road for full 5 M: runs along the side of Wynander-mere, with delicious views across [?] it, and almost from one end to the other. it is ten miles in length and at most a mile over, resembling the course of some vast and

magnificent river, but no flat marshy grounds, no osier
beds, or patches of scrubby plantation on its banks.
at the head two vallies open among the mountains,
one, that by which we came down, the other Langsledale
in which *Wrynose* and Hard-Knot two great mountains
rise above the rest. from thence the fells visibly sink
and soften along its sides, sometimes they run into it,
(but with a gentle declivity) in their own dark and
natural complexion, oftener they are green and cultivated with farms interspersed and round eminences on
the border cover'd with trees : towards the South it
seems to break into larger bays with several islands
and a wider extent of cultivation. the way rises
continually till at a place called *Orresthead* it turns to
S:E: losing sight of the water.

Passed by *Ings* Chappel and *Staveley*, but I can say
no farther for the dusk of the evening coming on
I entered *Kendal* almost in the dark, and could distinguish only a shadow of the castle on a hill, and tenter
grounds spread far and wide round the town, which
I mistook for houses. my Inn promised sadly having
two wooden galleries (like Scotland) in front of it. it
was indeed an old ill contrived house, but kept by civil
sensible people, so I stayed two nights with them, and
fared and slept very comfortably.

Oct: 9. W^d N:W: clouds and sun air as mild as
summer. all corn off the ground, sky larks singing
aloud (by the way I saw not one at Keswick, perhaps
because the place abounds in birds of prey). went up
the Castle-hill. The town consists chiefly of three
nearly parallel streets almost a mile long. except these
all the other houses seem as if they had been dancing
a country-dance and were out : there they stand back
to back, corner to corner, some up hill some down
without intent or meaning. along by their sides runs
a fine brisk stream, over which are three stone bridges,
the buildings (a few comfortable houses excepted) are
mean, of stone and covered with a bad rough cast.
near the end of the town stands a handsome house of
Col. Wilson's and adjoining to it the Church, a very

large Gothick fabrick with a square tower, it has no particular ornaments but double Isles and at the east end four Chappels or Choirs, one of the Parrs, another of the Stricklands, the 3ᵈ is the proper choir of the church, and a 4ᵗʰ of the Bellinghams, a family now extinct.

There is an altar-tomb of one of them dated 1577 with a flat brass, arms and quarterings and in the window their arms alone, Arg: a hunting-horn, sab: strung-Gules in the *Strickland's* chappel—several modern monuments, and another old altar-tomb, not belonging to the family: on the side of it ; a Fess dancetty between 10 Billets (Deincourt). In the *Parr* chappel is a third altar-tomb in the corner, no fig: or inscription, but on the side cut in stone an escutcheon of *Roos* of Kendal (3 Water-Budgets) quartering *Parr* (2 bars in a bordure engrailed). 2ndly an escutcheon, Vaire, a Fess (for Marmion). 3rdly. an escutcheon three Chevronels braced and a Chief (which I take for Fitzhugh) at the foot is an escutcheon surrounded with the Garter, bearing *Roos* and *Parr* quarterly, quartering the other two before mentioned. I have no books to look in, therefore cannot say, whether this is the Ld. *Parr of Kendal* (Queen Catharine's Father) or her Brother, the Marquis of Northampton. Perhaps it is a Cenotaph for the latter who was buried at Warwick in 1571.

The remains of the castle are seated on a fine hill on the side of the river opposite to the town. almost the whole enclosure of walls remains with 4 towers, 2 square and 2 or 3 round, but their upper part and embattlements are demolish'd. it is of rough stone and cement ; without any ornament or arms, round enclosing a court of like form and surrounded by a mote, nor ever could have been larger than it is, for there are no traces of outworks. there is a good view of the town and river with a fertile open valley thro' which it winds.

After dinner went along the *Milthrop* turnpike 4 m. to see the falls (or force) of the river *Kent :* came to Siserge (pronounce Siser) and turn'd down a lane to

the left. *Siser*, the seat of the *Stricklands* an old
Catholick family is an ancient Hall-house with a very
large tower embattled: the rest of the buildings added
to this are of later date, but all is white, and seen to
advantage on a back ground of old trees; there is
a small park also well wooded. opposite to this turned
to the left and soon came to the river. it works its way
in a narrow and deep rocky channel overhung with
trees. the calmness and brightness of yᵉ evening, the
roar of the waters, and the thumping of huge hammers
at an iron-forge not far distant made it a singular walk,
but as to the falls (for there are two) they are not 7 feet
high. I went on down to the forge, and saw the Demons
at work by the light of their own fires: the iron is
brought in pigs to *Milthrop* by sea from *Scotland*, and
is here beat into bars and plates. two miles farther at
Levens is the seat of L. Suffolk, where he sometimes
passes the summer. it was a favourite place of his late
Countess, but this I did not see.

Oct: 10. went by *Burton* to Lancaster. Wᵈ N:W:
Clouds and sun: 22 miles. very good country well
inclosed and wooded, with some common interspersed.
passed at the foot of *Farlton-Knot* a high Fell, four
miles north of Lancaster on a rising ground called
Bolton (pronounce Bouton) we had a full view of
Cartmell-sands, with here and there a Passenger riding
over them (it being low water) the points of Furness
shooting far into the sea, and lofty mountains partly
covered with clouds extending north of them. Lancaster
also appeared very conspicuous and fine, for its most
distinguished features, the Castle and the Church
mounted on a green eminence, were all, that could be
seen. Woe is me! when I got thither, it was the second
day of their fair. the Inn in the principal street was
a great old gloomy house full of people, but I found
tolerable quarters, and even slept two nights in
peace.

Ascended the Castle hill in a fine afternoon. it takes
up the higher top of the eminence on wᶜʰ it stands, and
is irregularly round encompassed with a deep mote.

in front towards the Town is a magnificent Gothick Gateway, lofty and huge, the over-hanging battlements are supported by a triple range of Corbels, the intervals pierced thro' and showing the day from above. on its top rise light watch-towers of small height. it opens below with a grand pointed arch : over this is a wrought tabernacle, doubtless once containing its Founders figure, on one side a shield of France semy-quarter'd with England, on the other the same with a label ermine for John of Gant D: of Lancaster. this opens to a court within, which I did not much care to enter being the County Gaol and full of Prisoners, both Criminals and Debtors. from this gateway the walls continue and join it to a vast square tower of great height, the lower part at least of remote antiquity for it has small round-headed lights with plain short pillars on each side of them ; there is a third tower also square and of less dimensions—this is all the castle : near it and but little lower stands the Church a large and plain Gothick fabrick. the high square tower at the west end has been rebuilt of late years, but nearly in the same style. there are no ornaments of arms, &ct. &ct. any where to be seen. within it is lightsome and spacious ; but not one monument of Antiquity, or piece of painted glass is left. from the Church-Yard there is an extensive sea-view (for now the tide had almost covered the sands, and filled the river), and besides greatest part of Furness I could distinguish *Peel*-Castle on the Isle of Fowdrey wᶜʰ lies off the southern extremity. the town is built on the slope, and at the foot of the Castle-hill more than twice the bigness of Auckland, with many neat buildings of white stone, but a little disorderly in their position ad libitum like Kendal. many also extend below on the Keys by the river-side, where a number of ships were moor'd, some of them 3 mast vessels, decked out with their colours in honour of the Fair. here is a good bridge of 4 arches over the Lune, which runs when the tide is out in two streams divided by a bed of Gravel, which is not covered but in spring tides. below the town it widens to near the breadth of the Thames at London, and meets the sea at 5 or 6 miles distance to S:W:

Oct: 11 : W^d S:W: Clouds and Sun : warm and a fine dappled sky : crossed the river and walked over a peninsula 3 miles to the village of *Pooton* wch stands on the beach. an old fisherman mending his nets (while I enquired about the danger of passing those sands) told me in his dialect a moving story, how a brother of the trade, a Cockler (as he styled him) driving a little cart with two daughter (women grown) in it, and his Wife on horseback following, set out one day to pass the 7 mile sands, as they had frequently been used to do ; for nobody in the village knew them better than the old Man did. when they were about half way over, a thick fog rose, and as they advanced, they found the water much deeper than they expected. the old man was puzzled, he stop'd, and said he would go a little way to find some mark he was acquainted with. they staid a little while for him but in vain. they call'd aloud, but no reply. at last the young women pressed their mother to think where they were, and go on, she would not leave the place, she wander'd about forlorn and amazed. she would not quit her horse, and get into the cart with them. they determined after much time wasted to turn back, and give themselves up to the guidance of their horses. the old Woman was soon washed off and perish'd. the poor Girls clung close to their cart, and the horse sometimes wading and sometimes swimming brought them back to land alive, but senseless with terror and distress and unable for many days to give any account of themselves. the bodies of their parents were found soon after (next ebb) ; that of the father a very few paces distant from the spot, where he had left them.

In the afternoon wandered about the town and by the key till it was dark. a little rain fell.

Oct^br 12. W^d N:E: sky gloomy, then gleams of sunshine. set out for Settle by a fine turnpike road, twenty-nine miles.

Rich and beautiful enclosed country diversifyed

with frequent villages and churches very uneven ground, and on the left the river Lune winding in a deep valley, its hanging banks clothed with fine woods thro' which you catch long reaches of the water, as the road winds about at a considerable height above it ; passed the Park (Hon: Mr Clifford's, a Catholick) in the most picturesque part of the way : the grounds between him and the river are indeed charming : the house is ordinary, and the Park nothing but a rocky fell scattered over with ancient hawthorns. came to Hornby a little town on the River Wanning, over which a handsome bridge is now in building. the Castle in a lordly situation attracted me, so I walked up the hill to it. first presents itself a large but ordinary white Gentleman's house sash'd, behind it rises the ancient keep built by Edward Stanley, Lord Mounteagle (inscribed Helas et quand ?) in Henry the 8^{ths} time. it is now a shell only, tho' rafters are laid within it as for flooring : I went up a winding stone-staircase in one corner to the leads, and at the angle is a single Hexagon watchtower rising some feet higher fitted up in the taste of a modern *Toot*, with sash-windows in gilt frames, and a stucco cupola, and on the top a vast gilt eagle, by Mr Charteris, the present possessor. but he has not lived here since the year 1745, when the people of Lancaster insulted him, threw stones into his coach and almost made his wife (Lady Katharine Gordon) miscarry. since that he has built a great ugly house of red stone (thank God it is not in England) near Haddington, which I remember to have passed by. he is the second son of the Earl of Wemyss, and brother to the Ld Elcho ; Grandson to Col. Charteris, whose name he bears. from the leads of the tower there is a fine view of the country round and much wood near the Castle. Ingleborough, which I had seen before distinctly at Lancaster, to N:E: was now compleatly wrapt in clouds, all but its summit, which might have been easily mistaken for a long black cloud too, fraught with an approaching storm. now our road began gradually to mount towards the Apenine, the trees growing less and

thin of leaves till we came to Ingleton 18 miles : it is
a pretty village, situated very high and yet in a valley
at the foot of that huge creature of God *Ingleborough*. two
torrents cross it with great stones rolled along their bed
instead of water : over them are two handsome arches
flung.   Here at a little ale-house were Sr Bellingham
Graham and Mr Parker, Lord of the manor, (one of
them six feet & $\frac{1}{2}$ high and the other as much in breadth)
come to dine.   the nipping air (tho' the afternoon was
growing very bright) now taught us we were in Craven ;
the road was all up and down (tho' no where very
steep).   to the left were mountain-tops : waryside to
the right a wide valley : (all inclosed ground) and
beyond it high hills again.   in approaching Settle the
crags on the left drew nearer to our way ; till we
ascended Brunton-Brow, into a chearful valley, (tho'
thin of trees), to *Giggleswick*, a village with a small
piece of water by its side cover'd with coots : near it
a Church, which belongs also to Settle, and half a mile
further having passed the Ribble over a bridge arrived
at Settle.   it is a small market-town standing directly
under a rocky fell, there are not a dozen good-looking
houses, the rest are old and low, with little wooden
Portico's in front.   my Inn pleased me much (tho'
small) for the neatness and civility of the good woman
that kept it, so I lay there two nights, and went

Oct. 13, to visit *Gordale-scar*.   W^d N:E: day gloomy
and cold.   it lay but 6 m: from Settle, but that way was
directly over a Fell, and it might rain.   so I went round in
a chaise the only way one could get near it in a carriage,
wch made it full thirteen miles : and half of it such a
road !   but I got safe over it, so there's an end ;   and
came to Malham (pronounce Maum) a village in the
bosom of the mountains, seated in a wild and dreary
valley ;   from thence I was to walk a mile over very
rough ground, a torrent rattling along on the left hand :
on the cliffs above hung a few goats : one of them
danced and scratched an ear with its hind foot in
a place where I would not have stood stockstill for all
beneath the moon : as I advanced the crags seem'd to

close in ; but discovered a narrow entrance turning to
the left between them. I followed my guide a few
paces, and lo, the hills open'd again into no large space,
and then all further way is bar'd by a stream, that at
the height of above 50 feet gushes from a hole in the
rock, and spreading in large sheets over its broken
front, dashes from steep to steep, and then rattles away
in a torrent down the valley. the rock on the left rises
perpendicular with stubbed Yew trees and shrubs,
staring from its side to the height of at least 300 feet :
but those are not the things : it is that to the right
under which you stand to see the fall, that forms the
principal horror of the place. from its very base it
begins to slope forwards over you in one black and solid
mass without any crevice in its surface ; and over-
shadows half the area below with its dreadful canopy.
when I stood at (I believe) full 4 yards distance from
its foot, the drops wch perpetually distill from its brow,
fell on my head, and in one part of the top more
exposed to the weather there are loose stones that hang
in the air, and threaten visibly some idle Spectator with
instant destruction : it is safer to shelter yourself
close to its bottom, and trust the mercy of that
enormous mass, which nothing but an earthquake can
stir. the gloomy uncomfortable day well suited the
savage aspect of the place and made it still more
formidable.

I stay'd there (not without shuddering) a quarter of
an hour, and thought my trouble richly paid, for the
impression will last for Life : at the ale-house where
I dined in Malham, Vivares, the landscape painter, had
lodged for a week or more : Smith and Bellers had also
been there ; and two prints of Gordale have been
engraved by them : I returned to my comfortable Inn :
night fine : but windy and frosty.

Oct: 14 Went to Skipton 16 miles : W^d N:E: gloomy :
at one o'clock a little sleet falls : from several parts of
the road, and in many places about Settle, I saw at
once the three famous hills of this country, Ingleborough, Penigent, and Pendle : the first is esteemed

the highest : their features are hard to describe, but I could trace their outline with a pencil. Craven after all is an unpleasing country, when seen from a height : its valleys are chiefly wide and either marshy or enclosed pasture with a few trees : numbers of black cattle are fatted here, both of the scotch breed and a larger sort of oxen with great horns : there is little cultivated ground except a few oats.

Oct 15. W^d N:E: gloomy, at noon a few grains of sleet fell, then bright and clear. went thro' Longpreston and Gargrave to Skipton 16 miles : it is a pretty large market town in a valley with one very broad street gently sloping downwards from the Castle, which stands at the head of it ; this is one of our good Countesses buildings, but on old foundations, it is not very large ; but of a handsome antique appearance with round towers, a grand gateway, bridge, and mote, and many old trees about it. in good repair, and kept up as a habitation the Earl of Thanet ; though he rarely comes thither : what with the sleet and a foolish dispute about chaises that delayed me, I did not see the inside of it : but went on 15 miles to *Ottley* : First up Shodebank, the steepest hill I ever saw a road carried over in England : for it mounts up in a straight line (without any other repose for the horses, than by placing stones every now and then behind the wheels) for a full mile. then the road goes on a level along the brow of this high hill over Rumbold Moor, till it gently descends into *Wharfdale*, so they call the Vale of the Wharf : and a beautiful vale it is : well wooded, well cultivated, well inhabited, but with high crags at distance, that border the green country on either hand, thro' the midst of it, deep, clear, full to the brink and of no inconsiderable breadth runs in long windings the river ; how it comes to pass that it should be so fine and copious a stream here, and at Tadcaster (so much lower) should have nothing but a wide stony channel without water, I cannot tell [you] ; I passed through *Long-Addingdam*, Ilkeley (pronounce Eccla) distinguished by a lofty brow of loose rocks to the right ; Burley, a neat and pretty village among trees; on the opposite side of the river lay *Middleton-lodge*, belonging to a Catholick gentleman of that name: *Weston* a venerable stone fabrick with large offices, of Mr Vavasor: the meadows in front gently descending to the water, and behind a great and shady wood. Farnley: (Mr Fawkes') a place like the last; but larger and rising higher on the side of the hill. *Ottley* is a large airy town, with clean but low rustic buildings, and a bridge over the Wharf. I went into its spacious Gothick church, which has been new roofed with a flat stucco cieling. in a corner of it is the monument of Thomas Ld Fairfax and Helen Aske, his Lady, descended from the Cliffords and Latimers, as her epitaph says. the figures not ill cut: particularly his in armour, but bareheaded; lie on the tomb. I take them for the Grandparents of the famous Sr Thomas Fairfax.

199. To Stonehewer
(By Caxton Bag.)

Cambridge, November 2, 1769.

My Dear Sir,—I am sincerely pleased with every mark of your kindness, and as such I look upon your last letter in particular. I feel for the sorrow you have felt, and yet I cannot wish to lessen it; that would be to rob you of the best part of your nature, to efface from your mind the tender memory of a father's love, and deprive the dead of that just and grateful tribute which his goodness demanded from you.

I must, however, remind you how happy it was for him that you were with him to the last; that he was sensible, perhaps, of your care, when every other sense was vanishing. He might have lost you the last year, might have seen you go before him, at a time when all the ills of helpless old age were coming upon him, and, though not destitute of the attention and tenderness of others, yet destitute of *your* attention and *your* tenderness. May God preserve you, my best friend, and, long after my eyes are closed, give you that last

satisfaction in the gratitude and affection of a son,
which you have given your father.

I am ever most truly and entirely yours,   T. G.

200. To Norton Nicholls. [From de
Bonstetten & Gray]

Cambridge the 6 Jan. 1770.

Hence, vain deluding Joys is our mottor hier, written
on every feature, and ourly spoken by every solitary
Chapel bel ; So that decently you can't expect no other
but a very grave letter. I realy beg you pardon to
wrap up my thoughts in so smart a dress, as an in
quarto sheet. I know they should apear in a folio
leave, but the Ideas themselves shall look so solemn as
to belie their dress. Tho' I wear not yet the black
gown, and am only an inferior Priest in the temple of
Meditation, yet my countenance is already consecrated.
I never walk but with even steps and musing gate, and
looks comercing with the skyes ; and unfold my
wrinkles only when I see mr. Gray, or think of you.
Then notwithstanding all your learnings and knowledge,
I feel in such occasions that I have a heart, which you
know is as some others a quite prophane thing to carry
under a black gown.

I am in a hurry from morning till evening. At
8 o Clock I am roused by a young square Cap, with
whom I follow Satan through Chaos and night. He
explaind me in Greek and Latin, the *sweet reluctant
amorous Delays* of our Grandmother Eve, We finish
our travels in a copious breakfast of muffins and tea.
Then apears Shakispair and old Liñeus struggling
together as two ghost would do for a damned Soul.
Sometimes the one get the better sometimes the other.
Mr. Gray, whose acquaintance is my greatest debt to
you, is so good as to shew me Macbeth, and all witches
Beldams, Ghost and Spirits, whose language I never
could have understood without his Interpretation.
I am now endeavouring to dress all those people in
a french dress, which is a very hard labour.

I am afraid to take a room, which Mr. Gray shall keep much better. So I stop hier my everrambling pen. My respectful Compliments to M^d Nichole. Only remember that you have no where a better or more grateful friend than your   de Bonstetten.

I loosd Mr. Wheeler letter and his direction.]

I never saw such a boy : our breed is not made on this model. he is busy from morning to night, has no other amusement, than that of changing one study for another, likes nobody that he sees here, & yet wishes to stay longer, tho' he has pass'd a whole fortnight with us already. his letter has had no correction whatever, and is prettier by half than English.

Would not you hazard your journal : I want to see, what you have done this summer though it would be safer & better to bring it yourself, methinks !

Complimens respectueux à Mad: Nichole, et à notre aimable Cousine la *Sposa*.

T. G.

201. To [NORTON NICHOLLS ?]

March 20. 1770.

DEAR SIR,—I am sorry for your disappointment and my own. Do not believe that I am cold to M^r Cl:^s translation : on the contrary, I long to see it, & wonder you should hesitate for want of Franks (wch here I have no means of getting) do I care about postage, do you think ?

On Wednesday next, I go (for a few days) with Mons: de B: to London. his cursed F:^r will have him home in the autumn, & he must pass thro' France to improve his talents & morals. He goes for Dover ·on Friday. I have seen (I own) with pleasure the efforts you have made to recommend me to him, *sed non ego credulus illis*, nor I fear, he neither. he gives me too much pleasure, and at least *an equal share* of inquietude. you do not understand him so well as I do, but I leave my meaning imperfect, till we meet. I have never met with so extraordinary a Person. God bless him ! I am unable to talk to you about anything else, I think.

I wondered you should think of Paris at the time of the Dauphin's marriage : it will be a frippery spectacle, and the expence of everything triple. As to *Wales*, doubtless I should wish it this summer, but I can answer for nothing, my own employment so sticks in stomach, and troubles my conscience. when I return hither, I will write to you better and more fully. Adieu ! I am very sincerely yours.

(No signature)

202. To Norton Nicholls

4 April 1770. P: Hall:

At length, my dear sir, we have lost our poor de B:^{n}, I pack'd him up with my own hands in the Dover machine at four o'clock in the morning on Friday, 23d March, the next day at 7 he sail'd and reached *Calais* by noon, & *Boulogne* at night. the next night he reach'd *Abbeville*, where he had letters to Mad: Vanrobais, to whom belongs the famous manufacture of cloth there. from thence he wrote to me, & here am I again to pass my solitary evenings, wch hung much lighter on my hands, before I knew him. this is your fault ! Pray let the next you send me be halt & blind, dull, unapprehensive, & wrong headed. for this (as Lady Constance says) *Was never such a gracious creature born !* and yet—but no matter ! burn my letter that I wrote you, for I am very much out of humour with myself, and will not believe a word of it. you will think I have caught madness from him (for he is certainly mad) and perhaps you will be right. oh ! what things are Fathers & Mothers ! I thought they were to be found only in England, but you see.

Where is Capt: Clarke's Translation ? where is your journal ? do you still haggle for me to save sixpence, you niggard ? why now I have been in Town & brought no franks with me yet. the translation of *Gruner* cannot be had this month or six weeks, so I am destitute of all things. this place never appeared so horrible to me as it does now. could not you come for a week or

fortnight ? it would be sunshine to me in a dark night !
even Dr Hallifax wishes, you would come. at least
write to me out of hand, for I am truly & faithfully

Yours

TG:

' Vous ne voyez plus que de la misere et de la gayeté.
les villages sont plus rares, plus petits : le silence dans
ces deserts annonce par tout un Maitre, il me sembloit,
que je devois demander a ces hommes en guenilles, qui
leur avoit pris leurs habits, leurs maisons ; quelle peste
avoit ravagé la nation.   mais ils ont le bonheur de ne
penser point, & de jouer jusqu'au moment qu'on les
egorge.

' Mais gardons notre indignation pour çeux qui sont
si stupides, qu'ils prennent de pareilles mœurs pour
modeles.'

203. To Charles de Bonstetten

Cambridge, April 12, 1770.

Never did I feel, my dear Bonstetten, to what a
tedious length the few short moments of our life may
be extended by impatience and expectation, till you
had left me ; nor ever knew before with so strong
a conviction how much this frail body sympathizes
with the inquietude of the mind. I am grown old in
the compass of less than three weeks, like the Sultan in
the Turkish tales, that did but plunge his head into
a vessel of water and take it out again, as the standers
by affirmed, at the command of a Dervise, and found
he had passed many years in captivity, and begot a
large family of children. The strength and spirits that
now enable me to write to you, are only owing to your
last letter a temporary gleam of sunshine. Heaven
knows when it may shine again ! I did not conceive
till now, I own, what it was to lose you, nor felt the
solitude and insipidity of my own condition before
I possessed the happiness of your friendship. I must
cite another Greek writer to you, because it is much
to my purpose : he is describing the character of

a genius truly inclined to philosophy. ' It includes,' he says, ' qualifications rarely united in one single mind, quickness of apprehension and a retentive memory, vivacity and application, gentleness and magnanimity ; to these he adds an invincible love of truth, and consequently of probity and justice. Such a soul,' continues he, ' will be little inclined to sensual pleasures, and consequently temperate ; a stranger to illiberality and avarice ; being accustomed to the most extensive views of things, and sublimest contemplations, it will contract an habitual greatness, will look down with a kind of disregard on human life and on death ; consequently, will possess the truest fortitude. Such,' says he, ' is the mind born to govern the rest of mankind.' But these very endowments, so necessary to a soul formed for philosophy, are often its ruin, especially when joined to the external advantages of wealth, nobility, strength, and beauty ; that is, if it light on a bad soil, and want its proper nurture, which nothing but an excellent education can bestow. In this case he is depraved by the public example, the assemblies of the people, the courts of justice, the theatres, that inspire it with false opinions, terrify it with false infamy, or elevate it with false applause ; and remember, that extraordinary vices and extraordinary virtues are equally the produce of a vigorous mind : little souls are alike incapable of the one and the other.

If you have ever met with the portrait sketched out by Plato, you will know it again : for my part, to my sorrow I have had that happiness. I see the principal features, and I foresee the dangers with a trembling anxiety. But enough of this, I return to your letter. It proves at least, that in the midst of your new gaieties I still hold some place in your memory, and, what pleases me above all, it has an air of undissembled sincerity. Go on, my best and amiable friend, to shew me your heart simply and without the shadow of disguise, and leave me to weep over it, as I now do, no matter whether from joy or sorrow.

204. To Norton Nicholls

Camb: 14 Apr: 1770.

I thought my mysteries were but too easy to explain, however you must have a little patience, for I can hazard only word of mouth. What you say of poor B: is so true, & (let me add) expresses so well my own feelings, that I shall transcribe your words, & send them to him : were I in his place, I should be grateful for them ! by this time I should think you may have received a letter from him yourself, for in that I received from Abbeville, 31 March, he spoke of his intention to write to you. I wrote to you myself as soon as I return'd from London, the 1st (I think) of April.

I am coming to see you, my good Friend, that is, on Monday se'nnight I mean to call on Palgrave for a few days in my way to Blundeston. as to Wales you may do with me, what you please, I care not. There is this inconvenience in our way, that I must call on Mason at Aston (& so may you too) for a little while, the last week in May : from thence we strike across to Chester, & enter Wales. For the summer of next year (tho' I shall be dead first) I am your Man, only I desire it may be a secret between ourselves, till the time comes, as you love your life.

I rejoice to see, you are so great a Gardiner & Botanist : my instructions will be very poor : De B:, with five lessons from Miller (before he departed for Sumatra) and his own matchless industry, could have told you much more than I can. it would be strange if I should blame you for reading Isocrates. I did so myself 20 years ago, & in an edition at least as bad as yours. the *Panegyrick*, the *De Pace*, *Areopagitica*, & *Advice to Philip*, are by far the noblest remains we have of this Writer, & equal to most things extant in the Greek tongue : but it depends on your judgement to distinguish between his real and occasional opinion of things, as he directly contradicts in one place what he has advanced in another ; for example, in the *Panathe-*

maic & the *De Pace*, &c: on the naval power of Athens : the latter of the two is undoubtedly his own undisguised sentiment.

Talk your fill to me, & spare not. it would perhaps be more flattering if you lived in the midst of an agreable society : but even as it is, I take it in good part, & heartily thank you, for you have given me a late instance of your partiality and kindness, that I shall ever remember.

I received on yᵉ 10ᵗʰ of this month a long letter from Paris lively and sensible as usual : but you will see it, & I shall hope for a sight of such as you have got by you. there are two different directions. A Mons: M:ʳ B: *a l'hotel de Luxembourg, rue des Petits Augustins, Fauxbourg Sᵗ Germain, Paris.* The other to the same, *chez Messʳˢ Lullin, Freres, & Rittiel,* rue Thevenot, Paris. the latter seems the safer, but then I am uncertain, whether I read it right. what shall I do ? I have tried both ways, but do not know yet with what success. Adieu, Dear Sʳ, I am very faithfully

Yours

TG:

205. To Thomas Warton

Pembroke Hall, April 15, 1770.

Sɪʀ,—Our friend, Dr. Hurd, having long ago desired me, in your name to communicate any fragments or sketches of a design, I once had, to give a History of English Poetry, you may well think me rude or negligent, when you see me hesitating for so many months, before I comply with your request, and yet, believe me, few of your friends have been better pleased than I, to find this subject (surely neither unentertaining nor unuseful) had fallen into hands so likely to do it justice. Few have felt a higher esteem for your talents, your taste, and industry. In truth, the only cause of my delay, has been a sort of diffidence, that would not let me send you anything, so short, so slight, and so imperfect as the few materials I had begun to collect, or the observations I had made on them. A sketch of the division or arrangement of the subject, however, I venture to transcribe; and would wish to know, whether it corresponds in any thing with your own plan, for I am told your first volume is in the press.

INTRODUCTION.

On the Poetry of the Gallic or Celtic nations, as far back as it can be traced. On that of the Goths, its introduction into these islands by the Saxons and Danes, and its duration. On the origin of rhyme among the Franks, the Saxons, and Provençaux. Some account of the Latin rhyming poetry, from its early origin, down to the fifteenth century.

PART I.

On the School of Provence, which rose about the year 1100, and was soon followed by the French and Italians. Their heroic poetry, or romances in verse, allegories, fabliaux, syrvientes, comedies, farces, canzoni, sonnetts, ballades, madrigals, sestines, etc. Of their imitators, the French; and of the first Italian School, commonly called the Sicilian, about the year 1200, brought to perfection by Dante, Petrarch, Boccace, and others. State of poetry in England from the Conquest, 1066, or rather from Henry the Second's time, 1154, to the reign of Edward the Third, 1327.

PART II.

On Chaucer, who first introduced the manner of the Provençaux, improved by the Italians into our country. His character, and merits at large. The different kinds in which he excelled. Gower, Occleve, Lydgate, Hawes, Gawen Douglas, Lyndesay, Bellenden, Dunbar, etc.

PART III.

Second Italian School, of Ariosto, Tasso, etc., an improvement on the first, occasioned by the revival of letters, the end of the fifteenth century. The Lyric Poetry of this and the former age, introduced from Italy by Lord Surrey, Sir T. Wyat, Bryan Lord Vaulx, etc., in the beginning of the sixteenth century.

PART IV.

Spenser, his character. Subject of his poem, allegoric and romantic, of Provençal invention, of Provençal invention : but his manner of tracing it borrowed from the second Italian school.— Drayton, Fairfax, Phineas Fletcher, Golding, Phaer, etc. This school ends in Milton. A third Italian school, full of conceit, began in Queen Elizabeth's reign, continued under James, and Charles the First, by Donne, Crashaw, Cleveland ; carried to its height by Cowley, and ending perhaps in Sprat.

PART V.

School of France, introduced after the Restoration.— Waller, Dryden, Addison, Prior, and Pope,—which has continued to our own times.

You will observe that my idea was in some measure taken from a scribbled paper of Pope, of which I believe you have a copy. You will also see, I had excluded Dramatic poetry entirely ; which if you had taken in, it would at least double the bulk and labour of your book,—I am, sir, with great esteem, your most humble and obedient servant.

THOMAS GRAY.

Pembroke Hall April 15, 1770.

206. TO WHARTON

18 April, 1770.

MY DEAR SIR,—I have been sincerely anxious for Miss Wharton, whose illness must have been indeed severe, if she is only now recovering. let us hope everything from the spring, wch begins (tho' slowly) to give new life to all things, & pray give my best respects to her, & thanks for remembering me & my dictionary at a time, when she well may be excused for thinking of nothing but herself.

. . . I have utterly forgot, where my journal left off, but (I think) it was after the account of Gordale near Settle. if so, there was little more worth your notice : the principal things were *Wharfdale* in the way from Skipton to Ottley, & *Kirstall-Abbey* 3 miles from

Leedes. the first is the valley form'd by the River
Wharf, well-cultivated, well-inhabited, well-wooded,
but with high rocky crags at distance, that border the
green country on either hand : thro' the midst of it
runs the river in long windings deep, clear, & full to
the brink, and of no inconsiderable breadth. how it
comes to be so fine & copious a stream here, & at
Tadcaster (so much lower) should have nothing but
a wide stony channel with little or no water, I cannot
tell you. *Kirstall* is a noble ruin in the Semi-Saxon
style of building, as old as K: Stephen toward the end
of his reign, 1152. the whole Church is still standing
(the roof excepted) seated in a delicious quiet valley on
the banks of the river *Are*, & preserved with religious
reverence by the Duke of Montagu. adjoining to the
church between that & the river are variety of chappels
and remnants of the abbey, shatter'd by the encroach-
ments of the ivy, & surmounted by many a sturdy tree,
whose twisted roots break thro' the fret of the vaulting,
& hang streaming from the roofs. the gloom of these
ancient cells, the shade & verdure of the landscape, the
glittering & murmur of the stream, the lofty towers
& long perspectives of the church, in the midst of a
clear bright day, detain'd me for many hours & were
the truest subjects for my glass I have yet met with
any where. as I lay at that smoky ugly busy town of
Leedes, I drop'd all farther thoughts of my journal, &
after passing two days at Mason's (tho' he was absent)
pursued my way by Nottingham, Leicester, Harborough,
Kettering, Thrapston, & Huntingdon to Cambridge,
where I arrived, 22 Oct:, having met with no rain to
signify, till this last day of my journey. there's luck
for you !

I do think of seeing Wales this summer, having never
found my spirits lower than at present, & feeling that
motion & change of the scene is absolutely necessary
to me. I will make Aston in my way to Chester, and
shall rejoice to meet you there, the *last week in May* ;
Mason writes me word, that he wishes it, & tho' his old
house is down & his new one not up, proposes to receive

us like Princes in grain. Adieu, my dear S^r and believe
me most faithfully yours,   TG:

My best compliments to Mrs Wharton & the family.
our weather till Christmas continued mild & open.
28 Dec: some snow fell but did not lie. The 4th of Jan:
was stormy & snowy, wch was often repeated during
that month, yet the latter half of it was warm & gentle.
18 Feb: was snow again, the rest of it mostly fine.
snow again on 15th March; from 23 to 30 March was
cold & dry, W^d E: or N:E:. on ye 31st rain. from
thence till within a week past, W^d N:W: or N:E: with
much hail & sleet; and on 4 Apr: a thunder-storm. it
is now fine spring-weather.

1 March. first violet appear'd. frogs abroad.
4   Almond blow'd, & Gooseberry spread its leaves.
9   Apricot blow'd.
1 April.   Violets in full bloom, & double Daffodils.
   ,,   Wren singing. double Jonquils.

To Thomas Wharton Esq of Old Park near Darlington Durham.

207. To Charles de Bonstetten

April 19, 1770.

Alas! how do I every moment feel the truth of
what I have somewhere read, 'Ce n'est pas le voir, que
de s'en souvenir;' and yet that remembrance is the
only satisfaction I have left. My life now is but
a conversation with your shadow—the known sound
of your voice still rings in my ears—there, on the
corner of the fender, you are standing, or tinkling on
the piano-forte, or stretched at length on the sofa. Do
you reflect, my dearest friend, that it is a week or
eight days before I can receive a letter from you, and
as much more before you can have my answer; that all
that time I am employed, with more than Herculean
toil, in pushing the tedious hours along, and wishing to
annihilate them; the more I strive, the heavier they
move, and the longer they grow. I cannot bear this
place, where I have spent many tedious years within

less than a month since you left me. I am going for a few days to see poor N:, invited by a letter, wherein he mentions you in such terms as add to my regard for him, and express my own sentiments better than I can do myself. 'I am concerned,' says he, 'that I cannot pass my life with him; I never met with any one who pleased and suited me so well: the miracle to me is, how he comes to be so little spoiled: and the miracle of miracles will be, if he continues so in the midst of every danger and seduction, and without any advantages but from his own excellent nature and understanding. I own I am very anxious for him on this account, and perhaps your inquietude may have proceeded from the same cause. I hope I am to hear when he has passed that cursed sea, or will he forget me thus *in insulam relegatum?* If he should it is out of my power to retaliate.'

Surely you have written to him, my dear Bonstetten, or surely you will! he has moved me with these gentle and sensible expressions of his kindness for you: are you untouched by them?

You do me the credit, and false or true it goes to my heart, of ascribing to me your love for many virtues of the highest rank. Would to heaven it were so! but they are indeed the fruits of your own noble and generous understanding, which has hitherto struggled against the stream of custom, passion, and ill company, even when you were but a child; and will you now give way to that stream when your strength is increased? Shall the jargon of French Sophists, the allurements of painted women *comme il faut,* or the vulgar caresses of prostitute beauty, the property of all who can afford to purchase it, induce you to give up a mind and body by nature distinguished from all others, to folly, idleness, disease, and vain remorse? Have a care, my ever amiable friend, of loving what you do not approve. Know me for your most faithful and most humble despote.

208. To Charles de Bonstetten

May 9, 1770.

I am returned, my dear Bonstetten, from the little journey I made into Suffolk, without answering the end proposed. The thought that you might have been with me there, has embittered all my hours : your letter has made me happy, as happy as so gloomy, so solitary a being as I am, is capable of being made. I know, and have too often felt the disadvantages I lay myself under, how much I hurt the little interest I have in you, by this air of sadness so contrary to your nature and present enjoyments : but sure you will forgive, though you cannot sympathize with me. It is impossible with me to dissemble with you ; such as I am I expose my heart to your view, nor wish to conceal a single thought from your penetrating eyes. All that you say to me, especially on the subject of Switzerland, is infinitely acceptable. It feels too pleasing ever to be fulfilled, and as often as I read over your truly kind letter, written long since from London, I stop at these words : ' La mort qui peut glacer nos bras avant qu'ils soient entrelacés.'

209. To James Beattie

Pembroke Hall, July 2, 1770.

I rejoice to hear that you are restored to a better state of health, to your books, and to your muse once again. That forced dissipation and exercise we are obliged to fly to as a remedy, when this frail machine goes wrong, is often almost as bad as the distemper we would cure ; yet I too have been constrained of late to pursue a like regimen, on account of certain pains in the head (sensation unknown to me before), and of great dejection of spirits. This, Sir, is the only excuse I have to make you for my long silence, and not (as perhaps you may have figured to yourself) any secret reluctance I had to tell you my mind concerning the specimen you so kindly sent me of your new Poem.

On the contrary, if I had seen anything of importance to disapprove, I should have hastened to inform you, and never doubted of being forgiven. The truth is, I greatly like all I have seen, and wish to see more. The design is simple, and pregnant with poetical ideas of various kinds, yet seems somehow imperfect at the end. Why may not young Edwin, when necessity has driven him to take up the harp, and assume the profession of a Minstrel, do some great and singular service to his country? (what service I must leave to your invention) such as no General, no Statesman, no Moralist could do without the aid of music, inspiration, and poetry. This will not appear an improbability in those early times, and in a character then held sacred, and respected by all nations. Besides, it will be a full answer to all the Hermit has said, when he dissuaded him from cultivating these pleasing arts; it will shew their use, and make the best panegyric of our favourite and celestial science. And lastly (what weighs most with me), it will throw more of action, pathos, and interest into your design, which already abounds in reflection and sentiment. As to description, I have always thought that it made the most graceful ornament of poetry, but never ought to make the subject. Your ideas are new, and borrowed from a mountainous country, the only one that can furnish truly picturesque scenery. Some trifles in the language or versification you will permit me to remark. . . .

I will not enter at present into the merits of your *Essay on Truth*, because I have not yet given it all the attention it deserves, though I have read it through with pleasure; besides I am partial, for I have always thought David Hume a pernicious writer, and believe he has done as much mischief here as he has in his own country. A turbid and shallow stream often appears to our apprehensions very deep. A professed sceptic can be guided by nothing but his present passions (if he has any) and interests; and to be masters of his philosophy we need not his books or advice, for every child is capable of the same thing, without any study at

all. Is not that *naïveté* and good humour, which his
admirers celebrate in him, owing to this, that he has
continued all his days an infant, but one that has
unhappily been taught to read and write ? That
childish nation, the French, have given him vogue and
fashion, and we, as usual, have learned from them to
admire him at second hand.

210. To Wharton

MY DEAR DOCTOR,—It happened, that I was in
London at the time, when St: received your letter
relating to Mr. L:ˢ request. as my name was mentioned
in it, I ought to make my excuses to you as well as he,
wᶜʰ it is indeed easy to do, as I could by no means ask
anything but thro' him, & (tho' this had been in my
power) it would have been a very bad plea to say, my
Lᵈ, you have done me a very unexpected favour not
long since ; & therefore I must beg you to do another
at my desire, for a Friend of mine. but the truth is, at
this time our application could not have had any
success, as our Principal would certainly never apply
to three different Persons, with whom he has no
connection ; nor care to be refused, or even obliged by
them. the inside of things cannot be well explained
by letters ; but if you saw it, you would immediately
see in its full light the impracticability of the thing.

I am lately return'd from a six weeks ramble thro'
Worcestershire, Gloucestershire, Monmouthshʳᵉ: Here-
fordshʳᵉ: & Shropshire, five of the most beautiful
counties in the kingdom. the very light, & principal
feature in my journey was the river *Wye*, wᶜʰ I descended in a boat for near 40 miles from Ross to Chep-
stow : its banks are a succession of nameless wonders !
one out of many you may see not ill described by
Mr. Whateley, in his *Observations on Gardening* under
the name of the *New-Weir* ; he has also touched upon
two others, *Tinterne-Abbey*, and *Persfield* (Mʳ Morris's),
both of them famous scenes, & both on the Wye.
Monmouth, a town I never heard mention'd, lies on the

same river in a vale, that is the delight of my eyes, & the very seat of pleasure. the vale of Abergavenny, Ragland & Chepstow-Castles, Ludlow, Malvern-hills, Hampton Court near Lemster, the Leasowes, Hagley, the three Cities & their Cathedrals, & lastly Oxford (where I past two days in my return with great satisfaction), are the rest of my acquisitions, & no bad harvest to my thinking. I have a journal written by the companion of my travels, that serves to recall & fix the fading images of these things.

I desire to hear of your health, & that of your family. are Miss Wh^n: & Miss Peggy quite recover'd ? My respects to M^{rs}. Wharton & them. I am ever

Yours

TG

Pemb: Coll: Aug: 24. 1770.

To Thomas Wharton Esq of Old-Park near Darlington Durham.

211. To Norton Nicholls

Dear Sir,—Venga, venga, V: S: si serva ! I shall be proud to see you both. the lodgings over the way will be empty, but such an entry, such a staircase ! how will Mrs. N: be able to crowd thro' it ? with what grace, when she gets out of her chair, can she conduct her hoop-petticoat thro' this augre-hole, and up the dark windings of the *grand escalier* that leads to her chamber? it is past my finding out. So I delay, till I hear from you again, before I engage them. I believe there may be a bed for you, but is there room for Mrs. Kipiffe, Mamma's Maid ? I am sure, I know not.

I was very ill, when I received your letter, with a feverish disorder, but have cured it merely by dint of *sage-tea*, the beverage of life. It is a polydynamious plant, take my word : though your Linnæus would persuade us it is merely *diandrious*. I applaud your industry ; it will do you a power of good one way or other, only don't mistake a Carabus for an Orchis, nor a Lepisma for an Adenanthera. Here is Mr Foljambe

has got a Flying Hobgoblin from the E: Indies, & a
power of rarities; and then he has given me such
a *Phalœna*, with looking glasses in its wings; & a
Queen of the *White Ants*, whose belly alone is as big as
many hundred of her subjects, I do not mean their
bellies only, but their whole persons: and yet her head
and her *tetons* and her legs are no bigger than other
people's. oh, she is a jewel of a pismire!

I hear the triumphs & see the illuminations of Alloa
hither, but did Mrs. E: lie a night at Edinburgh in her
way thither? does she meet with no signs of mortality
about her castle? Are her subjects all civet-cats and
musk-deer?

My respects to your Mother. Adieu! I have had an
infinite letter from Bonst: he goes in October to
Rocheguion on the Loire, with the Dutchess d'Enville.
The people in several provinces are starving to death
on the highways. the King (in spite to his parliaments
and nation) it is thought, will make the Duke d'Ai-
guillon his chief Minister.

To the Revd Mr Nicholls, at William Turner's Esq at
Richmond Surrey. Sept: 14. 1770.

212. To WALPOLE
Sept: 17. 1770. Pemb: Coll:

I write, having nothing essential to say, merely
because you are ill, & have but too much time to
read me. I plead no merit in my sympathy, because
I have the same enemy, & am daily expecting her
attacks, the more violent perhaps for having been now
for some years suspended. talk not of round windows,
nor of dying in them: our distemper (remember) is the
means of health & *long life*, now this latter is only the
name of another distemper, of wch I know enough
already to say, when the gout pinches me, *'tis well, it is
nothing worse*. I do not understand, why (with your
temperance) you are treated so severely; but suspect,
it is owing to a little indolence & want of motion
between the fits, as I have lately heard you complain of

a tenderness in your feet, that would not let you walk as usual. Man is a creature made to be jumbled, & no matter whether he goes on his head or heels, move or be moved he must. I am convinced, I owe my late & present ease to the little expeditions I always make in summer. the smartness of the pain you undergo, is an undoubted sign of strength & *youth*, & the sooner it will be over. I know, this is poor comfort: but I flatter myself, that in some few days you will be at ease, & will have the good nature to tell me so.

I have neither seen Tyson, nor Cole of late, but will take care they shall know, what you say. the latter lives at Milton near the Ely road. for myself I shall hardly be in Town before the end of November. Adieu! I am

Yours ever

TG:

To the Honble Horace Walpole in Arlington Street London.

213. To Mason

Pembroke Hall, October 24, 1770.

DEAR MASON,—I have been for these three weeks and more confined to my room by a fit of the gout, and am now only beginning to walk alone again. I should not mention the thing, but that I am well persuaded it will soon be your own case, as you have so soon laid aside your horse, and talk, so relishingly of your old port.

I cannot see any objection to your design for Mr. Pierce. As to Wilson we know him much alike. He seems a good honest lad; and I believe is scholar enough for your purpose. Perhaps this connection may make (or mar) his fortune. Our friend Foljambe has resided in college, and persevered in the ways of godliness till about ten days ago, when he disappeared, and no one knows whether he is gone a hunting or a . . . The little Fitzherbert is come a pensioner to St. John's, and seems to have all his wits about him. Your *élève* Lord Richard

Cavendish, having digested all the learning and all the beef this place could afford him in a two months' residence, is about to leave us, and his little brother George succeeds him. Bishop Keene has brought a son from Eton to Peterhouse ; and Dr. Heberden another to St. John's, who is entered pensioner, and destined to the Church. This is all my university news ; but why do I tell you ? come yourself and see, for I hope you remember your promise at Aston, and will take us in your way as you go to your town residence.

You have seen Stonhewer, I imagine, who went northwards on Saturday last ; pray tell me how he is, for I think him not quite well. Tell me this, and tell me when I may expect to see you here.—I am ever yours, T. G.

214. To Norton Nicholls

25 Nov: 1770.

I do not see, why you should suppose that *you* only are to have the privilege of being ill. for me, from the time you left me (till within these three days) I have been only one day out of the walls of this college. that day was employ'd in going to the Hills by way of airing after the gout, & in catching such a cold & cough as has given me no rest night or day, & has only now taken its leave of me. I sent away your letter to B: directly : I saw no reason against it. He was then at Aubonne, near Geneva, with his Brother, and is now at Berne. the picture is not arrived, nor (I suppose) ever will ; tho' he says, he has sent it, but by what conveyance, or by what hand he does not say.

You do me wrong : I have thought very frequently of you, especially since S^r A: Allen's death. I am rather glad his family were about him, tho' I know not well why, for he perhaps was insensible to it. these sort of deaths are alarming to the Spectator ; but perhaps the best for the Sufferer. I have now every day before my eyes a Woman of ninety, my Aunt, who has for many years been gradually turning into chalk-stones : they are making their way out of the joints of both feet, and the surgeon twice a day comes to increase the torture. She is just as sensible & as impatient of pain, & as intractable, as she was 60 years ago. she thinks not at all of death, and if a mortification does not come to release her, may lie in this agony for months (at least), helpless and bed-rid. this is what you call a *natural* death !

It is well, you live in a dry country, but do not your lakes overflow ? Can anything get from Norwich to Blundeston ? 200,000 acres are drown'd in the Fens here, and cattle innumerable. our friends at Worcester, Gloucester, &c: are sailing through the streets from house to house. Adieu ! The Post is impatient. my respects to Mrs. N:, I am

Faithfully yours
TG:

To the Revd Mr Nicholls at Blundeston near Leostoff Suffolk.

215. To Norton Nicholls

26 Jan: 1771
Pemb: Coll:

Dear Sir,—I want to know a hundred things about you. are you fix'd in your house, for I hear many vague reports of Miss A^s: inclination to part with the estate, & that the Loves are desirous of the purchase, & would bid high ? what part of the mansion (where I used to tremble at a breath of air) was blown down in the high wind ? did not you bless your stars for that dreary flat that lay between you & Corton, & bar'd all sight of the sea in its fury, & of the numberless wrecks that strew'd all your coast ? as to our little & unpicturesque events, you know them, I find, & have congratulated Mr Presendent, who is now our Master, in due form : but you do not know, that it never rains but it pours : he goes to town on Monday for institution to the Living of Streatham in the Isle of Ely worth from two to three hundred pound a-year, and given him by the King's Majesty. the detail is infinite, the attacks, the defences, the evasions, the circumventions, the sacrifices, the perjuries, are only to be told by word of mouth : suffice it to say that it is carried swimmingly and triumphantly against two Lords temporal & one spiritual, who solicited for their several Protegés in vain : so our good Uncle Toby will have about 400£ a year, no uncomfortable pittance ! I have had several capricious letters from Berne. he has sent me some pretty views of his native country, and its inhabitants. The portrait too is arrived, done at Paris, but no more like *than I to Hercules* : you would think, it was intended for his Father, so grave & so composed : doubtless he meant to look like an Englishman or an owl. pray send me the letter, & do not suppose I grudge postage.

I rejoice you have met with Froissart : he is the Herodotus of a barbarous age. had he but had the luck of writing in as good a language, he might have been immortal ! his locomotive disposition (for then there was no other way of learning things) his simple curiosity, his religious credulity, were much like those of the old Grecian. our Ancestors used to read the Mort d'Arthur, Amadis de Gaul, & Froissart, all alike, that is, they no more suspected the good faith of the former than they did of the latter, but took it all for history. when you have *tant chevauché* as to get to the end of him, there is Monstrelet waits to take you up, and will set you down at *Philip de Comines*. but previous to all these, you should have read *Ville-hardouin* & *Joinville*. I do not think myself bound to defend the character of even the best of Kings. Pray slash them, & spare not. My best compliments to Mrs Nicholls. I am very sincerely,

Yours

TG:

Your friend Mr. Crofts has just left me. he is a candidate for the University & will succeed in the room of De Grey, now Chief-Justice of ye Common Pleas.

216. To WHARTON

2 Feb: 1771. Pemb: Coll:

It never rains, but it pours, my dear Doctor. you
will be glad to hear, that M^r Br: has added to his
Mastership (wch is better than 150£ a-year) a living
hard by Cambridge, Stretham in the isle of Ely, worth,
as it was lett above 40 years ago, at least £240 more.
It was in the gift of the Crown during the vacancy of
the See of Ely, & that its value is really more than
I have said, you will hardly doubt, when you hear, it
was carried against an Earl, a Baron, & a Bishop, the
latter of the three so strenuous a Suitor, that he still
persisted above a week after I had seen the Presentation sign'd to M^r B: by the King's own hand, nay, he
still persisted a day, after the King had publicly declared
in the Drawing-room, that he had given it M^r B: by
name. and who was this bishop ? no other than your
friend, who wanted it for a Nephew of his, a *poor
unfortunate* Nephew, that had been so imprudent many
a year ago to marry a Farmer's daughter, where he
boarded, when Curate ; & continued ever since under
a cloud, because his uncle would give him nothing. as
to us, we had a Duke, an Earl, a Viscount, & a Bishop
on our side, & carried it so swimmingly you would stare
again. there was a prologue & an exegesis & a peripe-
teia, and all the parts of a regular drama ; & the Heroe
is gone to London, was instituted yesterday, and to-day
is gone to Lambeth, for the Archbishop too spoke
a good word for us & at a very critical time. the old
Lodge has got rid of all its harpsichords, & begins to
brighten up : its inhabitant is lost like a Mouse in an
old cheese. He has received your generous offer of
a benefaction to the common good, but it is too much
to tax yourself : however we all intend to bring in our
mites, & shew the way to the high & mighty : when
a fund is once on foot, they will bestirr themselves.

I am sincerely concerned to find Miss Wharton is still
an Invalide. I believe, you must send her into the
milder regions of the South, where the sun dispells all

maladies. We ourselves have had an untoward season enough : vast quantities of rain instead of winter, the thermom^r: never below 40 deg:, often above 50, before Christmas ; unusual high winds (wch still continue) particularly the 19th of Dec: at night it blew a dreadful storm. The first grain of snow was seen on X^{mas} D^{ay}, of wch we have had a good deal since, but never deep or lasting. the 2^d week in Jan: was really severe cold at London, & the Thames frozen over. One morning that week the glass stood here (at 8 in the morning) at 16 degrees, wch is the lowest I ever knew it at Cambridge. at London it never has been observed lower than 13 (understand me right : I mean, 13 above Zero of Farenheit) & that was 5 Jan, 1739. now it is very mild again, but with very high winds at N:W:.

I give you joy of our awkward peace with Spain. Mason is in Town taking his swing, like a Boy in breaking-up-time. remember me kindly to Mrs Wharton, & all the good family. did I tell you of my breaking up, in summer, in the midland counties, & so as far as Abergavenny one way, & Ludlow the other ? I have another journal for you, in several volumes. I have had a cough for above three months upon me, wch is incurable. Adieu !

I am ever yours

TG:

217. To NORTON NICHOLLS

DEAR SIR,—Your friend *Jean Froissart*, son of Thomas by profession a Herald-painter, was born at Valenciennes in Haynault, about the year 1337. was by nature fond of every *noble* diversion, as hunting, hawking, dress, good-cheer, wine, & women (this latter passion commenced at 12 years old), and was in his own time no less distinguished by his gallant poesies (still preserved in MSS) than by his historical writings, wch he began at the desire of *Robert de Namur*, Seigneur de Beaufort, when he was barely 20 years of age. at 24 he made his first voyage into England, & presented the first part of his history to Edw: the 3^d's Queen, Philippa of Haynault, who appointed him *Clerk of her chamber*, that is, Secretary, by wch he became one of the Household in that Court. after the death of this Queen in 1369 he had then the living of *Lessines* in his own country given him, & must then consequently be a priest. He attach'd himself to Wenceslaus of Luxemburg, Duke of Brabant, who dying in 1384, he became Clerk of the Chappel to Guy Comte de Blois, who probably gave him a canonry in the collegiate Church of *Chimay* near Marienbourg in the county of Haynault. he also had obtain'd of the Pope a reversion of another canonry in the church of Lisle ; but of this he never could get possession. After 27 years absence from England he made a third voyage thither in 1395, and stay'd in it only 3 months. his Patron Guy de Blois died in 1397, & Froissart survived him certainly 4 years, but how much more is uncertain. these & many more particulars are taken from the account of his life & writings, collected by Mons: *de la* Curne de St Palaye, in ten Tome of the *Mem: de l'Acad: des Inscript:^{ns}* &c., where you may see much more about him. the same Author defends him strongly against the suspicions, that have been entertain'd, of his partiality to the English Nation.

A Man at arms was a complicated machine, consisting of about seven Men, *i:e:* the Knight or gentleman himself compleatly and heavily arm'd & mounted on his great war-horse caparison'd and arm'd as strongly as the Rider : the rest were his Esquires, rather meant to assist him & watch his motions in the combat, than to engage in action themselves. all of them were (as I apprehend) on horseback, and thus taken together, made the principal strength and principal expence of armies in those days. *Ecuyers* were the sons of Gentleman, train'd up in quality of *Pages* till 12 years old (commonly not in their Father's Castle, but in that of some famous Knight, his Friend), after wch age they assumed the title of *Esquires*, were exercised daily in feats of arms & curtesy, attended the person of their

Lord at home & abroad, and at 21 were qualified to receive themselves the order of knighthood. read the same St. Palaye's *Mem: de l'ancienne Chevalerie*, 2 v. 8vo 1759, Paris. if you would have me say anything to T: you must remind me, what period of time he inquired about, for my memory fails me.

You may be sure of a month's notice from me if I undertake the voyage, wch seems to me next to impossible. I received a letter from B^n: last night, wch mentions you kindly, & seems very desirous, we should come this summer. what you mention of herrings I know not : I have never seen or heard of them !

Monstrelet reaches from A:D: 1400 to 1467, & there are additions at the end of him, that come down to 1516. it is a splendid and very substantial folio, publ^d: in 1572. Adieu ! My respects to Mrs. Nicholls.

(Signature torn away.)

218. To NORTON NICHOLLS

3 May 1771
Pemb: Coll:

DEAR SIR,—I can not tell you, what I do not know myself ; nor did I know you staid for my determination to answer B^s: letter. I am glad to hear you say, you shall go at all events, because then it is sure, I shall not disappoint you ; & if (wch I surely wish) I should be able to accompany you, perhaps I may prevail upon you to stay a week or fortnight for me : if I find it will not do, you certainly shall know it.

Three days ago I had so strange a letter from B: I hardly know how to give you any account of it, & desire you would not speak of it to anybody. that he has been *le plus malheureux des hommes*, that he is *decidé à* quitter son pays, that is, to pass the next winter in England : that he cannot bear *la morgue* de l'aristocratie, et *l'orgueil armé* des loix, in short, strong expressions of uneasiness & confusion of mind, so much as to talk of *un pistolet & du courage*, & all without the shadow of a reason assign'd, & so he leaves me. he is either disorder'd in his intellect (wch is too possible) or has done some strange thing, that has exasperated his whole family & friends at home, w^ch (I'm afraid) is at least equally possible. I am quite at a loss about it. you will see and know more : but by all means curb these vagaries & wandering imaginations, if there be any room for counsels.

You aggravate my misfortunes by twitting me with Temple, as if a pack of names of books & editions were any cure for his uneasiness, & that I witheld it from him. I have had neither health nor spirits all the winter, & never knew or cared what weather it was, before. the spring is begun here, Swallows were seen 23d April, the Redstart on ye 26th, the Nightingale was heard on ye 29th, & the Cuckow, on 1st of May. methinks I could wish that *Wheeler* went with you, whether I do or not ! Adieu ! I am

Truly yours
TG:

(On back)
To the Revd Mr Nicholls at Blundeston near Leostoff Suffolk by London.

219. To NORTON NICHOLLS

London. 20 May. 1771
at Frisby's, Jermyn-Street.

I received your letter inclosing that of poor T: the night before I set out for London. I would by all means wish you to comply with his request. you may say many things to L^d L: with a better grace than he can. I trust to the cause, & to the warmth of your own kindness, for inspiration : there is little of management required, nothing to conceal, but the full persuasion (I trust) we both have, that L^d L: knows the distress of his circumstances at least as well as we do. this doubtless must be kept out of sight, lest it carry too keen a reproach with it. in all the rest you are at full liberty to expatiate on his good qualities, the friendship you have long had for him, the pious imprudence, that has produced his present uneasy situation, & above all, your profound respect for Lord L^s: character & sensibility of heart. who knows what may be the consequence ? Men sometimes catch that feeling from a Stranger, wch should have originally sprung from their own heart. as to the means of helping him, his own schemes are perhaps too wild for you to mention them to L^d L: & (if they are to separate him from his wife and family) what is to come of them in the mean time ? I have a notion that the Chaplainship at Leghorn is still vacant by the death of a young Mr Byrom. at least I have never heard it was filled up. it depends on recommendation to the principal Italian merchants, wch seems much in L^d L^s: power. The B^p of Derry (I apprehend) is at Nice, or somewhere in Italy, for his health : it is true he has a great patronage in Ireland, and sometimes (from vanity) may do a right thing. the other projects do not strike me as anything, but (if L^d L: can be brought to mean him well) many different means will occur, by which he may serve him.

I shall pass a fortnight here, & perhaps within that time may see you in Town, at least I would wish so to do. I am but indifferently well, & think, all things consider'd, it is best not to keep you in suspense about my journey. [The sense of my own duty, which I do not perform, my own low spirits (to which this consideration not a little contributes) and (added to these) a bodily indisposition make it necessary for me to deny myself that pleasure, which perhaps I have kept too long in view. I shall see, however, with your eyes, and accompany you at least in idea. Write or come, or both soon. I am ever yours sincerely,   T. G.

My respects to Mrs. Nicholls. Clarke (I hear) is in town at Claxton's.]

220. To Wharton

Dear Doctor,—I was really far from well in health, when I received your last letter : since that I am come to Town, & find myself considerably better. Mason has pass'd all the winter here with Stonhewer in

Curzon-Street, May-fair, but thinks of returning home-
ward in a week or ten days. he had your letter (wᶜʰ
had gone round by Aston) and was applying to Mʳ
Fraser & others for proper recommendations in case
poor Mrs. E: should be obliged to make use of them:
but now you have given us some hopes, that these
expedients may not be necessary. I for my own part
do heartily wish, you may not be deceived, & that so
cool a Tyrant as her Husband seems to be, may willingly
give up the thoughts of exercising that tyranny, when
it is most in his power: but, I own, it seems to me very
unlikely. however I would not have you instrumental
(but at her most earnest entreaty) in sending her out
of his reach. no persuasion or advice on this head
should come from you: it should be absolutely her
own firm resolution (before sure witnesses) for that is
the only thing, that can authorise you to assist her. it
must have been her own fault (at least her weakness)
that such a decision as that of these Delegates could
find any grounds to go upon. I do not wonder, that
such an event has discomposed you: it discomposed
me to think of the trouble & expense it has brought on
you!

My summer was intended to have been pass'd in
Switzerland: but I have drop'd the thought of it,
& believe my expeditions will terminate in Old-park:
for travel I must, or cease to exist. till this year
I hardly knew what (mechanical) low-spirits were:
but now I even tremble at an east-wind. It is here the
height of summer, but with all the bloom & tender
verdure of spring. At Cambridge the Laurustines
& Arbutus kill'd totally: Apricots, Almonds, & Figs
lost all their young shoots. Stʳ: has had a melancholy
journey: tomorrow we expect him here. Adieu!

I am ever
Yours
TG:

at Frisby's, in Jermyn-Street, St. James's.
24 May. 1771.

221. To Norton Nicholls

Jermyn-Street. 28 June. 1771.

DEAR SIR,—The enclosed came a few days after you left us, as I apprehend, from Temple. I continue here much against my will. the gout is gone, the feverish disorder abated, but not cured; my spirits much oppress'd, and the more so I foresee a new complaint, that may tie me down perhaps to my bed, and expose me to the operations of a Surgeon. God knows what will be the end of it.

It will be an alleviation to my miseries, if I can hear you are well, & capable of enjoying those objects of curiosity, that the countries you are in promise to afford you. the greater the detail you give me of them the happier I shall be. Mr. Clarke called on me yesterday, & desires to be remember'd. I know nothing new here, but that Mr. T: Pitt is going to be married to a Miss Wilkinson, the daughter of a rich Merchant, who gives her 30,000£ down, & at least as much more in expectation. Adieu! I am faithfully

Yours
TG:

Wilkes is like to lose his election.

THE
WORLD'S
CLASSICS

OXFORD UNIVERSITY PRESS

The World's Classics

❧

THE best recommendation of *The World's Classics* is the books themselves, which have earned unstinted praise from critics and all classes of the public. Some millions of copies have been sold, and of the volumes already published very many have gone into a second, third, fourth, fifth, sixth, seventh, eighth, ninth, tenth, or later impression. It is only possible to give so much for the money when large sales are certain. The clearness of the type, the quality of the paper, the size of the page, the printing, and the binding—from the cheapest to the best—cannot fail to commend themselves to all who love good literature presented in worthy form. That a high standard is insisted upon is proved by the list of books already published and of those on the eve of publication. Many of the volumes contain critical introductions written by leading authorities.

❧

A NUMBER of the volumes are issued in the *Oxford Library of Standard Works*, the size and type as *The World's Classics*, but bound in antique leather, in Italian, thin boards, gilt design, gilt top, and in Suède, yapp edges, gilt top, each with bookmarker. These are specially recommended for presentation. (The volumes are obtainable only through the booksellers.)

Pocket size, 6 × 3¾ inches.   Large type, on thin opaque paper.
Obtainable either in superfine art cloth or sultan-red leather.

LIST OF THE SERIES

The figures in parentheses denote the number of the book in the series

Aeschylus. The Seven Plays. Translated by LEWIS CAMPBELL. (117)

Ainsworth (W. Harrison). The Tower of London. (162)

À Kempis (Thomas). Of the Imitation of Christ. (49)

Aksakoff (Serghei). Trans. J. D. DUFF.
A Russian Gentleman. (241)   Years of Childhood. (242)
A Russian Schoolboy. (261)

Apocrypha, The, in the Revised Version. (294)

Aristophanes. Frere's translation of the Acharnians, Knights, Birds, and Frogs. Introduction by W. W. MERRY. (134)

Arnold (Matthew). Poems. Intro. by Sir A. T. QUILLER-COUCH. (85)

Aurelius (Marcus). Thoughts. Trans. J. JACKSON. (60)

Austen (Jane). Emma. Introduction by E. V. LUCAS. (129)

Bacon. The Advancement of Learning, and the New Atlantis. Introduction by Professor CASE. (93)   Essays. (24)

Barham. The Ingoldsby Legends. (9)

Barrow (Sir John). The Mutiny of the Bounty. (195)

Betham-Edwards (M.). The Lord of the Harvest. (194)

Blackmore (R. D.). Lorna Doone. Intro. by Sir H. WARREN. (171)

Borrow. The Bible in Spain. (75)   Lavengro. (66)
The Romany Rye. (73)   Wild Wales. (224)

Brontë Sisters.
Charlotte Brontë. Jane Eyre. (1)   Shirley. (14)   Villette. (47)
The Professor, and the Poems of Charlotte, Emily, and Anne Brontë. Introduction by THEODORE WATTS-DUNTON. (78)
Life of Charlotte Brontë, by E. C. GASKELL. (214)

Emily Brontë. Wuthering Heights. (10)

Anne Brontë. Agnes Grey. (141)
The Tenant of Wildfell Hall. (67)

Brown (Dr. John). Horae Subsecivae. Intro. by AUSTIN DOBSON. (118)

Browning (Elizabeth Barrett). Poems: A Selection. (176)

Browning (Robert). Poems and Plays, 1833–1842. (58)
Poems, 1842–1864. (137)

Buckle. The History of Civilization. 3 vols. (41, 48, 53)

Bunyan. The Pilgrim's Progress. (12)

Burke. 6 vols. Vol. I. General Introduction by Judge WILLIS and Preface by F. W. RAFFETY. (71)
Vols. II, IV, V, VI. Prefaces by F. W. RAFFETY. (81, 112-114)
Vol. III. Preface by F. H. WILLIS. (111)
Letters. Selected, with Introduction, by H. J. LASKI. (237)

Burns. Poems. (34)

Byron. Poems: A Selection. (180)

Carlyle. On Heroes and Hero-Worship. (62)
Past and Present. Introduction by G. K. CHESTERTON. (153)
Sartor Resartus. (19)
The French Revolution. Intro. C. R. L. FLETCHER. 2 vols. (125, 126)
The Life of John Sterling. Introduction by W. HALE WHITE. (144)

Cervantes. Don Quixote. 2 vols. With a frontispiece. (130, 131)

Chaucer. The Works of. 3 vols. Vol. I (42); Vol. II (56); Vol. III,
containing the whole of the Canterbury Tales (76)

Cobbold. Margaret Catchpole. Intro. by CLEMENT SHORTER. (119)

Coleridge. Poems. Introduction by Sir A. T. QUILLER-COUCH. (99)

Collins (Wilkie). The Woman in White. (226)

Congreve. The Comedies, with Introduction by BONAMY DOBRÉE. (276)
The Mourning Bride; and Miscellanies. (277)

Cooper (J. Fenimore). The Last of the Mohicans. (163)

Cowper. Letters. Selected, with Introduction, by E. V. LUCAS. (138)

Czecho-Slovak Short Stories. Translated, with a preface, by MARIE
BUSCH. (288)

Darwin. The Origin of Species. With a Note by GRANT ALLEN. (11)

Defoe. Captain Singleton. Intro. by THEODORE WATTS-DUNTON. (82)
Robinson Crusoe. (17)

De Quincey. Confessions of an English Opium-Eater. (23)

Dickens. Barnaby Rudge. (286)   Edwin Drood. (263)
Great Expectations. 6 Illustrations. (128)   Hard Times. (264)
Old Curiosity Shop. (270)   Oliver Twist. 24 Illustrations. (8)
Pickwick Papers. With 43 Illustrations. 2 vols. (120, 121)
Tale of Two Cities. With 16 Illustrations by 'PHIZ'. (38)

Disraeli (Benjamin). Sybil. With an Introduction by WALTER SICHEL.
(291)

Dobson (Austin). At Prior Park, &c. (259)
Eighteenth-Century Vignettes. Three Series. (245-7)
Four Frenchwomen. (248)   Old Kensington Palace, &c. (258)
A Paladin of Philanthropy, &c. (256)   Rosalba's Journal, &c. (260)
Selected Poems. (249)   Side-walk Studies. (257)

Dufferin (Lord). Letters from High Latitudes. Illustrated. (158)

Eliot (George). Adam Bede. (63)   Felix Holt. (179)
Romola. (178)   Scenes of Clerical Life. (155)
Silas Marner, &c. (80)   The Mill on the Floss. (31)

Emerson. English Traits, and Representative Men. (30)
Essays. Two Series. (6)   Nature; and Miscellanies. (236)

English Critical Essays. (Nineteenth Century.) (206)
(Sixteenth to Eighteenth Centuries.) (240)

English Essays. Chosen and arranged by W. PEACOCK. (32)

English Essays, 1600-1900 (Book of). Chosen by S. V. MAKOWER
and B. H. BLACKWELL. (172)

English Essays, Modern. Chosen by H. S. MILFORD. (280)

English Letters. (Fifteenth to Nineteenth Centuries.) (192)

English Prose. Chosen and arranged by W. PEACOCK.
  Mandeville to Ruskin. (45)   Wycliffe to Clarendon. (219)
  Milton to Gray. (220)   Walpole to Lamb. (221)
  Landor to Holmes. (222)   Mrs. Gaskell to Henry James. (223)

English Prose: Narrative, Descriptive, and Dramatic. Selected by H. A. TREBLE. (204)

English Short Stories. (Nineteenth Century.) (193)
  Second Series. (Nineteenth and Twentieth Centuries.) (228)

English Songs and Ballads. Compiled by T. W. H. CROSLAND. (13)

English Speeches, from Burke to Gladstone. (191)

Fielding. Journal of a Voyage to Lisbon, &c. Intro. A. DOBSON. (142)

Francis (St.). The Little Flowers of St. Francis. In English Verse by J. RHOADES. (265)

Franklin (Benjamin). Autobiography. (250)

Froude (J. A.). Short Studies on Great Subjects. First Series. (269)

Galt (John). The Entail. Introduction by JOHN AYSCOUGH. (177)

Gaskell (Mrs.). Introductions by CLEMENT SHORTER.
  Cousin Phillis, and Other Tales, &c. (168)
  Cranford, The Cage at Cranford, and The Moorland Cottage. (110)
  Lizzie Leigh, The Grey Woman, and Other Tales, &c. (175)
  Mary Barton. (86)   North and South. (154)
  Right at Last, and Other Tales, &c. (203)
  Round the Sofa. (190)   Ruth. (88)   Sylvia's Lovers. (156)
  Wives and Daughters. (157)   Life of Charlotte Brontë. (214)

Ghosts and Marvels: a Selection of Uncanny Tales made by V. H. COLLINS, with an Introduction by MONTAGUE R. JAMES. (284)

Gibbon. Decline and Fall of the Roman Empire. With Maps. 7 vols. (35, 44, 51, 55, 64, 69, 74)
  Autobiography. Introduction by J. B. BURY. (139)

Goethe. Faust, Part I (with Marlowe's Dr. Faustus). (135)

Goldsmith. Poems. (123)   The Vicar of Wakefield. (4)

Gray (Thomas). Letters, selected by JOHN BERESFORD. (283)

Hawthorne. The House of the Seven Gables. (273)
  The Scarlet Letter. (26)

Hazlitt. Characters of Shakespeare's Plays. Introduction by Sir A. QUILLER-COUCH. (205)
  Lectures on the English Comic Writers. Introduction by R. BRIMLEY JOHNSON. (124)   Lectures on the English Poets. (255)
  Sketches and Essays. (15)   Spirit of the Age. (57)
  Table-Talk. (5)   Winterslow. (25)

Herbert (George). Poems. Introduction by ARTHUR WAUGH. (109)

Herrick. Poems. (16)

Holmes (Oliver Wendell). The Autocrat of the Breakfast-Table. (61)
  The Poet at the Breakfast-Table. Intro. Sir W. R. NICOLL. (95)
  The Professor at the Breakfast-Table. Intro. Sir W. R. NICOLL. (89)

Homer. Translated by POPE. Iliad. (18)   Odyssey. (36)

Hood. Poems. Introduction by WALTER JERROLD. (87)

Horne (R. H.). A New Spirit of the Age. Intro. W. JERROLD. (127)

Hume. Essays. (33)

Hunt (Leigh). Essays and Sketches. Intro. R. B. JOHNSON. (115)
      The Town. Introduction and Notes by AUSTIN DOBSON. (132)

Irving (Washington). The Conquest of Granada. (150)
      The Sketch-Book. Introduction by T. BALSTON. (173)

Johnson (Samuel). Letters, selected by R. W. CHAPMAN. (282)
      Lives of the Poets. Intro. A. WAUGH. 2 vols. (83, 84)

Keats. Poems. (7)

Keble. The Christian Year. (181)

Kingsley (Henry). Geoffry Hamlyn. (271)   Ravenshoe. (267)

Lamb. Essays of Elia, and The Last Essays of Elia. (2)

Landor. Imaginary Conversations. Selected, with Introduction, by
      Prof. E. DE SÉLINCOURT. (196)

Lesage. Gil Blas. Ed. J. FITZMAURICE-KELLY. 2 vols. (151, 152)

Letters written in War Time. Selected by H. WRAGG. (202)

Longfellow. Evangeline, The Golden Legend, &c. (39)
      Hiawatha, Miles Standish, Tales of a Wayside Inn, &c. (174)

Lytton. Harold. With 6 Illustrations by CHARLES BURTON. (165)

Macaulay. Lays of Ancient Rome; Ivry; The Armada. (27)

Machiavelli. The Prince. Translated by LUIGI RICCI. (43)

Marcus Aurelius. See Aurelius.

Marlowe. Dr. Faustus (with Goethe's Faust, Part I). (135)

Marryat. Mr. Midshipman Easy. (160)

Melville (Herman). Moby Dick. Intro. VIOLA MEYNELL. (225)
      Typee. (274)   Omoo. (275)   White Jacket. Intro. C. VAN DOREN
      (253)

Mill (John Stuart). On Liberty, &c. Intro. Mrs. FAWCETT. (170)
      Autobiography. Intro. H. J. LASKI. (262)

Milton. The English Poems. (182)
      Selected Prose. (293)

Montaigne. Essays. Translated by J. FLORIO. 3 vols. (65, 70, **77**)

Morier (J. J.). Hajji Baba of Ispahan. With a Map. (238)
      Hajji Baba in England. (285)

Morris (W.). The Defence of Guenevere, Jason, &c. (183)

Motley. Rise of the Dutch Republic. 3 vols. (96, 97, 98)

Nekrassov. Who can be happy and free in Russia? A Poem. Trans.
      by JULIET SOSKICE. (213)

Palgrave. The Golden Treasury. With additional Poems, including
      FITZGERALD's translation of Omar Khayyám (133)